CW01090626

Delville Wood   Oct. 4 1918

DELVILLE WOOD.

THE HISTORY OF THE
SOUTH AFRICAN FORCES
IN FRANCE

BY

JOHN BUCHAN

The Naval & Military Press Ltd

Published by

The Naval & Military Press Ltd

Unit 10 Ridgewood Industrial Park,
Uckfield, East Sussex,
TN22 5QE England

Tel: +44 (0) 1825 749494
Fax: +44 (0) 1825 765701

www.naval-military-press.com
www.nmarchive.com

PREFACE.

IN the autumn of 1916 I was asked by the Union Government to undertake the official History of the South African Forces in Europe. At the time I was serving in France, and had therefore an opportunity to see something of the Infantry Brigade. For various reasons I was unable to begin the work until after the signing of the Armistice: since which date I have had at my disposal all official papers, and have received the assistance of many South African officers. I desire to express my gratitude to Major-General Sir H. T. Lukin, Brigadier-General Dawson, Brigadier-General Tanner, and the various battalion and battery commanders for the help they have given me. I would especially thank Major H. P. Mills of the Third Regiment, but for whose unwearying co-operation the book could not have been written. My aim has been to tell as simply as possible the story of a great military achievement, to my mind one of the finest in the whole history of the campaigns; and, at the same time, to provide a detailed account of the operations of the infantry and the other services, which, I trust, may be of interest as a war record both for the men who fought and for the country which sent them forth.   J. B.

CONTENTS.

APPENDICES.

LIST OF ILLUSTRATIONS.

LIST OF MAPS.

THE HISTORY OF THE SOUTH AFRICAN FORCES IN FRANCE.

CHAPTER I.

THE RAISING OF THE BRIGADE.

The Purpose of the Book—South Africa in History—Her Problem
at the Outset of War—General Botha's Proposal to Furnish
a Contingent for Europe—The Composition of the Brigade—
The Officers—Brigadier-General Lukin—The Heavy Artillery
Batteries—The Field Ambulance—The Medical Services—
The Contingent arrives in England—The Situation at the close
of 1915—The Brigade ordered to Egypt.

THIS book is the tale of a great achievement in
war. It is a record of the deeds of that expeditionary force which represented South Africa on
the front in the West. There were South Africans in
many British battalions, in cavalry regiments, in the Flying
Corps, in every auxiliary service ; but here we are concerned only with the contingent which, with its appurten-
ances, was the direct contribution of the Union Government to the main battle-ground. It is a tale to be proud
of, for among the many brigades in that field the South
African Infantry Brigade may be said, without boasting,
to have had no superior and not many equals. In the
fellowship of war great deeds go to a common stock, and

the credit of one is the credit of all. But it is permitted to detach the doings of a single unit, not to make petty comparisons, but to hearten ourselves with the contemplation of exploits which offer an incontrovertible proof of manly virtue and civic vigour. In such a spirit let this story be told.

South Africa is no newcomer among the nations, for she has interested the world for three thousand years. She was the port of Phœnician adventurers centuries before the birth of Christ ; she was the goal of the great Portuguese captains in the first dawn of the Renaissance ; Holland claimed her when Holland was the first of sea-Powers ; she received the flower of the Huguenots scattered by the French religious wars. During the century which has elapsed since Britain first acquired an interest in her soil, she has been the theatre of many wars, as she has been the cradle of many industries. " From Africa comes always some new thing "—the proverb is as old as Aristotle ; and the ancient continent has not lost her power to surprise the world. South Africa has had some magic in her to beguile the hearts of all races, and he who has once been captured by the love of her wide sun-steeped spaces will never forget them, and, though he leave her, will assuredly return. For her charm lies in the paradox that she is long-descended and old, and yet eternally young. Distant as she is from the main centres of the world, scarcely one of the great crises of modern history has left her untouched ; and it was right, nay inevitable, that in a war of nations she should play a conspicuous part. She who had passed through so many furnaces, could not stand aside when that for which her sons had often fought was challenged, and the hard-won gains of civilization stood in jeopardy.

Of all the nations of the British Commonwealth she had at the outbreak of war the most intricate task. Australia and New Zealand, once the Pacific Islands were cleared, were free to look to Europe ; Canada had no nearer enemy than the Germans in France and Flanders ; but South Africa had foes within and without her gates. She had to contend with internal revolution and with the enemy across her border, while a thousand miles off, in German East Africa, there awaited a problem which she must help to solve. Hence the first business of her Government was her own security. When on September 8, 1914, General Botha announced that, after due consideration, he and his colleagues had resolved to carry the war into German territory, " in the interests of South Africa as well as of the Empire," he could not foresee what this most honourable resolution involved. Germany had been engaged for years in putting temptation in the way of restless spirits within the Union. In a month Maritz was in revolt in the north-east part of the Cape Province, and conducted a guerilla campaign till the end of October, when Brits and Van Deventer drove him over the German frontier. About the same time, within the confines of the Union, rebellion broke out under De Wet and Beyers, and it was not till the close of the year that the treason was crushed by Botha with firmness and far-sighted humanity. Early in 1915 began that great " drive " in German South-West Africa which brought the troops of the Union on 12th May to

Windhoek, and on 2nd July to Otavifontein, and on 9th July forced the enemy remnant to an unconditional surrender. Of this campaign let General Smuts speak : " Not only is this success a notable military achievement, and a remarkable triumph over very great physical, climatic, and geographical difficulties. It is more than that, in that it marks in a manner which history will record for all time the first achievement of the United South African nation, in which both races have combined all their best and most virile characteristics, and have lent themselves resolutely, often at the cost of much personal sacrifice, to overcome extraordinary difficulties and dangers in order to attain an important national object."

General Botha did not rest on his laurels. He saw the great war in its true perspective, and recognized that no part of it was alien to South Africa's interest. She was as intimately concerned in the decision now being sought on the battlefields of Europe as in clearing her own borders. He was in the highest sense a patriot, for, while abating nothing of his loyalty to the land of his birth, he saw that the fortunes of that land were indissolubly bound up with the fortunes of the British Commonwealth, and of that civilization which Germany had outraged. Hence, he could not acquiesce in South Africa's inaction after the close of the German South-West campaign. But the old problems were still there. He dared not denude the country of too many of her most loyal and vigilant citizens so soon after the Rebellion. Moreover, there remained German East Africa, where at the moment the British troops were precariously situated, and it was already becoming clear that

South Africa must take a hand in that campaign. As early as April 1915, the Union Government had discussed the matter with the Imperial Government, for it was reasonable to suppose that the troops would return from German South-West Africa shortly after midsummer, and it was necessary to decide on a plan. In July the Imperial Government *July* 1915. accepted General Botha's proposal to furnish a contingent for Europe. South Africa's exchequer, already depleted by her local wars, could not undertake the equipment and payment of these troops throughout the campaign. It was accordingly arranged that the contingent should be equipped, as far as possible, from stores in hand and paid by the Union up to the date of their embarkation. Thereafter they would be paid at the rate of British regular troops,* and have the status of the new service battalions of the British army.

The War Office had asked especially for infantry, and an infantry contingent was bound to be raised largely from the inhabitants of British blood. The Dutch had provided mounted troops, who had done fine service in German South-West, and were to do still finer work the following year in German East Africa. They were natural light-cavalrymen, and the infantry service had not for them the same attraction.† But throughout the land there were men who had served in the war of 1899–1902—some of them old regulars ;

---

* On January 1, 1917, the pay of privates was raised to 3s. a day, but other ranks continued to draw pay at Imperial rates.

† About 15 per cent. of the original Brigade was Dutch. The proportion rose to something like 30 per cent. before the end of the campaign.

there were the various volunteer regiments; and there were many young men in town and country whose eyes turned naturally towards Europe. Sir Charles Crewe was appointed Director of Recruiting, and there was no lack of response to the appeal. It was generally agreed that, considering the smallness of her white population and the complexity of her other tasks, a brigade of infantry was the most that South Africa could raise and keep up to strength. The war in Europe was costly in men; 15 per cent. per month was the estimated rate of reinforcements required, and in the event of heavy fighting it was clear that this figure must be exceeded. Accordingly a brigade of four battalions was decided upon, and at the same time it was resolved to dispatch to Europe five batteries of Heavy Artillery, a General Hospital, a Field Ambulance, and a Signal Company to be attached to the Royal Engineers. The battalions were designed to represent the main divisions of the Union, and recruits were given the option of joining the regiment affiliated to their own province.

The four battalions were constituted as follows: the 1st South African Infantry was the Cape of Good Hope regiment, drawn largely from the " Old Colony ; " the 2nd South African Infantry was the Natal and Orange Free State regiment ; the 3rd South African Infantry was the Transvaal and Rhodesia regiment ; the 4th South African Infantry was the South African Scottish regiment, recruited from the Scottish regiments existing in the Union, the 1st and 2nd Transvaal Scottish and the Cape Town Highlanders, and from the members of the various Caledonian societies. This last regiment is of special interest to the historian, for it had a long ancestry. It descended from the 77th (Atholl) High-landers, through the Scottish Horse and the Transvaal Scottish regiments, and had, therefore, something of the continuity in tradition of the old regular Army.* As originally formed it numbered 1,282 of all ranks, of whom 337 were Scottish born, 258 English, 30 Irish, 13 Welsh, 595 South African, and 49 of other origin. In nearly every company the Scots were stronger than any other element except the South African born, who, of course, included a large proportion of men of Scottish descent. We may take the constitution of the 4th as in other respects typical of all the regiments. It showed 292 men not older than twenty years, 350 between twenty and twenty-five, 232 between twenty-five and thirty, 212 between thirty and thirty-five, and 196 be-tween thirty-five and forty. Only 344 of the rank and file were without previous military training ; of the rest 64 had been in the Regular Army, 760 in territorial, volunteer, or irregular units, 97 in both regulars and irregulars, and 17 in the police. Occupations were thus represented : mining, 234 ; agriculture, 69 ; police and military, 21 ; government service, 145 ; business, 722 ; and the various professions, 91.

Few of the new brigades were better supplied with men of the right kind of experience, for many of the old South African irregular corps had records of which any army might be proud ; and no brigade showed a better standard of physical well-being. It should also be remembered that the level of education and breeding

* The regiment wore the tartan of the Atholl Murrays. The story of the Atholl Highlanders may be read in *The Military History of Perthshire,* by the present Duchess of Atholl.

was singularly high.   The Brigade resembled indeed the famous 51st Division of Highland Territorials, which was largely a middle-class division.   In the slow intricacies of a modern campaign there is need of intelligence and responsibility and power of initiative in every man ; and these are found at their best among those who fight not only because they like it, but because they have much to fight for, and are determined to get the job finished.   The possession of some education and a serious purpose in no way lessens dash and tenacity in the field.   This was the moral of the Highland Territorials who were given first place in Germany's catalogue of her most formidable opponents, and it was also the moral of the South African Brigade.

Sir Charles Crewe was appointed Honorary Colonel of the 1st Battalion, General Botha of the 2nd, General Smuts of the 3rd, and Colonel Dalrymple of the 4th. The commanding officers selected were all permanent members of the Union Defence Force.   They were— for the 1st, Lieutenant-Colonel F. S. Dawson, who was then in command of the 4th South African Mounted Rifles ;   for the 2nd, Lieutenant-Colonel W. E. C. Tanner, District Staff Officer, Pietermaritzburg ;   for the 3rd, Lieutenant-Colonel E. F. Thackeray, District Staff Officer, Kimberley ;   for the 4th, Lieutenant-Colonel F. A. Jones, D.S.O., District Staff Officer, Johannesburg.   Major J. Mitchell Baker, of the General Staff of the Union Defence Force, was Brigade Major ; Captain A. L. Pepper, Staff Captain ;   and Lieutenant-Colonel P. G. Stock, Senior Medical Officer.   The depot of the Brigade was fixed at Potchefstroom, where there existed large cantonments and all facilities for mobilization.

Major-Gen. SIR HENRY TIMSON LUKIN, K.C.B., C.M.G., D.S.O., Commanding South African Brigade to December 1916, and 9th Division from December 1916–February 1918.

To the command of the Brigade was appointed Brigadier-General Henry Timson Lukin, C.M.G., D.S.O., the Inspector-General of the Union Forces. General Lukin was a man of fifty-five, who had had a long and distinguished record in South African campaigns. He had fought in the Zulu War, and had been severely wounded at Ulundi. He was in Basutoland in 1881, and in the Langeberg affair in 1896–7. In the war of 1899–1902 he commanded the artillery at the siege of Wepener, and was thereafter in charge, first of a mounted column, and then of the 1st Colonial Division in Cape Colony. In the German South-West campaign he commanded a mounted column in the northern force under Botha, which marched east from Walfisch Bay; after Botha's departure he was entrusted with the details of the final German surrender; and at the time of his appointment to the Brigade was the General Commanding the Union Forces in German South-West Africa. He was the essential fighting man, inured to the hardships of war; but a life spent in campaigning had in no way impaired his genial humanity. By virtue of his wide experience and his resourceful temper he was a commander well fitted for a brigade so varied in composition and destined to fight on such diverse battle-grounds.

At the same time the five batteries of heavy artillery were assembled. In the German South-West campaign a Heavy Artillery Brigade, armed with 4.7 and 4-inch naval guns, had been formed at Cape Town, the *personnel* being drawn from non-commissioned officers of the Royal Marine Artillery and from the various South African artillery regiments. In June 1915 this Brigade was disbanded, and in July, largely from the old Brigade, a regiment of heavy artillery was recruited for Europe. Only men of fine physique and of a standard height of 5 feet 8 inches were accepted, and the roll was closed when it reached a total of 600. The regiment contained five batteries, the 1st representing the Western Cape Province, the 2nd the Eastern Cape Province, the 3rd the Transvaal, the 4th Kimberley and the Diamond Fields, and the 5th Natal. Before they appeared on the fighting front the War Office decided that they should be rated as siege artillery, armed with 6-inch howitzers, and affiliated to the Royal Garrison Artillery. This involved each battery receiving an R.G.A. number. The 1st Battery became the 73rd Siege Battery, R.G.A., under the command of Major Brydon ; the 2nd, the 74th, under Major Pickburn ; the 3rd, the 71st, under Major Harrison ; the 4th, the 72nd, under Major Alston ; the 5th, the 75th, under Major Tripp.*

The 1st South African Field Ambulance was mobilized at Potchefstroom during August, under Lieutenant-Colonel G. H. Usmar, S.A.M.C., and was attached to the Infantry Brigade. This was a departure from the usual practice, for a field ambulance is classed as divisional troops under the orders of the Assistant-Director of Medical Services in the division, and a new-formed brigade usually meets its field ambulance for the first time when it joins its division. The General Hospital mobilized at Wynberg, its *personnel* being largely composed of volunteers from the staffs of No. 1 General Hospital, Wynberg, and No. 2 General Hospital, Maitland, and included representatives from all the

* See Appendix I.

provinces of the Union. It accompanied the Brigade to England, and provided the staff for the depot there, and for the South African Military Hospital at Richmond, as well as for No. 1 South African General Hospital in France.*

Between the 28th of August and the 17th of October the whole contingent embarked at Cape Town for England. The Infantry numbered 160 officers and 5,648 other ranks ; the Heavy Artillery, 34 officers and 636 other ranks ; and the Signal Company, 6 officers and 198 other ranks. By *Aug.–Oct. 1915.* the beginning of November all the services were safely established on English soil—the Infantry being quartered at Bordon, the Field Ambulance at Fleet, and the Heavy Artillery at Bexhill. For two months the units were busy with their training, varied by the customary inspections. On 3rd November the Brigade was reviewed by General Sir Archibald Hunter, the G.O.C. Aldershot Command, and on the 19th the same officer, accompanied by the Duke of Atholl, visited the 4th Battalion. On the 9th the South Africans furnished a detachment for the Lord Mayor's Show. On the 21st the senior officers went to France for three days' duty with the army in the field, and on 2nd December the Brigade was reviewed by the Queen.

* A medical unit with South African *personnel* for service with the French Army was formed in South Africa in the autumn of 1914 by the Société Française du Cap. Early in 1915 this unit was established by the French military authorities at the Hôtel Beau-Rivage at Cannes, which was equipped as a hospital for the reception of French sick and wounded. It did admirable work under the auspices of the French Red Cross, with which it was affiliated.

It was an obscure and critical moment in the war. The great Russian retreat had come to an end, but Mackensen had overrun Serbia and driven the Allies back to the entrenched camp of Salonika. Gallipoli was about to be evacuated. The ambitious attacks of Loos and Champagne had achieved no decision. The first instalment of the new British levies had taken the field ; Sir Douglas Haig had replaced Sir John French as the British Commander-in-Chief, and had begun that elaborate system of training which was to make his army in two years the most formidable in the world. The early hopes of the Allies had been dashed, and men were slowly recognizing that the war was a longer and grimmer business than they had foreseen. Already there were mutterings of that storm in the west which in two months time was to break around Verdun. The South African Brigade was at first attached to the 16th (Irish) Division, and it was expected that the middle of December would see it in France. But on 7th December the plans were altered. For its first taste of war the Brigade

Dec. 30. was to retrace its course, and return again to the continent which it had left. On 30th December the four battalions embarked at Devonport for Alexandria.

CHAPTER II.

AT the close of 1915 the main British force in Egypt was concerned with the defence of the Suez Canal against a threatened attack by the Turks from their Syrian bases. The Canal, as Moltke had long before told his countrymen, was for Britain a vital artery, and Egypt was the key of all her activities in the Near and Middle East. Suddenly, as is the fashion in the Orient, a new trouble blew up like a sandstorm in the desert. The Western frontier, some 700 miles long, adjoined the Italian possessions in Tripoli ; but, though the Treaty of Lausanne had given Italy the suzerainty of that province, her writ ran feebly in the interior and her occupation had never been effective beyond the coast-line. When she declared war on Austria, she was compelled to leave the inland tribes to their own devices, and, stirred up by German and Turkish agents, they prepared for mischief. The chief of the Turkish agents was Nuri Bey, a half-brother of Enver, and about April 1915 a certain Gaafer arrived from Constantinople with large supplies of money and arms. His instructions were to mobilize the Arab and Berber tribes of the Libyan plateau for a dash upon Egypt from the west.

The hope of the Turks in that region lay in the support of the great Senussi brotherhood. The Senussi form one of those strange religious fraternities familiar to the student of Northern Africa. Their founder had been a friend of Britain and had refused to cast in his lot with the Mahdi. He had preached a spiritual creed which orthodox Islam repudiated, and his followers had stood outside the main currents of Moslem life, holding apart from all secular politics, and declining any share in the propaganda of Pan-Islamism. Their headquarters were the oases of the Northern Libyan desert, and they looked without disfavour upon the rule of Britain in Egypt. Their Grand Sheikh, Sidi Ahmed, had at the outbreak of the war given assurance of friendliness to the Anglo-Egyptian authorities, and his official representatives dwelt on the banks of the Nile in good relations with the Government of Cairo.

But the overtures of Nuri and Gaafer proved too much for the loosely organized tribesmen of the Senussi, and ultimately for the Grand Senussi himself. The Egyptian littoral as far as the Tripoli frontier was sparsely populated, consisting only of a few coastguard stations and the strip of flat land between the Libyan plateau and the sea. The Khedival highway, a rough unmacadamized road cut as a relief work during famine, ran to Sollum on the border, and a railway ran west from

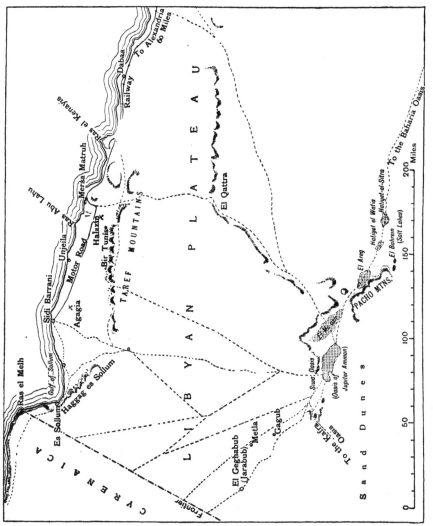

OPERATIONS ON THE WESTERN FRONTIER OF EGYPT.

Alexandria to Dabaa. It was only at the north end that the frontier had to be guarded, where were many little oases linked up by caravan-tracks, for to the south lay the impassable wastes of the Libyan desert. The possibility of trouble was suspected in May 1915, but it was not till August that the first hostile incident took place, when two British submarines, sheltering from bad weather on the Tripoli coast, were treacherously fired upon by Arabs, under a white officer. In the first week of November the crews of the *Tara* and the *Moorina*, torpedoed by enemy submarines, landed in Cyrenaica, and were taken captive by the Senussi. On the 6th of that month, the little port of Sollum was shelled by U-boats, and an Egyptian coastguard cruiser sunk. After that Sollum and Sidi Barrani were subjected to repeated attacks by land, and it became necessary to admit a state of war.

The frontier posts were drawn in to Mersa Matruh, which, with a railway eighty miles distant and the sea at its door, was well-equipped as a base to defend the marches. On 11th December Major-General Wallace, in command of the hastily-collected Western Frontier Force, moved out from Mersa Matruh and drove the enemy from the Wadi Senaab. On the 13th his column dispersed with considerable losses some 1,200 Arabs near Beit Hussein. Towards the end of the month an enemy force of some 5,000, under Gaafer, concentrated eight miles south-west of Matruh, and on Christmas Day General Wallace marched *Dec. 25, 1915.* against it with two columns, one composed of English Yeomanry and Australian Light Horse, and the other of the 15th Sikhs, a battalion of the New

Zealand Rifle Brigade, and a territorial battalion of the Middlesex. The action was of the familiar type—a frontal attack by the infantry, and a wide circling movement by the horse, and it resulted in a substantial check to the enemy. He lost nearly 500 killed and prisoners, and most of his transport and supplies, and the Grand Senussi and his staff retired to Unjeila and Bir Tunis.

But the enemy was checked and not routed, and early in January 1916 he reappeared in force some twenty-five miles south-west of Matruh. It was clear that to safeguard the frontier he must be driven westward out of Egyptian soil and south into the desert, and General Wallace had not at his command the troops for such an operation. It was at this time that the South African Brigade arrived in Alexandria.

The contingent had had a fair voyage after the first few days at sea. Submarines were active in the Mediterranean, and stringent precautions had to be taken in the way of guards and boat drills, which, combined with the congestion of the ship, made life on board a Spartan business. At Malta the Governor, Lord Methuen, was prevented by illness from greeting his old friends, but he wrote to General Lukin : " South Africa has been a second home to me. Fourteen years of my life have been spent there, and you know the love we bear for each other. I look back as the proudest and happiest time of my life on the helping hand I gave to General Botha and General Smuts in the formation of your great citizen army, that true bond of union between Englishmen and Dutchmen. We little thought how soon and how splendidly you would be called upon to show its value." On 10th January the *Saxonia* reached Alexandria, and the *Corsican*, bringing the 4th South African Regiment and the Field Ambulance, arrived three days later. The Brigade encamped under canvas at Mex Camp, six miles west of the city, where they spent some days in training and in perfecting the local defences. On 18th January they were inspected by the G.O.C. of the Forces in Egypt, Lieutenant-General Sir John Maxwell, who years before had been Military Governor of Pretoria. " The South African Brigade," he wrote, " is evidently fit to take its place alongside the best troops in the army," and he expressed the hope that it might soon have the chance of meeting the enemy. His hope was speedily realized, for next day came orders for part of the Brigade to move towards the western marches.

An infantry battalion was required at once to reinforce General Wallace for his attack upon the enemy concentration south-west of Matruh. The 2nd South African Regiment was chosen, and two companies, under Major Christian, embarked on the afternoon of the 19th on their sixteen-hours voyage.* Next day the remainder of the regiment followed, and by the evening of the 21st, after a weary time in bucketing little coasters, the 2nd South Africans, *Jan. 21, 1916.* under Lieutenant-Colonel Tanner, were at Matruh awaiting orders. The whole force moved out next afternoon to Bir Shola, eighteen miles distant, and the South Africans, still fagged from their journey, found their first day in the field a high test of endurance. They

* Troops could not be moved to Dabaa by rail from lack of rolling stock.

bivouacked for the night at Bir Shola, and at six o'clock
Jan. 23. on the morning of the 23rd, General Wallace
began his preparations for attack. He disposed his troops in two columns. One on the right,
consisting mainly of infantry, under Lieutenant-Colonel
J. L. R. Gordon, included the 2nd South Africans, the
15th Sikhs, the 1st Battalion New Zealand Rifle Brigade,
and a squadron of the Duke of Lancaster's Yeomanry ;
the second, echeloned on its left front and moving parallel
with it, consisted of squadrons of the Dorset and Herts
Yeomanry, the Royal Bucks Hussars, and the Australian
Light Horse, under Brigadier-General Tyndale Biscoe.

About 8.30, when the infantry were some seven miles
from Bir Shola, the mounted column became engaged
with the enemy, who was occupying as his advanced
position a half-moon of ridge, on which he had prepared
trenches not easy to locate. The ground, except for
the undulations, was utterly featureless and treeless,
and a morning mirage increased its difficulty. The
mounted column found itself checked, and the infantry
were ordered to attack the enemy centre and left, while
the cavalry covered its left flank and worked round the
enemy right. There followed a stubborn battle, the
ground traversed being often no better than a swamp,
owing to the abnormal rains. The 15th Sikhs led, with
the 2nd South Africans in support, and the attack, spread
over a mile and a half of ground destitute of any cover,
gave a fine target to the enemy artillery and machine
guns. There were many casualties, and, since the hostile
positions were in the shape of a semicircle, it was impossible to avoid flanking fire. But the infantry steadily
pressed on, and after the first three-quarters of a mile

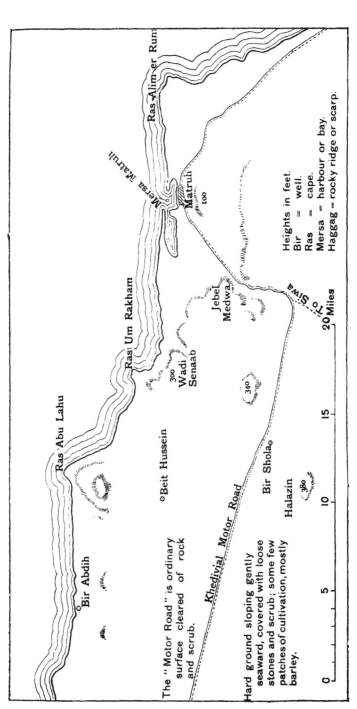

Bir Abdih

Ras Abu Lahu

Ras Um Rakham

Mersa Matruh

Ras Alimer Run

Matruh

100

The "Motor Road" is ordinary
surface cleared of rock
and scrub.

Beit Hussein

300

Wadi
Senaab

Jebel
Medwa

340

Hard ground sloping gently
seaward, covered with loose
stones and scrub; some few
patches of cultivation, mostly
barley.

Bir Shola

Halazin

380

Khedivial Motor Road

To Siwa

Heights in feet.
Bir = well.
Ras = cape.
Mersa = harbour or bay.
Haggag = rocky ridge or scarp.

0   5   10   15   20 Miles

SCENE OF EARLIER OPERATIONS NEAR MERSA MATRUH.

had been covered, the South Africans, hitherto in support of the Sikhs, were ordered to extend the attack to the right. The Senussi were forced back from their forward lines, and retreated slowly and with much skill the three miles to their main camp at Halazin, resisting all our efforts to get to close quarters. About two in the afternoon the Sikhs in the centre, the South Africans on the right, and the New Zealanders on the left, were close on the main enemy position, but their flanks were in jeopardy, for the Senussi still kept their semicircular formation, and their horns threatened envelopment. Tanner was obliged to leave a company to protect his right flank, and the reserve battalion of the column, the 1/6th Royal Scots, had to be put in to avert danger from the same quarter.

By 2.30 our infantry had broken into the main position, but the mounted troops on their left were less happily fated. They had been compelled to give ground, and were now nearly a thousand yards behind, so that Colonel Gordon had to detach two companies of the New Zealanders to assist the cavalry and protect his left rear. This proved sufficient, and by 4.30 the Senussi were in retreat, and their camp given to the flames. But the sun was now low in the west, our horses were too exhausted to pursue, and the baggage camels of the enemy were allowed to retire unmolested. Our troops were compelled to bivouac on the ground won—a comfortless bivouac, for it rained in sheets, and they had no supplies or blankets, seeing that the transport was bogged in the mud three miles west of Bir Shola. Mud, indeed, had been the trouble of the day. It had hindered the cavalry from giving due support to the infantry, and it had deprived the latter of the Royal Naval Armoured Car Division, which had been detailed to defend their right flank. The following *Jan. 25.* morning the troops struggled through the quagmires to Bir Shola, and on the 25th, in better weather, returned to Matruh.

The South Africans had come well out of their baptism of fire. They had lost in killed, one officer (Captain J. D. Walsh) and seven other ranks ; one officer (Lieutenant W. G. Strannock) and two other ranks died of wounds ; four officers and 102 other ranks were wounded. It must be remembered that no time to rest had been given them after a fatiguing voyage, and that they were already weary before the battle began. Yet all observers bore testimony to the " invincible dash and resolution of their attack." * In that desert fighting we relied much upon the work of our airmen, and it is interesting to note that among the most brilliant members of the Royal Flying Corps attached to the Western Frontier Force was a South African, Lieutenant van Ryneveld.

The Western Frontier Force was now completely reconstituted. General Wallace's health did not permit him to continue in the command, and his place was taken by Major-General W. E. Peyton, who had commanded the 2nd Mounted Division at Suvla Bay. The 2nd Mounted Brigade replaced the composite Yeomanry Brigade, and the place of the Sikhs and New Zealanders was filled by the South African Brigade, which by the middle of February had arrived in its entirety at Matruh.

* The phrase is Sir John Maxwell's in his dispatch of March 1, 1916.

Sufficient camel transport had now been provided to make the columns really mobile, and to enable them to follow up any success.

Early in February it became clear that the main Senussi forces were near Barrani, with a smaller body at Sollum, and that to pacify the country these forces must be beaten and dispersed. It was difficult to land troops at Sollum, for the place was commanded by encircling ridges, and, since it would be necessary to sweep the mines at the entrance to the harbour, a surprise was impossible. General Peyton accordingly resolved to attack by land. His object was to occupy Barrani and Sollum, after which supplies would be available by sea. The problem before him was largely one of physical difficulties, for the land was almost devoid of water. An advance depot was established at Unjeila on the 16th of February, and on 20th February a column under General Lukin *Feb. 20.* moved out from Matruh with orders to occupy Barrani, as the first stage on the road to Sollum.

The column consisted of the 3rd South African Regiment, the Dorset Yeomanry, the Notts Battery, R.H.A., one squadron of the Royal Bucks Hussars, the 1/6th Royal Scots, and two field ambulances. Its course lay north of the Khedival highway, practically along the line of an old Roman road. The scanty wells were as often as not the ruins of Roman cisterns, so that the new defenders of civilization followed in the steps of the greatest empire of the past. The weather had changed since the January fighting at Halazin. Scorching winds and a glaring sun made the march arduous, but since the route ran close to the sea the men could refresh themselves with sea-bathing at the different halting places. Bir Abdih was reached on the afternoon of the 21st, and Unjeila, 32 miles from Matruh, on the 22nd. Here the 1st South Africans, who had gone on ahead on the 16th, joined the column, and the greater part of the Royal Scots remained as garrison. On the 24th Lukin was at Maktil, where his column rested for a day. The Senussi had been located at Agagia, 14 miles south-east of Barrani, and it was ascertained from captured Bedouin that both Nuri and Gaafer were with them.

During the 25th, while the troops rested in camp, the enemy was observed in considerable numbers about *Feb. 25.* three miles to the south, and a good deal of sniping followed. Lukin had decided to make a night attack, moving off at 7 p.m. ; but Gaafer anticipated him, for about half-past five he opened on our camp with two field guns and at least one machine gun. Lukin at once moved forward the Royal Scots on his right, and the 1st South Africans on his left, with the 3rd South Africans in reserve. The enemy guns had been located, and were quickly silenced by our artillery, and in half an hour, with the loss of one man killed and one man wounded, the threatened assault was frustrated. The incident compelled Lukin to cancel the orders for the night march, and he resolved to advance against the enemy at daybreak.

A Yeomanry reconnaissance sent out at dawn on the 26th, reported that Gaafer had evacuated his posi-*Feb. 26.* tion of the previous night ; and presently we learned from our aircraft that he was back on his old ground near Agagia. At 9.30 Lukin moved out his whole force, leaving 300 Royal Scots to guard his

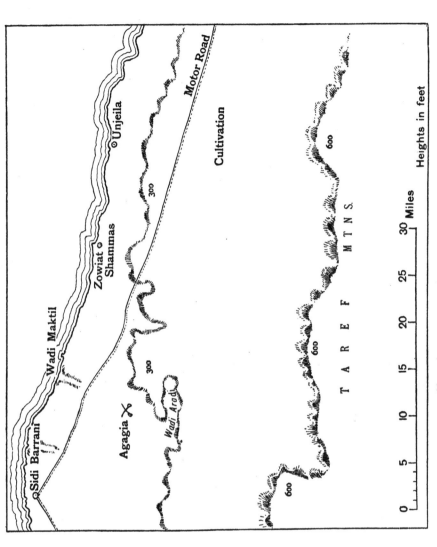

THE ADVANCE TO AGAGIA AND BARRANI.

camp. He had now with him six armoured cars, under Major the Duke of Westminster, which had just arrived. Three-quarters of an hour later the Yeomanry seized a little hill rather more than two miles north of the enemy's position. This enabled us to reconnoitre the field, and at eleven it was possible to join battle. In the centre the 3rd South Africans, under Lieutenant-Colonel Thackeray, advanced on a front of about 1,700 yards, with Yeomanry and armoured cars on either flank. The 1st South Africans formed the general reserve. The guns were brought up to a point about 4,500 yards from the enemy, but were outranged, and played little part in the beginning of the action. Presently Lukin moved them to 3,500 yards range, where their shrapnel was more effective.

The battle which followed was a model of a successful desert action. Lukin had his main strength in mounted troops on his right, and it was his plan that these, when the infantry had broken the enemy, should swing round his flank and rear, prevent him breaking west, and round up his retreat. As the 3rd South Africans advanced with admirable steadiness the enemy opened a heavy fire upon them with rifle and machine gun and more than one field piece. Then, following his old practice, Gaafer attempted an encircling movement against our left. Lukin ordered Lieutenant-Colonel Dawson to send a company of the 1st South Africans to that flank, and so checked the enemy manœuvre. As soon as this danger was past he withdrew the squadron of Yeomanry on his left to augment the mounted troops on his right. The firing line was now within 300 yards of Gaafer's posts. In order to gain fire superiority at once, Lukin brought the greater part of his reserves into the fight, and sent a message to Colonel Souter, commanding the Yeomanry on his right, that now was the time to push forward. In a few minutes the company of the 1st South Africans on the left flank broke into the enemy position, the 3rd South Africans followed immediately, and presently the whole enemy lines were in our hands.

It was now the turn of the Yeomanry. When Colonel Souter received Lukin's message about one o'clock, he resolved to let the enemy retreat get clear of the sandhills, and then attack it in the open. His pursuit, therefore, took a line parallel to the enemy's retirement, and about a thousand yards to the west of it. The rest is best told in Colonel Souter's own words : " About 2 p.m. I saw for the first time the whole re-treating force extend for about a mile, with a depth of 300 to 400 yards. In front were the camels and baggage, escorted by irregulars, with their proper fighting force (Mahafizia) and maxims forming their rear and flank guard. I decided to attack mounted. About 3 p.m. I dismounted for the last time to give my horses a breather and to make a careful examination of the ground over which I was about to move. By this time the Dorset Regiment was complete, and, as the squadron of the Bucks Yeomanry had gone ahead and could not be found, I attacked with Dorsets alone. The attack was made in two lines, the horses galloping steadily and well in hand. Three maxims were brought into action against us, but the men were splendidly led by their squadron and troop leaders, and their behaviour was admirable. About 50 yards from the position I gave the order to charge, and with one yell the Dorsets hurled themselves upon the enemy, who immediately broke.   In the middle of the enemy's lines my horse was killed under me, and, by a curious chance, his dying strides brought me to the ground within a few yards of the Senussi General, Gaafer Pasha."

This very complete success, due to the perfect co-ordination of infantry and yeomanry, and General Lukin's power of prompt decision after the action had begun, was not gained without severe losses.   These were chiefly among the mounted troops, for when their officers were killed the men were apt to carry on too far.   The infantry casualties—almost all incurred by the 3rd South Africans—were 1 officer (Lieutenant Bliss) and 13 other ranks killed, and 5 officers and 98 other ranks wounded.   The capture of Gaafer and his staff deprived the enemy of his principal general, and two days later Barrani was occupied by us without a blow.

" It was the Battle of Agagia," General Peyton subsequently wrote, " which sealed the fate of the combined Turks and Senussi who had contemplated an attack on Egypt."   The possession of Barrani enabled us to bring to that port supplies by sea and to make of it a new advanced base.   After the action at Halazin the 2nd South African Regiment had been employed in furnishing escorts for convoys between Matruh and Unjeila.   This task was now accomplished, and by 8th March the 2nd and 4th Regiments had joined Lukin at Barrani, together with the rest of the 2nd Mounted Brigade and two sections of the Hong-Kong and Singapore Mountain Battery.   After their defeat the Senussi had retreated westward towards Sollum, and the Egyptian Bedouin, notably the Aulad Ali tribes, began to desert in large numbers and sue for pardon. The time had not yet come, however, for negotiations. The enemy had occupied his old camp near Sollum, which had been the Grand Senussi's headquarters before the campaign began, and there was the danger that he might receive reinforcements from Tripoli. It therefore behoved General Peyton to strike again without delay, and to clear Egyptian soil up to the frontier.

To Sollum there were two routes : one by the Khedival road along the coast, the other inland by the high ground of the plateau. For military purposes the latter was to be preferred, for the ridges rise steeply behind Sollum, and to attack the enemy's camp from the coast would have been no light undertaking. It was better to move inland and come upon the Senussi from the south and south-east. The main problem, as in all desert warfare, was that of the water supply; but General Peyton's intelligence led him to believe that there were sufficient wells by the inland route to supply his force if it moved in two parts and made careful use of its reserve water park.

On 9th March a column, under Lukin, left Barrani to secure the plateau by way of the pass called the Nagb *Mar.* 9. Medean. The troops were the whole South African Brigade, a squadron of the Dorset Yeomanry, the Hong-Kong and Singapore Mountain Battery, and a Camel Supply column and train, and it was arranged that they should be joined later by the Armoured Car Battery and a company of the Australian Camel Corps. Sollum lay 50 miles off along the coast,

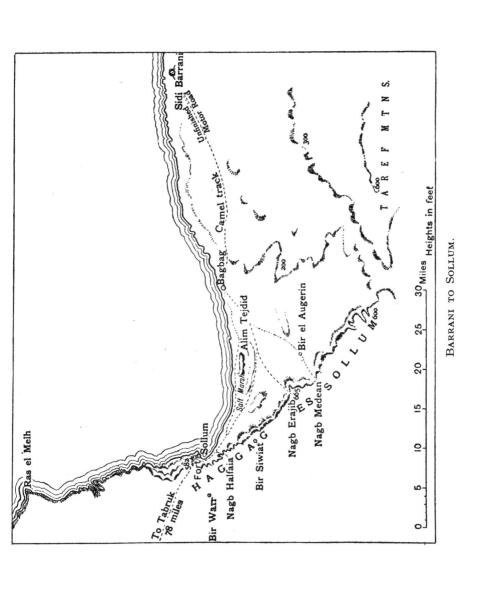

Ras el Melh

To Tabruk 78 miles

Bir Warr°

Nagb Halfaia

Bir Siwiat°

Nagb Erajib

Nagb Medean

Fort Sollum

Salt Marsh

Alim Tejdid

Bir el Augerin

S O L L U M

°Bagbag

Camel track

Unfinished Road
Motor Road

Sidi Barrani

T A R E F   M T N S.

Heights in feet

BARRANI TO SOLLUM.

and to turn its encircling escarpment the plan was to march to Bagbag, and then strike south-west for Bir-el-Augerin, after which an attempt would be made to seize the passes which led from the south-east to the Sollum tableland, notably the Nagb Medean and the Erajib. These passes could not be used by the armoured cars, so it was arranged that they should go further south by a practicable route, and join the column when the Medean pass had been taken by the infantry. General Peyton had planned that the second column, consisting of mounted troops and camel transport, should leave Barrani two days later than Lukin, and reach Augerin after the Medean pass had been secured. This would have concentrated the whole force at Augerin, with its outposts on the south-eastern scarp of the Sollum plateau, ready to make its final attack on the enemy's camp.

The water difficulty became serious for Lukin as soon as he left Barrani. The first night a Roman cistern was found, which gave a fair supply. On the night of the 10th the column bivouacked on the seashore, where the Roman wells were found to be silted up with sand, and had to be opened up by the engineers. On the 11th Bagbag was reached, but the water proved scanty and infamous, much of it being too sulphurous to be drunk by men or beasts. The best that could be done was to dig new wells in the sand. On the morning *Mar.* 12. of the 12th Lukin was at Augerin, and that afternoon the 1st and 4th South Africans made good the Medean pass without opposition, and were presently joined by the armoured cars.

Now appeared an unexpected difficulty. The Roman cistern at the top of the Medean pass, which it had been hoped would provide water for the whole column, proved to be dry, as were the wells at Siwiat further along the ridge. This compelled General Peyton to revise his plan. Clearly, he could not send the second column by the same route as the first ; indeed, the water supply made it impossible for the first column in its entirety to continue on its original line. He therefore made a new disposition of his forces. Lukin was ordered to push along the top of the escarpment with the 1st and 4th South Africans, the armoured cars, the Hong-Kong and Singapore Battery, and a company of the Australian Camel Corps. The rest of the infantry and the mounted troops were directed to proceed from Augerin along the coast to the foot of the Halfaia pass. Lukin's force carried their water in " fantasies " on camels, and their total supply, which had to last for forty-eight hours, was limited to eight pints per man.

The movement began on the 13th. At midnight Lukin was four miles from the Halfaia, the rest of the infantry at Alim Tejdid, and the cavalry at Bagbag. At daybreak on the 14th the armoured cars moved forward to the Halfaia pass, which they occupied without opposition. At 9 a.m. we learned that the enemy had evacuated Sollum the previous evening and was retiring to the south-west. There was now no obstacle in front *Mar. 15.* of the two columns, and the mounted troops joined Lukin on the high ground. Next day, 15th March, General Peyton entered Sollum.

As soon as the news of the enemy's evacuation reached Lukin, he dispatched the Duke of Westminster with the armoured cars in pursuit. The battery consisted of nine cars and one open Ford car mounting a machine gun, and the total *personnel* was only thirty-two. They made for the enemy's camp at Bir Warr, where a straggler was captured, who was afterwards to prove a most valuable prize. Dashing along the Tabruk road, which runs westward into the Libyan desert, they came presently upon the *débris* of the retreat. After 23 miles had been covered, the leading cars, as they turned a bend in the road, came suddenly in view of the enemy's camp at the Bir Asisa well a few hundred yards to the south. The camels were standing loaded, one ten-pounder and two machine guns were in position, and the enemy masses were just beginning to move. The battery swung into line and charged. Their machine guns silenced the Turkish guns, and the shells from the ten-pounder burst far behind them. The Senussi were surprised and wholly demoralized. Most of them flung down their rifles and fled. To prevent the escape of the supply train some 50 camels already on the move were shot— in several cases with extraordinary results, for the unhappy beasts were laden with petrol and bombs, and blew up under our fire with terrific explosions. At least 50 of the enemy were killed, 40 prisoners were taken, including 3 Turkish officers, and all the Senussi guns and much of the supplies were captured. The British loss in this brilliant affair was one officer slightly wounded.

The final exploit in the campaign fell also to the credit of the armoured cars, and the war has shown few more romantic incidents. It will be remembered that the previous November the survivors from the *Tara* and *Moorina* had been taken prisoner by Arabs and moved into the interior. By a coincidence which would scarcely be credited in a work of fiction, the man captured at Bir Warr proved to have been employed as one of the guards of the prisoners, and disclosed their whereabouts. The place was 75 miles west of Sollum, and with General Peyton's consent, the Duke of West-

Mar. 17. minster set out on the morning of the 17th to their rescue. He had with him, besides his cars, a number of motor ambulances. The guide proved faithful, and after a journey of 120 miles over featureless desert the prisoners' camp was found at a place called the Hidden Spring. The men were naked skeletons, and no language can describe their amazement and joy at this miraculous rescue. By the morning of the 18th the cars with the released captives were safely back at Sollum, having travelled in 24 hours some 300 miles. It was an enterprise which in normal times would have been considered to belong rather to the realms of wild romance than to the sober chances of war, and it did signal credit to the intrepidity and resource of its originator. In the words of Sir John Maxwell's dispatch, " to lead his cars through perfectly unknown country against an enemy of unknown strength was a feat which demanded great resolution, and which should not be forgotten even in this war, where deeds of rare daring are of daily occurrence." *

So ended the first invasion of Egypt from the west since the Fatimite attempt of the tenth century. The occupation of Sollum and the achievement of the

* The Duke of Westminster received the Distinguished Service Order ; he was recommended for the Victoria Cross.

armoured cars put an end to the menace from the Senussi. In less than a month General Peyton had driven the enemy back 150 miles, had scattered his forces beyond the frontier, had captured his commander and taken all his guns. If Germany hoped to make of the Arabs and Bedouin of the Tripoli hinterland a fanatical horde which would sweep to the gates of Cairo, she had wholly misjudged their temper. To build up armies from such material was like an attempt to make ropes of desert sand. Thereafter hostilities degenerated into frontier brigandage and police patrols. A year later the Grand Senussi, who had been living in the Siwa oasis, made an attempt to shift his quarters. Major-General Watson, who then commanded the Western Frontier Force, sent a column of armoured cars, which on February 3, 1917, broke up his camp, drove him into the outer deserts, and destroyed for good any little military prestige that remained to him. The main problem left to the British Government was that of feeding the starving tribes, for the futile war had prevented the raising of the usual barley crop. After our humane fashion we beat the enemy and fed his belongings.

On the afternoon of 16th March a parade of all arms was held in Sollum, and General Peyton thanked his men for the victory which they had won. On 28th March the South African Brigade began its return journey by sea to Alexandria, and on its arrival there was joined by a draft of 8 officers and 400 other ranks, under the command of Captain L. W. Tomlinson. On 10th April it was inspected by Sir Archibald Murray, the G.O.C. of the Forces in Egypt, and next day it received orders to embark for Marseilles. The three

April 11.
months in North Africa had given it its first field training in war, and it had emerged with increased physical and moral strength from the trial. The difficult weather, when hailstorms and great cold were diversified with long spells of scorching heat, and the weary and waterless desert marches, had toughened the fibre of every soldier. It was fortunate that the Brigade had such a preparation, for it was about to take its place in a classic division on the Western Front, and to enter one of the most desperate struggles of the campaign.

CHAPTER III.

THE transports *Megantic, Oriana, Scotian,* and *Tinto-
retto,* carrying the Brigade, left Alexandria between
the 13th and 15th of April, and reached Marseilles
during the night of the 19th, about the same time as
the Russian division dispatched to the aid of France
from Vladivostok. Owing to a case of contagious sickness on board the *Oriana,* the 4th Regiment and part
of the 1st were placed in quarantine, while the remainder
of the troops entrained at once for Flanders. Steenwerck was reached on the morning of the 23rd, and
the 2nd and 3rd Regiments marched to their billeting
area along roads wholly under water. It
was the first sight which the South Africans *April 23.*
had of the delectable land in which for four years the

British Army made war. Headquarters were established at Bailleul, and the Brigade was attached to the 9th (Scottish) Division, under Major-General W. T. Furse. For three weeks detachments of the two regiments took their place in the trenches for instruction, and on 11th May the 4th Regiment and the rest of the 1st arrived from their quarantine at Marseilles. On 14th May the 28th Brigade of the 9th Division disappeared, being absorbed in other divisions, and the South African Brigade took its place in the fighting unit to whose glory it was so worthily to contribute.*

The 9th Division belonged to the " First Hundred Thousand " of the New Army, and at the start was wholly Scottish. The famous Scottish battalions of the old regulars had drawn their men from every quarter of Britain ; but the 9th Division had few in its ranks who did not hail from north of the Tweed. It had already made a name for itself at Loos, where, under Major-General George Thesiger, who fell in the battle, it had captured the Hohenzollern Redoubt and the ill-omened Fosse 8, and held the latter till it was utterly outflanked. It had fought in the toughest part of the whole line, and all the troops, Highland and Lowland, had borne themselves like veterans. The division had spent the winter in the Ypres salient as part of Sir Herbert Plumer's Second Army, and during the spring

---

* The 9th Division was now composed of the 26th Infantry Brigade, comprising the 8th Black Watch, the 7th Seaforths, the 5th Camerons, and the 10th Argyll and Sutherland Highlanders ; the 27th Infantry Brigade, comprising the 11th Royal Scots, the 12th Royal Scots, the 6th K.O.S.B. and the 9th Scottish Rifles ; and the South African Infantry Brigade. The Pioneer Battalion was the 9th Seaforths.

had occupied the front around Armentières. It was a proof of the respect in which the South African Brigade was held by the British Command that it should be made part of so notable a division ; and it was not less fortunate for the 9th Division that it received a brigade so competent to sustain its record.

The April of 1916 was a critical month in the Western campaign. On the 9th the first and deadliest stage of the German assault on Verdun had closed with the failure of the attackers. Pétain's thin lines had held their ground; the little city was still inviolate; and, though France had lost terribly, she had wrecked the plans of her enemy, inflicted upon him irreparable loss, and by her heroism won that quiet confidence which is the surest guarantee of victory. When the Imperial Crown Prince opened the battle, one part of his purpose had been to induce a British counter-offensive. That counter-offensive did not come, for General Joffre did not desire it. He preferred to wait until Germany had spent her strength, and to use the armies of France and Britain in a great movement against a weakened foe. Our task, therefore, during the first months of 1916 had been to wait. The duty had been costly, for on our front the average daily toll of loss in trench fighting was not far from 1,000. It was a difficult time, for there was no great objective to quicken the spirit, and those indeterminate months imposed a heavy strain upon the *moral* of our troops. Yet the apparent stagnation was not without its advantage, for it gave the new British Commander-in-Chief time to complete his field army and perfect its education. When Sir Douglas Haig took over the supreme command he set himself to the work which Sir John Moore had undertaken more than a century before. He had to train his men for a new kind of warfare, and the whole British front became one vast seminary. To quote from his dispatch at this date : " During the periods of relief all formations, and especially the newly-created ones, are instructed and practised in all classes of the present and other phases of warfare. A large number of schools also exist for the instruction of individuals, especially in the use and theory of the less familiar weapons, such as bombs and grenades. There are schools for young staff officers, and regimental officers, for candidates for commissions, etc. In short, every effort is made to take advantage of the closer contact with actual warfare, and to put the finishing touches, often after actual experience in the trenches, to the training received at home."

Moreover, during these months of waiting our strength in munitionment had grown beyond belief. The Allied offensives of 1915 had failed largely because there was no sufficient weight of shells and guns behind them. But by June of 1916 Britain was manufacturing and issuing to the Western front weekly as much as her whole pre-war stock of land service munitions. In heavy guns the output in the year had increased sixfold. The weekly production of machine guns had increased fourteen-fold, and of rifles three-fold—wholly from home sources. In small-arm ammunition the output was three times as great, and large reserve stocks had been accumulated. The production of high explosives was sixty-six times what it had been in the beginning of 1915, and the supply of bombs for trench warfare had been multiplied by thirty-three. At last

"Nancy," the 4th Regiment Mascot, on the Somme Battlefield.

(*By permission of the Imperial War Museum.*)

The springbok "Nancy" was presented to the Regiment in August 1915 by Mr. D. M'Laren Kennedy of Driefontein, Orange Free State. She accompanied the 4th to Egypt, and thence to France, where she was with the Brigade in all its battles. She was wounded in 1917. She died at Hermeton, in Belgium, on 28th November 1918.

we were providing a machine which would put our infantry on equal terms with the enemy.

The South African Brigade was inspected on 29th April by Sir Douglas Haig, and on 4th May by Sir Herbert Plumer. The next two months were devoted to its initiation in the methods of trench warfare, which were wholly new to it. During May it held a portion of the front line, and on 4th June the whole Brigade and the Field Ambulance moved into the Steenbecque and Morbecque training area. Battalion training was followed by skeleton Brigade training until 14th June, when orders were received for the division *June* 14. to move to the Somme. The Brigade was quartered in the neighbourhood of Ailly-sur-Somme, whence parties of officers and N.C.O.'s visited the front line in the Maricourt region. Meantime the 2nd and 3rd Regiments were attached to the 30th Division, to assist in the work of preparation for the coming attack.

Few men who were then in Picardy will ever forget that strange month before the great battle opened—the pleasant summer weather, the quiet of the front, the endless activity of the British hinterland, where every road was thronged with guns and transport, the curious breathless sense of expectation. On 23rd June the Brigade moved to Corbie and Sailly-le-Sec, where it was within a few miles of the line. Next morning, Saturday, the 24th, in grey, cloudy weather with flying showers of rain, the main bombardment opened.

The South Africans, as they moved east from Corbie along the Picardy downs, beheld a landscape which, in the heat and dust of midsummer, must have recalled their own country. The Somme, with its acres of swamp and broad lagoons, was not unlike some river of the bushveld. The " tawny ground," which Shakespeare's Henry V. had summoned his men to colour with their blood, had something of the air of the high-veld—yellow-green ridges and slopes falling away to an infinite distance. As they topped the hill behind Méaulte and faced the long lift of land towards Bapaume, they had the kind of spectacle which is common enough beyond the Vaal. In the hollows around the water-courses was the light green of crops ; then a great stretch of unfenced country patched with woods, which were curiously clean-cut like the coppices in the park of a country house. It was such a view as a man may see from Haenertsberg, looking north towards the Wood-bush. The weather, too, was the soft, shimmering mist which one meets on the edge of the Berg. Our bombardment had only just begun, and the countryside was not yet devastated. Fricourt was still a pleasant wood-land village, Bernafay and Trônes were as yet little forests, and the spire of Mametz church was more than a tooth of masonry.

The story of the Battle of the Somme belongs to history written on a larger scale than this, for here we are concerned with only a part of it. But to understand that part it is necessary to grasp the purpose of the whole action. The enemy was suffering from a lack of immediate reserves, and the depression of *moral* due to his failure at Verdun and the recent successes of Brussilov in Galicia. He had boasted so loudly of his " war map," and the amount of conquered territory which he held, that he dared not resort to the expedient of shortening his long line. He trusted to the great natural and artificial strength of his positions in the West to repel the Allies, whatever weight of men and guns might be brought against him. In no part of the Western front were these positions stronger than between Arras and the Somme, where he held in the main the higher ground, and had in the rear many fortified woods and villages which could be linked together into reserve lines.

The Allies had learned the lesson of the futile offensives of 1915, and of the long-drawn contest at Verdun. They no longer dreamed of breaking the enemy's front by a sudden bound, for they realized the depth of his fortified zone. They had accepted the principle that an attack should proceed by stages, with, as a preliminary to each, an elaborate artillery " preparation ; " and they realized, too, that, since the struggle must be protracted, fresh troops must be used for each stage. Their new plan was simply attrition on a colossal scale. It was like the mighty head of water which hydraulic engineers apply to a mountain in order to wash it away. The governing idea was not a breach in the front, though that might come incidentally, but such a steady, unrelenting pressure as would first cripple and then destroy the enemy's machine. Their method was that of " limited objectives," with new troops and a new bombardment for each phase, and they had certain tactical devices in reserve which they hoped to apply with good effect at the right moment. To quote what I have written elsewhere, the scheme might be suggested by the metaphor of a sea-dyke of stone in a flat country where all stone must be imported. " The waters

crumble the wall in one section, and the free reserves
of stone are used to strengthen that part. But the
crumbling goes on, and to fill the breach stones are
brought from other sections of the dyke. Some day
there must come an hour when the sea will wash through
the old breach, and a great length of the weakened dyke
will follow in the cataclysm." This method of attrition
presupposed the continuance of the war on two fronts.
When Russia fell out of line the situation was utterly
changed, and the plan became futile against an enemy
with a large new reservoir of recruitment. But at the
time of its inception, uninspired and expensive as it was,
it was a sound plan, and *ceteris paribus* would have given
the Allies victory before the end of 1917. Even as
things turned out, in spite of the unlooked-for *débâcle*
in the East, the Battle of the Somme struck a blow at
the heart of Germany's strength from which she never
wholly recovered.

A strategy of active attrition demands a battle, and
a battle requires certain definite objectives. Our aim
was to crumble the enemy's defences on the Bapaume
Ridge so completely that he could not find an alter-
nate position of equal strength, and would be slowly
forced into open warfare. The British front of attack
was from Gommecourt in the north to Maricourt in
the south, whence the French carried the battle across
the Somme to a point opposite the village of Fay. It
was Sir Douglas Haig's intention to make his main
attack between the Ancre and Maricourt, and it is clear
from his dispatch that he regarded the movement of his
left wing as a subsidiary operation. The final campaign of 1918 proved that in this he judged wrongly,

and that the Bapaume Ridge was most vulnerable to a flanking attack from the north. The effort of the British left on the first day failed, and thereafter the battle became a stubborn frontal attack up the slopes from the west. The enemy's fortress was assaulted on its most formidable side, and when after six months he admitted defeat and fell back, he yielded not to any strategical brilliance in our plan, but to the incomparable valour and tenacity of the Allied troops.

On 30th June, the day before the battle began, the South African Brigade, comprising the four infantry battalions, the 64th Field Company R.E., the 28th Brigade M.G. Company, and the South African Brigade Trench Mortar Battery, moved to Grove Town, a large dump on the outskirts of Bray, the 9th Division being in general reserve to Sir Walter Congreve's XIII. Corps. That night the weather suddenly cleared to a blue midsummer evening. Next morning, Saturday, 1st July, at half-past seven, under a cloudless and *July* 1. windless sky, the Allied infantry went over the parapets, and the battle began.

The result of that day was that the German first line was carried almost everywhere from the Ancre southward. In no part of the field was the success more notable than in the area of Congreve's XIII. Corps, which took Montauban, and came to the edge of Bernafay Wood. For the next few days, while our centre was struggling for Ovillers and Contalmaison, Congreve, on the British right wing, working in co-operation with the French, was endeavouring to clear the woods of Trônes and Bernafay, which intervened between the first and second German positions. Bernafay soon fell; but Trônes Wood, being commanded from the south by the Maltzhorn Ridge and from the north by the German position at Longueval, was a hard nut to crack, and though we took most of it, we could not hold it. The place became a Tom Tiddler's ground, which neither side could fully claim, since it was at the mercy of both the British and German artillery fire. That was the position by the 13th of July, when the capture of Contalmaison allowed Sir Douglas Haig to begin the second stage of the action.

Meantime the South Africans had entered the fringes of the battle. On the night of 2nd July the Brigade moved forward to Billon Valley to relieve the 27th Brigade, which was advancing into the line. On 4th July General Furse ordered Lukin to relieve the 21st Brigade in divisional reserve, and the 89th Brigade in the Glatz sector of the front.* This relief was completed by 3.15 a.m. on the morning of 5th *July* 5. July. The position now was that the 1st and 4th South Africans held the line from the junction with the French to Briqueterie Trench east of Montauban, the 2nd South Africans were in divisional reserve at Talus Boise, and the 3rd South Africans were in support in the old British and German front-line trenches immediately to the north-west of Maricourt.

The first experience of the South Africans in the battle was the difficult task of holding a piece of captured front in the face of heavy enemy shelling. The 27th Brigade had cleared Bernafay Wood on the night of the 4th, and during the following days the French

* Both of these brigades belonged to Major-General Shea's 30th Division.

(General Nourrisson's 39th Division of the famous XX. Corps*) were assiduously attacking towards Maltzhorn Farm, while the British right division, the 30th, was labouring to secure the wood of Trônes. The South Africans were stationary except for the contingent which, as we shall see, assisted the 30th Division in Trônes Wood. Their position was uncomfortable, for they were close to the angle of our front, where it bent southward, and were thus exposed to sniping and gun-fire from both front and flank. On the 5th General Lukin began those faithful pilgrimages along the front-line trenches which from the first marked him out among brigade commanders. He was on his feet that day for no less than fifteen hours. Next day, the 6th, there was a great shelling, and the two South African regiments suffered some twenty casualties, among the killed being Lieutenant Oughterson at Glatz Redoubt, and Lieutenant W. N. Brown in Chimney Trench. On the 7th the shelling continued, and that afternoon, in pouring rain, the relief began of the 1st South Africans by the 18th Manchesters of the 21st Brigade. That evening came the preliminary orders from General Headquarters for the second stage of the battle, which for the 9th Division was an attack upon the German line at Longueval.

At dawn on the 8th the only South Africans in the line were the 4th Regiment, holding the Briqueterie Trench and the section from Dublin Trench to Dublin Redoubt. The 2nd Regiment, which had been in

* The XX. Corps held the Grand Couronné of Nancy in September 1914, and delivered the counter-attack at Douaumont on February 26, 1916, which turned the tide at Verdun.

reserve at Talus Boise, was ordered to relieve the 12th Royal Scots and the 6th K.O.S.B. of the 27th Brigade, which were holding a portion of Bernafay Wood. " A " and " C " Companies were detailed for the task, and the following day they were joined by " D " Company. During the 10th these companies of the 2nd South Africans were replaced by two companies of the 4th. The 2nd during its short time in the line was most severely shelled, and incurred some 200 casualties, including Captain H. E. Clifford and Lieutenants C. L. H. Mulcahy, L. Greene, and B. N. Macfarlane, the first two dying of their wounds.

The 4th Regiment, now the only part of the Brigade in the line, was about to be drawn into the fight for Trônes Wood, where the 30th Division had made a lodgment on Saturday, the 8th. There were heavy counter-attacks all through the Sunday, and on Mon-

July 10. day, the 10th, an attack was ordered to clear the place. At 11 p.m., on the 9th, " A " Company of the 4th was sent to support the 90th Brigade, a platoon was dispatched to the garrison of the Briqueterie, and the 3rd Regiment was held in reserve at the disposal of the 30th Division. At dawn on the 10th came the attack, and troops of the 30th Division, together with " A " Company of the 4th South Africans, advanced through the southern half of the wood, and reported it clear of the enemy. But it could not be held. The half-moon of German artillery positions around it made communication with our rear too perilous, and the denseness of the covert, cut only by the railway clearings and the German communication trenches, rendered organized movement

Lieutenant-Colonel F. A. JONES, C.M.G., D.S.O.,
Commanding 4th Regiment, South African Infantry.   Killed at
Bernafay Wood, 11th July 1916.

impossible within it. In the afternoon a German counter-attack lost us most of our gains, and the company of the 4th, when it returned to its trenches, was subjected to a desperate shelling, in which its commander, Captain Russell, was mortally wounded.

On the 11th the fighting in Trônes continued, and the 4th South Africans, whose " A " and " C " Companies were in the neighbourhood of Glatz *July* 11. Redoubt, and whose headquarters and " B " and " D " Companies were in Bernafay Wood, came under the barrage with which the enemy prepared his counter-attacks. That day the Brigade suffered a grievous loss in the death from a shell-splinter of Lieutenant-Colonel F. A. Jones, the commanding officer of the 4th Regiment. He had served in the old South African War with the Welsh Regiment, and won the D.S.O., and in German South-West Africa had been Brigade major to Colonel Beves, commanding the 1st Infantry Brigade. " Fatty " Jones was beloved throughout the contingent for his gay and imperturbable temper, his ready humour, and his complete coolness and gallantry. It was a tragic fate which cut him off on the eve of a battle for which his whole life had been a preparation. The command of the 4th Regiment now passed to Major D. M. MacLeod.

On the 13th orders were issued for the attack on the German second line, and the 4th Regiment was relieved by the 2nd Royal West Surreys and the 7th Middlesex of the 55th Brigade in the 18th Division. That evening the whole South African Brigade was concentrated at Talus Boise as the reserve brigade of the 9th Division. Its week in the front line had been costly. In the 1st Regiment there were 50 casualties, in the 2nd 205, in the 3rd 91, and in the 4th 191, and these included 7 officers killed and 9 wounded. Almost all the losses were from shell-fire, and the severity of the German bombardment may be gathered from the fact that the 3rd Regiment, which was in the support trenches, had 91 losses, mainly among its working and carrying parties.

In the cloudy dawn of Friday, the 14th of July, Haig launched his attack against a section of the Ger-

July 14. man second position—the four miles of front from a point south-east of Pozières to Longueval and Delville Wood. It was the business of Congreve's XIII. Corps to take Bazentin-le-Grand, Longueval, and Delville Wood, and to clear Trônes Wood and form a defensive flank. The result of the day was that we carried all our objectives from Bazentin-le-Petit to Longueval, a front of over three miles, and at one moment had all but penetrated the enemy third position at High Wood. Here we are concerned only with the British right flank, the attack of the 9th Division against Longueval, and of the 18th Division, under Major-General Ivor Maxse, on its right at Trônes Wood.

This section was beyond doubt the most difficult in the battle-front. To begin with, we were fighting in a salient, and our attack was under fire from three sides. This enabled the enemy to embarrass seriously our communications during the action. In the second place, the actual ground of attack presented an intricate problem. The land sloped upwards from Bernafay and Trônes Wood to Longueval village, which was shaped like an inverted fan, broad at the south end, where the

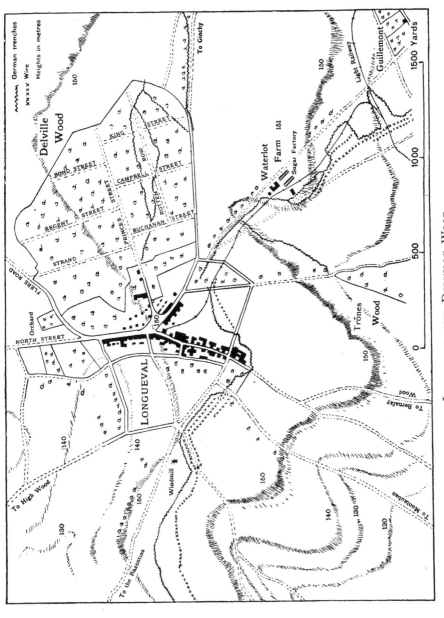

LONGUEVAL AND DELVILLE WOOD.

houses clustered about the junction of two roads, and straggling out to the north-east along the highway to Flers. Scattered among the dwellings were many little enclosed gardens and orchards. To the east and north-east of the hamlet stretched the wood of Delville, in the shape of a blunt equilateral triangle, with an apex pointing northward. The place, like most French woods, had been seamed with grassy rides, partly obscured by scrub, and the Germans had dug lines of trenches along and athwart them. It had been for some days a target for our guns, and was now a mass of splintered tree-trunks, matted undergrowth, and shell-holes. The main German positions were to the north, north-east, and south-east, at a distance of from 50 to 200 yards from its perimeter, where they had strong entrenchments manned by machine guns. It was Sir Douglas Haig's aim to carry Longueval, and make it the flanking buttress of his new line, from which a defensive flank could be formed running south-east to the junction with the French. But it was obvious that the whole of Longueval could not be held unless Delville were also taken, for the northern part, where the road climbed towards Flers, was commanded by the wood. Nothing short of the whole village would make an adequate pivot ; and, with the wood still in German hands, there would be no good leaping-off ground from which to press outward in the direction of Ginchy and Guillemont.

The attack on Longueval on the morning of the 14th was entrusted to the 26th Brigade of the 9th Division—the 8th Black Watch and the 10th Argyll and Sutherlands leading, the 9th Seaforths in support, and the 5th Camerons in reserve. The 27th Brigade moved behind them to " clean up," and the intention of General Congreve was that day to make good Longueval and also Delville Wood, if the latter should prove practicable—a heavy task for two brigades. Shortly after dawn Lukin received orders to put a battalion at the disposal of the 27th Brigade to assist in clearing the Longueval streets, and the 1st Regiment was sent forward for the purpose. The 3rd Regiment was also allotted to the 26th Brigade, but this order was subsequently cancelled.

The assault of the Highlanders was a most gallant performance. They rushed the trenches outside the village, and entered the streets, where desperate hand-to-hand fighting took place among the houses, for the enemy made a resolute defence. Before noon all the west and south-west part of Longueval was in our hands ; but it had become clear that the place in its entirety could not be held, even if won, until Delville Wood was cleared. At 1 p.m. General Furse informed Lukin that, as soon as the other two brigades had taken Longueval, the South Africans should capture and consolidate the outer edge of Delville Wood. For this purpose the whole of the Brigade was available with the exception of the 1st Regiment. Lukin thereupon drew up his orders for the operation. The first hour suggested for the attack was 5 p.m. that afternoon ; the time was later changed to 7 p.m., and then to 7.30 p.m. ; but owing to the fact that the village was not entirely captured these orders were suspended. A staff officer of the Brigade, Lieutenant Roseby, was sent forward to ascertain the position in Longueval ; and from his report it was apparent that the northern part was not in our hands, and that, consequently, it would be

LONGUEVAL VILLAGE AFTER THE BATTLE.

(*By permission of the Imperial War Museum.*)

impossible to form up on a line west of Longueval and advance to the attack from that direction. At a conference with General Furse at Montauban that evening it was arranged that the attack should take place at 5 a.m. on the following morning. The orders were that the wood was to be taken at all costs, and that the advance was to proceed, even if the 26th and 27th Brigades failed to capture the northern part of the village.

Lukin called together his battalion commanders and gave them instructions. These were that if, on arrival at Longueval, they found the northern part still held by the enemy, they should attack Delville from the south-west corner, moving forward on a one-battalion front. To the 2nd and 3rd Regiments, the latter leading, was entrusted the assault, with the 4th Regiment in support. Meantime during that day the 1st Regiment, under Lieutenant-Colonel Dawson, had been heavily engaged in Longueval. At 2 p.m. it had deployed along the line held by the two Scottish brigades, having been brought through a severe artillery fire in eight lines of sections in file without a single casualty. Its business was to attack the remainder of the village, and its leading companies, " A " and " B," reached their first objectives about four o'clock, but were unable to advance owing to the machine-gun fire from front and flank. During the night three parties—under Lieutenants Burgess, Henry, and Bate—were sent out to capture the enemy posts which were checking the advance, and found that the whole village in its northern part was a nest of machine guns. On the morning of the 15th, after the other three regiments had started for Delville Wood, the 1st returned to Lukin's command.

Two hours before dawn the three other regiments of the Brigade had moved forward from Montauban. *July* 15. It was a cloudy morning, but as the sun rose the sky lightened above the Bapaume Ridge, and men noticed amid the punctual shelling how small birds still sang in the ruined coverts, and larks rose from the battered ridges. Before them on their right front lay the shadow which was Delville Wood, and the jumbled masonry, now spouting like a volcano, which had been the hamlet of Longueval. On the way orders came from the division to put two companies at the disposal of the 26th Brigade in Longueval, and accordingly " B " and " C " Companies of the supporting battalion, the 4th, were instructed to report to the officer commanding the 5th Camerons there. The rest of the Brigade, under Lieutenant-Colonel Tanner, who was in charge of the attack, moved over the broken ground under heavy fire till they were close on the southern edge of the village.

It was Tanner's first business to find out the situation. His patrols reported that the Germans still held the northern part of Longueval and all the wood adjoining the streets, but that the position in the rest of the wood was obscure. Some of the 5th Camerons were holding a trench running into Delville from the south-west corner, and in rear of this trench the 2nd and 3rd Regiments assembled about six o'clock. In such a posture of affairs, Lukin's instructions had been to attack the wood from the south-west. As the coming action was fought in a narrow area where the smallest landmark had its importance, it is necessary to understand the nature of the place. From the road junction

Brigadier-General W. E. C. TANNER, C.B., C.M.G., D.S.O.,
Commanding 2nd South African Regiment, and later South
African Brigade.

in Longueval there ran nearly due east a long ride which our men called Princes Street. Subsidiary rides branched off it to the north and south extending to the perimeter ; these were in order from west to east, on the north side the Strand, Regent Street, and Bond Street ; and on the south side Buchanan Street, Campbell Street, and King Street—an odd mixture of the nomenclature of London and Glasgow. Another ride, parallel to Princes Street and about half-way between it and the southern edge, ran from Buchanan Street to the eastern perimeter, and was named Rotten Row. Tanner decided to occupy the wood by first clearing the southern part—that is, the area south of Princes Street—and then pushing north from Princes Street, and occupying the Strand and the perimeter from its northern end round to the south-west corner. This would give him the whole of Delville except the north-west corner, which abutted on the uncaptured part of Longueval village.

At first the attack moved swiftly. By seven o'clock the 3rd South Africans, supported by one company of the 2nd, held everything south of Princes Street. Thereupon Tanner sent the remaining three companies of the 2nd to occupy the Strand and the northern perimeter. This proved to be a heavy undertaking. The three weak companies reached their objective, and found themselves compelled to hold a front of some 1,300 yards on which it was almost impossible to maintain connection. They were well supplied with shovels, and did their best to dig themselves in and wire the ground they had won ; but as soon as they reached the edge the whole wood was violently shelled by the enemy, while machine-gun and rifle fire broke out from the strong German lines around the perimeter. Meantime, in the southern and eastern parts, two patrols of the 3rd Regiment, under the command of Captains Medlicott and Tomlinson, had managed to get to close quarters with the enemy, and had captured three officers, 135 other ranks, and a machine gun.

At 2.40 p.m. Tanner reported to Lukin that he had won the whole wood with the exception of strong points in the north-west abutting on Longueval and the northern orchards. He had succeeded brilliantly in the first part of his task, but the problem of Delville was far less to carry the wood than to hold it. Lukin's plan had been to thin out the troops in the wood as soon as the perimeter was reached, leaving it to be held by small infantry detachments with machine guns. But now came the enemy's counter-attack which made this plan impossible, for every available man was needed to resist the German pressure. About three o'clock elements of the 6th Bavarian Regiment of the 10th Bavarian Division attacked in force from the east, but were driven back by rifle-fire. At 4.40 p.m. Tanner reported that the enemy was also massing for an attack at the northern end, and at 6.30 he again reported an enemy concentration to the north and north-east. He informed Lukin that his casualties had been heavy, one company of the 2nd South Africans having virtually been destroyed, and he asked for reinforcements. He had already received a company of the 4th South Africans, and another company of that regiment was sent forward to reinforce the 3rd South Africans. The 1st Regiment had now returned to Lukin's command, and one of its companies was dispatched to reinforce the

2nd. At 7 p.m. Lukin sent a staff officer to obtain full details of the position in the wood. The officers commanding the 2nd and 3rd Regiments were urged to see that their battalions, in spite of their fatigue, dug themselves in, since heavy shell-fire might be expected on the morrow. This had already been done, for unless the men had been well dug in they could not have lived where they were. The officer commanding the 1st Regiment was ordered to detail special carrying platoons to keep up the supply of ammunition, and to put up a Vickers and a Lewis gun at the south-west corner of the wood to command the southern edge.

As the sun went down the activity of the enemy's guns increased, and the darkness of night was turned by shells and liquid fire into a feverish and blazing noon. The German rate of fire was often as high as 400 shells a minute. The position that evening was as follows :—The north-west corner of the wood was in the enemy's hands. The north-east corner was held from left to right by one and a half companies of the 2nd Regiment, with one company of the 1st in support, and by one company of the 3rd Regiment, with one company of the 4th in support. The south-east corner was held by two companies of the 3rd Regiment. The southern face from left to right was held by one company of the 2nd Regiment and by one company of the 3rd, with one company of the 4th in support. A half company of the 2nd Regiment held the western third of Princes Street, with two companies of the 1st forming a defensive flank on the side of the village. The headquarters of the 2nd and 3rd Regiments were at the junction of Buchanan Street and Princes Street. Machine guns were in position round the perimeter—four at the northern apex, four at the eastern end of the north-eastern face, and two in the eastern half of the southern face.   It will be seen that twelve companies of infantry, now gravely weakened, were holding a wood little less than a mile square with a long, rambling perimeter—a wood on which every German battery was accurately ranged, and which was commanded at close quarters by a semicircle of German trenches.   Moreover, since the enemy held the north-west corner, he had a covered way of approach into the place.   The only reserves of the South African Brigade were one company of the 1st Regiment and the two companies of the 4th which had been lent to the 26th Brigade, and were due to return the following morning.

To complete the story of the day, we must record the doings of these two companies.   On the 14th the 18th Division had cleared Trônes Wood, and established their line up to Maltzhorn Farm.   They joined hands with the 9th Division just west of Waterlot Farm, where, in the ruined sugar factory, the enemy had a position of great strength.   On the morning of the 15th the 5th Camerons were attacking this point, and the two companies of the South African Scottish were to be used as troops to follow and consolidate.   Major Hunt, who was in charge of the companies, sent a platoon from each to occupy the trenches close to the farm, which they did under heavy fire from the concealed posts to the south and east.   The farm was not taken till the following day, and the work of the South Africans was therefore less that of consolidation than of protecting the skirts of the Cameron attack under a heavy German barrage. About six in the evening an enemy force was detected coming from Guillemont, but this was checked by our artillery barrage. An hour later the two companies were ordered to fall back and construct a strong point, and at 2.30 on the morning of the 16th they were relieved by the Camerons and withdrawn to the sunken road behind Longueval.

All through the furious night of the 15th the troops in Delville Wood were working for dear life at entrenchments. At the time it was rumoured that the South Africans were a little negligent in digging, trusting rather to their courage and their marksmanship than to trenches. The criticism was unjust. No soldiers ever worked harder with the spade, but their task was nearly impossible. In that hard soil, coagulated by incessant shellfire, and cumbered with a twisted mass of roots, wire, and tree trunks, the spade could make little way. Nevertheless, when the Sunday morning dawned, a good deal of cover had been provided.

At 2.35 a.m. Lukin received orders from the division that at all costs the northern entrance into Longueval must be blocked, and that for this purpose his Brigade must complete the cap- *July* 16. ture of the northern perimeter of the wood, and advance westward till they joined hands with the 27th Brigade. There was a lane called North Street, which was a continuation of the main street of Longueval from the point where the Flers Road branched off to the northeast. Between these roads lay an orchard, the tactical importance of which will be obvious from the map. The plan was for the 27th Brigade to push north through the village and capture that orchard and the other enclosures east of North Street, and to join hands with the South Africans on the Flers Road. This was to be the work of the 11th Royal Scots ; while two companies of the 1st South Africans (those which, as has been already explained, had formed a defensive flank at the south-west corner of the wood) were to push north from the Princes Street line. The situation did not allow of a previous artillery bombardment ; but it was arranged that a " preparation " by trench mortars should precede the infantry attack.

The advance was made at ten on the Sunday morning and failed completely, since the Royal Scots were held up in their area by a strongly-wired stone redoubt, and the South Africans by machine-gun fire from the ominous orchard between the two roads. It was then that Private W. F. Faulds of the 1st Regiment won the first Victoria Cross which fell to the lot of the Brigade. Lieutenant Craig had attempted to reach a German trench with a bombing section, and had fallen severely wounded half-way between the lines. He was rescued by Private Faulds, who, along with Privates Baker and Estment, crossed the parapet in broad daylight under a drenching machine-gun and rifle fire.

After this failure the attacking troops fell back to the trenches midway in the wood, and for the rest of the day had to endure a steady concentrated fire to which they had no means of effective reply. It was hot, dusty weather, and the enemy's curtain of shells made it almost impossible to bring up food and water or to remove the many casualties. That afternoon Lieutenant-Colonel Dawson, commanding the 1st Regiment, met Lukin in Longueval, and reported that his men were greatly ex-

LIEUTENANT W. F. FAULDS, V.C.,
1st Regiment, South African Infantry.

hausted. He asked for an early relief ; but Lukin could only repeat his divisional commander's instructions that at all costs the wood must be held. At the same time he was so impressed with the signs of strain and fatigue on the faces of the men that he submitted the matter to General Furse. The situation, indeed, was becoming desperate. Longueval and Delville had proved to be far too strongly held to be overrun at the first attack by one division. At the same time, until they were taken, the objectives of the battle of the 14th had not been achieved, and the stability of the whole right wing of our new front was endangered. Fresh troops could not yet be spared for the work, and the thing must be attempted again by the same weary and depleted battalions. It was a vicious circle. Longueval could not be won and held without Delville ; Delville could not be won and held without Longueval ; so what strength remained to the 9th Division had perforce to be divided between two simultaneous objectives.

That Sunday evening it was decided to make another effort against the north-west corner next morning. At 10.30 p.m. orders were received to withdraw all the infantry in Longueval village to a line south of Princes Street, and all infantry in the wood to the area east of the Strand, in order that the north-west corner of Delville and the north end of Longueval might be bombarded. The bombardment was to cease at 2 a.m. on the morning of Monday, the 17th, when the 27th Brigade and two companies of the 1st South Africans were to repeat their attack of the Sunday. Lieutenant-Colonel Tanner, commanding in the wood, was instructed to order the men of the 2nd Regiment, who were now holding the Strand, to move slowly forward so as to narrow the front of the 1st Regiment attacking from Princes Street.

The attack was made shortly before dawn, and did not succeed. Once again machine-gun fire from the fatal enclosures blocked any advance from west or south. The enemy, too, was in force just inside the angle of the wood. The 2nd South Africans, moving west from the Strand according to plan, met with a stubborn resistance, and were forced to fall back to their original position.

July 17.

That morning Lukin visited Delville and discussed the position with his commanding officers. He had now no troops which had not been in action for at least forty-eight hours. It was the most wearing kind of battle, for there was rarely a chance of getting to close quarters with the enemy. Now and then the brilliant marksmanship of the South Africans was given its opportunity ; but for the most part they had to wait under a continuous machine-gun and artillery fire, contending with a distant and impalpable foe. Their general was gravely concerned both at the fatigue of the men and the impossibility of making the wood anything but a death-trap. On his return to Brigade Headquarters he discussed the situation on the telephone with General Furse, but could get no hope of relief or reinforcements. General Congreve's instructions stood that Delville must be held at any cost.

There was no change in the situation during the Monday afternoon. Lieutenant Roseby, the Brigade Intelligence Officer, was sent forward to get information, and was mortally wounded. During the evening

Tanner was hit, and Lieutenant-Colonel Thackeray, commanding the 3rd Regiment, succeeded him in charge of the troops in the wood. That afternoon the news came that the 9th Division was drawing in its left flank, and that the 3rd Division, under Major-General Aylmer Haldane, was to attack Longueval that night from the west. About half-past seven Lukin received orders to take before the next dawn the enemy trench parallel to and 200 yards distant from the south-east edge of the wood. The perimeter facing this trench was held by two companies of the 3rd South Africans, and their commanding officer reported that the enemy trench before them was very strongly manned, and contained several machine guns. He added that he could not furnish more than 200 men for the attack without endangering the whole position. On receiving this news General Furse cancelled the operation. At half-past ten that night the Corps informed Lukin that as soon as the 3rd Division completed the occupation of the village they would establish machine guns on the north-west edge of the wood to protect his men. The attack was to take place at 3.45 a.m. on the 18th, and was to advance as far east as the Strand.

During the night all available reinforcements were pushed up to the perimeter, where they had to face a strong enemy attack. In the southern area the Germans advanced as far as Buchanan Street and Princes Street, and drove the South Africans out of some of their new trenches. A counter-attack cleared the ground, but only at the cost of heavy casualties. At a quar- *July* 18. ter to four the 76th Brigade of the 3rd Division succeeded in obtaining a footing in the orchard between Flers Road and North Street. At eight in the morning Thackeray was ordered to send up patrols to get in touch with this brigade, and directed the company of the 1st Regiment, then occupying the Strand and the western part of Princes Street, to move forward for the purpose. They were not seriously opposed, and presently they joined hands with the 1st Gordons just west of the orchard.

On that morning, the fourth of the battle, came the crisis for the defenders of Delville. The arrival of the company of the 1st Regiment at the outskirts of the wood was the signal for the enemy to open a bombardment of unprecedented fury. Every part of the area was searched and smothered by shells, but the fire was most intense around the perimeter and down the Strand. Major Burges, the officer in command of the company, was wounded, and shortly afterwards killed. At the same time the 76th Brigade was driven in, and the Germans began to enter the wood on the exposed left flank of the South Africans. About nine o'clock an officer and fifty other ranks were dispatched as reinforcements. All through the morning the wearied handful, now rapidly thinning, held out as best they could. Their one relief was when the enemy came on to reap the fruits of his shelling, for then their admirable rifle-fire took heavy toll of him.

About half-past two in the afternoon the position had become desperate. Lieutenant-Colonel Dawson was ordered to take forward as reliefs all the men available under his command—a total of 150 from the 1st Regiment. These men had just been withdrawn

LIEUTENANT-COLONEL E. F. THACKERAY, C.M.G., D.S.O.,
Commanding 3rd South African Regiment.

after having been continuously in action for four days ; they had had no rest ; but their one thought when they were ordered forward was to get to grips with the enemy. On arriving at Longueval Dawson placed his men in a trench at the south-east corner of the village, and went into the wood to find Thackeray. At the same time the men of the Trench Mortar Battery, numbering three officers and some eighty other ranks, under Lieutenant Phillips, were brought up from Montauban and placed at Dawson's disposal. Dawson found Thackeray in serious straits. In many parts of the wood the garrisons had been utterly destroyed, and everywhere north of Princes Street the few survivors had been forced back. Thackeray was now holding only the south-west corner, defined by Buchanan Street and the western part of Princes Street. The wounded filled the trenches, for it was impossible to remove them, since all the stretcher-bearers of the 3rd Regiment were casualties, and no men could be spared to take their places. Dawson, acting under Lukin's instructions, did his best to cope with the situation. He sent Lieutenant Phillips and the Trench Mortar Battery men to reinforce Thackeray, and through the division procured additional stretcher-bearers from the cavalry, in addition to those from the 1st Regiment.

At 6.5 p.m. that evening came the welcome intelligence that that night the South Africans would be relieved by the 26th Brigade. But a relief under such conditions was a slow and intricate business. By midnight the work had been partially carried out, and portions of the two companies of the 1st Regiment and the two companies of the 4th were withdrawn.

But, as at Flodden, when

" they left the darkening heath
More desperate grew the strife of death."

The enemy had brought up a new division—the 8th of the 4th (Magdeburg) Corps—and made repeated attacks against the Buchanan Street line. For two days and two nights the little remnant under Thackeray clung to the south-west corner of the wood against impossible odds, and did not break. The German method of assault was to push forward bombers and snipers, and then to advance in massed formation simultaneously from the north, north-east, and north-west. The three attacks on the night of the 18th were repelled with heavy losses to the enemy ; but in the last of them the South Africans were assaulted on three sides. Thackeray's adjutant, Captain M'Donald, had been wounded, and he was left with only two officers—Lieutenant Garnet Green of the 2nd and Lieutenant Phillips of the 3rd—to assist him, who, though wounded themselves, were able to keep on their feet. All through the 19th the gallant handful suffered incessant shelling and sniping, the latter now from very close quarters. It was the same on the 20th, but still relief tarried. At last, at six o'clock that evening, troops of the 76th Brigade in the 3rd Division were able to take over what was left to us of Longueval and the little segment of Delville Wood. Thackeray marched out with two officers, both of whom were wounded, and 140 other ranks, made up of details from all the regi-

July 20. ments of the Brigade. He spent the night at Talus Boise, and next day joined the rest at Happy Valley.

It is not easy to reproduce the circumstances of a battle so that a true impression may be made upon the minds of those who have not for themselves seen the reality of modern war. The six days and five nights during which the South African Brigade held the most difficult post on the British front—a corner of death on which the enemy fire was concentrated at all hours from three sides, and into which fresh German troops, vastly superior in numbers to the defence, made periodic incursions only to be broken and driven back—constitute an epoch of terror and glory scarcely equalled in the campaign. There were positions as difficult, but they were not held so long ; there were cases of as protracted a defence, but the assault was not so violent and continuous. The closest parallel is to be found, perhaps, in some of the incidents at Verdun, and in the resistance of units of the old British regulars at the point of the Ypres salient in 1914 ; but even there we shall scarcely find an equal feat of tenacity, and certainly none superior. Delville Wood was not finally taken till the 25th of August, a month later, when the 14th Light Division cleared it for good. The high value set upon it by the enemy is proved by the fact that he used his best troops against it—successively the 10th Bavarian Division, the 8th Division of the 4th Corps, and the 5th of the 3rd Corps. The South Africans measured their strength against the flower of the German army, and did not draw back from the challenge. As a feat of human daring and fortitude the fight is worthy of eternal remembrance by South Africa and Britain, but no historian's pen can give that memory the sharp outline and the glowing colour which it deserves. Only the sight of the place in the midst of the battle—that corner of splinters and churned earth and tortured humanity—could reveal the full epic of Delville Wood.

Let us measure it by the stern register of losses. At midnight on 14th July, when Lukin received his orders, the Brigade numbered 121 officers and 3,032 men. When Thackeray marched out on the 20th he had a remnant of 143, and the total ultimately assembled in Happy Valley was about 750. The casualties were—for the 1st Regiment, 558 ; for the 2nd, 482 ; for the 3rd, 771 ; and for the 4th, 509. These figures included 23 officers who were killed, 7 who died of wounds, 47 who were wounded, and 15 who were prisoners or missing. All the commissioned ranks of the 2nd and 3rd Regiments who were in the wood became casualties, as did all the officers of the Machine-Gun Company attached to the Brigade.* It is such a record as that of the 1st Coldstream or the 2nd Royal Scots Fusiliers at First Ypres. But the price was not paid in vain. The Brigade did what it was ordered to do, and did not yield until it was withdrawn.

I take two quotations from personal narratives which, better than any words of mine, reflect the grimness of the battle. One is from Private J. A. Lawson of the 3rd Regiment. He is describing the fight of Tuesday, the 18th—the great German attack when the garrison was forced back to the south-west corner. That morning Thackeray was holding the wood with nine and a

---

* If we take the casualties from the 1st of July, the total is 2,815—made up of 502 killed, 1,735 wounded, and 578 missing. Tanner, MacLeod, and Thackeray were all wounded. General Lukin was slightly gassed.

half companies, a strength of about 1,500 men ; two
days later he had 140 ; so we may judge the fury of
the conflict.

" Our little party had to wait in their cramped position of
tortured suspense till nearly 3 p.m. for the only relief we now
looked for—the relief afforded by the excitement of desperate
fighting against great odds. The enemy now launched an attack
in overwhelming numbers, amid the continued roar of artillery.
Once more they found us ready—a small party of utterly worn-
out men, shaking off their sleep to stand up in the shallow trench.
As the Huns came on they were mowed down—every shot must
have told. Our rifles smoked and became unbearably hot ; but
though the end seemed near, it was not yet. When the Huns
wavered and broke, they were reinforced and came on again. We
again prevailed, and drove them back. Only one Hun crossed
our trench, to fall shot in the heart a few yards behind it. The
lip of our trench told more plainly than words can how near they
were to not failing. Beyond, in No Man's Land, we could do
something to estimate the cost of their failure. . . . Exhaustion
now did what shell-fire and counter-attacks had failed to do, and
we collapsed in our trench, spent in body and at last worn out
in spirit. The task we had been set was too great for us. What
happened during the next two hours or so I do not know. Numbed
in all my senses, I gazed vacantly into space, feeling as if the whole
thing had been a ghastly nightmare, out of which I was now only
awaiting complete deliverance. From this state of coma I was
awakened by a shell which exploded just over me, and instantane-
ously I passed into unconsciousness. When I regained conscious-
ness a few minutes after, my first sensation was that of having
been thoroughly refreshed by sleep. But on moving I found that
the fight for me was over. . . . I tried to rouse my friend, who
had fallen face downward beside me. Getting no response, I
lifted his head, calling upon him by name, but I could not arouse
him. I then began with pain and difficulty to walk down the
line. I found that the last two hours of shelling had done their
work—only six remained alive in the trench. I aroused one
sleeper, and told him I had been badly hit, and was going to try
and walk out. He faced me for a second, and asked me what
he was to do. I said there was nothing to do but carry on, as

the orders of Saturday morning had not been countermanded. His brave ' Right-o ! ' were the last words I heard there—surely fitting words as the curtain fell for me."

The second quotation is from the late Captain Welsh, M.C., D.C.M., who was then a staff sergeant with the stretcher-bearers. The work of the Field Ambulance and of the regimental medical officers during these days deserved the highest praise, and it was due to their gallantry and resource that the sufferings of the men in the wood were not more horrible. The weather was now hot sun, now drenching rain, and the task of getting out the casualties was one long nightmare.

" The road from Longueval to Bernafay Wood was in an indescribable condition. It was impossible to carry from the front of the Regimental Aid Posts in Longueval, owing to the sniping, which was at times very severe and accurate. The rear was a mass of ruins, wire entanglements, garden fences, fallen and falling trees, together with every description of *débris* and shattered building material. It is one thing to clear a path along which reinforcements may be brought, but quite another to make a track on which four men may carry a stretcher with a modicum of comfort to the patient. . . . Besides this road there was a narrow sunken lane, which at first afforded some safety, but later became so pitted with shell-holes that the bearers were compelled to take to the open. In addition to these difficulties, it must be remembered that these roads were shelled heavily day and night. At times the enemy would put up a barrage with heavy stuff, which meant that no stretcher-bearing could be done until the fire was over. Parties who were unfortunate enough to be caught in one of these barrages spent moments of nerve-racking suspense, crouching in shell-holes or under banks, or wherever cover was available. One of the worst experiences of this kind was when it was decided to shell Longueval once more. Very short notice was given to clear all the Regimental Aid Posts, and only two men per stretcher could be spared. Padres, doctors, and odd men were pressed into service to enable all patients to be removed. As the party left, the bombardment began on both sides. Scrambling, pushing, and slipping amid a tornado of shell-fire, they headed for Bernafay Wood. It was impossible to keep together, and in the darkness squads easily became detached and lost touch. The noise of bursting shells was incessant and deafening, while the continuous sing of the rifle and machine-gun bullets overhead tried the nerves of the hardiest. To crown all, it was raining, and the roads were almost impassable for stretcher work. In fact, had it not been for the light of the German star shells, the thing could not have been worked at all. As the night wore on squad after squad of tired, soaked, and mud-covered men stumbled into Bernafay Wood. Here came a medical officer covered with grime and mud from top to toe, carrying a stretcher with a kilted Scot. Then a tall parson, unrecognizable under a coating of mud, with a stretcher-bearer as partner, whose orders he obeyed implicitly. When word was passed round in the morning that all had returned alive, some were so incredulous that they started an inquiry of their own."

I quote, too, from the records of the Field Ambulance a bare summary of a very gallant deed :—

" On the 18th it was again decided to shell Longueval, in which Captain Lawrie had established a Regimental Aid Post. It was found to be quite impossible to move all the stretcher cases, so he decided to remain behind in his station. The Aid Post was in a building, and as the Germans were counter-attacking and our troops going out, the windows and doors were barricaded with mattresses, furniture, and anything that might stop a bullet. The bombardment was opened by both British and German guns, and for about nine hours a hurricane of shells was poured into the village. By nothing short of a miracle the Regimental Aid Post was practically the only place that did not get a direct hit. During the night, dressing the wounded was carried out under great difficulty, as only a small electric torch or candle could be used. Captain the Rev. E. Hill, who had also remained to help, managed to keep up a constant supply of tea and coffee, apparently from supernatural sources. On the morning of the 19th a counter-attack was driven well home, and Captain Lawrie's party was thus saved from capture."

There is no more solemn moment in war than the parade of men after battle. The few hundred haggard survivors of the Brigade in the bright sunshine in Happy Valley were too weary and broken to realize how great a thing they had done. Tributes had come to them from high quarters. Sir Douglas Haig had sent his congratulations. The commander of the Fourth Army, Sir Henry Rawlinson, had written that " in the capture of Delville Wood the gallantry, perseverance, and determination of the South African Brigade deserves the highest commendation." They had earned the praise of their own intrepid commanding officers, who had gone through the worst side by side with their men. " Each individual," said Tanner's report, " was firm in the knowledge of his confidence in his comrades, and was, therefore, able to fight with that power which good discipline alone can produce. A finer record of this spirit could not be found than the line of silent bodies along the Strand over which the enemy had not dared to tread." But the most impressive tribute was that of their Brigadier. When the remnant of his Brigade paraded before him, Lukin took the salute with uncovered head and eyes not free from tears.

NOMINAL ROLL OF OFFICERS OF THE SOUTH AFRICAN INFANTRY BRIGADE—DELVILLE WOOD, JULY 1916.*

Brigadier-General H. T. LUKIN, C.B., C.M.G., D.S.O.
Major J. MITCHELL-BAKER, D.S.O.
Captain A. L. PEPPER.
Lieutenant F. R. ROSEBY . . . . . Died of wounds.
Sec.-Lieutenant F. W. S. BURTON.

1ST REGIMENT.

Name and Rank.	Remarks.
Lieut.-Col. F. S. DAWSON, C.M.G. . .	
Major F. H. HEAL	With transport.
„ E. T. BURGES	Killed.
Captain G. J. MILLER	Killed.
„ H. H. JENKINS	Wounded.
„ P. J. JOWETT	Missing (assumed dead).
Lieutenant T. O. PRIDAY (Adjutant) . .	Wounded.
„ S. W. E. STYLE	Wounded.
„ C. B. PARSONS	Killed.
„ C. F. S. NICHOLSON . . .	
„ E. A. DAVIES	Transport Officer.
„ W. S. DENT	Wounded.
„ J. M. HOLLINGWORTH . .	Missing (assumed dead).
„ A. W. CRAIG	Wounded.
„ L. I. ISSACS	
„ H. G. CHAPMAN	Wounded.
„ F. S. ENGLISH	
„ A. C. HARRISON	Wounded.
„ W. D. HENRY · · · · ·	{ Wounded and missing (since prisoner of war).
„ W. A. LARMUTH	Wounded.
„ A. W. LEIFELDT · . . .	Wounded.
„ C. W. REID	Wounded.
„ W. N. BROWN	Killed.
„ A. STUCKEY	
„ E. J. BURGESS	Wounded.
Sec.-Lieut. A. C. HAARHOFF	Killed.

* The roll is exclusive of the Machine Gun Company, the Trench Mortar Battery, the Field Ambulance, and the 64th Field Company Royal Engineers, all of which took part in the battle.

Sec.-Lieut. A. E. Brown . . . . . Killed.
    ,,   E. A. L. Hahn . . . . . Killed.
    ,,   W. Tempany . . . . . Wounded.
    ,,   P. W. Furmidge . . . . Wounded.
    ,,   C. I. Bate . . . . . . Prisoner.
    ,,   R. M. Lyne . . . . .
Q.M. and Hon. Captain A. C. Wearner
          Attached.
Chaplain and Captain E. St. C. Hill .

2ND REGIMENT.

Name and Rank.	*Remarks.*
Lieut.-Col. W. E. Tanner, C.M.G. . .	Wounded.
Major H. H. Gee	Died of wounds.
Captain H. W. M. Bamford (Adjt.) .	Wounded.
,, C. R. Heenan	Wounded.
,, E. Barlow	Wounded.
,, H. E. Clifford	Died of wounds.
,, W. F. Hoptroff	Killed.
,, W. J. Gray	Killed.
Lieutenant H. E. F. Creed	Killed.
,, L. Greene	Wounded.
,, W. J. Hill	Killed.
,, F. M. Davis	Wounded.
,, C. T. K. Letchford . . .	Killed.
,, C. L. H. Mulcahy	Died of wounds.
,, R. Beverley	Wounded.
,, W. J. Perkins	Wounded.
Sec.-Lieut. T. W. Bru-de-Wold . . .	Killed.
,, E. V. Tatham	Killed.
,, A. R. Knibbs	Wounded.
,, R. G. Miller	Killed.
,, B. N. Macfarlane . . .	Wounded.
,, E. C. Bryant	Injured.
,, R. P. Tatham	Killed.
,, F. G. Walsh	Transport officer.
,, A. T. Wales	Killed.
,, G. Green	Wounded.
,, W. H. Flemmer	Died of wounds.
,, N. Fenix	Wounded.

Sec.-Lieut. J. G. CONNOCK . . . . Killed.
Q.M. and Hon. Captain E. A. LEGGE .
Attached.
Chaplain and Captain P. J. WALSHE .

3RD REGIMENT.

Name and Rank.	*Remarks.*
Lieut.-Col. E. F. THACKERAY, C.M.G. .	Wounded. (At duty.)
Captain (Acting-Major) J. W. JACKSON	Killed.
„ R. F. C. MEDLICOTT . . .	Prisoner.
„ D. R. MacLACHLAN . . .	Killed.
„ E. V. VIVIAN	Wounded.
„ L. W. TOMLINSON	Wounded.
„ A. W. H. M'DONALD (Adjt.) .	Wounded.
LieutenantO. H. DE B. THOMAS · · ·	{Wounded and missing (since prisoner of war).
„ J. B. BAKER	Wounded.
„ A. L. PAXTON	Wounded.
„ A. M. THOMSON	Wounded.
„ B. H. L. DOUGHERTY . . .	Wounded.
„ D. A. PIRIE.	Prisoner.
„ H. M. HIRTZEL.	Prisoner.
„ H. G. ELLIOTT	Missing (assumed dead).
„ E. J. PHILLIPS	Wounded.
Sec.-Lieut. S. B. STOKES	Wounded.
„ D. JENNER	Wounded.
„ A. E. BARTON	Killed.
„ A. E. SHARPE	Gassed.
„ F. K. ST. M. RITCHIE . .	Prisoner.
„ D. M. ABEL.	Wounded.
„ H. W. GOVE	Missing (assumed dead).
„ C. H. DICK	Killed.
„ F. H. SOMMERSET	Killed.
„ A. C. HANKS	Died of Wounds.
„ S. PEARSON	Wounded.
„ S. J. GUARD	Wounded and prisoner.
„ W. SCALLAN	Wounded.
„ H. N. HEELEY	Wounded.
„ D. J. W. GOWIE	Shell shock.

Q.M. and Hon. Lieut. W. H. CARDING .

Attached.

Captain S. LIEBSON, S.A.M.C . . .	Wounded.
Chaplain and Captain G. T. COOK . .	Killed.

4TH REGIMENT.

Name and Rank.	*Remarks.*
Lieut.-Col. F. A. JONES, C.M.G., D.S.O.	Killed.
Major D. M. MACLEOD	Wounded.
„ D. R. HUNT	
Captain E. C. D. GRADY	Wounded.
„ T. H. ROSS	
„ C. M. BROWNE (Adjutant) .	Wounded.
„ S. C. RUSSELL	Died of wounds.
„ W. ANDERSON	Shell shock.
„ G. E. W. MARSHALL . . .	Shell shock.
„ F. McE. MITCHELL . . .	Attached 26th Brigade.
Lieutenant A. M. CAMERON	Wounded.
„ J. L. SHENTON	Wounded.
„ H. M. NEWSON	Prisoner.
„ T. FARRELL	Gassed.
„ C. M. GUEST	Staff.
„ A. H. BROWN	Killed.
„ J. WATKINS	Wounded.
„ R. D. GRIERSON	Gassed.
„ W. McLEAN	Brigade Staff.
„ A. S. TAYLOR	Wounded.
„ H. G. OUGHTERSON . . .	Killed.
„ R. B. THORBURN	Killed.
„ G. SMITH	Wounded.
„ A. V. CHASE	Wounded.
„ J. S. FRY	Killed.
„ A. YOUNG, V.C.	Wounded.
Sec.-Lieut. C. S. BELL	Killed.
„ D. ROSS	Killed.
„ W. H. KIRBY	Wounded.
„ C. A. A. MACLEAN . . .	Wounded.
„ E. F. DALGETY	
Q.M. and Hon. Lieut. Z. B. BAYLY.	

Attached.

Major M. B. POWER, S.A.M.C. . . .	
Chaplain and Captain S. THOMSON . .	

CHAPTER IV.

THE BATTLE OF THE SOMME : THE BUTTE DE WARLENCOURT.

(July–December 1916.)

The Brigade attached to the First Army—In the Trenches at Vimy —The Difficulties of the Later Stages of the Battle of the Somme—The Country around the Butte de Warlencourt— —The Brigade enters the Line at Eaucourt l'Abbaye—The Attack of 12th October—The Capture of the Pimple—The Attack of 18th October—The Fighting of the 18th and 19th —The Brigade withdrawn to the Arras Area—General Lukin takes Command of the 9th Division.

AFTER the fight at Longueval and Delville Wood the 9th Division left the Somme and was transferred from the XIII. Corps in the Fourth Army to the IV. Corps, under Lieutenant-General Sir Henry Wilson, in Sir Charles Monro's First Army. The South African Brigade marched to Maricourt on 23rd July, where it entrained for Hengest, *July 27.* and on the 27th arrived in the Frévillers area, north of the main road between Arras and St. Pol.

Here its first task was reorganization. Drafts to the number of 40 officers and 2,826 other ranks had been sent from Bordon during July, and their training had to be completed before they could be absorbed into the different regiments.* On 5th August, the Army Com-

* Lieutenant-Colonel Tanner was wounded on 17th July and his second-in-command, Major Gee, took over the 2nd Regiment. Major

mander, Sir Charles Monro, inspected the Brigade, which at the moment showed a parade strength of 62 officers and 2,523 men. On the 11th the King visited Frévillers and walked down the village street, which was lined by the 1st Regiment in fatigue dress. By the third week in the month the Brigade was sufficiently rested and reconstituted to take its place once again in the front line, and on 23rd August it took over from the 26th Brigade the Berthonval and Carency sections of the Vimy area. At that date the Germans held the crown of the celebrated ridge, and the British front ran along its western slopes. Different battalions of the Brigade held the first-line trenches until 23rd September, and thereby enlarged their experience of modern war, for they were enabled to realize for the first time the discomfort of trench fighting amid perpetual rain. For the greater part of the time the weather was abominable, the men were standing in two feet of water, and the last few days it rained so heavily that the parapets crumbled, and every available man had to be employed on their repair. It was a foretaste of what awaited them in October.

Aug. 11.

Aug. 23.

Vimy was a quiet area, for the great battle on the Somme continued, and this stage was for the Brigade almost barren of incident. The exception was a raid into

Gee was killed almost at once, and as there were no senior officers of the 2nd left Major Heal of the 1st took over command. This he held till the arrival from England at the end of August of Lieutenant-Colonel Christian, who took command of the 2nd Regiment. After the death of Lieutenant-Colonel Jones the 4th Regiment was under Major D. M. MacLeod. He was wounded on 17th July, after which Major D. R. Hunt took over, and continued in command till December 31, 1916.

the enemy's trenches on the night of the 13th September, carried out by parties from " B " and " D " Companies of the 2nd Regiment, under the command of Lieutenants Lilburn and Walsh. *Sept.* 13. There was a bright moon occasionally obscured by passing clouds ; but the raiding parties managed to reach the enemy's side of our wire without being observed. Our artillery put down a barrage, and under its cover the men doubled across No Man's Land and jumped into the German trenches, the barrage lifting as they arrived there. Prisoners were secured, dug-outs were bombed, and at a prearranged signal the raiders returned to their lines before the German barrage began. Their casualties were only two, though one was so severely wounded that he could not be moved from the German lines. Sir Charles Monro sent a message to General Lukin to express his admiration for the way in which the raid had been conducted—the meticulous care in its preparation, and the gallantry and enterprise displayed in its execution.

On 23rd September the Brigade was relieved, and on the 25th it moved to a new training area, that of the Third Army. On 5th October the 9th Division was restored to the Fourth Army, *Sept.* 23. and on the 7th the South Africans marched southward to the Somme. Next day, in heavy rain, they relieved the 141st Brigade of the 47th (Lon- *Oct.* 8–9. don Territorial) Division in Mametz Wood, now a bleak desolation, and on the 9th moved to High Wood, where they took over from the 142nd Brigade. The 9th Division was now side by side with another famous Scottish division, the 15th, and part of General Pulteney's III. Corps.

Since the 20th of July much had happened on the Somme. The advance of 1st July had carried the first enemy position on a broad front ; but the failure of the attack north of the Ancre had made the breach eight miles less than the original plan. The advance of 14th July gave us the second enemy position on a still narrower front—from Bazentin-le-Petit to Longueval. The danger now was that any further movement might result in the formation of a sharp and precarious salient ; so Haig broadened the breach by striking out to left and right, taking first Pozières and the high ground at Mouquet Farm, and then on the other flank Guillemont and Ginchy. This made the gap in the second enemy line seven miles wide, and brought us in most places to the highest ground, from which direct observation could be had over the slopes and pockets to the east. On 3rd

Sept. 3. September the Allies everywhere between Thiepval and Estrées were facing the German third line. At the outset of the battle this third position had been only in embryo, but before the assault of 14th July it had been for the most part completed, and by the beginning of September it had been elaborately fortified, and a fourth position prepared behind it. The third line was based on a string of fortified villages which lay on the reverse slopes of the main ridge—Courcelette, Martinpuich, Flers, Lesbœufs, and Morval. Behind it was an intermediate line, with Le Sars, Eaucourt l'Abbaye, and Gueudecourt as strong points in it. Further back lay the newly-made fourth line, just west of the Bapaume-Péronne road, covering the villages of Sailly-Saillisel and Le Transloy. This was the line protecting Bapaume, and at the moment the final German prepared position.

The fighting during July and August had greatly weakened the enemy forces. All the most famous German units had appeared—the pick of the Bavarians, the 5th Brandenburgers, and every division of the Guard and Guard Reserve Corps. The time was ripe early in September for a new attack which should accelerate the enemy's decline, and give the British front a new orientation. Haig's immediate aim was to break through the German third line ; but his ultimate objective was a thrust north-eastward across the Upper Ancre, so as to get behind the great slab of unbroken enemy positions from Thiepval northward. The moment was propitious for a new blow. The French on the British right had won conspicuous successes ; Brussilov was still pinning down the Austro-German forces on the Eastern front ; Sarrail had just launched an offensive in the Balkans ; Rumania had entered the war, and was pouring troops into Transylvania ; and the recent changes in the German High Command had for the time being slightly dislocated the machine.

On Friday, 15th September, Haig struck from a point south-east of Thiepval to Ginchy, with a force the larger part of which, such as the Guards, the Canadians, and the New Zealanders, was fresh *Sept.* 15. to the Somme area. He used for the first time the new British tanks, and in one day advanced to an average depth of a mile on a front of more than six, taking Courcelette, Martinpuich, and Flers. Only on his right, where the Guards were faced with an impossible task, was there any serious check. On 25th September he struck again between Combles and Martinpuich, and for the second time advanced one mile on a front of

six, and took Morval, Lesbœufs, and Gueudecourt, while
on the 26th the right wing of Sir Hubert
Sept. 25–
26.
Gough's Fifth Army carried Thiepval and
the whole of that crest.   That evening the
Allied fortunes in the West had never looked brighter.
The enemy was now back in his fourth line, and had
lost all the advantages of the higher ground.   His *moral*
was seriously shaken, and it appeared as if his great
machine was getting out of gear.   If heaven granted a
fine autumn there was good hope that a further advance
might drive him from the Bapaume ridge and crumble
his whole front between Arras and Péronne.

That hope was destined to fail.   The guns were
scarcely silent after the attack of the 26th when the
weather broke, and October was one succession of
tempestuous gales and drenching rains.   Now appeared
the supreme difficulty of trench warfare.   For three
months the Allies had been slowly advancing, blasting
their way forward with their guns before each infantry
attack, and the result was that the fifty square miles of
old battleground which lay behind their front lines had
been tortured out of recognition.   The little country
roads had been wholly destroyed, and, since they never
had much of a bottom, the road-menders had nothing
to build upon.   New roads were hard to make, for the
chalky soil had been so churned up by shelling that it
had lost all cohesion.   In all the area there were but
two good highways, and by the third month of the
battle even these showed signs of wear.   The consequence was that there were now two No Man's Lands
—one between the front lines, and one between the old
enemy front and the front we had won.   The second

was the bigger problem, for across it must be brought the supplies of a great army. It was a war of motor transport, and we were doing what the early Victorians had pronounced impossible—running the equivalent of steam engines not on prepared tracks but on high-roads, running them day and night in endless relays. The problem was difficult enough in fine weather, but when the rain came it turned the whole land into a morass. Every road became a watercourse, and in the hollows the mud was as deep as a man's thighs. The army must be fed, troops must be relieved, guns must be supplied, so there could be no slackening of the traffic. Off the roads the ground was one vast bog, dug-outs crumbled in, and communication trenches ceased to be. Behind the British front lay six miles of sponge, varied by mud torrents. It was into such miserable warfare, under persistent rain in a decomposing land, that the South African Brigade was now flung.

The line of the Fourth Army from a point northeast of Courcelette ran southward for the most part along the foot of the slopes which culminated in High Wood, and which were known to us as the Thiepval-Morval ridge. But a special topographical feature must be noted, for on it depended the fighting in October. From that ridge a series of spurs descended eastward into the hollow, one of which specially concerns us— the hammer-headed spur immediately west of Flers, at the end of which stood the odd tumulus called the Butte de Warlencourt. Below the eastern edge of this spur lay the German fourth position. It was a position on reverse slopes, and thus screened from direct observation, though our command of the high ground to the west gave us a view of its hinterland. Our own possession of the heights, great though the advantages were, had this drawback, that our communications had to descend the reverse slopes, and were thus partly exposed to the enemy's observation and long-range fire. The task of Sir Henry Rawlinson's Fourth Army in this sector was, therefore, to carry the spurs, and so get within assaulting distance of the German fourth line. The spurs were not part of the German main front, but were held as intermediate positions, every advantage being taken of sunken roads, of ruins, and of the undulations of the country. They represented for the fourth German line what Contalmaison had represented for the second ; till they were carried no general assault on the main front could be undertaken. Further, their capture would relieve our difficulties by giving us certain cover for our advanced gun positions, and shelter for the bringing up of supplies.

At first things went well. From Flers north-westward, in front of Eaucourt l'Abbaye and Le Sars, ran a very strong trench system which we called the Flers line, and which was virtually a switch connecting the old German third line, now in our hands, with the intermediate positions on the spurs. The capture of Flers gave us the south-eastern part of this line, and during the last days of September and the beginning of October we won the rest of it. On the 1st of October the 50th and 47th Divisions carried the Flers line north of Destremont Farm, and the ruined abbey of Eaucourt, though in the latter remnants of the 6th Bavarian Division made for some days a stout resistance. On 7th October the 23rd Division took the village of Le Sars, on the Albert-Bapaume road ; but the 47th Division, on their right, failed to reach the Butte de Warlencourt. These two divisions were now relieved, and the 15th and the 9th took their places, with orders to carry the Butte and the German intermediate line.

During the day of 9th October the 2nd South African Regiment, under Lieutenant-Colonel Christian, to the strength of 20 officers and 578 other ranks, took over the portion of the front line to be held by the Brigade. The relief, with the exception of *Oct. 9.* two posts, was complete by 1.25 a.m. on the 10th, and shortly before daybreak the missing posts were discovered. During that night a number of wounded, belonging to the outgoing 141st Brigade, were brought in by the South Africans.

The attention of the reader is now requested to the map opposite page 92. The boundary of the 9th Division on the left was the road from the Butte de Warlencourt to Martinpuich, where it ran along the depression of the ground west of Eaucourt. The South African Brigade was on the left of the division, and its brigade boundary ran through the ruins of Eaucourt l'Abbaye, beyond which the 26th Brigade held the front. The 27th Brigade was in divisional reserve. " B " and " C " Companies of the 2nd Regiment held the front line, as shown in the map, together with two strong posts, Nos. 58 and 77, on their left and right fronts respectively. " A " and " D " Companies were in the support trenches of the old Flers line running along the south-west side of Eaucourt l'Abbaye. The German front trenches, known to us as Snag and Tail, lay about 1,000 yards from our front line, and conformed roughly to its shape. Beyond them, running through the Butte de Warlencourt, was the enemy main intermediate position, cutting the Albert-Bapaume road beyond Le Sars. The confused fighting of the past weeks and the constant rains had made the whole front on both sides indeterminate. Odd lengths of fantastically-named trenches abounded, and at any one moment it was doubtful which were held by the Germans and which could be claimed by the British. Sir Henry Rawlinson's first task was to clear the ground up to the Butte, which would bring him directly in front of the German fourth position, running through Le Transloy and Ligny-Thilloy.

On the left of the South African front, and under their control, stood the ruins of a mill. The first instructions of the 2nd Regiment were to link up the posts 58 and 77 with the mill ; but owing to the slowness of the relief this could not be done till the second night, when some 600 yards of trench were dug. During the whole of the 10th and the 11th the 2nd Regiment was heavily shelled ; but their casualties were not large. On the 11th General Furse issued orders for an attack during daylight on the 12th in conjunction with the 26th Brigade on their right, and the 44th Brigade of the 15th Division on their left. The enemy's trenches were accordingly reconnoitred, and a certain number of machine guns located. So far as could be judged, there was no wire in the immediate vicinity. Orders were issued to push out a post to the point marked 93, and to link it up with the mill, but this instruction

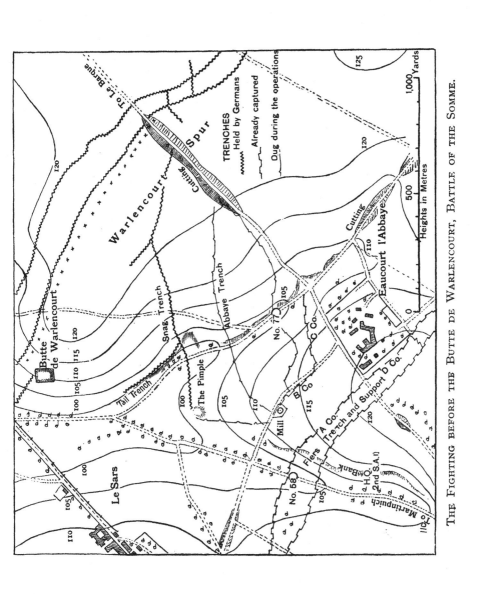

The FIGHTING BEFORE THE BUTTE DE WARLENCOURT, BATTLE OF THE SOMME.

was presently cancelled.   A new communication trench was dug between Flers trench and the front line.

The attack on the 12th was fixed for 2.5 in the afternoon.   The assault was to be carried out on a one-battalion front by the 2nd and 4th Regiments, the 2nd Regiment leading, with the *Oct. 12.* 3rd and 1st in reserve.   There were two objectives; the first the enemy trenches called Snag and Tail, and the second the main intermediate line through the Butte de Warlencourt.   The cloudy morning dissolved after midday in a drizzle of rain.   At 2.5, after a well-arranged barrage, the 2nd Regiment crossed the parapets, closely followed by the 4th, under Major Hunt.   One minute after zero an enemy barrage of exceptional violence began, with the result that in a quarter of an hour the telephone wires to the front line were cut, and no reports were received for some time.   In the misty weather it was impossible to see any distance, and the difficulty was increased owing to a smoke barrage, which we had laid down around the Butte, drifting in our direction. Presently it appeared that the enemy was following a new practice.   The ground over which we were attacking was a gentle slope, perfectly suited to machine-gun fire.   He had his machine guns placed well back in prepared positions, and caught our attack at long range. Under this blast no troops could live, and presently the impetus of the assault died away, long before the first objective had been obtained.

At 4 p.m. General Lukin received a message from Captain Ross of the 4th Regiment that he, with some details of the 2nd, was holding a line of shell-holes and a shallow trench half-way between our old front line and the first objective, and that in front of him, near the first objective, was a company of the 4th, while a part of the 2nd seemed to be farther forward. Lukin had already sent forward a company of the 3rd Regiment to hold the old front line, and he now ordered two officers' patrols from this company to clear up the situation. They reported during the evening that the Brigade had nowhere reached its first objective. As the attacking battalions had suffered heavily, and were now more or less disorganized, Lukin ordered the 3rd Regiment to relieve them, while the 1st was moved up in support. The relief was no light task, owing to the congested state of the communication trenches, and the difficulty of obtaining reliable guides ; and it was not till after dawn on the 13th that the 2nd and 4th Regiments were brought back to High Wood.

Early on the 13th it was discovered that Lieutenants Pearse and Donaldson, with about sixty men, had dug

Oct. 13. themselves in at a very exposed point near the enemy's line, and due south of the post at point 93. Lieutenant-Colonel Thackeray, commanding the 3rd Regiment, instructed Captain Montgomery, who commanded " C " Company in it, to open up visual communication with Lieutenant Pearse, and tell him that he could not be relieved till after dark. This was found to be impossible ; but Lieutenant Cruddas succeeded in reaching the place and ascertaining the exact position of the party, with the result that they were brought back safely during the evening. Meantime much work had been done in digging trenches and establishing what ground had been won. A new trench, afterwards known as Pearse's Trench, was dug from our old line to the point which he had held, and made a jumping-off ground for future operations.

Orders were received from the division at 6.15 p.m. to reconnoitre the deserted strong-point 93, with the object of occupying it. A patrol, under Lieutenant Mallett, reached it with little opposition, and found there many signs of German occupation, including a field and two machine-gun emplacements and a deep dug-out. This place was soon to become only too familiar to us under the name of the Pimple, a little mound some 60 feet long, 12 feet wide, and from 12 to 15 feet high.* The patrol did not return till daybreak, so it was impossible to occupy the Pimple that night ; but the 3rd Regiment were instructed that the following evening, as soon as the dark fell, they must enter into possession of the place, so that it might be linked up with the rest of the line. Accordingly, early on the night of the 14th, " B " Company of the 3rd Regiment, under Captain Sprenger, *Oct. 14.* was detailed for the work. Lieutenant Mallett led the advance for 400 yards and reached the mound, which was thereafter garrisoned by a party under Lieutenant Medlicott. Lieutenant Mallett then entered the trench running from the Pimple towards the enemy position in Snag and Tail trenches, and bombed the enemy out of a portion of this till he was driven back by machine-gun fire and severely wounded. Another party, however, under Lieutenants Harris and Estill, continued the work, and succeeded in taking and holding a considerable part of this section of the old German communications. That night the place was heavily bombed

* In its origin it was probably a big-gun emplacement.

by Germans moving along the trenches, and soon after dawn on the 15th a working party was seen approaching. As they were in close order, a Lewis gun was turned on them, and the squad was dispersed with many casualties. The garrison of " B " Company continued to hold the Pimple and the captured trenches until relieved by " A " Company of the 3rd on the night of the 15th. The casualties during the operation amounted to 3 officers (Lieutenant Medlicott killed, Captain Sprenger and Lieutenant Mallett wounded, the latter subsequently dying of his wounds) and 35 other ranks. It was one of the most gallant exploits during this stage of the battle.

On the night of the 16th the 3rd Regiment retired to the support line, and their place in the front trenches was taken by the 1st, under Lieutenant-Colonel Dawson. Meantime, large working parties had been employed in widening and deepening the communication trench between the Pimple and our front line and back to Flers Switch. During the 17th Dawson took his company commanders round the whole trench system, pointing out the limits of each company's front and the points to be attacked, for on that day orders had come from the division for an assault in the early morning of the 18th against the same objectives which had been attacked without success on the 12th. Such coaching was a most needful preliminary, for every hour, under the shelling and the weather, the landscape was growing more featureless. To the eye it was only a waste of wrinkled grey mud.

All that evening and for most of the night heavy rain fell, so that the trenches and parapets were mere

Oct. 16–17.

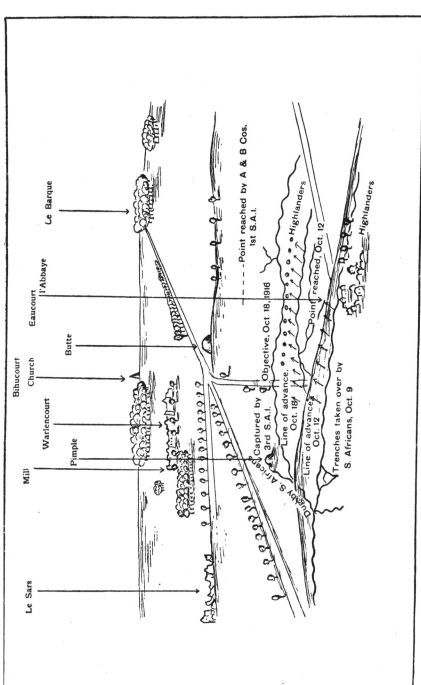

Le Sars   Mill   Pimple   Warlencourt   Church   Butte   Eaucourt   l'Abbaye   Le Barque

Bihucourt

Point reached by A & B Cos. 1st S.A.I.

Objective, Oct. 18, 1916

Point reached, Oct. 12

Highlanders

Highlanders

Captured by 3rd S.A.I.

Line of advance, Oct. 18

Line of advance, Oct. 12

Dug in S. Africans

Trenches taken over by S. Africans, Oct. 9

SCENE OF SOUTH AFRICAN BRIGADE'S ADVANCE AGAINST THE BUTTE DE WARLENCOURT POSITION.

undulations in a quagmire. The front-line trench being deep and narrow with few fire-steps, it was difficult for the men to leave it, and realizing this, the company commanders began getting their troops out more than an hour before the time fixed for the attack. Zero hour was at 3.40 a.m., and when it came the three *Oct. 18.* assaulting companies of the 1st Regiment were already for the most part formed up in No Man's Land.

Keeping as close as they dared to their barrage, the South Africans advanced, with " C " Company on their left, " B " Company in the centre, and " A " on the right. They disappeared into the rain, and for several hours were unheard of. When news came it was news of failure. " C " Company, under Captain Jenkins, passed the communication trench leading south from the Pimple, and came to that junction of Tail and Snag trenches which we called the Nose of the Switch. Here they were held up by wire at the foot of a steep bank in front of the German line, and were also heavily bombed from the trenches themselves. The leading platoon was almost entirely shot down, and though an officer and six men of the following platoon managed to get into the German trench, they, too, immediately fell. The only officer left was Captain Jenkins, who was himself wounded ; and, seeing that the enemy line was so strongly held, and that there was no hope of success for what remained of his company, he ordered the company sergeant-major to withdraw the survivors to their original line. The casualties of " C " Company were 69 out of the 100 who crossed the parapet.

The fate of " A " and " B " Companies was still harder, and to understand it the reader must again turn to the map. The two companies advanced rapidly behind our barrage and entered Snag Trench, Captain Whiting, who commanded " B " Company, being mortally wounded half-way across. They failed, however, to realize that they had reached their objective, and continued beyond it. The whole place was so battered by shell-fire that the trench outlines had become obscure. They saw about 600 yards on their right some of the Highlanders of the 26th Brigade, but they had now wholly lost touch with their flanks, and the enemy was filtering in between them and their old front. Lieutenant Stapleton with a few stragglers succeeded in returning, after killing some twelve Germans and taking nineteen prisoners ; two officers and sixteen other ranks were captured ; but with these exceptions all the men of " A " and " B " Companies were killed.*

At daybreak a gallant attempt was made by Major Ormiston, commanding the troops on the Pimple, to bomb along the trench leading to the junction of the Tail and Snag trenches, but it broke down under machine-gun fire from the German strong-point at the Nose. A block was established about 50 yards up the trench from the Pimple, but no further progress could be made, since the trench dipped into a hollow, and was wholly commanded by the Germans at the Nose.

Such was the position on the morning of the 18th. During the night a company of the 3rd Regiment, under Captain Langdale, had been moved forward to the front

* " One saw a large party of South Africans at full stretch with bayonets at the charge—all dead ; but even in death they seemed to have the battle ardour stamped on their faces." Lieut.- Col. Croft's *Three Years with the 9th Division*, p. 84.

line and put at Dawson's disposal, and a company of the 4th Regiment was sent to replace it in the support line. Presently Langdale took up his position in Pearse's Trench, and on Dawson's instructions sent out a patrol to look for " A " and " B " Companies. The patrol returned at two in the afternoon, having obtained no information. The situation, therefore, was that " C " Company had failed in the attack with heavy losses, and that " A " and " B " Companies had disappeared. The key of the enemy position was clearly the Nose, and until this could be thoroughly bombarded progress was impossible. Communications, however, were so difficult that all day Dawson was asking for the bombardment of the Nose, and all day our guns were firing on the wrong point.

That afternoon Dawson was ordered to renew the attack at 5.45 p.m. He decided that " D " Company of his own 1st Regiment should attack from the Pimple, while Captain Langdale's Company of the 3rd should advance from Pearse's Trench. If the Nose was to be taken it must be attacked along Snag Trench from the east. Owing to the appalling condition of the trenches, which were now all but impassable, Captain Langdale advanced with only one platoon and two Lewis gun teams. He entered Snag Trench without opposition, and moved along it to the right for some 200 yards, where he made a block and left a Lewis gun. He then moved westward to a point about 25 yards from the Nose, where he came upon three German machine guns in action. He did not feel strong enough to attack them himself, and after remaining there about an hour withdrew his men to the original front line. The bombing attack from the Pimple had also failed. Dawson ordered Captain Langdale to return at once and re-occupy Snag Trench, and this was done between twelve and one on the morning of the 19th.

Meanwhile Lukin had sent forward a company of the 4th Regiment, under Captain Ross, with instructions to carry out a fresh attack at the junction of Snag and Tail trenches. Captain Ross reached the front line about 4 a.m. on the morning of the 19th. At about five o'clock the enemy launched an assault with bombs and *flammenwerfer* against Captain Langdale's and Captain Ross's men in Snag Trench, and drove them out, with heavy casualties to Captain Ross's company. The leader was wounded, and Lieutenant Young, V.C., killed. The position now was that Snag and Tail trenches were held in force by the enemy, and that we were everywhere back in our old line except on the extreme right, where some details of the 3rd and 4th Regiments seemed to be on the left flank of the 26th Brigade.

Oct. 19.

On the morning of the 19th it was decided to make another attempt to clear Snag Trench, and for the purpose a company was dispatched from the 3rd Regiment, under Lieutenant Elliott. All that morning the two machine guns at the Pimple, under Major Ormiston, had enfiladed the trench. It often happened that small bodies of Germans, unable to stand the strain, would leave cover and bolt across the open towards the Butte, making an excellent target for our snipers and machine gunners.* By the afternoon few of the enemy were left

---

* When the Nose was finally occupied by the 6th K.O.S.B. they found over 250 German dead lying around it.

in Snag Trench ; but the machine guns were still at the Nose, and our artillery seemed unable to touch them.

At noon Lieutenant Elliott reported to Dawson, and was instructed to enter Snag Trench, to get in touch with the 26th Brigade on his right, and then to work his way towards the Nose and drive out the enemy there. At five minutes to three Lieutenant Elliott entered Snag Trench without difficulty, but failed— apparently owing to insufficient bombs—to advance towards the Nose, beyond which Major Ormiston was waiting to attack as soon as there was a supporting movement from the east. The thing had now become hopeless. Dawson had not a single officer or man, with the exception of his adjutant, fit to make another journey to the front line. The mud was so thick that rifles, machine guns, and Lewis guns were constantly jamming, and among the little party on the Pimple there was not one rifle which could be fired. In many of the trenches the mud was three feet deep, and the wounded had to be dug out at once before they suffocated. Every man was utterly exhausted.*

That night the remnant under Dawson was relieved by the 6th K.O.S.B. from the 27th Brigade, and early on the morning of the 20th all were back in High Wood. *Oct. 20.*

So ended the tale of the South Africans' share in the most dismal of all the chapters of the Somme, a chapter which, nevertheless, deserves to rank high in

---

* The atrocious condition of the ground was partly due to our use of the delay-action fuse, which caused shells to explode well below the soil and so led to big subsidences which speedily became mudholes.

the record of British hardihood. The enemy held his ground with admirable skill and resolution. The fighting had not the swift pace and the obvious successes of the earlier battles. We were striving for minor objectives, and such a task lacks the impetus and exhilaration of a great combined assault. Often the action resolved itself into isolated struggles, a handful of men in a mud-hole holding out till their post was linked up with our main front. Rain, cold, slow reliefs, the absence of hot food, and often of any food at all, made those episodes a severe test of endurance and devotion. So awful was the mud that each stretcher required eight bearers, and at the end battalion runners, though carrying no arms or equipment, took from four to six hours to cover the thousand odd yards between the front line and battalion headquarters. To show the utter exhaustion of the troops, at High Wood after the relief many men were found lying fast asleep without overcoats or blankets, and stiff with frost. To add to their discomfort, there was a perpetual and inevitable confusion of mind. The front was never at any one moment clearly defined, and officers led and men followed in a cruel fog of uncertainty. Such fighting could not be other than costly. In the ten days from the 9th to the 19th October the South African casualties were approximately 1,150, including 45 officers, 16 of whom were killed.*

On 21st October the Brigade, with the exception of the 3rd Regiment, which was in High Wood in reserve

* The Butte de Warlencourt was never taken during the Battle of the Somme, though early in November the 50th Division made a gallant attempt. It was occupied by us in the last week of February 1917, when the enemy retreated.

BRIG.-GEN. FRED. STEWART DAWSON, C.M.G., D.S.O., A.D.C.
Commanding 1st South African Regiment, and later South African
Brigade.

to the 27th Brigade, moved to Mametz Wood. On the 23rd orders were received that the Brigade would be in reserve in the attack to be carried out by the 9th Division on the 25th. Presently these orders were cancelled, and the entire division was taken out of the line. At the end of the month it moved north to an area south of the Doullens-Arras road, and became part of Major-General Aylmer Haldane's VI. Corps in Sir Edmund Allenby's Third Army.

During November the 1st South African Regiment was in huts at Duisans, the 2nd at Lattre St. Quentin, the 3rd at Wanquetin, and the 4th billeted in Arras, where it was engaged in improving the defences of that city. The other regiments were occupied in training, in the construction of new roads and cable trenches, and in the other preliminary work necessary in the area of a coming battle. For it had already been decided by Sir Douglas Haig that the great thrust of the spring would be from Arras eastward.

November of that year was not the sodden downpour of October. There were seasons of high wind and sharp frost, which were a grateful relief after the monotony of the Butte de Warlencourt fighting. On 2nd December General Lukin was promoted to the command of the 9th Division, with the rank of Major-General, on General Furse's *Dec. 2.* appointment as Master-General of the Ordnance. All South Africans felt their Brigadier's advancement to be a personal tribute to the Brigade which he had so gallantly led. He was succeeded in its command by Lieutenant-Colonel Dawson of the 1st Regiment, who was succeeded in turn by Major F. H. Heal.

CHAPTER V.

IN November 1916 a conference of representatives of
all the Allied Powers was held at French General
Headquarters, and a plan made for the campaign of
the following year. In 1917 Sir Douglas Haig desired
to undertake a great offensive in Flanders, with a view to
clearing the Belgian coast, for in that area he believed
that success would give the highest strategic reward.
But before this movement began it was desirable to reap
the fruits of the Battle of the Somme. In November
the enemy was penned in an awkward salient between
the valleys of the Ancre and the Scarpe. The British
Commander-in-Chief proposed early in the spring to
attack this salient simultaneously on two sides—the
Fifth Army moving on the Ancre front, and the Third
Army attacking from the north-west about Arras. At

the same time the First Army was to carry the Vimy Ridge, the possession of which was necessary to secure the left flank of our operations farther south. So soon as this was completed, the Flanders campaign would begin with an assault on the Messines Ridge, to be followed by an attack eastward from the Ypres salient.

The reasons for Sir Douglas Haig's plan are clear. He was fully aware of the new great German position which had been preparing during the winter, and which was known as the Hindenburg or Siegfried Line, and he did not think it good policy to make a frontal assault upon it. He knew that the Battle of the Somme had seriously weakened the enemy, and he believed—it was, indeed, a mathematical certainty—that the tactics of the Somme, if persisted in during 1917, and supported by a reasonable pressure from the Russian front, would give the Allies victory before the close of that year. He wished, therefore, to stage a second battle of the Somme type—to stage it in an area where its strategic results would be most fruitful ; and to begin it sufficiently early in the season to allow a decision to be reached before the close of the good weather.

This plan had to be wholly recast. The British and French Governments decided that Haig must take over a longer front, and before the end of February 1917 the British right was as far south as a point opposite the town of Roye. Again, the retreat of the Germans during February and March 1917 destroyed the salient which Haig had purposed to attack. There now remained nothing of the preliminary movement as originally planned, except the carrying of the Vimy Ridge. But a fresh scheme had been proposed by the French

and accepted by the British Government. Under the
new French Commander-in-Chief, Nivelle, an ambitious operation was conceived on the heights of the
Aisne, which, it was trusted, would open the way to
Laon. In this action the old method of limited objectives was to be relinquished ; and Nivelle hoped, by
means of his new tactics and by an unexampled concentration of troops, to break through the enemy lines
on a broad front and restore the war of movement.
This attack was fixed for the middle of April. It would
operate against the southern pivot of the Siegfried zone,
and it was arranged that Haig should use his forces
against the northern pillar east of Arras, and should
strike a week before.

The position was, therefore, that the Arras battle,
which Haig had regarded as only a preparation for the
main campaign of the season in Flanders, became the
principal task of the British Army during the first half of
1917. This battle in turn was conceived as an action
subsidiary to the greater effort of the French in the south.
It was admittedly an attack in a region where, except
for an unexampled piece of fortune, great strategic
results could scarcely be obtained. The British success
depended upon what the French could do on the Aisne.
If Nivelle failed, then they, too, must fail in the larger
strategic sense, however valuable might be certain of
their local gains. If, however, Nivelle succeeded, the
pressure from Arras in the north would beyond doubt
greatly contribute to the enemy's discomfiture. The
danger of the whole plan was that the issue might be
indeterminate and the fighting at Arras so long protracted, without any decisive success, that the chances

of the more vital Flanders offensive later in the summer would be imperilled. This, as we shall see, was precisely what happened.

In December 1916 the 9th Division relieved the 35th Division, which was then holding the trenches in front of Arras. The front held by the South African Brigade extended now for 1,800 yards northward from the River Scarpe.* For three months they remained in this section, during the severest winter known in France for many years. For most of December it rained, and in January and February there came heavy snow and bitter frost. On 14th *Jan.* 14, January the 9th Division passed from the 1917. VI. Corps to the XVII. Corps, commanded by Lieutenant-General Sir Charles Fergusson, and this involved an alteration in the divisional boundaries. The 26th Brigade, which was holding a line of trenches south of the Scarpe, now relieved certain Canadian units; and the whole of the new corps front, since several of its divisions had not yet arrived, was held by the 9th Division, with all three brigades in line. Early in February the 51st (Highland Territorial) Division took over the ground held by the 26th Brigade, and the 34th Division relieved the 27th Brigade, so that the 9th Division's front from St. Pancras Trench to the Scarpe was held by the South Africans.

These months were filled with preparations for the great spring attack. New trenches had to be made and old trenches diverted; headquarters had to be found for battalions and brigades, and emplacements con-

* Their right flank was in a marsh, where duck-shooting could be enjoyed within 800 yards of the German trenches.

structed for artillery and trench mortars. In addition to this, patrols and wiring parties were busy every *Jan.* 3. night. On January 3, 1917, a party from the 3rd South African Regiment, commanded by Lieutenants B. W. Goodwin and W. F. G. Thomas, made a successful raid on the German trenches. The men were picked volunteers, who, for the week before, had been thoroughly trained in the work, so that each knew exactly the task before him. All had blackened faces, and used only the Zulu language. After our barrage had drenched the enemy front line the raiders entered the German trenches, which were found to be very deep and magnificently constructed, though badly damaged by our gun-fire. Only one prisoner was brought in, but a number of dug-outs and concrete machine-gun emplacements were destroyed, and the enemy suffered many casualties.

On 4th March the South Africans were relieved by the 26th Brigade, and marched from Arras to the neigh- *March* 4. bourhood of Ostreville, where they began their intensive training for the coming offensive. Their casualties during the previous three months in the line had been 2 officers and 49 other ranks killed, and 5 officers and 166 other ranks wounded. The health of the men, considering the severity of the weather, had been extraordinarily good, and only twenty-eight cases of trench feet were reported. As was dryly observed, the doubt as to whether they could stand a northern winter was settled by keeping them continuously in the trenches. On 5th March Sir Douglas Haig inspected the 1st and 4th Regiments, and complimented them highly on their smartness ; and on 11th

March the 1st, 2nd, and 4th Regiments were inspected by the Colonial Secretary, Mr. Walter Long.

While the South Africans were beginning their intensive training, the Germans were completing their retirement from the Bapaume Ridge to the Siegfried Line. At the hamlet of Tilloy-lez-Mofflaines, on the Arras-Cambrai road, this line branched off from the old front. Beaurains was now ours, and Arras was therefore free from its former encirclement in the south. The German position from the northern pivot of the new Siegfried Line to Lens was very strong, consisting of three main systems, each constructed on the familiar pattern of four parallel lines of trenches studded with redoubts, and linked up by numerous switches. A special and very powerful switch line ran for 5½ miles from the village of Feuchy northward across the Scarpe to beyond Thélus, and constituted what was virtually a fourth line of defence. The whole defensive belt was from two to five miles deep, but the German High Command were not content with it. They had designed an independent line running from Drocourt, south-east of Lens, to the Siegfried Line at Quéant as an alternative in case of an assault on the Arras salient. Towards the close of March this position, which was to become famous as the Drocourt-Quéant Switch, was not complete. It was intended as a protection to Douai and Cambrai, the loss of which would have made the whole Siegfried system untenable. But it was designed only as an extra precaution, for there was every confidence in the mighty ramified defences between Lens and Tilloy and in the resisting power of the northern Siegfried section. The country through which the German positions ran was peculiarly suited to their purpose. It represented the breakdown of the Picardy wolds into the flats of the Scheldt, the last foothills of the uplands of northern France. Long, low spurs reach out to the eastward separating the valleys of the Scarpe, the Cojeul, and the Sensée, and their sides are scored with smaller valleys —an ideal terrain for a defensive battle.

It will be seen that Sir Douglas Haig had a formidable problem before him. The immediate key of the area was Vimy Ridge, the capture of which was necessary to protect the flank of any advance farther south. It was clear that no strategic result could be obtained unless the Drocourt-Quéant Switch were breached, and that meant an advance of well over six miles. But this position was still in the making ; and if the fates were kind, and the first three German systems could be carried at a rush, there was good hope that the Drocourt-Quéant line would never be manned, and that the drive of the British, assisted by the great French attack on the Aisne, might bring them to Douai and Cambrai. It was a hope, but no more. A result so far-reaching demanded a combination of fortunate chances, which as yet had not been vouchsafed to us in any battle of the campaign.

The city of Arras, situated less than a mile inside the British lines, was, like Ypres, the neck of a bottle, and through it and its environs went most of the transport for the new battle front. For two years it had been a place of comparative peace. It had been badly shelled, but mainly in the autumn and winter of 1914. The cathedral, a poor rococo edifice, had been destroyed, and looked far nobler in its ruin than it had ever done in its integrity. The beautiful old Hôtel de Ville had been wrecked, and much damage had been done among the exquisite Spanish houses of the Grande Place. Few buildings had altogether escaped, but the place was still a habitable though a desolated city. Entering it by the Baudimont Gate on a summer's day the stranger saw the long white street running intact towards the railway station, and it was not till he looked closer that he noted shell marks and broken windows and the other signs of war. There were many hundreds of civilians still living there, and children could be seen playing on the pavement. Visitors came often, for it was the easiest place in all France from which to enter the first lines. Across the railway, a short walk in communication trenches, or even on the open road, and you were in the actual battle front west of Blangy or in the faubourg of St. Sauveur. An inn, the Hôtel de Commerce, was still open, and men could dine there in comfort before proceeding to their posts in the line. But up to April 1917 the place had the air of a tomb. It was like a city stricken with the plague: whole, yet untenanted. Especially eerie did it seem in the winter twilight, when in the long echoing streets the only sign of life was an occasional kilted Scot or South African, or a hurrying peasant woman, and the rumble of the guns beyond Vimy alone broke the heavy silence. The gaunt ruins of the cathedral rose like a splendid headstone in a graveyard.

Towards the close of March 1917 Arras awoke to an amazing change. Its streets and lanes were once more full of life, and the Roman arch of the Baudimont Gate saw an endless procession of troops and transport. A city makes a difficult base for a great attack. It must be the route of advancing infantry and their billeting area, and it is a mark which the enemy guns can scarcely miss. To minimise this danger the British generals had recourse to a bold plan. They resolved in this section to assemble their armies underground. After the fashion of old French towns, Arras had huge ancient sewers, like those of Paris which may be read of in *Les Misérables*. A map of them was found, and the underground labyrinth was explored and enlarged. Moreover, the town had grown over the quarries from which the older part of it had been built, and these also were discovered. The result was that a second city was created below the first, where three divisions could be assembled in perfect security. The caverns were lit by electricity, plans and sign-posts were put up as if it had been a Tube railway, and a dressing station with 700 beds was constructed. Here it was arranged that the greater part of the VI. Corps should assemble for the attack due east of the city. As a matter of fact the thing was not needed. The Germans shelled the town intermittently, but there was no real bombardment, and before Arras could be methodically destroyed the enemy had been pushed many miles eastward.

The South African Brigade, like the other troops of assault, were trained for the battle with scientific precision. Models in clay of the German trenches were constructed on the training ground, which was laid out as near as possible to correspond to the enemy front in depth and breadth. Here the attack was practised until each man was made familiar with his proper task. During these days the British artillery was very busy. So great was the concentration of guns that they could have been placed wheel to wheel from end to end of the battle front. Various " Chinese " attacks were organized, as rehearsals and to mislead the enemy. In the third week of March a systematic cutting of the German wire began, and our heavy artillery shelled their back areas *April 5.* and communications. On Thursday, the 5th of April, a steady bombardment opened against all the main German positions, more especially the great fortress of the Vimy Ridge. Wonderful counter-battery work was done, and battery after battery of the enemy was put out of action, located partly by direct observation from the air, and partly by our new device for sound-identification. These were for the most part days of clear, cold, spring weather, with the wind in the north-east ; and from dawn to dark our airplanes fought on their own account a mighty battle. The history of that week must rank as an epoch in the campaign in the air. It was a time of heavy losses, for at all costs the foe must be blinded, and the British airmen kept up one continuous offensive. Forty-eight of our own planes failed to return, and forty-six of the enemy's were destroyed or driven down out of control. The attackers, as was natural, paid the heavier price.

The British front of attack was slightly over twelve miles long, from Givenchy-en-Gohelle in the north to a point just short of Croisilles in the south. On the left was the right Corps of Sir Henry Horne's First Army— the Canadian Corps under Sir Julian Byng, with one British brigade, directed against the Vimy Ridge. On their right lay Sir Edmund Allenby's Third Army. Its northern Corps, next to the Canadians, was the XVII., under Sir Charles Fergusson, with three divisions in line— from left to right the 51st (Highland Territorial), the 34th, and the 9th ; and one, the 4th, in support. The central Corps was Aylmer Haldane's VI., with, in line, the 15th, 12th, and the 3rd Divisions, and the 37th in support. On the right of the battle was Sir Thomas Snow's VII. Corps, with the 14th, 56th, and 30th Divisions in line, and the 21st forming a pivot on the right. It is interesting to note that in its constituents the army of assault was largely Scottish. Thirty-eight Scots battalions were destined to go over the parapet—a larger number than the British at Waterloo, and many times the force that Bruce commanded at Bannockburn.

On 13th March the 9th Division had received the plan of attack, and from 5th April onward its divisional guns—269 pieces in all—were busy with the preliminary bombardment. On Friday, 6th April, the South African Brigade—with the exception of the 1st Regiment, which was in line—was inspected by Lieutenant-General J. C. Smuts, but lately returned from his East African campaign. He was deeply impressed by the fine condition of the men. They had passed through one of the worst winters on record without losing any of their ardour of spirit or vigour of body. So far their experience in battle had been bitterly hard— the long-drawn-out torture of Delville Wood, and the misery of the hopeless struggle at the Butte de Warlencourt. Now for the first time they were about to engage in a great forward movement, long and patiently prepared, and amply supported by artillery. Every man among them was strung to that pitch of expectation and confidence which is the mood of all successful offensives.

A proof of their spirit was given the following day. It was necessary to identify more carefully the German

April 6.

troops against them, and the 1st Regiment was ordered to carry out a daylight raid. The attempt was origi- nally timed for eleven in the morning, but *April 7.* it was subsequently postponed to three in the afternoon. At that hour, under cover of our barrage, a party of 5 officers and 50 other ranks, under Captain T. Roffe, crossed our parapets, and reached the German trenches without a casualty. A large dug-out was found, out of which three Germans of the 8th Bavarian Regiment were taken prisoner. Their object having been accomplished the party retired, and reached their own lines with the loss of one killed and three wounded. On their way back, however, a private with a broken thigh was seen by Lieutenant Scheepers to be lying in front of the German parapet. He and Captain Roffe went back to help him; but, coming under heavy fire, were compelled to take cover in a shell-hole in No Man's Land, where they remained until, under the cloak of darkness, they were able to bring in their wounded man.

That night the Brigade, less the 1st Regiment, marched from its training area to Arras, and took up its quarters in the northern outskirts. The artillery preparation continued to be intense till the *April 8.* next day, Sunday, 8th April, the day origi- nally fixed for the attack. That Sunday the weather was clear and calm, with a foretaste of spring. A lull seemed to fall upon the British front, and the ear-splitting din of the past week died away into sporadic bombardments. It is possible that this sudden quiet outwitted the enemy. He was perfectly aware of the coming attack, and he knew its area and objectives. He had expected it each day, and each day had been disappointed. On the Sunday he began to reply, and rained shells at intervals into the streets of Arras, but he did little harm. The troops of attack there were waiting comfortably in cellars and underground assembly stations. In the late evening the weather changed, the wind shifted to the west, and blew up to rain and squalls of snow. During the night there were long spells of quiet, broken by feverish outbreaks of enemy fire from Vimy to Croisilles. Our own batteries were for the most part silent.

That night the South Africans began to assemble in the front and support lines preparatory to their attack. The 9th Division was holding some 1,800 yards of front from the river Scarpe to a point just north of the Bailleul road. It had the 26th Brigade on its right next the river, the South Africans in the centre, and the 27th Brigade on its left. Three objectives had been given to the division, known as the Black, the Blue, and the Brown lines. The Black Line, from the river Scarpe to Chantecler, including the village of Laurent-Blangy, represented the last line of the enemy's front system, and was approximately 800 yards away from our own front trenches. To reach this line two, and in places three, trench lines had to be taken and passed. The Blue Line was 900 yards east of the first objective, and represented the enemy's second trench system on the Arras-Lens railway. The Brown Line, from 800 to 1,000 yards farther east, was the German third system, running from the village of Athies to the Point du Jour. To reach the Brown Line a distance of some 2,700 yards had to be traversed. If the Brown Line were taken, General Lambton's 4th Division was to pass through the 9th, and capture the Green Line, including the village of Fampoux—the last German system before the Drocourt-Quéant Switch.

The arrangements for the South African Brigade were that they should attack on a two-battalion front of 600 yards, with the 4th Regiment on the left and the 3rd on the right, each battalion attacking on a two-company front, supported by its two remaining companies, while each company in turn would be on a two-platoon front. The 2nd Regiment was in support on the left, and the 1st on the right. When the first two objectives were taken the two battalions in support were to become the attacking battalions for the third objective —the Brown Line—while the two original assaulting battalions remained in support. The 1st Regiment was under Lieutenant-Colonel Heal, the 2nd under Lieutenant-Colonel Tanner, the 3rd under Lieutenant-Colonel Thackeray, and the 4th under Lieutenant-Colonel Christian. Pontoons were thrown across the Scarpe during the night to facilitate the march of the men to the assembly area ; and the Royal Engineers attached to the Brigade blew twenty-six craters in No Man's Land to accommodate the leading waves of the attack. By 2 a.m. on the morning of Easter Monday, 9th April, all four battalions of the Brigade were in position. *April* 9.

Zero hour was at 5.30 in the morning. At 4 a.m. a drizzle began which changed presently to drifts of thin snow. It was intensely cold, and it was scarcely half-light, so the troops waiting for the signal saw before them only a dark mist flecked with snowflakes. But at the appointed moment the British guns broke into such a fire as had not yet been seen on any battleground on earth. It was the first hour of the Somme repeated, but tenfold more awful. As our men went over the parapets they felt as if they were under the protection of some supernatural power, for the heaven above them was one canopy of shrieking steel. There were now no enemy front trenches; there were no second-line trenches; only a hummocky waste of craters and broken wire, over which our barrage crept relentlessly.

The great deeds of that day are known to all : how the Canadians at a bound reached the crest of Vimy ; how the 15th Division carried the Railway Triangle and Feuchy ; how the fortress of the Harp fell to the 3rd Division ; how Telegraph Hill fell to the 14th and Observation Hill to the 12th, and Neuville-Vitasse to the 56th. We are here concerned with only one part of the battle—the doings of the 9th Division, and especially of the South African Brigade.

At zero hour our barrage opened fifty yards in front of the first German trenches, and under its cover the 3rd and 4th South African regiments advanced to the attack. On the left " C " Company (Lieutenant Smith) and " D " Company (Captain Reid) of the 4th led, followed by " A " Company (Captain Grady) and " B " Company (Lieutenant Morrison). On the right " A " Company (Captain Vivian) and " D " Company (Lieutenant Money) of the 3rd led, followed by " B " Company (Lieutenant Elliott) and " C " Company (Lieutenant Ellis). Close on their heels came the supporting companies of the 1st and 2nd Regiments, and occupied some trenches just beyond the German front line, as the supporting point to the attack on the first objective. The 3rd Regiment, as it crossed the parapet and moved over No Man's Land, met with heavy machine-gun fire on its right flank, and suffered many casualties, includ-

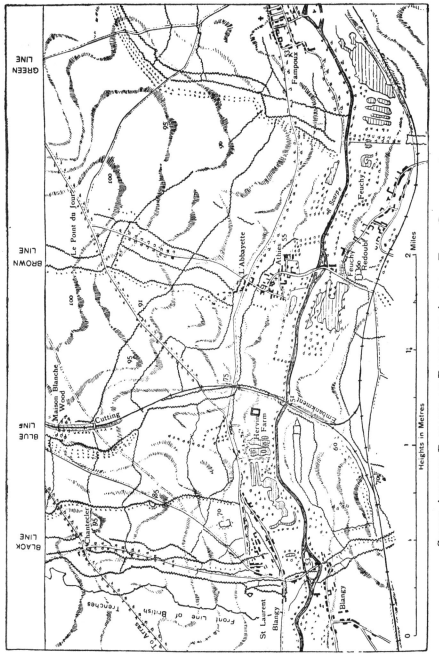

SOUTH AFRICAN BRIGADE AT BATTLE OF ARRAS. FIRST STAGE OF ADVANCE.

ing Lieutenant Burrows killed, and Lieutenants Elliott, Money, Hyde, Gray, Thomas, Van Ryneveld, and Lee wounded. Our barrage, however, was perfect, and the skilful use of smoke shells blinded the enemy's vision. n thirty-four minutes the Black Line was reached. The 4th Regiment on the left had fewer losses, though its leading companies had some casualties from approaching too close to our own barrage. The " mopping-up" detachments, consisting of fifty men from the 4th Regiment, two platoons from the 1st, and two platoons from the 2nd, reached the trenches with the first wave, and cleared out the dug-outs, taking many prisoners, and meeting with little resistance.

At 7.30 the advance was continued towards the Blue Line, supported not only by the artillery, but by a creeping barrage of twenty machine guns. At first sight this was a far more formidable objective, for it included the cutting of the Arras-Lens railway, and the attackers had to descend a slope where were a number of wire entanglements not fully destroyed. It was at this point that most of the casualties occurred, for the passes through the wire were commanded by snipers on the edge of the railway cutting. Once down the slope some protection was given by the bank beside the railway. Mounting this, our men looked down into the cutting, where the enemy were sheltering from our guns in their dug-outs. Here there were many machine-gun posts, which, being visible to us, were engaged by our Lewis guns. There was one awkward incident. The South African attack had pushed slightly in advance of the 26th Brigade on its right, thus causing a gap ; and the Germans were able to open machine-gun and rifle fire along the railway. Captain Vivian, however, of the 3rd Regiment, pushed forward some details of the 26th Brigade who had joined him, and cleared out the German machine gunners and snipers. The Blue Line, which lay on the eastern side of the cutting, was then consolidated. Part of it was a veritable fortress, and in the cutting itself concrete machine-gun posts had been built. By the time the whole Brigade had reached the second objective it was just on 10 o'clock.

The attack on the final objective, the Brown Line, was timed to start at 12.45. The 1st and 2nd Regiments took the place of the 3rd and 4th, who became the supporting battalions. The 1st Regiment was on the right, with a strength of 20 officers and 488 other ranks ; on the left was the 2nd, with a strength of 20 officers and 480 other ranks. Punctual to time the final advance began under the same methodical barrage. The German wire in the valley just west of the Brown Line was found to be very strong and untraversable, except through a passage cut by the enemy and a communication trench. Had there been serious resistance the attack might have been long delayed at this point, but already there were signs that the enemy was breaking. Few prisoners were found in the trenches, but groups were seen to advance from the Green Line and surrender. About 2 o'clock the Brown Line was occupied, where the trenches were found in almost perfect order, having suffered little from our bombardment.

The work of the South Africans was now accomplished. General Lambton's 4th Division, about 3 o'clock, moved up and passed through the 9th Division to the assault of the final Green Line—an operation now tried for the first time on the British front.

Thanks to the admirable training of both divisions, the experiment was a brilliant success. Before dark the Green Line had fallen, the strong-post of the Hyderabad Redoubt was rushed, and Lambton was in Fampoux. This was the apex reached on the first day of the battle. The right of the XVII. Corps and the left of the VI. Corps formed a salient on both sides of the Scarpe, the point of which was facing no prepared position nearer than the Drocourt-Quéant line.

The record of the 9th Division that day was not excelled by any other unit in the battle. All three brigades had performed to the full the tasks allotted to them. They had taken the strength of a brigade in prisoners—51 officers and 2,088 other ranks ; they had taken 7 howitzers, 10 field guns, and 84 machine guns. As regards the South Africans, whose advance was literally unbroken, the casualties were far less than the number of prisoners. The enemy was demoralized by our barrage, and then surprised and routed by the steady infantry pressure behind it. Seven officers fell— Major H. C. Symmes and Lieutenant Hardwich of the 2nd Regiment; Lieutenants Godfrey, Burrows, and Lee of the 3rd Regiment ; and Lieutenants Hunt and Dorward of the 4th Regiment. The total casualties were : in the 1st Regiment, 15 killed and 69 wounded or missing ; in the 2nd Regiment, 20 killed and 68 wounded or missing ; in the 3rd Regiment, 53 killed and 226 wounded or missing ; in the 4th Regiment, 57 killed and 186 wounded or missing. From dawn to dusk the troops were in the highest spirits. In the words of General Dawson : " The men are on their toes, and the wounded do not want to leave the fighting line."

Throughout the day the work of the Field Ambulance was admirably performed. The advance was so rapid that the task of the stretcher-bearers was a heavy one, for the distance from the farthest objective to the nearest collecting post was more than 3,000 yards. Had the weather been fine, the difficulties would have been great enough, but the drizzle and sleet showers soon converted the battle area into a sea of mud. Nevertheless, by working without rest, under the brilliant direction of Captain Lawrie, before 6 o'clock that evening all the wounded of the Brigade had been collected and evacuated by the South African Field Ambulance, who had also dealt with casualties from the other two brigades of the 9th Division, and from the 34th and 4th Divisions.

The result of the first day of Arras was that all the enemy's front positions had gone, and his final position, short of the Drocourt-Quéant line, had been breached on a front of $2\frac{1}{2}$ miles. Unfortunately the weather became his ally. It changed to intense cold and wet, and with the sodden ground it took long to bring up our guns. He held us up with machine guns in pockets of the ground, which prevented the use of our cavalry, and there was no chance of a dramatic *coup de grâce*. The infantry could only push forward slowly and methodically, and complete the capture of the remains of his position. We had made a breach, a genuine breach, on a broad front in his line, but we could not exploit our success owing to the nature of the ground and the weather. Our remarkable gains, won at small cost the first day, could only be increased by small daily additions, for the elaborate preliminaries of Arras could not be improvised, and the infantry must wait on the advance of the guns.

Tuesday, 10th April, was spent by the South African Brigade in the Blue and Black lines, in cleaning rifles and equipment and replenishing ammuni- *April* 10. tion. The Brigade was then placed at the disposal of the 4th Division, and early on Wednesday, the 11th, orders were received for it to re- *April* 11. lieve the 10th Brigade, which was then holding the Brown Line. That day Lambton was attacking at noon, and the 1st and 2nd South African Regiments moved up to a forward post under cover of a ridge 500 yards behind the Green Line to act in support. The attack of the 4th Division gained some ground, but failed in its main purpose ; and after dark the 1st, 2nd, and 4th South African Regiments took up a position running north-west from Fampoux, with the 3rd Regiment in reserve. At that moment the enemy held a line running from south to north from Rœux through the Chemical Works and the railway station along the Gavrelle road. Behind it to the east lay the slopes of Greenland Hill.

An attack was ordered for the following day against this position. The 9th Division was to advance against the line between Rœux and the roadside inn which lay a thousand yards east of the Hyderabad Redoubt, with the 15th Division holding the front south of the Scarpe, and the 4th Division to protect the northern flank of the attack. There were two objectives—the first being the road from the inn to the station ; and the second, the Chemical Works and buildings south of the railway, the wood called Mount Pleasant, and the village of Rœux. The South African Brigade on the right and the 27th Brigade on their left were to capture the first objective, after which the 26th Brigade would advance south of the railway.

At 3 p.m. on the 12th the 1st, 2nd, and 4th South African Regiments assembled in Fampoux. The enemy *April 12.* was evidently prepared, for though this movement was carried out in file, with intervals between companies, it was subjected to a heavy and steady bombardment, which cost us many casualties.

The prospects of success were not bright. All three brigades of the 9th Division were very tired, having been hard at work under shell-fire for three days, and having had no sleep for four nights, three of which they had spent lying in the snow without blankets and many without greatcoats. There was no chance of an adequate bombardment, and there was no time to reconnoitre the ground. The country between Fampoux and Rœux station was perfectly open, and was commanded in the south by a high railway embankment and three woods, all of them held by the enemy ; while in the north it sloped gradually to the inn around which the Germans had organized strong-points. It was impossible, therefore, to prevent the movement of troops being observed by the enemy. The South African dispositions were the 1st Regiment on the left and the 2nd on the right, with two companies of the 4th in support of each. The 3rd Regiment was held in brigade reserve. As the different companies began to deploy from the shelter of the houses in the east end of Fampoux they were met with heavy machine-gun and rifle fire.

The attack was timed for 5 p.m., when our guns opened fire. Unfortunately our barrage dropped some 500 yards east of the starting-point, and behind the first enemy line of defence, so that the South Africans had a long tract of open ground to cover before they could

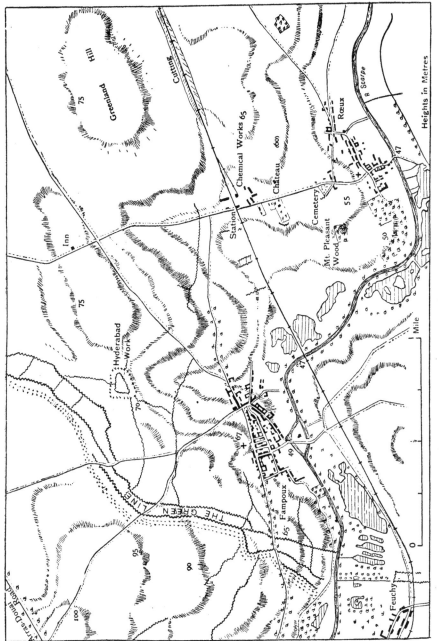

BATTLE OF ARRAS. FINAL STAGE OF ADVANCE.

come up with it. Our artillery, too, seemed to miss the enemy machine-gun posts on the railway embankment, which, combined with the flanking fire from the woods in the south and the south-east and from the direction of the inn, played havoc with both the attacking brigades.

The result was a failure. A gallant few of the South Africans succeeded in reaching the station, a point in their objective, where their bodies were recovered a month later when the position was captured. For the rest, only one or two isolated parties reached points as much as 200 yards east of the line held by the 4th Division. But as a proof of the quality of the troops, it should be recorded that before the attack was brought to a standstill, the casualties of the 2nd Regiment, who went in 400 strong, amounted to 16 officers and 285 men, while the 1st Regiment lost 2 officers and 203 men, and the 4th, 6 officers and 200 men.* Among the dead were Captain Grady, who commanded " A " Company of the 4th ; and Lieutenants J. M. Ross, Lees, and Porteous. Since the first part of the assault had failed, the 26th Brigade, which was waiting to advance on Rœux, was not called upon. That night it took over the line from the Scarpe to the Hyderabad Redoubt, where it linked up with the 4th Division, and the South Africans withdrew to the Green Line. They were finally relieved on the night of the 15th, *April* 15. having, in the three days since the 12th, suffered 720 casualties.

In the unsuccessful operations in front of Fampoux the Field Ambulance, which had a collecting station in

* The casualties of the 27th Brigade in this ill-fated action were nearly as high as those of the South Africans.

that village, had a heavy task. The stretcher-bearers were under constant shell-fire, and Captain Welsh was mortally wounded on the 12th—an irreparable loss to the unit. Many of the stretcher-bearers had been working without rest for three days, but they continued to do their duty till they dropped from sheer exhaustion. The work of one man, Private R. W. Nelson, deserves special mention. He had carried continuously from the morning of the 9th, and was already worn out when the attack opened on the 12th. He worked on steadily, until he collapsed late in the evening. Nevertheless, he refused to be relieved, and after a short rest returned to his post, and carried seven cases before morning.

The Brigade was to have no further part in the long-drawn-out struggle lasting till far on in May, which the failure of the French attack on the Aisne compelled us to continue in the Arras area. It was in the Monchy-Breton district during the latter part of April. On 5th May a composite battalion, consisting of a company from each of the 1st, 2nd, and 3rd Regiments, was formed under the command of Major Webber, and moved to Arras, where it was placed at the disposal of the 27th Brigade. It took its share in holding the front line till May 14th, when it was demobilised. On the 13th of that month Sir Edmund Allenby inspected the Brigade, and congratulated the men on the distinguished part they had played in the late battle. In June it was in Arras as divisional reserve, and on 5th June two composite battalions were formed to assist in the attack on Greenland Hill. That attack, carried out by troops of the XVII. Corps, was so successful that the supports were not called upon, and these battalions rejoined their Brigade on the 6th.

Its numbers had now grown sadly thin. It had suffered severe casualties in April, and there had been the usual wastage from sickness which is inevitable in any force on active service. It was clear that if the Brigade was to preserve its identity on the British front it must get larger reinforcements than it had received in the past. To replace losses, drafts to the strength of 1,448 had been sent to France between the end of April and the end of June, but even with these it was gravely under strength. On 30th June the strength of the different regiments was as follows : 1st Regiment, 38 officers, 680 other ranks ; 2nd Regiment, 37 officers, 601 other ranks ; 3rd Regiment, 35 officers, 691 other ranks ; 4th Regiment, 39 officers, 818 other ranks.

In July the Brigade moved to the Somme area for training, and on the 27th of that month, along with the rest of the 9th Division, was transferred to the IV. Corps. On the 28th it relieved the 174th Infantry Brigade in the Trescault section of the line, *July 28.* north of Havrincourt Wood and along the Canal du Nord. This was then a quiet region, and beyond a few minor raids there was no incident to record. During the summer, while the Brigade was in training, the weather had been all but perfect ; but by the close of July it had broken in a deluge of rain, and August recalled the October of the past year on the Somme. The great battle had begun in the north, the fight on which Haig had placed his highest hopes, and with it had begun that epoch of mists and gales and torrents which were more fatal to our success than any German tactics.

CHAPTER VI.

THE THIRD BATTLE OF YPRES.
(July–November 1917.)

The Change in the Military Situation—Haig's Plan for Third Ypres—The Nature of the Problem—Von Armin's Defensive Tactics—The " Pill-boxes "—The Attack of 31st July—The Attack of 16th August—The British Front reorganized—The 9th Division enters the Salient—Its " Pill-box " Tactics —The Night Assembly—The Attack of 20th September—The Fall of Potsdam Redoubt—The First Objective gained—The Second Objective gained—The Difficulties on the Left Flank—The Result of the Battle—Individual Exploits—The Brigade's Losses—The Field Ambulance Work—The Brigade returns to the Salient—Moves to the Belgian Coast—The Close of Third Ypres.

WHEN, on the last day of July 1917, Sir Douglas Haig launched his attack in the Ypres salient, the nature of the war had dramatically changed. The great plan conceived for 1917, of which the Somme had been the logical preliminary, had proved impossible. This was not due wholly or mainly to the failure of the ambitious offensive in April at Arras and on the Aisne. The real cause was the defection of Russia, for, by the failure of one great partner, the old military coherence of the Alliance had gone. The beleaguering forces which had sat for three years round the German citadel were wavering and straggling on the East. The war on two fronts, which had been Germany's chief handicap, looked as if it might change presently to a war on a single front. Whatever victories might be won during the remainder of 1917, it was now certain that a decisive blow could not be delivered. The Teutonic League, just when it was beginning to crumble, had been given a new tenure of life. Up till then the campaign had been fought on data which were familiar and calculable. The material and human strength of each belligerent was known, and the *moral* of each was confidently assessed. But with the Russian revolution new factors had suddenly appeared out of the void, and what had seemed solid ground became sand and quagmire. It was the old Europe which waged war up till the spring of 1917 ; but a new Europe had come into being by midsummer in which nothing could be taken for granted. Everywhere in the world there was the sound of things breaking.

Haig was compelled to protract the fighting in the Arras area so long as the French on the Aisne required his aid ; but by the end of May he was free to turn his attention to the plan which, as early as the previous November, had been his main preoccupation. This was an offensive against the enemy in Flanders, with the aim of clearing the Belgian coast and turning the northern flank of the whole German defence system in the West. It was a scheme which, if successful, promised the most far-reaching results. It would destroy the worst of the submarine bases ; it would restore to Belgium her lost territory, and thereby deprive Germany of one of her most cherished bargaining assets ; it would cripple the enemy communications with the depôts of the Lower Rhineland. But time was the essence of the business.

The blow must be struck at the earliest possible hour, for each week's delay meant the aggrandisement of the enemy.

Haig's first business was to clear his flanks for the coming attack, and on the 7th June, by one of the most *June 7.* perfect operations in the campaign, he won the Messines-Wytschaete ridge at a single bound. His next step was the advance east of Ypres. The famous Salient had during three years been gradually contracted till the enemy front was now less than two miles from the town. The Germans held all the half-moon of little hills to the east, which meant that any preparations for attack would be conducted under their watchful eyes. They were very conscious of the importance of the position, and the wary general who now commanded their IV. Army was not likely to be taken by surprise. This was Sixt von Armin, who had commanded the 4th Corps at the Somme, and had there shown himself one of the most original and fruitful tacticians on the enemy's side.

The Battle of Messines was over by the 12th June, but for various reasons it was not till late in July that the date of the main advance could be fixed. It was now more than ever a race against time, for the precarious weather of autumn was approaching; and, unless the advance proceeded strictly according to time-table, it ran a grave risk of failure. The high ground east of the Salient must be won in a fortnight to enable us to move against the enemy bases in West Flanders and clear the coast-line. The nature of the countryside made any offensive a gamble with the weather, for the Salient was, after Verdun, the most tortured of the

Western battlefields. Constant shelling of the low ground west of the ridges had blocked or diverted the streams and the natural drainage, and turned it into a sodden wilderness. Weather such as had been experienced on the Somme would make of it a morass where tanks could not be used, and transport could scarcely move, and troops would be exposed to the last degree of misery.

The coming attack was much canvassed in Germany beforehand, and von Armin, having learned the lesson of his defeat at Messines, had prepared his defences. In Flanders the nature of the ground did not permit of a second Siegfried Line. Deep dug-outs and concreted trenches were impossible because of the water-logged soil, and he was compelled to find new tactics. His solution was the " pill-box." These were small concrete forts, sited among the ruins of a farm or in some derelict piece of woodland, often raised only a yard or two above the ground level, and bristling with machine guns. The low entrance was at the rear, and the " pill-box " could hold from eight to forty men. It was easy to make, for the wooden or steel framework could be brought up on any dark night and filled with concrete. They were echeloned in depth with great skill, and, in the wiring, alleys were left so that an unwary advance would be trapped among them and exposed to enfilading fire. Their small size made them a difficult mark for heavy guns, and since they were protected by concrete at least three feet thick, they were impregnable to the ordinary barrage of field artillery.

Von Armin's plan was to hold his first line—which was often a mere string of shell craters—with few men, who would fall back before an assault. He had his guns well behind, so that they should not be captured in the first rush, and would be available for a barrage if his opponents became entangled in the " pill-box " zone. Finally, he had his reserves in the second line, ready for the counterstroke before the attack could secure its position. It will be seen that these tactics were admirably suited for the exposed and contorted ground of the Salient. Any attack would be allowed to make some advance ; but if the German plan worked well, this advance would be short-lived and would be dearly paid for. Instead of the cast-iron front of the Siegfried area, the Flanders line would be highly elastic, but it would spring back into position after pressure with a deadly rebound.

The " preparation " for the battle lasted for the greater part of July, and every part of the Salient was drenched with our fire. On the last day of the month *July* 31. came the advance on a front of 15 miles— from the river Lys to a little north of Steenstraate, the main effort being that of the Fifth Army, under Sir Hubert Gough, on the 7½ miles between Boesinghe and the Zillebeke-Zandvoorde road. With the attack the weather broke. Gough's purpose was to carry the enemy's first defences, situated on the forward slope of the rising ground, and his second position along the crest. The opening day saw a brilliant success, for everywhere we captured the first line, and in many parts the second. But the weather prevented the series of cumulative blows which we had planned. For a fortnight we were compelled to hold our hand, since till the countryside grew dryer advance was a stark impossibility.

The second stage of the Ypres struggle began on 16th August, when the Fifth Army attacked the German third position, the Gheluvelt-Langemarck line, which ran from the Menin road along *Aug.* 16. the second of the tiers of ridges which rimmed the Salient on the east. These tiers, the highest and most easterly of which was the famous Passchendaele crest, had the common features that they all sprang from one southern boss or pillar, the point on the Menin road marked 64 metres, which we knew as Clapham Junction, and all, as they ran northward, lost elevation. The attack, which took place at dawn, made a considerable gap in the German third line, but it was very far from attaining its main objectives. That day, indeed, showed at its best von Armin's new defensive method. The weather was in his favour, for the air was thick and damp, making airplane observation difficult, and therefore depriving us of timely notice of the enemy's counter-strokes. The ground was sloppy, and made tangled and difficult with broken woods ; and the whole front was sown with " pill-boxes," against which we had not yet discovered the proper weapon. The result was a serious British check. The splendid courage of the Fifth Army had been largely fruitless. Fine brigades had been hurled in succession against a concrete wall, and had been sorely battered. The troops felt that they were being sacrificed blindly ; that every fight was a soldiers' fight, and that such sledge-hammer tactics were too crude to meet the problem. For a moment there was a real ebb of confidence in British leadership.

Sir Douglas Haig took time to reorganize his front and prepare a new plan. He extended Sir Herbert

Plumer's Second Army northward, so that it should take over the attack on the enemy front on the Menin road. Sorely tried divisions were taken out of the line, and our whole artillery tactics were revised. The "pill-box" problem was studied, and a solution was found, not by miraculous ingenuity, but by patient and meticulous care. Early in September the weather improved, and the sodden Salient began slowly to dry. That is to say, the mud hardened into something like the *séracs* of a glacier, and the streams became streams again and not lagoons. But the process was slow, and it was not till the third week of the month that the third stage in the battle could begin.

For this third stage the 9th Division was brought up from the Somme. It arrived at Brandhoek on *Sept.* 14. 14th September, where it became part of Sir E. A. Fanshawe's V. Corps of Sir Hubert Gough's Fifth Army. The next few days were spent in careful training for the impending attack. The terrain over which the advance was to be made was explained to all ranks, and, as before Arras, clay models were built and part of the training ground taped off to represent the area of assault for each brigade. No division had made a more elaborate study of the "pill-box" problem. Lukin had worked out the subject in detail with the brigadiers who were to lead the coming assault—General Dawson of the South African Brigade and General Frank Maxwell, V.C., of the 27th Brigade; and the division had reached its own conclusions as to the failure of our past efforts. The objectives set before it had already been attacked fruitlessly more than once, and the reason of failure seemed to be clear. The enemy

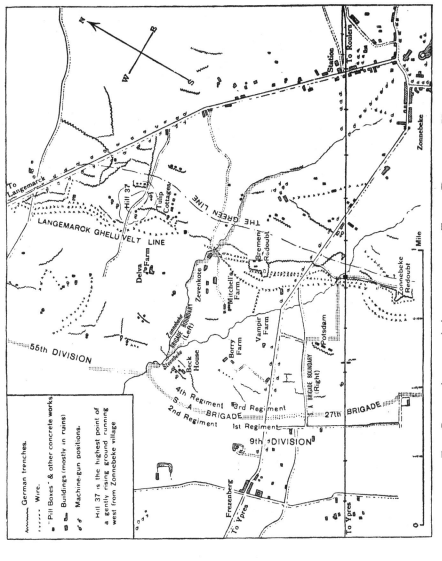

THE SOUTH AFRICANS' ATTACK AT THE THIRD BATTLE OF YPRES.

came out of holes and dug-outs behind the attacking wave, and held up the second wave and isolated the first one. Hence Lukin and his brigadiers trained their men to stop at every " pill-box," trench, or dug-out, and clear out all occupants, the troops behind them passing through them to a further attack. This leap-frog system was obviously dangerous and difficult against an irregular and intermittent line, for if part of the advance stopped the whole front might halt. Again, the men in the second wave would be apt to halt when they saw the advance in front of them cease. Nevertheless, in spite of its difficulties, it was beyond doubt the only method which offered a reasonable chance of success. The 9th Division also had its own views about artillery methods. The " pill-boxes " in front of it were carefully reconnoitred and located. In the attack it was arranged that the field-gun barrage should lengthen on both sides of a " pill-box," so that the advancing troops, hugging their barrage, might get round its unprotected rear. The barrage was to be high-explosive instead of shrapnel, for the path of the former could be more exactly noted and closely followed.

The front allotted to the 9th Division was some 2,000 yards north of the Ypres-Menin road. Through its centre ran the Ypres-Roulers railway. On its right was the 2nd Australian Division, and on its left the 55th Division of West Lancashire Territorials. The 9th Division formed the right of the Fifth Army. Its attack was to be on a two-brigade front, the South Africans on the left and the 27th Brigade on the right, while the 26th Brigade was held in reserve. The South Africans were disposed as follows : the 3rd Regiment, under Lieutenant-Colonel Thackeray, on the right, and the 1st, under Lieutenant-Colonel Heal, in support ; on the left the 4th Regiment, under Lieutenant-Colonel MacLeod,* supported by the 2nd, temporarily under Major Cochran. When the first objective had been taken, the two supporting battalions were to pass through, and attack the second and third objectives.

The British line at the moment lay on the east side of the Frezenberg Ridge. The first objective for the South Africans was roughly the line of the Steenbeek stream.† The second was a line running north and south a little west of the junction of the Ypres-Zonnebeke road and the Ypres-Roulers railway. This was now the main German position, part of the great Langemarck-Gheluvelt line. The final objective, known as the Green Line, was very slightly east of the second, and involved an advance mainly on the left wing of the attack. The purpose was to win the ridge which gave observation of Zonnebeke, and which, until it was captured, hindered all advance further north. The countryside was to the last degree blind and desperate. Not only was there a stream to cross, and many yards of swamp to struggle through, but the area included some of the most formidable " pill-boxes " on the German front, while in the main enemy line stood the Bremen Redoubt, and the stronghold made out of Zevenkote village.

---

* MacLeod took over the 4th from Christian on 25th April when he returned from sick leave, Christian going to the XVII. Corps School of Instruction as Commandant.

† On some maps this is given as the Hansbeek, or Hannebeek, but it is more convenient to keep this name for the larger stream which runs by St. Julien.

The starting-point being what it was, a night assembly in such an area was the most intricate of problems.   On 17th September the South Africans moved into the front line, relieving the 125th *Sept. 19.* Brigade.   Wednesday, the 19th, was a clear, blowing day; but about ten o'clock in the evening the rain began, and fell heavily all that night.   During the darkness the Brigade was getting into position for attack. The black night and the slippery ground made the whole operation extraordinarily difficult in a place devoid of communication trenches and honeycombed with shell-holes. The ground was so cut up that it was possible to move only by duck-board tracks, and it was hard to get reports back from the different units.   Nevertheless, long before zero hour, the attacking battalions were in their place.

At dawn the drizzle stopped, but a wet mist remained, which blinded our air reconnaissance.   At twenty minutes to six, preceded by a barrage of high explo- *Sept. 20.* sive and smoke shells, the attacking troops moved into the desert of mud.   In the dim light, obscured by smoke, it was impossible to see their objective.   The advance had scarcely begun when the German barrage came down on our old front line, so that the supporting battalions had to close up as near as possible to the leading troops.

The right battalion, the 3rd Regiment, had " A " Company, under Captain Vivian, on its right ; " B " Company, under Captain Sprenger, in the centre ; and " C " Company, under Captain Ellis, on the left ; with " D " Company, under Captain Tomlinson, in support. Its strength was 20 officers and 617 other ranks.   The left battalion, the 4th Regiment, had a strength of 21 officers and 511 other ranks. It had on its left " A " Company, under Captain Farrell; " B " Company, under Captain McCubbin, in the centre; and " C " Company, under Major Browne, on its right; with " D " Company, under Captain Gemmell, in support. Now was seen the value of their careful training. The 4th Regiment took the strong-points known as Beck House and Borry Farm in their stride, and by half-past six had reached their first objective. Seeing the place called Mitchell's Farm in front of them, a party went through our own barrage and captured it, killing most of its garrison. A machine gun across the brook on their left flank gave trouble, so a platoon, under Second-Lieutenant Saphir, crossed the stream and took the German post there, bringing back the gun and twenty prisoners.

In the meantime the left wing of the 3rd Regiment had taken Vampir Farm and reached its objective. Its right, however, was held up by the position of the left battalion of the 27th Brigade, the 12th Royal Scots, who, in their area, had encountered the formidable redoubt known as Potsdam, which, in addition to other defences, included three " pill-boxes." When " A " Company and part of " B " Company of the 3rd Regiment reached their objective they were too far in advance of their neighbouring brigade, and were subjected to a heavy enfilading fire from Potsdam. Captain Vivian of " A " Company immediately organized an attack on that point, leading the assault in person, but he, together with Lieutenants Coxen and Newbery, was killed. Captain Sprenger of " B " Company then collected all the men he could, both from the 3rd Regiment and the 1st, and with two Lewis guns and one machine gun he advanced by rushes from shell-hole to shell-hole against the redoubt. This gallant attack, combined with the pressure of the 27th Brigade from the west, brought about the fall of the place. The enemy was seen bolting south towards the Ypres-Roulers railway line, and in a quarter of an hour the fort was in our hands.

A halt was called for an hour before the attack on the second objective. After passing Potsdam it had been arranged between Dawson and Maxwell, with Lukin's approval, that the area of the South African Brigade would be extended to the right till it included the northern bank of the railway. This made it important to clear that northern bank. Second-Lieutenant Lawrence of the 1st Regiment had accordingly been sent forward as soon as the attack began, and had met with no opposition till he came under machine-gun fire on the west side of Potsdam. Finding no troops near him, he retired till he fell in with some derelict tanks, when he turned south-east and reached the railway. Here he found some South Africans, who had become separated from the rest, clearing a dug-out on the south side of the line. Going eastward he found a large dug-out, where he took twenty German prisoners and captured three machine guns. He then found touch with the 12th Royal Scots, which had been his main object, and rejoined his battalion before the second stage of the battle began.

Just previous to the opening of this stage Lieutenant-Colonel Heal of the 1st Regiment saw some men of the 1st and 3rd Regiments, headed by Sergeant Frohbus, advance through our own barrage against a large " pill-box " immediately on their front. It was a place which would give trouble in the next advance, so he joined the

party and took command. On calling on the inmates of
the " pill-box " to surrender, some thirty or forty came
out, but the remainder declined to move. All the loop-
holes and openings of the structure were closed, but a
certain "Mike" Fennessy of the 3rd Regiment, a Johannesburger whose past career had been largely outside the
confines of the law, managed to get a bomb either through
a ventilator in the roof or through a window which had
been blown open by a grenade. This set fire to the
wood lining, and the garrison broke out and were shot
down. Four machine guns were captured in the place.*
The doings of this Johannesburger are a comment on
the value of the scallawag in war. As the shepherd said
to Dr. John Brown about his dog : " There was a deep
sariousness about him, for he could never get eneuch o'
fechtin'." Twice in former battles he had gone over
with the first wave, and when their work was done
managed to continue with their successors. At Arras he
actually finished the day with a wholly different division,
which he found had the farthest to go.

The 3rd and 4th Regiments now remained at the first
objective and consolidated the ground, and the two
supporting battalions at 7 a.m. moved against the
second objective, the main Langemarck-Gheluvelt line.
The 1st Regiment was on the right with a strength of
20 officers and 546 other ranks, and the 2nd on the left
with a strength of 20 officers and 566 other ranks. The
task of the 1st Regiment was easy, and it advanced
smoothly towards its second objective. At 7.50 Colonel
Heal was able to report that his section of the main

* Private C. E. Fennessy was awarded the Military Medal for
this exploit.

German line had been taken. The 2nd Regiment, however, on his left, had a heavier duty. Mitchell's Farm
had been previously taken by the 4th, but the enemy was
still holding Waterend Farm, and from beyond the
stream was galling their flanks with machine-gun and
rifle fire from the high ground at the place called Tulip
Cottages and Hill 37—all in the area of the 55th Division.
Before them, too, lay the strong Bremen Redoubt and
the fortified village of Zevenkote. Nevertheless, the
Bremen Redoubt and Zevenkote were carried, and with
them the second German position. But the situation
on his left made Major Cochran uneasy. The men of
West Lancashire were held up by the enemy at Hill 37,
and the South Africans had therefore an exposed flank.
He extended his left, and captured Waterend Farm, together with three machine guns and seventy prisoners, and
thereby found touch with the 55th Division, and formed
a defensive flank. It was not till the afternoon that
the Lancashire troops gallantly stormed Hill 37, which
enabled the South African left to advance to the Green
Line, the final objective, where they held a position
consisting mainly of a string of shell-holes.

Meantime there was no word of von Armin's usual
counterstroke. The troops against us were some of
the best in the German Army, part of the 2nd Guard
Reserve. But the speed and fury of the advance
of the 9th, the accuracy of their artillery barrage, and
the skill with which they accounted for " pill-box "
after " pill-box " had paralyzed the enemy. During
the morning there seemed to be a concentration for a
counter-attack near Bostin Farm, but this was dispersed
by our guns. Only small parties moving from shell-

hole to shell-hole advanced, and these never came nearer than 800 yards. By the evening of that day on nearly all the British front of attack the final objectives had been reached. The 9th Division had carried theirs in the record time of three hours.

That day's battle cracked the kernel of the German defence in the Salient. It showed only a limited advance, and the total of 3,000 prisoners had been often exceeded in a day's fighting ; but every inch of the ground won was vital. Few struggles in the campaign were more desperate or carried out in a more gruesome battlefield. The mass of quagmires, splintered woods, ruined husks of " pill-boxes," water-filled shell-holes, and foul creeks which made up the land on both sides of the Menin road was a sight which, to the recollection of most men, must seem like a fevered nightmare. It was the classic soil on which, during the First Battle of Ypres, the 1st and 2nd Divisions had stayed the German rush for the Channel. Then it had been a battered but still recognizable and featured countryside ; now the elements seemed to have blended with each other to make of it a limbo outside mortal experience and almost beyond human imagining. Only on some of the tortured hills of Verdun could a parallel be found. The battle of 20th September showed to what heights of endurance the British soldier can attain. It was an example, too, of how thought and patience may achieve success in spite of every disadvantage of weather, terrain, and enemy strength.

Delville Wood was still for the Brigade the most heroic episode in the War. But its advance on 20th September must without doubt be reckoned its most

SECOND-LIEUTENANT W. H. HEWITT, V.C.,
2nd Regiment, South African Infantry.

successful achievement up to that date in the campaign. It carried one of the strongest parts of the enemy's position, and assisted the brigades both on its right and left to take two forts which blocked their way. The day was full of gallant individual exploits. The regimental commanders led their men not only with skill, but with the utmost dash and fearlessness. Heal was struck by shrapnel, and once buried by a shell ; Thackeray was twice buried ; Cochran was knocked down, but rose unhurt, though all thought him killed. " The regimental officers," wrote Dawson on the 22nd, " were an awful sight this morning, haggard and drawn, unwashed and unshaven for four days, covered with mud and utterly tired, but very happy, and exceedingly proud of their men." One N.C.O. and two men of the 2nd Regiment took seventy prisoners. Another man of the 2nd Regiment engaged a German in a bayonet duel and killed him ; then a second, whom he also killed ; then a third, when each killed the other. In dealing with the " pill-boxes," individual courage and initiative were put to the highest test. It was for such an episode that Lance-Corporal W. H. Hewitt of the 2nd Regiment was awarded the Victoria Cross. He attacked a " pill-box " in his section, and tried to rush the doorway, but found a stubborn garrison within, and received a severe wound. Nevertheless he managed to reach the loop-hole, where, in his attempts to insert a bomb, he was again wounded. Ultimately he got a bomb inside, dislodged the occupants, and took the place.

On the 21st there was heavy shelling, but no serious counter-attack on the 9th Division, though the 55th, on their left, faced and defeated a strong enemy attempt.

Early on the morning of the 22nd the Brigade was relieved from the front line. Its casualties were not

Sept. 21–22. light. The 1st Regiment had 58 killed (including Captain J. T. Bain and Second-Lieutenant E. Spyker) and 291 wounded and missing; the 2nd Regiment had 61 killed (including Captain F. M. Davis, Lieutenant E. D. Lucas, and Second-Lieutenant A. B. Cooper) and 224 wounded and missing; the 3rd Regiment had 88 killed (including Captain E. V. Vivian, Captain and Adjutant A. W. H. M'Donald,* and Second-Lieutenants W. J. Blanchard, C. F. Coxen, N. Cruddas, N. T. Hendry, J. Newbery, W. P. Sweeney, and D. A. Williams) and 283 wounded and missing; the 4th Regiment had 56 killed (including Captain D. Gemmell and Second-Lieutenants B. D. Trethewy, A. Aitken, and W. G. S. Forder) and 197 wounded and missing. One death cast a gloom over the whole division, and might almost be regarded as a South African loss. General Frank Maxwell, the gallant commander of the 27th Brigade, was shot by a sniper on the morning of the 21st. He had won his Victoria Cross at Sanna's Post, and had been a familiar figure in South Africa as a member of Lord Kitchener's Staff. No one who remembers the old days in Pretoria can forget Frank Maxwell's boyish daring and humour. There was no braver man or better soldier in the British Army.

In recounting the doings of the Brigade in this battle the subsidiary services must not be forgotten. The Field Ambulance had the hardest task which they had yet faced, for their posts were under constant shell-

---

* He was mortally wounded on the 20th, and died the day after.

fire. In getting back the walking wounded they were much helped by the Décauville trains, which were run by a section of the South African railwaymen. Owing to the impossibility of making dug-outs the wounded, as they became numerous, had to be dressed in the open, and it was no light task to attend fifty wounded men on stretchers with shells dropping around. On the afternoon of the 21st, Captain Lawrie was wounded. About the same time a squad of Argyll and Sutherland stretcher-bearers was caught in a barrage, one being killed and another wounded. Sergeant Edgar of the South African Field Ambulance behaved with great gallantry in going into the barrage and rescuing the wounded man. In spite of every difficulty the arrangements worked with wonderful precision, and no casualties were ever better cared for than those of the Brigade. One small point may be mentioned to show General Dawson's careful thought for his men. During a battle it was his custom to give every officer and man who came into his headquarters a cup of tea with a tot of rum in it, and his mess servants entered into the spirit of his instructions, and dispensed general hospitality. On the night of the 21st, when the four regiments were relieved in the front line, the Brigade headquarters mess supplied 690 cups of tea, with a staff of one cook and one waiter and an equipment of eight teacups and one teapot.

The Brigade was not yet finished with Third Ypres. On 24th September it left the battle front, and on 4th October it was in the Houlle area, where for five days it underwent general training. On 10th October the

9th Division began to concentrate in the forward area of General Ivor Maxse's XVIII. Corps with a view to relieving the 48th Division in line. It thus became again the right division of the Fifth Army. On 12th
Oct. 12. October it entered the support line, along the canal bank at Ypres. The battle, in the meantime, had moved slowly. By 25th September we had won all the interior ridges of the Salient and the southern pillar ; but we were not yet within striking distance of the north part of the main Passchendaele Ridge. To attain this, we must lie east of Zonnebeke and the Polygon Wood, at the foot of the final slopes. Haig struck on the 26th September in fine weather, and took the Polygon Wood and Zonnebeke village. On 4th October, the very day fixed for a great German counter-attack, he struck again, and by a little after midday had gained all his objectives. He broke up forty German battalions, taking over 5,000 prisoners, and now held 9,000 yards of the crest of the ultimate
Oct. 13. ridge. On the night of the 13th the 2nd and 4th South African Regiments moved up to the front line, taking over trenches held by part of the 26th and 27th Brigades, which had been engaged in that attack on the 12th which was foiled by the disastrous weather. The relief was very difficult, for the whole country had become an irreclaimable bog, and the mud was beyond all human description. There was intermittent shelling during the 14th and 15th, and much bombing from enemy planes. On the night of the 16th the 2nd and 4th Regiments were relieved by the 1st and 3rd. For five more days the Brigade remained in the front trenches, taking part in no action,

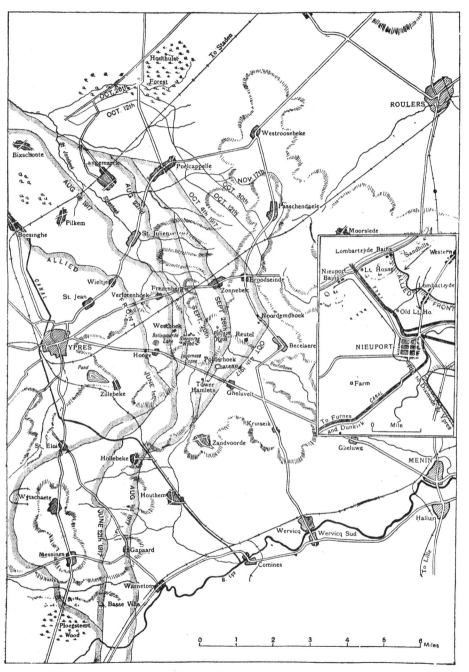

THE THIRD BATTLE OF YPRES.

but suffering heavily from the constant bombardment. Between the 13th and the 23rd of October, *Oct. 23.* when it moved out of the Salient, it had no less than 261 casualties in killed and wounded. The 9th Division now relieved the 41st Division in the Nieuport area, and remained on the Belgian coast till 20th November, a period of welcome rest. On 15th October Lieutenant-Colonel Tanner, who had commanded the 2nd Regiment since its formation, left the Brigade to take over the command of the 8th Brigade in the 3rd Division. He was succeeded by Lieutenant-Colonel Christian.

In November the struggle at Ypres reached its close. On Tuesday, the 6th, the Canadians carried the last fragment of the Passchendaele Ridge, and *Nov. 6.* wiped out the Salient, where for three years we had been at the mercy of the German guns. Sir Douglas Haig had not come within measurable distance of his major purpose, and that owing to no fault of plan, but through the maleficence of the weather in a terrain where weather was all in all. He gambled upon a normal August, and he did not get it. The sea of mud which lapped around the Salient was the true defence of the enemy. Consequently the battle, which might have had a profound strategic significance in the campaign, became merely an episode in the war of attrition, a repetition of the Somme tactics, though conspicuously less successful and considerably more costly than the fighting of 1916. Yet it will remain in history as a proof of the superb endurance and valour of the armies of Britain, fighting under conditions which for horror and misery have not been surpassed in war.

CHAPTER VII.

THE EVE OF THE GREAT GERMAN ATTACK.
(November 1917–March 1918.)

The New German Tactics—The Experiments at Riga, Caporetto, and Cambrai—The 9th Division moves to Gouzeaucourt—The South African Brigade in the Front Line—Hardships of this Period—The 3rd Regiment disbanded—General Lukin leaves the Division—The Memorial Service at Delville Wood —The Brigade again enters the Line—The British Scheme of Defence—The Quiet before the Storm—The Morning of the 21st March.

DURING the summer months there was a strange quiet on the Eastern front. The German armies did not advance, though the way seemed plain before them. But they were not idle. Ludendorff had seen the opportunity afforded by the downfall of Russia, and believed that long before America took the field in strength he could deal a decisive blow to the Allies in the West. He prepared most patiently for this final *coup*, and turned the whole of his Eastern front into one vast training camp, where picked divisions were practised in open fighting ; for his scheme demanded a high perfection of discipline and individual stamina. The history of the war had been the history of new tactical methods devised to break the strength of en-trenched defences. The Allies had tried repeatedly from Neuve Chapelle onward, each time changing their plan, and at last at the Somme they seemed to have found a method which, though slow and laborious in its working, was decisive in its results. But the defection of Russia put an end to the hopes of this plan, and once again the theory of war was recast. But while Byng at Cambrai was feeling his way towards new tactics, Germany had already decided upon a scheme. She had seen that surprise was essential, and that therefore a laboured artillery " preparation " was out of the question. She realized, too, that in order to get the full cumulative effect of a blow, division must follow division to strike while the iron was hot. If these two things—surprise and an endless chain of troops of assault—could be found, then it might be possible to deal the decisive blow within the narrow limits of time still permitted to her. A break here and a break there meant only a restricted advance, behind which the enemy's front grew solid in time, as concrete hardens with exposure. She therefore aimed not at a break-through in the older sense, but at a general crumbling.

Ludendorff's plan was based upon the highly specialized training of certain units, and was a legitimate conclusion from the German use of " storm troops." The first point was the absence of any preliminary massing near the front of attack. Men were brought up by night marches just before zero hour, and secrecy was thus obtained for the assembly. Again, there was no long bombardment to alarm the enemy, and the guns began at the moment when the infantry advanced, the enemy's back areas being confused by a deluge of gas shells. The assault was made by picked troops in open order, or rather in small clusters, carrying light trench mortars and many machine guns, with the field batteries close behind them in support. The actual mode of attack, which the French called " infiltration," may be likened to a hand, of which the finger-tips are shod with steel, and which is pushed into a soft substance. The picked troops at the finger-ends made gaps through which others poured, till each section of the defence found itself outflanked and encircled. A system of flares and rockets enabled the following troops to learn where the picked troops had made the breach, and the artillery came close behind the infantry. The men had unlimited objectives, and carried iron rations for several days. When one division had reached the end of its strength, another took its place, so that the advance resembled a continuous game of leap-frog.

This method was the opposite of the old German mass attack, which had seen a succession of hammer-blows on one section of front. It was strictly the filtering of a great army into a hostile position, so that each part was turned, and the whole front was first dislocated and then crumbled. This might be achieved by inferior numbers ; but a local numerical superiority was aimed at to ensure a complete victory by pushing far behind into unprotected areas. Advance was to be measured not by metres but by miles, and in any case was to proceed far enough to capture the enemy's artillery positions. Obviously the effect would be cumulative, the momentum of the attack would grow, and, if it was not stopped in the battle-zone, it would be far harder to stop in the hinterland. It was no case of an isolated stroke, but of a creeping sickness, which might demoralize a hundred miles of front. Ludendorff was confident, for he saw his way presently to a numerical superiority in the West, and he had devised tactics which must come with deadly effect upon an enemy prepared to meet only the old methods. But his plan demanded immediate success. A protracted battle would destroy the picked troops, and without them the new tactics were futile.

The first experiment was made early in September, when von Hutier captured Riga. But the true test came in October, when Otto von Below, with the VI. German Army, broke through the Italian front at Caporetto, and drove Cadorna behind the Piave. After that there could be no question of the value of Germany's plan. One other test, and her certainty was complete. On 20th November Byng struck at Cambrai, achieving by means of his tanks a genuine surprise. Ten days later came the German counterstroke—in two parts. The attack on the British left at Bourlon, carried out in the old fashion, signally failed. The attack on the British right between Masnières and Vendhuile, following the new fashion, as signally succeeded. But the Allied Staffs had not yet grasped the full meaning of the new method. Caporetto was explained by a breakdown in Italian *moral* and Cambrai by defective local intelligence. Neither explanation was sound, and four months later the armies of France and Britain read the true lesson in letters of fire.

On 20th November the 9th Division moved from the Belgian coast. The South African Brigade spent

some days in rest-billets in the Fruges area, engaged in
Nov. 20. training the recruits which had arrived to
replace the casualties of Third Ypres. On
the 30th news came of the counterstroke at Cambrai,
and the battalions were ordered to be ready to move
at short notice. On the morning of 1st December they
began their long march southward to the accompaniment of a deluge of rain and a sharp east wind. The
lorries which carried the kits and blankets did not turn
up, being required for some other purpose by the army
controlling that area, with the result that the men passed
three nights of bitter weather without adequate covering.
Presently came snow, and then a binding frost, and when,
Dec. 3. on 3rd December, the Brigade arrived at
Moislains, it was after three days of weary
marches in the worst of weathers and a freezing night
in the train.

During the night of the 3rd they were ordered to
relieve the 2nd Brigade of Guards at Gouzeaucourt,
nine miles off. The 9th Division became part of the
VII. Corps, under Sir Walter Congreve. By the night
of the 4th the 2nd and 4th South African Regiments
had taken over a section of the front line, with the
1st in support and the 3rd in reserve. The line now
held was that established by the Guards Division after
their brilliant advance on 1st December. It consisted
of a newly-dug trench on the east slope of Quentin
Ridge, extending from Gauche Wood, on the right, to
a point near the head of Flag Ravine. No communication trenches existed, and in the right battalion section all approaches to the front line were under enemy
observation. The trenches were neither fire-stepped nor

revetted, and no dug-outs or shelters existed in the forward area. There was also very little wire, the whole position having been extemporized during the recent battle. The relief was carried through successfully, and the commanding officer of a Coldstream battalion wrote to Lieutenant-Colonel Christian complimenting the 2nd Regiment on its work, adding that the Guards had long heard of the South Africans' reputation, and did not wish to be relieved by better troops.

As attacks on this part of the front were daily expected, the forward battalions had to detail troops to occupy the immediate support trenches as " counter-attack forces," while the reserve battalion constituted a counter-attack force for the Brigade. The next few weeks were filled with strenuous work. Material had to be salved or brought up for the defence of the area, a large number of British and German dead had to be buried, trenches had to be broadened and deepened, and shelters constructed. All through December the Brigade was heavily shelled. On the morning of the 8th, for example, the 2nd Regiment lost by shell-fire Captain E. C. Bryant and Second-Lieutenants V. S. Dickerson and G. J. S. Mandy killed, while Second-Lieutenants B. Pope-Hennessy and L. Arnold were wounded. On the night of the 8th the 2nd and 4th Regiments were relieved by the 1st and 3rd, the 4th becoming the Brigade reserve, while the 2nd formed the garrison of the support and reserve lines. During the first week the casualties averaged throughout the Brigade about thirty a day, which were severe for trench warfare. After that they slackened, but carrying parties at night continued to suffer heavily. The Brigade, by constant patrolling, maintained its ascendancy in No Man's Land, but the German outposts were exceptionally vigilant. The worst trial was the weather, which was first frost, then thaw, and then about the middle of the month a settled frost, which lasted until the New Year.

These violent changes added to the difficulty of the task by causing the trenches constantly to collapse, and the severity of the climate told heavily upon troops who had only lately been through a long action, and had had a peculiarly trying journey from the Belgian coast. Moreover, a large percentage of the new recruits were less able to withstand hardships than the older soldiers. Everything that was possible was done to ensure their comfort. Regimental kitchens were constructed so that the men could be supplied with hot meals during the night. A Brigade soup-kitchen was established in the support line under the superintendence of the chaplains, where men could receive hot soup at any hour. Nevertheless, during this month of December, the sickness returns were larger than at any similar period during the history of the Brigade. The chief malady was trench feet, but by the middle of the month rooms for the medical care of this ailment had been established at Heudicourt and Fins, and during rest periods all the men were sent there for preventive treatment.

On 13th January the Brigade came out of the line, *Jan.* 13, 1918. and for ten days was billeted in the villages of Moislains, Heudicourt, Fins, and Sorel-le-Grand. On the 23rd the 2nd and 3rd Regiments moved again into the line to relieve units of the 26th Brigade, and the 1st and 4th Regiments followed the next day. The relief was carried out without casualties. When the Brigade arrived at Heudicourt on 4th December it numbered 148 officers and 3,621 other ranks. By January 23rd *Jan.* 23. its total strength had shrunk to 79 officers and 1,661 men. On the last day of January all four battalions came out of the front trenches, and were moved to a back area for a much needed *Jan.* 31. month's rest.

That month was spent in training for the great battle which was now believed to be due in early March. One sad change had perforce to be made. It had been resolved to reduce the British divisions from a thirteen battalion to a ten battalion basis, and this meant that one battalion must disappear from each brigade. General Smuts and General Lukin, after consultation with General Dawson, decided to disband the 3rd (Transvaal and Rhodesia) Regiment, which had received the smallest number of recruits during the past twelve months. On 8th February Dawson visited the battalion to explain the decision. He promised that as far as possible complete companies would be sent as reinforcements to the other regiments of the Brigade, and that every assistance would be given to officers and men who might desire to transfer to outside units. Accordingly, on 18th February, the 3rd Regiment was finally disbanded, practically all the officers, *Feb.* 18. N.C.O.'s, and men joining the other South African regiments.

In the beginning of March General Lukin relinquished the command of the 9th Division to Major-

General Tudor, who formerly commanded the divisional artillery, and returned home on leave. While at home he was compelled because of the grave illness of his wife to accept the offer of a tour of duty in England. He had had more than two years of the most arduous service, first as brigadier and then as divisional general, and he left to the profound regret of all his colleagues.* It was a departure that could not be without its element of sadness, especially for the South Africans, for it meant a break in that continuity of tradition which they had hitherto preserved. They had begun with Lukin, and till March 1918 they had been directly or indirectly under Lukin. These changes were, as it were, symbolical of the change which was coming over the aspect of the war. The former things were passing away ; the long months of almost static trench warfare were about to give place to a stormy season, when all maps had to be redrawn and every conception of war revised. It was the eve of the ultimate phase which at long last was to determine the issue of the campaign.

* Of Lukin Sir Douglas Haig wrote : " Coming to France in April 1916, his skilful command of the South African Brigade soon induced me to select him for command of the 9th Division. This division he has commanded with skill and ability in many hard-fought battles, and I have looked on him as one of the most reliable divisional commanders in France." Lieut-Col. Croft in his *Three Years with the 9th Division* has this pleasant tale of Lukin at Third Ypres : " In the early stage of the night march we met the divisional commander, who, like all the divisional commanders of the 9th Division, spent most of his time near the front lines. He was on his way back, and this good old regimental officer insisted on getting off the track and up to his knees in mud while the men went by, saying, ' I have a comfortable dug-out to go back to,' when we offered to make way for him."

But before these changes came about one great episode in the past record of the Brigade was commemorated. On the 17th February all its regiments, including the vanishing 3rd, took *Feb. 17.* part in a memorial service at Delville Wood. On the south side of the place towards Longueval a tall wooden cross had been erected, bearing the inscription : " In Memory of the Officers and Men of the 1st South African Brigade who fell in Action in July 1916 in the Battle of the Somme." Before this cross, among the shattered tree-stumps, the drumhead service was held, and around in a square stood details of the four battalions. First came a lament on the pipes, composed by Pipe-Major Grieve of the 4th Regiment. The service was conducted by the chaplains of the English, Presbyterian, and Dutch Churches, and the hymns included the beautiful Dutch version of the Hundredth Psalm. Sir Douglas Haig wrote to General Lukin :—

" I send you these few lines to greet you and all South Africans who meet together on Sunday next in honour of those brave men who, at the call of justice and humanity, came from a distant continent to fight and die for the principles they held sacred. The story of the great struggle of July 1916 for the ridge on which Delville Wood stands, when South Africa played so conspicuous a part, will live for all time in the history of our Empire—a perpetual witness to the strength of those common ideals which bind together all British people. The task of those who fell in Delville Wood and by their gallant death made desolation glorious, has not yet been completed ; but I feel confident that those who remain will see to it that their blood shall not have been shed in vain."

It was a clear day of frost and bright sunshine, and in the pause of the hymns, like the sound of breakers heard afar off on a coast, came the drone of airplanes overhead, and the echo of the now distant guns. That ceremony was something more than a commemoration of a great thing in the past. It was a sacrament taken in preparation for a still greater test of manhood now impending. For before the next month had closed, the enemy flood had once again poured over the wastes of Delville, and the flower of the South Africans had fallen in a new Thermopylæ.

Early in March the Brigade moved up to the front area, and on the night of the 12th began to take over *March 12.* from the 116th Brigade of the 39th Division the sector east of Heudicourt. Ever since the close of 1917 the Allied Command in the West had been conscious that the situation had altered. The Germans were able now to resume the offensive at their will, and the next phase of the campaign must see the Allies on their defence. Haig and Pétain were aware that large reinforcements could be brought from the East, which would give Ludendorff a numerical superiority until such time as the Americans arrived to redress the balance. Nevertheless, the general temper of the armies of France and Britain was one of confidence. At the worst they believed that they would have to face a small preponderance in numbers; but they had faced greater odds at First Ypres and Verdun, and had held their ground. Let the enemy attack and break his head against their iron barriers. He would only be the weaker when the time came for their final advance.

But certain wiser heads among both soldiers and civilians were uneasy. They knew that the German

Staff would make a desperate effort to secure a decision while they still held their opponents at a disadvantage. The German defence had been conducted in a long-prepared fortified zone ; the battles of 1917 had given us a new line, in parts only a month or two old. How, it was asked, would we fare against a resolute assault ? Worst of all, we were deplorably short of men. Haig had not received during 1917 the minimum levies he had asked for, and had been compelled to put into the line of battle men imperfectly trained, and to strain good divisions to breaking point. There were other drawbacks which bore specially hard upon the British. Up to January 1918 their right wing had been Sir Julian Byng's Third Army. Before the middle of that month the Third Army was moved a little farther north, and the place on its right taken by Sir Hubert Gough's Fifth Army from the Ypres area, which replaced the French in front of St. Quentin. About the 20th the Fifth Army extended its right as far south as Barisis, across the Oise, thus making itself responsible for a line of 72,000 yards.

For this new duty Haig had not received proportionate reinforcements. He had now a front of 125 miles, and he did not dare to weaken his north and central sections, where, in the case of an attack, he had but little room to manœuvre. So he was compelled to leave the Fifth Army on his right in a condition of perilous weakness. Gough on his forty-mile front had no more than eleven divisions in line, and three infantry and two cavalry divisions in reserve. His right three divisions were holding 30,000 yards—an average of one bayonet to the yard, while the German average was four.

There was the further handicap that the Germans from their position inside the great salient in the west could concentrate with ease a force of attack, and until the actual assault was made the Allied Command would not know on which side of the salient the blow would fall. For Ludendorff's dispositions would threaten the French in Champagne as much as the British at St. Quentin. There was still no centralized command, though the Versailles Council provided something in the nature of a unified Staff. Hence it would not be easy to arrange for co-operation with Pétain and for the support of French reserves till the battle had developed, for the French commander would not unreasonably desire to keep his reserves at a point where they could be used with equal facility for St. Quentin or Champagne. Yet it was to French support that Gough must look in the first instance, since the available British reserves had been allotted to Byng, and it would take time to bring troops from Plumer and Horne in the north.

The British Command attempted to atone for its weakness in numbers by devising defences of exceptional strength. In front, along the ground held by Byng and Gough, lay the " forward zone " organized in two sections—a line of outposts to give the alarm and fall back, and a well-wired line of resistance. In both were a number of skilfully placed redoubts armed with machine guns, and so arranged that any enemy advance would be drawn on between them, so as to come under cross fire. The spaces between the redoubts were to be protected by a barrage of field guns and corps heavy guns. The line of resistance and the redoubts were intended to hold out till the last, and to receive no support from the rear, except for such counter-attacks as might be necessary. The purpose of this " forward zone " was to break up an advancing enemy, and the principle of its organization was " blobs " rather than a continuous line.

Behind the " forward zone," at a distance of from half a mile to three miles or more, came the " battle zone," arranged on the same plan, except that it had no outposts. It was a defence in depth, elaborately wired, and studded with strong-points. A mile or two in its rear lay the third and final defensive zone, which in March was little more than a sketch. The theory of the system was that the " forward zone " would break up the cohesion of any assault, and that the " battle zone " would be impregnable against an attack thus weakened. Consequently the alternative positions in the rear—the third zone and the Péronne bridgehead—were not serious defences. Considering the small number of men available, it was not possible to provide any further safeguards in the time. On the " battle zone " rested the hope of resistance for the Third and Fifth Armies. If it failed to stand, the situation would be grave indeed, for there were no prepared defences to fall back upon, and no immediate hope of reserves.

The 9th Division formed the extreme left of the Fifth Army, with, on its right, the 21st Division under Major-General David Campbell ; and on its left the 47th (London Territorial) Division under Major-General Sir G. F. Gorringe—the right flank of Byng's Third Army. The 9th held its front with two brigades, the 26th on the left and the South Africans on the right, with the

27th in reserve. The South African sector covered some 2,000 yards from just north of Quentin Redoubt to just south of Gauche Wood. The Brigade was distributed in depth—that is to say, it was responsible not only for the front line, but for all other trench lines to the depth of about a mile. This made it impossible for it to man the entire length of its trenches, so its front was held by a series of posts placed at key positions, and so arranged as to enable their occupants to cover the whole ground with their fire. As the hour of attack approached, the " forward zone " was held by the 2nd Regiment on the right and the 1st on the left, with the 4th Regiment in reserve in the " battle zone."

To understand the battle which followed, it is necessary to examine more closely the nature of the Brigade's position. The country around Gouzeaucourt is more deeply cut than most of the tableland, with small valleys and ravines running north by east. The South African " forward zone " lay west of the village of Villers-Guislain, and was separated from it by a well-defined hollow. The outpost line had two important points—Quentin Redoubt on the north, garrisoned by a company of the 1st Regiment ; and Gauche Wood on the south, held by a company of the 2nd Regiment. The line of resistance ran from near the point called Chapel Crossing on the railway, along the west side of the Gouzeaucourt valley, and along the east side of the ruins of Gouzeaucourt. The " battle zone " began about the same point, and its first line, following the high ground west of the valley, curved round the western end of Gouzeaucourt. The reserve line of this zone lay some three-quarters of a mile farther west, from Chapel Hill along the eastern

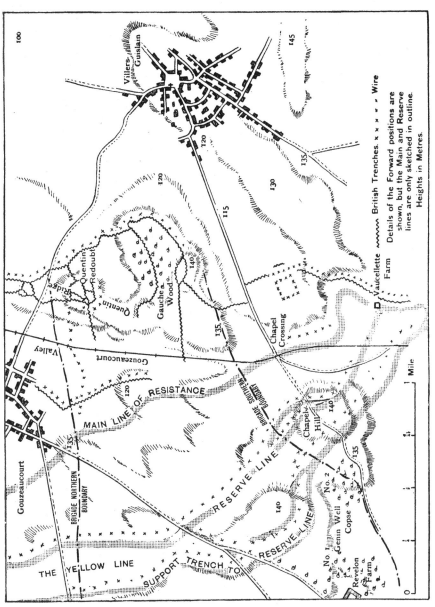

POSITIONS HELD BY THE SOUTH AFRICAN BRIGADE AT THE OUTSET OF THE GERMAN OFFENSIVE OF 1918.

slope of the ridges north of Revelon Farm. This was known to the Brigade as the Yellow Line. A few hundred yards farther back, on the western slopes of the same ridges, lay the Brown Line, the final line of the " battle zone." Three miles in the rear lay what was known as the Green Line, the third zone of defence, which, as we have seen, was still in embryo. Apart from the posts in the " forward zone," the specially fortified areas of resistance for the 9th Division were—for the 26th Brigade, Gouzeaucourt village and the place called Queen's Cross, south-east of Gouzeaucourt ; and for the South Africans, Revelon Farm, and, should that fail, the village of Heudicourt.

The first weeks of March saw the dry, bright weather of a Picardy spring. As early as the 14th our airplanes reported a big concentration well back in *March* 14. the enemy's hinterland, and the Third and Fitth Armies were warned of an approaching battle. The troops on our front waited on the future with composure. No one, perhaps, either in France or Britain, realized how much Germany was prepared to stake on this, her last blow, or the immense asset which her new tactics gave her. They did not know that Ludendorff had promised his country absolute and complete victory at the cost of a million and a half losses, and that she had accepted the price. Many raids undertaken during these days established the arrival of fresh enemy divisions in line ; but they gave us no notion of the real German strength. One fact however we learned—that Thursday, the 21st March, was the day appointed for the attack.

The last eight days were the quietest which the South African Brigade had ever known in the front line, and they had scarcely a casualty. On Tuesday, the 19th, the weather broke in a drizzle, but it cleared on the Wednesday, with the result that a thick mist was drawn out of the ground and muffled all the folds of the downs. That day was spent in an eerie calm, like the hush which precedes a storm. When the sun set, the men in the front trenches were looking into heavy fog, which grew thicker as darkness fell. There was no warning of any enemy movement, scarcely even a casual shell or the sputter of outpost fire.

About 2 a.m. on the morning of the 21st word was passed along our lines to expect an assault. The " forward zone " was always kept fully manned ;

March 21. but at half-past four the order went out to man the " battle zone." Still the same uncanny silence held, and the same clinging fog, under cover of which the Germans were methodically pushing up troops into line, till by dawn on the fifty odd miles of front between Croisilles and the Oise they had thirty-seven divisions within 3,000 yards of our outposts. Then, precisely at a quarter to five, the whole weight of their many thousand guns was released on the British forward and battle zones, headquarters, communications, and artillery posts, the back areas specially being drenched with gas, which hung like a pall in the moist and heavy air. Ludendorff had flung the dice for victory.

CHAPTER VIII.

THE SOMME RETREAT : GAUCHE AND MARRIÈRES WOODS.
(March 21–27, 1918.)

The German Assault—The Fight at Gauche Wood—The Brigade
Right Flank turned—The Fight for Chapel Hill—The Brigade
in the Yellow Line—The Fighting of 22nd March—Loss of
Chapel Hill and Revelon Farm—The Withdrawal to the Green
Line—The Situation on the Evening of the Second Day—
Gough decides to abandon the Péronne Bridgehead—The
Retreat of 23rd March—The Dangerous Position of the 9th
Division—General Tudor's Instructions to Dawson—The
Brigade retires to Marrières Wood—The Fight of Sunday
the 24th—The Brigade cut off—Death of Lieutenant-Colonel
Heal—The Last Stand—The End of the Brigade—The Splen-
dour of the Achievement—Its Value to the British Defence.

OUR artillery replied to the German barrage as well
as it might ; but no gunner or machine gunner
or observer could see fifty yards before him.
Under the cloak of the mist the vanguards of the enemy
were everywhere cutting the wire and filtering
between the Allied strongholds. The infantry *March* 21.
attack was timed differently along the front, in parts
beginning as early as eight o'clock, but by ten in the
morning it was general. The garrisons of the outposts,
beaten to the ground by the bombardment and struggling
amid clouds of gas, were in desperate case. In the

thick weather the enemy was beyond the places where the cross-fire of machine guns might have checked him long before the redoubts were aware of his presence. The first thing which most of the outposts knew was that the Germans were in their rear, and they were over-whelmed before they could send back warning. Even when they had longer notice, the S.O.S. signals were everywhere blanketed by the fog. Presently the bulk of the outpost line was gone, and the enemy was well into our forward zone. There the line of resistance held on gallantly for hours ; and long after the main battle had swept beyond it, messages continued to be received from odd posts, until that silence came which meant destruction. The havoc wrought among our communications kept the battle zone in the dark as to what was happening in front. Often, too, in those mad hours of fog, our guns received their first news of the assault from the appearance of German infantry on flank and rear. A little after eleven the brume lightened, and it was possible to see something of the landscape to the east. With the lightening came the German airplanes, flying low to attack with machine guns our troops and batteries. The men in the battle zone waited with anxious hearts till the shock of the assault should reach them.

We have seen that the main outposts of the forward zone held by the South African Brigade were Quentin Redoubt and Gauche Wood. At the first, where a company of the 1st Regiment was stationed, there was no attack.' The main enemy shock in that area fell upon the left Brigade of the 21st Division, and " B " Company of the 2nd South Africans in Gauche Wood.

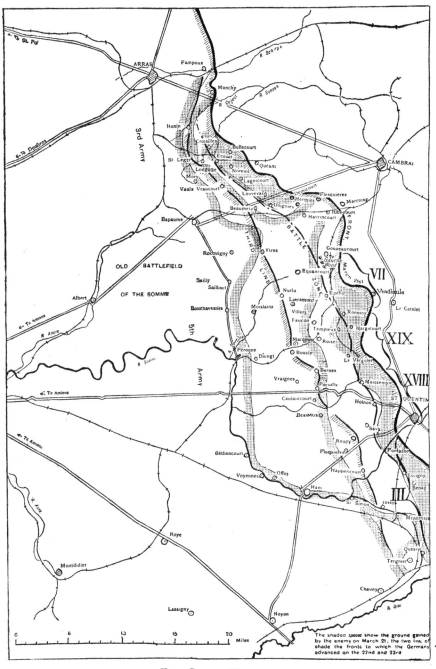

The shaded spaces show the ground gained by the enemy on March 21; the two lines of shade the fronts to which the Germans advanced on the 22nd and 23rd

THE SOMME RETREAT.

This company was under the command of Captain Garnet Green, an officer of the most proven courage and coolness, whose doings at Delville Wood I have already recounted. He had three strong-points inside the wood and one in the open on the south-west side ; there were also in the wood two machine guns and a detachment of the Brigade Trench Mortar Battery under Lieutenant Hadlow. Under cover of the fog the enemy worked his way into the wood from the east. Second-Lieutenant Kennedy fought his machine-gun till all his team were killed or wounded, and he himself was wounded and taken. About 10.15 Captain Green reported that the Germans were in the wood, but that the strong-points were intact. Presently the enemy began to creep in from the north, and the two posts in the eastern half, under Lieutenant Bancroft and Lieutenant Beviss, were overpowered. Bancroft and most of his men fell, and the rest were wounded and captured, with the exception of one who rejoined company head-quarters. Beviss, with nearly half his garrison, succeeded in cutting his way through and reaching Captain Green. The latter, finding that the enemy was on three sides of him in overpowering numbers, withdrew the garrison of the third post in the wood to join the fourth post in the open ground to the south-west. Every yard was fiercely contested, and, since the Germans exposed themselves recklessly, they lost heavily from Green's Lewis guns and rifles. They attempted to dig themselves in on the western edge of the wood, but our fire was too strong for them and they fell back in confusion into cover.

The situation was now clear to General Dawson.

He directed the fire of all the guns at his disposal on Gauche Wood. Further, before midday the mist had lifted and the garrison of Quentin Redoubt on the north were able to open a heavy flanking fire on the advancing enemy. Throughout the rest of the day Green, with his little band, was able to maintain his position on the western and south-western skirts of the wood. The situation, however, had become very serious farther south. At the first rush the Germans had forced back the left Brigade of the 21st Division and taken the cluster of ruined buildings called Vaucellette Farm. This they used as an assembly position for extending their attacks. The right flank of the South African Brigade at Gauche Wood was therefore wholly exposed, and by the early afternoon the enemy had worked his way more than a mile eastward, reaching the slopes of the little height called Chapel Hill.

Dawson was in a serious quandary. He had his line intact, except for the single point of Gauche Wood, which was an outpost of his forward zone; but with the enemy on Chapel Hill not only was the whole forward zone turned, but the first part of the battle zone, for this eminence commanded all the trench system in what was known as the Yellow Line. The front had now a singular formation, running back sharply from the extreme point of Quentin Redoubt in the north-east, by the west side of Gauche Wood to the north side of Chapel Hill, which itself was in the area of the 21st Division. The two forward battalions of the South Africans, the 1st and the 2nd, were most gravely menaced. After midday came worse news, for the enemy was reported to be as far west as Genin Well Copse.

At all costs it was necessary to recapture Chapel Hill,* so "A" Company of the 2nd Regiment, which had been reserved for a counter-attack, was sent early in the afternoon to strengthen the right flank. They found the Germans holding the trenches on the north ridge of the hill, and could make no further progress. Meantime the 4th Regiment, which, as we have seen, was manning the battle zone, was able to bring flanking fire to bear on the Germans at Genin Well Copse, and this, aided by a detachment of machine gunners at Revelon Farm, stayed further enemy progress on the south.

At 3.30 the 2nd Regiment reported that the Germans were concentrating in large numbers south-west of Vaucellette Farm for a further attack. It was difficult to check them with artillery, for the guns of the Brigade at the time were covering not only their own front, but 600 yards of that of the 21st Division. At half-past five Lieutenant-Colonel MacLeod, commanding the 4th Regiment, was ordered to send a company to retake Chapel Hill. "A" Company, under Captain Bunce, was detailed for the purpose, and by a spirited counter-attack they took the crest as well as the trenches on the south and south-east slopes, and so enabled posts to be established linking up the ridge with Genin Well Copse.

During the afternoon orders arrived from the division for a general retirement of all forward troops to the Yellow Line, and for Brigade Headquarters to fall back upon Sorel. The reason for this order lay in the

* Up till this, Chapel Hill had been in the area of the 21st Division, but Dawson that afternoon was ordered to assume responsibility for it.

general position of the battle. On the Fifth Army front the Germans had before midday broken into our battle zone at Ronssoy, Hargicourt, Templeux, and Le Verguier, and were threatening the valley of the Omignon. Later came news that the same thing had happened at Essigny and Maissemy. In the Third Army area the forward zone had gone at Lagnicourt and Bullecourt, and the fight was being waged in the battle zone northward from Doignies to the Sensée. Against 19 British divisions in line Ludendorff had hurled 37 divisions as the first wave, and before the dark fell not less than 64 German divisions had taken part in the battle—a number much exceeding the total strength of the British Army in France. In such a situation the Flesquières salient could not be maintained, though it had not been seriously attacked, and Byng's withdrawal from it meant a corresponding retirement by the 9th Division, which, except for Gauche Wood, had yielded nothing.

Accordingly during the evening and early night the South African Brigade fell back from the whole forward zone to the Yellow Line, the reserve position of the battle zone. The general line of the railway east of Gouzeaucourt was held up till 2 a.m. on the 22nd, and by 5 a.m. the retirement was complete.

March 22. During the night the left brigade of the 21st Division carried out a counter-attack, and re-established itself in the Yellow Line. By dawn on the 22nd the following was the disposition of the South Africans. On the left the 1st Regiment held the Yellow Line with three companies, one platoon of each in the front line, and two in support. Its fourth company was in the Brown Line, the last line of the battle zone system.

LIEUTENANT-COLONEL E. CHRISTIAN, D.S.O., M.C.,
Commanding 2nd Regiment, South African Infantry.

On the right the 4th Regiment was in the Yellow Line and on Chapel Hill with three companies, and the remaining company at Revelon Farm. Two companies of the 2nd assisted the 4th in holding the advance position on Chapel Hill, and the remainder of that battalion was in the Brown Line. So closed the first day of the battle. The Brigade had not received the full shock of the German onrush, and its main concern had been its right flank, where, by the gallant defence of Gauche Wood and the rapid counter-attack on Chapel Hill, it had checked for the moment the dangerous enemy infiltration in the area of the 21st Division.

The fog thickened again in the night, and by the dawn of Friday, the 22nd, it was as dense as on the previous morning. The first day of the battle had by no means fulfilled Ludendorff's expectations ; but he had time to spare, and had still the chance of complete victory. From the first light the enemy pressed heavily on the whole battle-front, but notably at the danger spots which the previous day had revealed in the line of the Fifth Army. Once again he made no serious attack on the South African Brigade, except on its right flank, where he laboured to work his way through it and the left brigade of the 21st Division. He had brought up a number of light trench mortars, and opened a heavy bombardment on Chapel Hill, Genin Well Copse, Revelon Farm, and Railton. Dawson had a most intricate task, for his headquarters were now at Sorel, from which he had no proper telephone communications ; and it was equally hard to direct the fire of our artillery and to obtain news of the fighting. He had received during the night the 11th Royal Scots from the 27th Brigade, which he used in the Brown Line in front of Heudicourt.

Throughout the morning, under cover of a heavy bombardment from artillery and trench mortars, the Germans gradually closed round Chapel Hill and Revelon Farm, both of which fell in spite of a most gallant defence. It was there that Captain Liebson, M.C., the medical officer of the 4th Regiment, was killed. Shortly after noon orders came from the division to give up the Yellow Line and fall back upon the Brown, the retirement to be complete by 4.30, and to be ready to retire later to the Green Line, three miles in the rear. The Green Line was the third defence zone, a partly completed line of trenches between Nurlu and Equancourt. The hour for the second withdrawal was to be announced later, but no message on the subject ever reached Dawson. Each battalion in the Yellow Line was directed to leave one section per company as a rearguard on its retirement to the Brown Line. The first part was carried out successfully. But as soon as the enemy noticed the withdrawal he advanced in close formation, and presently had reached the Brown Line in the 21st Division's area, had outflanked Heudicourt, and was occupying the high ground south-west of that village. The retirement of the 4th Regiment was only made possible by an accurate supporting fire from the 2nd. Dawson sent his Acting Brigade Major, Captain Beverley, about 3.30, on horseback, to give the battalions the message about the Green Line, which he succeeded in doing, after having his horse shot under him. All the troops had their instructions before five o'clock.

The disposition of the Brigade was now as follows.

On the right, at the quarry on the east of Heudicourt (the old Brigade Headquarters), was " B " Company of the 2nd, under Captain Green, with one company of the 11th Royal Scots and a few details of the 21st Division extending the line on the right. In the centre was the 4th Regiment, and on the left the 1st Regiment, both in the Brown Line. But the situation was full of peril, for the Brown Line was hopelessly outflanked on the right, and the enemy was moving northwards round the south end of Heudicourt. Communication with headquarters had become impossible, and a heavy responsibility fell upon the junior commanders, who flung out defensive flanks and fought rearguard actions with the coolness of veterans. While the guns were falling back, about thirty enemy airplanes, flying low, kept up a continual fire on the teams and also on the infantry in the trenches. Everything depended on whether the German advance could be stayed till darkness came, and under its cover the various units could reach the Green Line.

The Brigade Headquarters were at Sorel, and in the dusk the Germans could be seen in great strength moving westward south of the village. As our wounded and guns were passing through the place it was vital to defend it until the retirement was complete. The whole countryside seemed to be in flames ; Heudicourt was spouting like a volcano, and everywhere was the glare of burning stores and bursting shells. Dawson formed up his Brigade Headquarters Staff, and put them into the trenches east of Sorel, to give the guns and wounded time to get clear. About this time Major Cochran, the brigade major, returned from leave and resumed his duties—duties which, for the two days left to him on earth, he was to perform with a noble fidelity. The Headquarters details succeeded in arresting the enemy's advance, and, before he had time to reconnoitre or to organize an attack, the last guns had passed through Sorel, Brigade Headquarters withdrawing to Moislains. It was here that Lieutenant M. Webb was killed. Only darkness could save the Brigade, and the darkness was fast falling.

The gravest danger was in the south, for any further enemy advance there would turn the Green Line. Owing to the Germans moving northward behind our front it was impossible to keep to the original route of retirement, and all three units had to withdraw in a northern direction before striking west. The task of the 1st Regiment on the left was the least difficult. Under Lieutenant-Colonel Heal, it fell back upon Fins. Lieutenant-Colonel MacLeod, who commanded the 4th Regiment, was wounded during the afternoon, and the remnant, under Captain Bunce, moved along the Brown Line to the Fins-Gouzeaucourt road, and then westward from Fins. The most difficult operation fell to Lieutenant-Colonel Christian of the 2nd Regiment, but by a series of providential chances he extricated a large part of the regiment, following mainly the direction of the 4th. For " B " Company and its heroic commander, Captain Green, there was no chance of withdrawal. They were destroyed, fighting to the last. The details of the Brigade, to the strength of about 650 all ranks, had, on the 21st, been encamped at Heudicourt under Lieutenant-Colonel Young. Early on the 22nd they were ordered to fall back upon Nurlu, where,

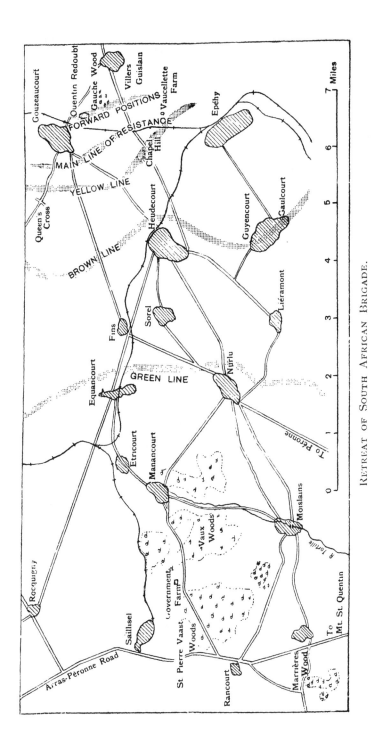

RETREAT OF SOUTH AFRICAN BRIGADE.

together with other 9th Division details, they laboured to improve the Green Line. The Brigade in its retreat passed through these details, and by about two in the morning of the 23rd had reached the Green Line and dug a position along the Nurlu-Péronne road south-east of Moislains.

The South Africans were now in divisional reserve. Their casualties during the first two days of the battle had been about 900 all ranks. Two weak companies of the 1st Regiment, under Captains Burgess and Ward, had become detached in the darkness, and for the next days fought along with the 26th Brigade. Of the 2nd Regiment, Captain Green and Lieutenants Bancroft and Terry had been killed, Captains Rogers and Stein wounded and captured, Lieutenant Beviss was missing, and Captains Jenkins and Pearse and Lieutenant Sprenger had been wounded. Of the 4th Regiment, all the senior officers—Lieutenant-Colonel MacLeod, Majors Clerk and Browne, and the Adjutant, Captain Mitchell, had been wounded. In the circumstances the withdrawal of the Brigade to the Green Line must be regarded as a very remarkable feat of arms. For two days they had fought with their flank turned, and only the tenacity and courage of the men and the extreme coolness and daring of the junior officers had prevented a wholesale disaster. At about five in the evening of the 22nd it might well have seemed that nothing could save them.

While we leave the South Africans secure for the moment in the Green Line we must note what happened elsewhere that day on the battle-front. Byng had been the less heavily engaged, and during the day yielded little ground. The enemy's main effort was against the Fifth Army, especially at the three critical points of the Cologne and Omignon valleys and the Crozat Canal. By midday the canal had been lost, and early in the afternoon Gough was almost everywhere in the third defensive zone. . By the evening that zone had been broken around Vaux and Beauvois. Our last reserves had been thrown in, and, save for a French division and some French cavalry, now heavily engaged on the Crozat Canal, there was no help available for the hard-pressed Fifth Army. The gaps could not be stopped, so at all costs our front must withdraw. At 11 p.m. that night Gough gave orders to fall back to the bridgehead position east of the Somme, a position which, as we have seen, was not yet completed. Maxse's XVIII. Corps was to retire to the river line; Watts' XIX. Corps and Congreve's VII. Corps were to hold the Péronne bridgehead on a line running from Voyennes through Monchy-Lagache to Vraignes, and thence continue in the third zone to the junction with the Third Army at Equancourt. This compelled Byng to fall back to conform, and his front ran now in the third zone to Hénin-sur-Cojeul, whence the old battle zone was continued to Fampoux.

The third zone was nowhere a real defence, and presently it was clear that the Péronne bridgehead was little better. During the thick night, while the divisions of the Fifth Army, now in the last stages of fatigue, struggled westward, Gough was faced with a momentous decision. He now knew the weight of the German attack; his right flank was in desperate peril; he had no hope of support for several days; and his men strung out on an immense front had been fighting without rest for forty-eight hours. If he faced a general engagement on the morrow he might suffer decisive defeat. There seemed no course open to him but to abandon the Péronne bridgehead, and fall back behind the river. It was a difficult decision, for it shortened our time for defending the river line and for clearing troops and material from the east bank. But the alternative was certain disaster, and beyond doubt in the circumstances Gough's judgment was right. Accordingly, very early on the morning of Saturday, the 23rd March, instructions were given to Watts to withdraw gradually to the river line, while Congreve, on his left, was to take up a position between Doingt and Nurlu. The front of the VII. Corps would now just cover Péronne on the north, and it would have behind it, flowing from north to south, the little river Tortille.

Saturday, 23rd March, dawned again in fog, and from an early hour it became clear that the position allotted to Congreve could not be held. *March 23.* That day von der Marwitz began the most dangerous movement of all—the attempt to drive a wedge between the Third and Fifth Armies. Very early in the morning he attacked the Green Line, which was held by details of the 9th Division. The advance was checked ; but the position was clearly untenable, and the South African details, under Lieutenant-Colonel Young, fell back to Bouchavesnes, where they again came under Dawson's orders.

That day the South Africans were nominally in reserve, holding a position in echelon on the right flank of the 27th Brigade. But a wavering front, faced by preposterous odds, called every man into the fight, and presently the Brigade was in the front line again on the right of the 27th, endeavouring to maintain touch with the 21st Division, which was compelled to retire by the withdrawal on its right from the Péronne bridgehead. During the morning Dawson fell back from Moislains, and took up ground about midday on the ridge south-west of that village, overlooking the Tortille River, where, during the afternoon, he was heavily shelled. Once again came the old menace on the right wing. The 21st Division, itself outflanked by the withdrawal farther south, was again retiring, and presently Dawson's flank was in the air, and the enemy in the immediate south was more than a mile behind his front. He had five tanks as a flank-guard, and he endeavoured to fling out posts as a defensive flank across the Péronne-Arras road. An officer and twenty men were sent to occupy the cutting on the summit of the ridge overlooking Mont St. Quentin. All afternoon the enemy poured down the slopes along the Péronne-Nurlu road, and before dark fell he had occupied Moislains and Haute-Allaines.

General Tudor visited Dawson in the evening. The situation of the whole 9th Division under von der Marwitz's thrust had grown desperate. It was holding an impossibly long line, and a gap had opened between its left and Fanshawe's V. Corps in the Third Army, of which the enemy had promptly taken advantage, in spite of gallant attempts to fill the breach made by the 47th London Division and a Brigade of the 2nd. On its right it was out of touch with the 21st Division ; so that that evening it was holding a salient of high ground with both flanks hopelessly in the air. There was no other course but to fall back, especially as the retirement of the 21st Division was by no means at an end. The 1st Regiment had been moved from the left of the South African Brigade to strengthen the right flank, but it could not hope to fill the breach, the more as the enemy was pressing hard from Moislains against this weak spot.

General Tudor told Dawson that instructions had come for the division to withdraw after dark to a position on the line from Government Farm by the east of St. Pierre Vaast Wood to the road just west of Bouchavesnes which led to Cléry. He informed him that Sir Walter Congreve had ordered that this line must be held " at all costs," and added that he presumed, if it was broken, it would be retaken by a counter-attack. These words of Tudor's are of importance, for they were Dawson's charter for the fighting of the next day. He was also bidden keep in close touch with the troops on his right —a counsel of perfection hard to follow, for Gough's decision on the night of the 22nd involved an indefinite retreat westward, and in such circumstances a unit which had orders to stand at all costs must inevitably be left in the void. Dawson saw his commanding officers, Heal and Christian (the remnants of the 4th had now been attached to the 2nd), and explained to them the gravity of the position. Whoever retired, the Brigade must stand.

The withdrawal started at 9.45 p.m., and the last troops had begun their retreat by 11 p.m. At 3 a.m. on the morning of the 24th all were in position in the new line. It was not the line which General Tudor had indicated, for by this time the left brigade of the

21st Division was more than a mile westward of that front, and if the South Africans were to stand they must find ground which, at any rate to begin with, was not hopelessly untenable. Dawson decided to occupy a ridge some 1,500 yards west of Tudor's line, so that by throwing back his right flank he might reduce the gap between him and the 21st to a less dangerous size. His Brigade Major, Cochran, was sent to prospect the position while it was still light, and to get into touch with the neighbouring Brigadier of the 21st, from whom he learned that immediately after dark that brigade intended to make a further retirement. In the South African withdrawal some of the posts flung out on the right flank lost their way, and wandered back to the transport lines. They were destined to be among the few survivors. During the night touch was obtained with the 21st Division, which, after retiring, had again advanced. The left flank of the Brigade was in touch with a company of the 6th K.O.S.B. of the 27th Brigade. The situation on that flank, however, was far from secure, for the K.O.S.B. did not know the whereabouts of the rest of their battalion or of their brigade. Dawson sent out patrols to look for them, but there was no sign of them anywhere in the countryside.

By dawn on Sunday, the 24th, the two regiments of the South Africans were holding a patch of front which, *March 24.* along with Delville Wood, is the most famous spot in all their annals. It lay roughly behind the northern point of Marrières Wood, running north-east in the direction of Rancourt, a little over two miles north-west of Bouchavesnes village. The ground sloped eastward, and then rose again to another ridge about

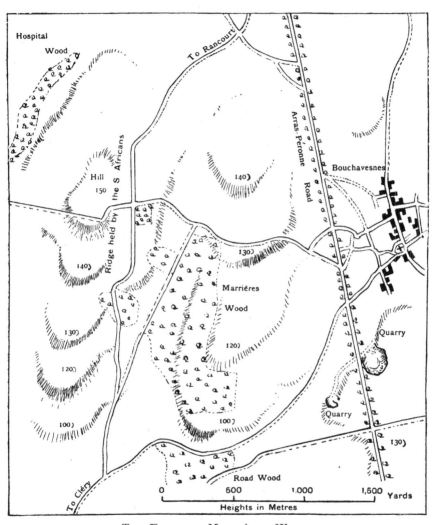

Hospital

Wood

To Rancourt

Arras-Péronne Road

Bouchavesnes

Hill
150

Ridge held by the S Africans

140)

130)

Marrières
Wood

140)

130)

120)

120)

100)

100)

Quarry

Quarry

130)

Road Wood

To Cléry

| 0 | | 500 | | 1.000 | | 1,500 | Yards |

Heights in Metres

THE FIGHT AT MARRIÈRES WOOD.

1,000 yards distant—a ridge which gave the enemy excellent chances for observation and machine-gun positions. There was one good trench and several bad ones, and the whole area was dotted with shell-holes. Dawson took up his headquarters in a support trench some 300 yards in rear of the front line. The strength of the Brigade was about 500 in all, composed of 478 men from the infantry, one section of the 9th Machine Gun Battery, and a few men from Brigade Headquarters. The previous day some officers had joined from the transport lines, and in consequence the number of officers was out of all proportion to the other ranks. The 2nd Regiment, for example, with a strength of 110, had no less than fourteen officers. Dawson's only means of communication with divisional headquarters was by runners, and he had long lost touch with the divisional artillery.

The South Africans seemed fated to have their greatest deeds linked always with some broken woodland. So far the proudest names in their record were those wraiths of copses, Delville and Gauche. To them must now be added a third, the splintered desert which had once been the wood of Marrières. It was a weary and broken little company which waited on that hilltop in the fog of dawn. During three days the 500 had fought a score of battles. Giddy with lack of sleep, grey with fatigue, poisoned by gas and tortured by the ceaseless bombardment, officers and men had faced the new perils which each hour brought forth with a fortitude beyond all human praise. But wars are fought with the body as well as with the spirit, and the body was breaking. Since the 20th of March, while the men had received rations, they had had no hot food or tea. Neither they nor their officers had any guess at what was happening elsewhere. They seemed to be isolated in a campaign of their own, shut out from the knowledge of their fellows and beyond the hope of mortal aid. Yet in a sense they were fortunate in their ignorance, for only the High Command knew how desperate was the position. When Ludendorff on the Saturday night announced that the first stage of the great battle had ended and counted his prisoners, he did not exaggerate his success. It was true that he had not yet broken the British line, but he had worn it to a shadow, and any hour might see that shadow dissolve.

The South African position was well placed for defence, for it had before it a long, clear field of fire. But it was a trap from which there could be no retreat, since all the land to the west was bare to the enemy's eyes. Dawson's 500, on the morning of the 24th, had, each man, 200 rounds of ammunition and a fair supply of Lewis gun drums. One section, however, of the Machine Gun Battery had only four belts of ammunition, and three of the guns with their teams were therefore sent back to the transport lines at Savernake Wood.

Soon after daylight had struggled through the fog the enemy was seen massing his troops on the ridge to the east, and about nine o'clock he deployed for the attack, opening with machine-gun fire, and afterwards with artillery. Dawson, divining what was coming, sent a messenger back to the rear with the Brigade records. He had already been round every part of the position, and had disposed his scanty forces to the best advantage. At ten o'clock some British guns opened an accurate fire, not upon the enemy, but upon the South African lines, especially on the trench where was situated Brigade Headquarters. Dawson was compelled to move to a neighbouring shell-hole. He sent a man on his last horse, followed by two runners, to tell the batteries what was happening, but the messengers do not seem to have reached their goal, and the fire continued for more than an hour, though happily with few casualties. After that it ceased, because the guns had retired. One of our heavies continued to fire on Bouchavesnes, and presently that, too, was silent.

It was the last the Brigade heard of the British artillery.

Meantime the enemy gun-fire had become intense, and the whole position was smothered in dust and fumes. Men could not keep their rifles clean because of the débris choking the air. The Germans were now some 750 yards from our front, but did not attempt for the moment to approach closer, fearing the accuracy of the South African marksmanship. The firing was mostly done at this time by Lewis guns, for ammunition had to be husbanded, and the men were ordered not to use their rifles till the enemy was within 400 yards. He attempted to bring a field gun into action at a range of 1,000 yards, but a Lewis gunner of the 1st Regiment knocked out the team before the gun could be fired. A little later another attempt was made, and a field gun was brought forward at a gallop. Once again the fire of the same Lewis gunner proved its undoing. The team got out of hand and men and horses went down in a struggling mass.

This sight cheered the thin ranks of the defence, and about noon came news which exalted every heart. General Tudor sent word that the 35th Division, which had arrived at Bray-sur-Somme, under Major-General Franks, had been ordered to take up position 1,000 yards in rear of the Brigade. For a moment it seemed as if they still might make good their stand. But the 35th Division was a vain dream. It was never during that day within miles of the South Africans. Dawson sent back a report on the situation to General Tudor.

It was the last communication of the Brigade with the outer world.

At midday the frontal attack had been held, an attack on the south had been beaten off, and so had a very dangerous movement in the north. The grass in that parched week was as dry as tinder. The enemy set fire to it and, moving behind the smoke as a screen, managed to work his way to within 200 yards of our position in the north. There, however, he was again checked. But by this time the German thrust elsewhere on the front was bearing fruit. Already the enemy was in Combles on the north and at Péronne and Cléry on the south. The 21st Division had gone, and the other brigades of the 9th Division were being forced back on the South African left. At about half-past two on that flank an officer with some thirty men began to withdraw under the impression that a general retirement had been ordered. As they passed Headquarters, Major Cochran and Captain Beverley, with Regimental Serjeant-Major Keith of the 4th Regiment, went out to stop them under a concentrated machine-gun fire. The party at once returned to the firing-line and were put into shell-holes on the north flank. Unhappily Cochran was hit in the neck by a machine-gun bullet and died within three minutes.

Dawson, early in the afternoon, attempted to adjust his remnant. The enemy now was about 200 yards from his front and far in on his flank and rear. Major Ormiston took out some twenty-five men as a flank-guard for the left, in which performance he was dangerously wounded. All wounded who could possibly hold a rifle were stopped on their way to the dressing-station, and sent back to the front line, and in no single instance did they show any reluctance to return. Ammunition was conserved with a noble parsimony, and the last round was collected from casualties. But it was now clear that the enemy was well to the west of the Brigade, for snipers' fire began to come from that direction. Unless the miracle of miracles happened the limit of endurance must be reckoned not in hours but in minutes. For the moment the most dangerous quarter seemed to be the north, and Lieutenant Cooper of the 2nd Regiment, with twenty men, was sent out to make a flank-guard in shell-holes 100 yards from Brigade Headquarters. The little detachment did excellent work, but their casualties were heavy, and frequent reinforcements had to be sent out to them. Lieutenant Cooper himself was killed by a fragment of shell.

As it drew towards three o'clock there came a last flicker of hope. The enemy in the north seemed to be retiring. The cry got up, " We can see the Germans surrendering," and at the same time the enemy artillery lengthened and put down a heavy barrage 700 yards to the west of the Brigade. It looked as if the 35th Division had arrived, and for a little there was that violent revulsion of feeling which comes to those who see an unlooked-for light in darkness. The hope was short-lived. All that had happened was that the enemy machine guns and snipers to the west of the Brigade were causing casualties to his troops to the east. He therefore assumed that they were British reinforcements.

About this time Lieutenant-Colonel Heal, commanding the 1st Regiment, was killed. He had already been twice wounded in the action, but insisted on remaining with his men. He had in the highest degree every quality which makes a fine soldier. I quote from a letter of one of his officers. " By this time it was evident to all that we were bound to go under, but even then Colonel Heal refused to be depressed. God knows how he kept so cheery all through that hell ; but right up to when I last saw him, about five minutes before he was killed, he had a smile on his face and a pleasant word for us all."

All afternoon the shell-fire had been terrific. Batteries of 7.7 cm., 10.5 cm., and 15 cm. were in action, many of them in full view of our men. A number of light trench mortars were firing against the north-east corner of our front and causing heavy losses. The casualties had been so high that the whole line was now held only by a few isolated groups, and control was impossible. About four o'clock Christian made his way to Dawson and told him that he feared his men could not hold out much longer. Every machine gun and Lewis gun was out of action, the ammunition was nearly gone, the rifles were choked, and the breaking-point had

LIEUTENANT-COLONEL F. H. HEAL, D.S.O.,
Commanding 1st South African Regiment. Killed at Marrières
Wood, near Bouchavesnes, 24th March 1918.

been reached of human endurance. The spirit was still unconquered, but the body was fainting.

Dawson had still the shadow of a hope that he might maintain his ground until the dark and then fight his way out. Like all good soldiers in such circumstances he was harassed by doubts. The Brigade was doomed; even if the struggle could be protracted till dusk, only a fragment would escape. Had he wished to withdraw he must have begun in the early morning as soon as the enemy appeared, for once the battle was joined the position was a death trap. He had orders from the division to hold his ground " at all costs "—a phrase often given an elastic interpretation in war, but in this case literally construed. He wondered whether the stand might be of value to the British front, or whether it was not a useless sacrifice. He could only fall back for comfort on his instructions. As he wrote in his diary : " I cannot see that under the circumstances I had any option but to remain till the end. Far better go down fighting against heavy odds than that it should be said we failed to carry out our orders. To retire would be against all the traditions of the service."

Some time after 4.15 enemy masses appeared to the east-north-east of Brigade Headquarters. It was the final attack, for which three fresh battalions had been brought up, and the assault was delivered in close formation. There were now only 100 South Africans, some of them already wounded. There was not a cartridge left in the front line, and very few anywhere except in the pistols of the officers. Had they had ammunition they might have held even this last attack ; as it was, it could be met only by a few scattered shots. The South

Africans had resisted to the last moment when resistance was possible ; and now they had no weapon. The Germans surged down upon a few knots of unarmed men. Dawson, with Christian and Beverley, walked out in front of a group which had gathered round them, and was greeted with shouts of " Why have you killed so many of us ? " and " Why did you not surrender sooner ? " One man said, " Now we will soon have peace," at which Dawson shook his head. Before he went eastward into captivity he was allowed to find Cochran's body and rescue his papers.

The Brigade had ceased to be. It had surrendered —such a surrender as Sir Richard Grenville made, when the *Revenge* fought for a day and a night against the fleets of Spain. Less than 100 unwounded prisoners fell to the enemy ; the rest were killed or crippled or lost, all but the little group of details and stragglers now in the transport lines. Heal and Cochran were dead, MacLeod was wounded, Dawson and Christian were prisoners. The rest of the 9th Division, along with the remnants of the 21st, were now fighting desperately north of the Somme behind Cléry, struggling to the line from Hem through Trônes Wood to Longueval, where the 35th Division and the 1st Cavalry Division were to come to their aid. It will be remembered that two companies of the South Africans had gone astray on the night of the 22nd and had since been fighting with other brigades. There were also the parties left behind in the Brown Line on that date, which had been unable to rejoin their units, and there were the posts which Dawson had flung out on his right flank on the 23rd, and which had lost their road in the last withdrawal. These oddments, along with the details and the transport of the Brigade, collected that evening half-way between Bray and Maricourt, and on the following day were formed into a composite battalion of three companies under Lieutenant-Colonel Young. Each company represented a regiment of the Brigade, No. 1 being under Captain Burgess, No. 2 under Lieutenant Jenner, and No. 3 under Lieutenant G. Smith. The fighting strength was some 450 rifles. On the 26th they were ordered to Dernancourt to report to General Kennedy of the 26th Brigade. They there *March 26.* found the 9th Division holding a line from that village to south of Albert, and took up a position in trenches and along the railway embankment south-east of the former place. This ground they held in spite of furious enemy efforts to dislodge them, until they were re- *March 27.* lieved by the Australians on the night of the 27th, when the whole division was withdrawn from the line.

In all that amazing retreat, when our gossamer front refused to be broken by the most fantastic odds, no British division did more nobly than the 9th. It held a crucial position in the line, and only by its stubborn endurance was a breach between Gough and Byng prevented. Among the brigades of the 9th, the chief brunt was borne by the South African. A great achievement is best praised in the language of the commanders themselves. General Tudor wrote :—

" I think everybody should know how magnificently the South African Brigade fought. None but the best could have got through on the 22nd from the Yellow Line with Heudicourt in the hands of the enemy. They were sadly thinned then, only about 900 rifles all told when they got back, but they left their mark on the Hun. The story of the magnificent stand made by the Brigade when afterwards surrounded can only be told by those who were with it to the last ; but this much is certain, that it was shortage of ammunition alone which made the survivors surrender. The division will not seem the same again without them, and it was they who bore the brunt of the fighting of the 9th on the 21st and 22nd."

Here are Dawson's words :—

" It is impossible for me to do justice to the magnificent courage displayed by all ranks under my command during this action. For the two years I have been in France I have seen nothing better. Until the end they appeared to me quite perfect. The men were cool and alert, taking advantage of every opportunity, and, when required, moving forward over the open under the hottest machine-gun fire and within 100 yards of the enemy. They seemed not to know fear, and in my opinion they put forth the greatest effort of which human nature is capable. I myself witnessed several cases of great gallantry, but do not know the names of the men. *The majority, of course, will never be known.* It must be borne in mind that the Brigade was in an exhausted state before the action, and in the fighting of the three previous days it was reduced in numbers from a trench strength of over 1,800 to 500."

Let us take the testimony of the enemy. During the German advance, Captain Peirson, the brigade major of the 48th Brigade of the 16th Division, was taken prisoner. When he was examined at German Headquarters, an officer asked him if he knew the 9th Division ; for, said he, " We consider that the fight put up by that division was one of the best on the whole of your front, especially the last stand of the South African Brigade, which we can only call magnificent." In the course of his journey to Le Cateau Captain Peirson was spoken to by many German officers, all of whom mentioned the wonderful resistance of the South Africans. There is a more striking tribute still. On the road to Le Cateau a party of British officers was stopped by the Emperor, who asked if any one present belonged to the 9th Division. " I want to see a man of that division," he said, " for if all divisions had fought like the 9th I would not have had any troops left to carry on the attack."

It was no piece of fruitless gallantry. Dawson, as he was tramping eastwards, saw a sight which told him that his decision had been right, and that his work had not been in vain. The whole road for miles east of Bouchavesnes was blocked by a continuous double line of transport and guns, which proved that the South Africans had for over seven hours held up not only a mass of German infantry, but all the artillery and transport advancing on the Bouchavesnes-Combles highway. Indeed, it is not too much to say that on that fevered Sabbath the stand of the Brigade saved the British front. It was the hour of von der Marwitz's most deadly thrust. While Gough was struggling at the river crossings, the Third Army had been forced west of Morval and Bapaume, far over our old battleground of the Somme. The breach between the two armies was hourly widening. But for the self-sacrifice of the Brigade at Marrières Wood and the delay in the German advance at its most critical point, it is doubtful whether Byng could ever have established that line on which, before the end of March, he held the enemy.

" The majority will never be known." That is the

comment which has to be made after every great episode
in war. The names of commanders stand out, and now
and then some single feat of gallantry emerges into
light ; but a great thing is achieved not only by the
spirit of the leaders, but by the faithfulness and devotion of those who disappear without record into the
dark, or are remembered only by a wooden cross on an
obscure grave. In that last stand every man of the
Brigade " took counsel from the valour of his heart,"
and the glory became less that of the individual than of
the race. Two strong stocks, coming together from the
ends of the earth, had each of them in their blood the
spirit that defends lost hopes and is undismayed by any
odds. The kinsfolk of the men who shattered Dingaan's
hordes and under Andries Potgieter beat off the indunas
of Mosilikatse at Vechtkop, and those who had in their
tradition the Ridge of Delhi and the laager at Rorke's
Drift, joined hands at the wood of Marrières in an
achievement more fateful and not less heroic than any
in their splendid past.

CHAPTER IX.

THE BATTLE OF THE LYS.
(March 27–May 5, 1918.)

The New Brigade—General Tanner takes Command—Ludendorff's
Strategy in the North—The Weakness of the British Position
—The Attack of 9th April—Von Armin attacks on the 10th—
The Brigade moves into Line—Attached to the 19th Division
—The Counter-attack on Messines—The Situation on the
Evening of the 10th—The South Africans forced back from
Messines—Plumer's General Withdrawal—The Brigade re-
lieved—The Fight for Mont Kemmel—The Brigade in the
Vierstraat Line—The Counter-attack on Wytschaete—Von
Armin's Failure of the 17th—The Brigade withdrawn—The
Composite Battalion formed—The New South African Brigade—
Attached to the 49th Division—The Attack of 26th April
—The Attack of 29th April—End of the Battle of the Lys—
The Forty-five Days.

THE old Brigade had come to an end, but the glory
which South Africa had won on the Western front
required that without delay it should have a suc-
cessor. The story of Marrières Wood, for all its tragedy,
was too great to be permitted to lack a fitting sequel.
General Botha, on behalf of the Union Government,
telegraphed to Haig during these days : " We are watch-
ing with appreciation the strenuous efforts which you and
your gallant men are making in this supreme struggle
for the liberty of mankind." To this the Commander-
in-Chief replied : " The fine part already played by South

Africa in this great battle is a symbol of the strength and unity of purpose that binds together all parts of the British Empire." When the composite battalion, under Lieutenant-Colonel Young, was withdrawn from the line on the night of 27th March, it marched along with the rest of the 9th Division to Candas, arriving there on *April 1.* 1st April. It detrained at Abeele on the morning of the 2nd, and moved into the Ridgewood area. Every man who could be found was brought from England, and during the next few days drafts to the number of 17 officers and 945 other ranks arrived. The reorganization of the Brigade was immediately begun, and General Tanner, the former leader of the 2nd Regiment, came from the 8th Brigade to its command. The presence of Tanner was in itself a pledge of continuity in tradition. Presently the Brigade had a strength of 39 officers and 1,473 other ranks, and the old regiments were once more in being, the 1st under Lieutenant-Colonel Young, the 2nd under Captain Jacobs, and the 4th under Captain Reid.

By the 6th of April the German thrust towards Amiens had failed, and for the moment the gate of *April 6.* the Somme was closed. Brought to a standstill, Ludendorff cast about for a diversion, for he could not permit the battle to decline into a stalemate, and so lose the initiative. His main purpose was the same, but he sought to achieve it by a new method. He would attack the British elsewhere on some part of the front where they were notoriously weak, and compel Foch to use up his reserves in its defence. Then, when the Allied "mass of manœuvre" had shrunk, he would strike again at the weakened door of Amiens. On Ludendorff's plan the operation was to be a strictly subsidiary one, designed to prepare the way for the accomplishment of his main task farther south. He proposed to allot only nine divisions for the initial stroke, and to choose a battle-ground where even a weak force might obtain surprising results.

That battle-ground was the area on both sides of the Lys between the La Bassée Canal and the Wytschaete Ridge. The German Staff were aware that it had already been thinned to supply ten divisions for the contest in the south, and that at the moment it was weakly held, mainly by troops exhausted in the Somme battle. Haig, as we know from his dispatch, had drawn especially upon this section, since a retreat there would not imperil the whole front so gravely as would the loss of ground between La Bassée and Arras. Nevertheless, it was a very real danger-point. The enemy had the great city of Lille to screen his assembly. Certain key-points of communications, like Béthune and Hazebrouck, lay at no great distance behind the British front. The British communications were poor, and the German were all but perfect. Any advance threatened the Channel Ports, and might be expected to cause acute nervousness in the mind of British Headquarters. Reinforcements would be demanded from Foch, and the place was far enough from the Amiens battle-ground to put a heavy strain upon the Allied power of reinforcement. Ludendorff's aim was by a sharp, short thrust to confuse the Allied plans and absorb their reserves. If he could break through at once between La Bassée and Armentières and capture Béthune, he could swing north-westward and take Hazebrouck and the hills beyond Bailleul, and so compel a general retirement west of Dunkirk and the floods of the river Aa. But to succeed he must have a broad enough front. He must take Béthune at once and the Messines Ridge soon after, for, if the British pillars of the gate at Givenchy and Messines should stand, his advance would be squeezed into narrows where even a weak and tired force might hold it.

On the 8th the South African Brigade moved to hutments along the road between La Clytte and the little hill of Scherpenberg. On the morning of Tuesday, 9th April, Ludendorff struck between the Lys and La Bassée with von Quast's VI. Army. He broke that part of the line held by the Portuguese, and in the afternoon had swept over the Lys on a broad front. But at one vital point he failed. The 55th (West Lancashire) Division still held the gate-post at Givenchy, and throughout the whole battle that key position was never yielded by British troops.

April 8–9.

That night General Tudor instructed Tanner that the South Africans would be placed at the disposal of the 19th Division, which, along with the 25th and 9th Divisions, was holding the Messines Ridge and the line just north of the Lys. The corps was the IX., under Lieutenant-General Sir A. Hamilton Gordon. Next morning, 10th April, at 5.30 a.m., the IV. German Army, under our old antagonist at Ypres, Sixt von Armin, attacked from Frelinghien to as far north as Hill 60. Under cover of the fog the enemy filtered into our positions from Ploegsteert Wood to Messines along the valleys of the Warnave and Douve streams. By noon he had taken Ploegsteert village and the south-east part of the wood, and had got Messines,

April 10.

while farther north he had driven in our line as far as
Hollebeke, and was close on the Wytschaete crest.
Ludendorff was striking hard against the northern pillar
of the gate.

At eight that morning the Brigade was ordered to
move to a position of assembly just south of the village
of Neuve Eglise, where they formed part of the reserve
of the IX. Corps.   During the morning the march was
accomplished, and for the first time the South Africans
saw the impact of war upon a land yet undevastated.
Tanner wrote in his diary : " The sights in that march
from La Clytte are never likely to be forgotten by those
who witnessed them.   With the falling back of our line
that morning the shelling of the back areas had greatly
increased, both in density and length of range.   As a
result, a large belt of country previously unmolested became subjected to a terrifying storm of long-range pro-
jectiles, and the inhabitants, who up to then had been
conducting peacefully their farming operations, were
compelled to flee for shelter beyond the reach of the
enemy guns.   As we approached Neuve Eglise the road
from Scherpenberg onward presented a constant stream
of fugitives, old men, women, and children, laden with
what household goods they could remove in carts,
wheelbarrows, and perambulators.   The most pitiable
sights were those of infirm old people being removed
in barrows, pushed or pulled by women and children."
That was a spectacle which British troops had already
seen east of Amiens, and it was not likely to weaken
their determination in the coming battle.

At noon Tanner saw Major-General Jeffreys, commanding the 19th Division, and received his orders.

The enemy had broken through between Messines and the place called Pick House on the Wytschaete road, and the situation at the moment was obscure. The South Africans were to counter-attack and retake that section of the crest of the ridge. The front established by the Messines victory of June 1917 had been more than two miles east of the crest, but that morning's fighting had brought it back generally to the western slopes. The counter-attack, in which the 57th and 58th Brigades of the 19th Division were to co-operate, was aimed at recovering the ridge and its eastern slopes. The area of the South African Brigade was between Messines village and Lumm's Farm. Their first objective was the Messines-Wytschaete road ; the second the original British third defence zone, bending round the village on the east from Bethlehem Farm in the south to Pick House in the north ; and the third the original battle zone. The defence system in this area had not the elaboration of that of the Somme, and the second and third objectives may be best described as the old British third and second lines.

At 5.15 p.m. the South Africans moved from their position of assembly to the line of the Steenebeek stream, where, at 5.45, they deployed for the attack. The 1st Regiment was on the right, and directed against Messines village ; the 2nd on the left against the front between the village and Pick House. The 4th was in support to both battalions, and one of its companies was allotted to the assistance of the attack of the 1st on Messines itself. The spring day had clouded over, and there was mist and a slight drizzle when the infantry advanced. The western slopes of the ridge were held

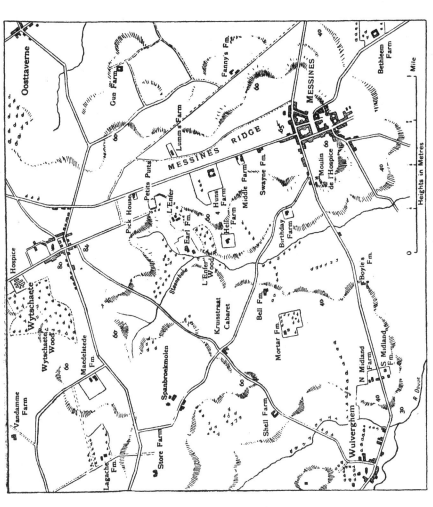

'ACTION OF SOUTH AFRICAN BRIGADE ON MESSINES RIDGE.'

at the time only by some units of the 19th Division. On the South African right was the 57th Brigade, and on their left, beyond Pick House, on the Wytschaete Ridge, the rest of the 9th Division.

In the mist it was not easy to keep close touch, and the 1st Regiment reached the western slopes ahead of the time, so that for a little its left flank was out of touch with the 2nd. As had been expected our artillery support proved very weak, and in no way affected the German machine gunners established in our old strong-points, and their snipers in shell-holes. As the South Africans approached the crest they were met by a heavy fire from the outskirts of the village, and from Middle Farm, Four Huns Farm, and Pick House. Nevertheless, by 6.30 the 2nd Regiment had won its first objective and crossed the Messines-Wytschaete road. Presently it had reached the second position, " D " Company, on the left, capturing Lumm's Farm with two machine guns, much ammunition, and part of the garrison, while the right companies, reinforced by part of the 4th Regiment, took Four Huns Farm, Middle Farm, and Swayne's Farm, together with four machine guns and many prisoners. Pick House itself, however, which consisted of three concrete pill-boxes, was too strongly held, and Captain Jacobs, commanding the 2nd, was compelled to swing back his left company to Earl Farm, where it formed a defensive flank in touch with the 5th South Wales Borderers in the 58th Brigade. Here it was heavily enfiladed from a strong-point north of Messines and from Pick House, and early in the night Jacobs took up a crescent-shaped line astride the Messines-Wytschaete road, with his right resting on Middle Farm, his left on Petits Puits, and his own headquarters at Hell Farm. His casualties on the left had been slight, but the companies of the 2nd on the right had lost some 50 per cent. of their effectives, among them Lieutenant Pope-Hennessy killed, and Lieutenant Jenner wounded.

In the meantime the 1st Regiment had met the enemy issuing from Messines, had charged him with the bayonet, and had driven him back well over the ridge. In the eastern outskirts of the village, however, they were held up by heavy machine-gun fire from the direction of Bethlehem Farm, and from various strong-points north of it. One of the latter was captured, and many prisoners were taken. For an hour there was severe hand-to-hand fighting, in which many casualties were sustained, all the officers in the vicinity being either killed or wounded. Among those who fell were Captain A. E. Ward and Lieutenants Hopgood and Griffiths, while Captains Burgess, Larmuth, and Tobias, and Lieutenants Lawrence, Neville, Spyker, Carstens, Christensen, and Clarke were wounded. Captain Burgess, in especial, gallantly led a small detachment through heavy fire to the east of the village. Owing to the shortage of men the position soon became untenable, and what was left of the 1st Regiment was compelled to withdraw to a line about 100 yards west of Messines. The headquarters of the 4th Regiment in support had been established at Birthday Farm.

The situation, therefore, on the Wednesday evening was as follows. The new German line ran from Hollebeke, east of Wytschaete, which was held by the 9th Division; along the crest of the Messines Ridge, and just west of the village; through the south-east corner of

Ploegsteert Wood, and west of Ploegsteert village.
Farther south the advance was deeper, for the enemy
were north of Steenwerck, north and west of Estaires,
just east of Lestrem and the Lawe River, and then cur-
ving south-eastward in front of the unbroken position at
Givenchy. It was a narrow front for a great advance,
for the pillars at Givenchy and the Messines Ridge were
still standing. The safety of the British front depended
upon the 55th, the 19th, and the 9th Divisions.

Little happened during the night of the 10th. The
South Africans retained their ground, and endeavoured
to gain touch with the troops of the 9th Division about
Pick House, while the 4th Regiment took over part of
the line of the depleted 1st. On the morning of the
11th the 108th Brigade was moved forward in
April 11.
support of the South Africans, and took up
a line along the Steenebeek stream. The South African
front at the time ran from the western skirts of Messines
through the Moulin de l'Hospice, then to Middle Farm
and Lumm's Farm northwards, and back to Petits Puits,
with an outpost at Rommen's Farm.

Early in the afternoon von Armin attacked with fresh
troops, and the situation north of the Lys became very
grave. On the British right the 40th Division was
forced well north of Steenwerck. On its left the 34th
Division was strongly attacked, and with difficulty succeeded in holding Nieppe, which, owing to the pressure
on the 25th Division from Ploegsteert, had now become
an ugly salient. That afternoon the crest of the Messines Ridge was lost. The enemy attacked in great force
on the South African left on the line between Middle
Farm and Petits Puits, and drove the 2nd Regiment

back to a front parallel to and about 600 yards west of the Messines-Wytschaete road. Captain Jacobs having been wounded during the morning, Captain L. Greene assumed command, and, with Lieutenant Thompson of the 4th Regiment, immediately counter-attacked and regained the lost ground. Presently, however, the enemy succeeded in working round the left flank, and the South Africans were compelled to retire to a line 200 yards east of Hell Farm, where they were in touch on their left with the 5th South Wales Borderers. In this position, in spite of repeated assaults, they were able to remain during the evening. There was also trouble on the right, where the 4th Regiment had relieved the 1st. Middle Farm had been strongly assaulted, and our counter-attack had sustained severe casualties. The 108th Brigade moved up in support, and for the moment the German advance was arrested.

The loss of the Messines Ridge, though the 9th Division was still standing south of Hollebeke and at Wytschaete, compelled Plumer to rearrange his front. Early on the night of the 11th he relinquished Nieppe, retiring the 34th Division to the neighbourhood of Pont d'Echelles. This involved the falling back of the 25th and 19th Divisions to a front about 1,000 yards east of Neuve Eglise and Wulverghem, and the consequent abandonment of the important point, Hill 63, just north of the western extremity of Ploegsteert Wood. South of the Lys there had been heavy fighting. The line of the Lawe had been lost, and by this time the enemy was in Merville. That night the British front ran from Givenchy to Locon, west of Merville, west of Neuf Berquin, north of Steenwerck and Nieppe, east of Neuve

Eglise and Wulverghem, west of Messines, and along the ridge just covering Wytschaete. The gate was open, but it was narrow, and the gate-posts still held.

About four on the afternoon of the 11th orders had been received from the 19th Division for a general withdrawal. The South Africans were to fall back to a line from North Midland Farm by Kruisstraat Cabaret and Spanbroekmolen to Maedelstaede Farm, with the 108th Brigade on their right and the 57th in reserve along the Neuve Eglise-Kemmel road. About eight o'clock the Germans were found to be working round the left flank in the vicinity of L'Enfer, and accordingly two companies of the 1st Royal Irish Fusiliers from the 108th Brigade were sent to the north of L'Enfer to obtain touch with the 9th Division. For the *April 12.* rest, the withdrawal was carried out without incident. By 5 a.m. on the 12th the South Africans were in their new front.

Up to now the enemy had not used more than sixteen divisions ; but on the morning of Friday, the 12th, he began to throw in his reserves at a furious pace. Elated by his rapid success, he turned what was meant as a diversion into a major operation, and dreamed of Boulogne and Calais. It was Ludendorff's first blunder, and it was fatal. It saved the Allied front, but for the moment it all but destroyed the British army. Our reinforcements were arriving from the south, but they could only gradually come into line. That day the enemy came very near to crossing the La Bassée Canal. He made an ugly gap in our line south-west of Bailleul, which let through detachments, who seized Merris and Oultersteene north of the railway. He was now close on Bailleul Station, pushing direct for Haze-brouck, and but for a gallant stand of a brigade of the 33rd Division, would have been through the breach. In the section of the 9th and 19th Divisions nothing happened. The enemy, having gained the Messines Ridge, was apparently content to rest there for a time, and made no further attack.

The South African Brigade was to have been relieved during the night of the 12th, but the relief was cancelled, since the troops detailed to take its place had to be used to restore the situation farther south. During the night Tanner established an outpost line along the Wulverghem-Wytschaete road. On the morning of *April* 13. Saturday, the 13th, his outposts reported that the Germans, under cover of the mist, were massing opposite Kruisstraat Cabaret. They were quickly dispersed by our artillery, which during the day dealt faithfully with similar concentrations. That night the Brigade was relieved in line by the 58th, and withdrew to hutments at La Clytte, where it came once more under the 9th Division.

The stand at Messines by the South Africans played a vital part in the battle of the Lys. For thirty hours the Brigade delayed the enemy's advance, and took heavy toll of him. In the words of the special order of the IX. Corps, " Its tenacity in the face of superior numbers and heavy firing undoubtedly relieved a serious situation, and obliged the enemy, when he was able to occupy the ridge, to be content to stay there during the whole of the 12th April without any further attempt to advance." Major-General Jeffreys, commanding the 19th Division, and Sir A. Hamilton Gordon, the Corps

Commander, bore testimony to the quality of the exploit. The latter wrote, " I wish to express to the General of the South African Brigade and to all his officers and men, my appreciation of their wonderful fighting spirit and most gallant doings in the great fight which we have been having in the last three days against heavy odds." Sir Herbert Plumer wrote that if any unit could be selected for exceptional praise it was the South African Brigade. Remember that the great majority of the men were new drafts, who had just arrived from home. Once again the Brigade had performed what seemed to be its predestined duty in an action—fighting outside its own area with its flank turned ; and, as was inevitable, it paid a heavy price. For the three days its casualty list amounted to 639 all ranks ; of these 89 were killed, 270 were wounded, and 280 were missing, of whom the majority were afterwards proved to be dead. Yet, as the men marched back from the line, their spirits seemed to be as high as when they had entered it.

The spell of rest was destined to be short. Von Armin was pressing hard for Mont Kemmel. On the 13th the 29th and 31st Divisions had fought a most gallant fight in front of Bailleul, where, with the assistance of the 4th Guards Brigade, they held the line till the 1st Australian Division could come up and organize positions east of the Forest of Nieppe. " No more brilliant exploit," wrote Sir Douglas Haig, " has taken place since the opening of the enemy's offensive, though gallant actions have been without number." All that day, too, the 33rd and 49th Divisions were hotly engaged in front of Neuve Eglise. In the evening the enemy made his way between that village and La Crèche, and so outflanked the left of the 34th. During the night Plumer withdrew to the high ground called the Ravelsberg, between Neuve Eglise and Bailleul, and the former village the following morning passed into German hands. The threat to Hazebrouck was now acute, for von Armin was on the edge of the line of upland from Mont des Cats to Kemmel, which commanded all the northern plain towards the Channel. On Sunday, the *April 14–15.* 14th, there was a little respite ; but on Monday morning the 19th Division was hard pressed at Wytschaete, and three fresh German divisions, including the Bavarian Alpine Corps, attacked our front on the Ravelsberg, and at nine in the evening entered Bailleul. About that time the remnants of the South African Brigade were moved to the Reninghelst area, with orders to be prepared to march at an hour's notice.

In the early hours of Tuesday, the 16th, the British front at Wytschaete and Spanbroekmolen was attacked *April 16.* in force, with the result that both places fell. At 8.30 came orders from the 9th Division that the South Africans should move at once to a position in the Vierstraat line from Desinet Farm, in the north, to La Polka, just east of Kemmel village. General Tudor was about to attempt the recapture of Wytschaete. By noon the South Africans were in position, the 1st Regiment on the right, 250 strong, and the 4th Regiment, with the same strength, on the left ; while the 2nd Regiment, 292 strong, was disposed in the second line along the

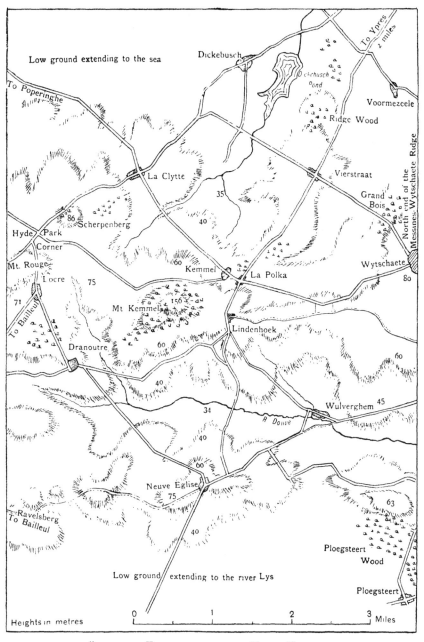

SCENE OF FIGHTING AROUND MONT KEMMEL.

whole front in the trenches which were known as Sack-
ville Street.

At 3.30 in the afternoon Tanner was instructed to
send 100 men of the 2nd Regiment to occupy an advanced
position between Store Farm and Van Damme Farm,
part of the line from which it was proposed to make
the counter-stroke. These men were required to form
a garrison there, while the attack was delivered by the
French. Meantime on the left the 26th Brigade of the
9th Division was to move on Wytschaete. The latter
attack was launched at 7.30 in the evening, but was held
up in the north-west of the village. A quarter of an
hour before midnight Tudor ordered Tanner to place
the 4th South Africans under the orders of Colonel
Mudie, the officer commanding the 7th Seaforth Highlanders, in order to assist in clearing up the situation.
At midnight the 1st South Africans and, two hours
later, the 2nd South Africans (less the garrison on the
Store-Van Damme Farm line) were also dispatched to
the Seaforths. The 4th Regiment on its arrival was
employed to fill a gap in the line on the north-west
skirts of the village, while the 1st and 2nd Regiments were
held in reserve. Some hours later Captain Farrell, who
was now in command of the 4th, reported that parties
of his men had succeeded in entering Wytschaete, but
on account of heavy machine-gun fire and the lack of
touch with their flanks, had been compelled to fall back.

Such was the situation on the morning of the 17th.
It was for the enemy the most critical moment, *April* 17.
perhaps, in the whole Battle of the Lys.
He had reached his greatest strength, and the British
troops were not yet reinforced at any point within sight

of security. That morning von Armin's right attacked in the Ypres salient, and wholly failed to break the Belgian front. At the same time his left, now that the possession of the Wytschaete Ridge gave him observation over all the land to the west, assaulted the wooded slopes of Kemmel, the key of the countryside. After an intense bombardment the German infantry advanced with great resolution from their new positions at Neuve Eglise and Wulverghem, but were repulsed at all points with heavy losses by the 34th, 49th, and 19th Divisions. Von Armin's cherished plan had signally failed. During the 17th the South African Brigade was temporarily placed under the 26th Brigade, and the 100 men of the 2nd in the Store-Van Damme Farm line rejoined their regiment in front of Wytschaete. In that position during the night the 1st and 2nd South Africans relieved the 4th Regiment and the 7th Seaforth Highlanders, the 4th returning to the La Polka-Desinet Farm section, where it came once again under Tanner.

Meantime Tudor had received the 62nd and 64th Brigades from the 21st Division as reinforcements, and contemplated a further attack upon Wytschaete. The *April* 18. 64th Brigade relieved the 26th, while the 1st and 2nd South Africans remained in line under the orders of the former Brigade. This plan, however, did not mature. During the morning of *April* 19- the 18th, under cover of mist, the enemy 20. assaulted the position held by the 1st Regiment, and captured its advanced posts, one officer, Lieutenant Hogg, being killed, and 48 other ranks missing. Save for this incident the situation remained unchanged that day. On the 19th 100 men of the 4th

Regiment were detailed to relieve some troops of the 19th
Division. On the night of the 20th, the 4th was relieved
in the southern part of the Vierstraat line and moved into
support, while the detachment lent to the 19th Division
rejoined its unit. Early on the morning of the 22nd
the 1st and 2nd Regiments were also relieved and moved
to Dickebusch, and on the 23rd the whole
Brigade reassembled in the Hopoutre area. *April 23.*

It was clear that the reconstructed Brigade could
not continue. The drafts received after the *débâcle* of
24th March had been used up in the heavy fighting on
the Messines-Wytschaete Ridge, and further reinforcements were not forthcoming to build it up to some
semblance of fighting strength. No other course was
possible but to organize the remnants into one battalion.
The history of the doings of the South Africans in France
is now the history of this composite unit, which was
commanded by Lieut.-Colonel H. W. M. Bamford, M.C.,
of the 2nd Regiment, with Major H. H. Jenkins of the
1st as second-in-command, and Second-Lieutenant
MacFie of the 4th as adjutant. The four companies were
made up of officers, N.C.O's, and men of the old regiments, and these, with the drafts arriving from England,
brought the battalion to a total strength of 59 officers
and 1,527 other ranks.

The name of the South African Brigade was still
to be retained, and the unit was to include, in addition
to the Composite Battalion, the 9th Scottish Rifles
(formerly in the 27th Brigade) and the 2nd Royal Scots
Fusiliers, that famous battalion which at Ramillies had,
along with the Buffs, led the decisive movement, and
which at First Ypres had been all but annihilated.

General Tanner was to be the Brigadier. To reconstruct a new brigade and a new battalion takes time, and while the work was in process the unfinished product had to be flung into the fight, for the Battle of the Lys was not over. Ludendorff had dipped too deeply in the north to withdraw easily. He had incurred great losses without gaining any real strategical objective, and he could not bring himself to write off these losses without another effort to pluck the fruit which was so near his grasp. If he could seize Kemmel Hill, he would broaden his comfortless salient and win direct observation over the northern plain. In front of Kemmel was the junction of the British and French lines, which he regarded as the weakest spot in our front. Accordingly on *April 25.* Thursday, the 25th April, he struck again for Kemmel.

In the early hours of that day a heavy enemy bombardment presaged the coming attack. At 3.35 a.m. the South African Battalion, which had been taken over on the 24th by Lieutenant-Colonel Bamford, was warned to be ready to move at fifteen minutes' notice. At 5 a.m. von Armin attacked with nine divisions, five of which were fresh. His purpose was to capture Kemmel by a direct assault on the French, and by a simultaneous attack on the British right south of Wytschaete to turn their flank and separate the two forces. At first he seemed about to succeed. By ten that morning he had worked his way round the lower slopes and taken Kemmel village and the hill itself, though isolated French troops still held out in both places. In the British area the 9th and 49th Divisions were hotly engaged west of Wytschaete, and before midday the right of the 9th was forced back to Vierstraat. In the afternoon the 21st Division, farther north, was also attacked, and by the evening the British front had been compelled to withdraw to positions running from Hill 60 in the north by Voormezeele and Ridge Wood to the hamlet of La Clytte on the Poperinghe-Kemmel road, where it linked up with the French.

By the next morning supports had arrived, and Plumer made a great effort to recapture the lost ground. The 25th Division, along with *April 26.* French troops and elements of the 21st and 49th Divisions, re-entered Kemmel village, but found themselves unable to maintain it against flanking fire from the northern slopes of the hill. After midday came the second wave of the German assault. It failed to make ground owing to the gallant resistance of the 49th (West Riding) Division, under Major-General Blacklock, and of troops of the 21st, 30th, 39th, and 9th Divisions, all four of which had been fighting for five weeks without rest. That afternoon the French recaptured Locre, on the saddle between Kemmel Hill and the heights to the west, so that our line in that quarter now ran just below the eastern slopes of the Scherpenberg, east of Locre, and then south of St. Jans-Cappel to Méteren.

At 2.15 that afternoon General Tanner took over command of the sector held by the 26th Brigade. He had the 9th Scottish Rifles in line, and the 8th Black Watch and the 5th Camerons (both of the 26th Brigade) in support and reserve, for the South African Battalion was still in divisional reserve at Hopoutre. Presently the Black Watch and the Camerons were relieved by the 2nd Royal Scots Fusiliers. The South African Brigade was for the moment under the command of the G.O.C. 49th Division. Tanner's line ran roughly from the crossroads called Confusion Corner, west of Vierstraat, to the southern end of Ridge Wood. The 9th Division was now back in support, and Tanner had on his right troops of the 49th, and on his left the 21st. The German attack came at 3 o'clock in the afternoon, and was repulsed with heavy losses ; but the 9th Scottish Rifles suffered so gravely that they were relieved by the 2nd Royal Scots Fusiliers. The night passed quietly, and on the 27th the South African Battalion, *April 27.* with a strength of 23 officers and 707 other ranks, moved forward and took up position in the La Clytte-Dickebusch support line. There it remained for two days under considerable shell-fire, which occasioned some 60 casualties.

On the 28th the fighting fell chiefly to the lot of the French at Locre, and there was no material change in the situation. But on the morning of Monday, the 29th, after one of the most intense *April 29.* German bombardments of the war, von Armin attacked the whole front from west of Dranoutre to Voormezeele. The Allied line at the moment ran round the eastern base of Mont Rouge, just covering Locre, across the low saddle of the range to the meadows in front of La Clytte, and thence by Voormezeele to the Ypres-Comines Canal. The British right was in the neighbourhood of the crossroads which we called Hyde Park Corner, on the saddle between the Scherpenberg and Mont Rouge. There lay the 25th Division as far as the little stream which runs from Kemmel to the Dickebusch Lake. On its left was the 49th Division as far as

Voormezeele, and beyond it the 21st Division to the canal. Von Armin made three main assaults—the first against the French to carry Locre and Mont Rouge; the second, at the junction of the French and the 25th Division, aimed at turning the Scherpenberg; and the third, between the 49th and 21st Divisions, to turn the obstacle of Ridge Wood.

The infantry attack was launched at 5 a.m. in a dense mist by at least eleven divisions—six against the French and five against the British. It was delivered in mass formation, the density being from six to eight bayonets to the yard. On the British front no ground was gained at all. The three divisions in line, with the assistance of troops of the 30th and 39th Divisions, not only stood firm, but in some cases advanced to meet the Germans and drove them back with the bayonet. By the end of the day the single German gain was the village of Locre, which was retaken by the French the following morning.

The battle of the 29th was a complete and most costly German repulse. The enemy had attacked with some 80,000 men, and his casualties were at least a quarter of his strength. The Royal Scots Fusiliers in Tanner's brigade had suffered heavily, and the South African Battalion was ordered to relieve them. The work was complete by four o'clock on the morning of the 30th. For the next five days the situation was unchanged, for the fight on the 29th was the last great episode of the Battle of the Lys. Lieutenant B. W. Goodwin was killed by shell-fire on the 30th, and throughout the time the South African lines were consistently shelled. The enemy posted at Kemmel dominated our trenches, and movement during the day was dangerous. Happily, however, the misty weather and the poor visibility were on the side of the defence. On the 4th, Second-Lieutenant E. C. Addison, who had but recently joined, was killed by a shell, and the total casualties in this part of the line were, approximately, 200. On the night of the 5th the Battalion was relieved, and moved back without losses, though a party of guides under Lieutenant Stokes, who had gone ahead of the main body, was less fortunate. Lieutenant Stokes, whose gallantry had been conspicuous during the past days, was severely wounded, and four of his men were killed. The Brigade had now rejoined the 9th Division.

May 5.

If we take 5th May as marking the close of the Battle of the Lys we may pause to reflect upon the marvels of the forty-five preceding days. More history had been crowded into their span than into many a year of campaigning. They had seen Ludendorff's great thrust for Amiens checked in the very moment of success. They had seen the not less deadly push for the Channel ports held up for days by weak divisions which bent but did not break, and finally die away with its purpose still far from achievement. In those forty-five days the South African Brigade had been twice destroyed as a unit, and in each case its sacrifice had been the salvation of the British army. At Marrières Wood it delayed the advance which would have made an irreparable breach between Gough and Byng ; on the ridge of Messines it maintained the northern pillar of our defence long enough to permit reserves to come up from the south. On 11th April Haig had issued his famous order, in which he warned his troops that they were fighting with their backs to the wall, and that every position must be held to the last man. The veterans of Marrières Wood and the new drafts of Messines obeyed this command to the letter. When the Composite Battalion was formed, there were men in it who had been fighting with Dawson or Tanner since the 21st of March. The few survivors of the forty-five days had behind them such a record of fruitful service as the whole history of the War could scarcely parallel.

CHAPTER X.

THE SUMMER OF 1918.
(May–September 1918.)

The Interlude—The Strategic Situation during the Summer—The Méteren Area—Awaiting the German Attack—The Action of 25th June—The Capture of Méteren on 19th July—The End of the Composite Battalion—The Brigade re-formed—Leaves the 9th Division and joins the 66th.

THE summer of 1918 may be regarded as an interlude in the history of the South African forces in France. The continuity was not broken, for there was still a titular South African Brigade, commanded by a South African general ; but the old regiments had shrunk to companies, and only one battalion was South African in its composition. Again, the summer months were for the northern part of the British line a time of comparative quiet. The great tides of war had flowed southward, and before May was out came Ludendorff's thrust on the Aisne, which drove the French back upon the Marne and in seventy-two hours advanced the enemy front by more than thirty miles. In that southern area the German tactics of April were repeated, and presently von Hutier pressed forward on the right, and carried the Lassigny hills. Then, after a delay of six weeks, came the last attack on the Marne, which was to open the way to Paris, and with it Ludendorff's final and irretrievable failure. But in the early summer that consummation could not have been fore-seen, and the months of May, June, and July were an anxious season for the Allied Command. When Foch became Commander-in-Chief his first problem was to create reserves, and his second to use just enough of them to hold the enemy. While the American armies were growing in numbers and efficiency he had to be ready, with still scanty resources, to face at any moment a new assault on any one of four sections of his long line. But his defence was not stagnant ; it was as vigilant and aggressive as any attack ; and there were two facts in the situation which might well seem to him of happy augury. He had devised an answer to the new German tactics, and formed his own scheme against the day of *revanche*. Again, the German strategy was clearly fumbling. The Lys had seen the decadence of the original plan, and the later adventures were blind and irrelevant hammer-blows. Germany, with waning strength, was being forced to stake all on a last throw ; if that failed, she might soon be helpless before the waxing might of the Allies.

The Brigade during the summer was with the 9th Division in the area of Plumer's Second Army. That front in the north was in no secure position, for the advance of the enemy in April had brought him too near to certain vital centres like Béthune and Haze-brouck, and he held the key-point of Kemmel. It was well within the domain of possibility that the next great stroke might fall in the north, and the British Army, which had been actively engaged for nine weeks, was

very tired. Hence there could be no sleeping anywhere on the line between Ypres and Arras. Till the
end of May an attack was hourly expected.

From the 10th to the 23rd May the Brigade was
busy training in the Heuringhem area. On the latter
date, with the 5th Cameron Highlanders in place of the
9th Scottish Rifles, it marched to Hondeghem, and next
day relieved the 26th Brigade in the support line, the
South African Battalion, on the left, being available as
a counter-attack battalion. On the 25th, since
May 25. a German attack seemed to be imminent, it
was decided to hold the 9th Division sector with a
two-brigade front : on the left the 26th Brigade, with
two battalions in line and one in support ; on the right
the South African Brigade, with one battalion in line,
one in support, and the South African Composite Battalion in divisional reserve in the village of Thieushoek.
The 27th Brigade was at Hondeghem in corps reserve.

The enemy was believed to be aiming at Mont des
Cats, the western end of the Kemmel range, the possession of which would directly threaten Hazebrouck
and the whole northern plain. At that time our front
ran in this area from Locre by the north of Bailleul and
just west of the village of Méteren to a point half-way
between Strazeele and Merris. The sector taken over
by the Brigade lay facing Méteren from the Méteren-
Cassel road to the tiny watercourse called Méteren
Becque, which ran south-east from Flêtre. The defences were organized in two zones. The front line
consisted of sections of trenches covered by an outpost
line between 150 and 200 yards in front of them, in
close touch with the enemy ; a support line, with the

strong-point of Princboom in it ; and a reserve line based on Flêtre. This forward zone was almost completely over-looked by the enemy in Méteren, and any movement by day there was impossible. The second zone, some 2,000 yards in the rear, included the fortified village of Caestre.

During these days patrols were busy on the quest for prisoners, and from the intelligence thus gathered it appeared that the German attack was fixed for the morning of the 29th. Much work was done in strengthening the defences, and a special battalion was formed of Brigade details, which was held at Caestre in divisional reserve. But nothing happened on the 29th. That night the South African battalion moved into the support line, and on the 1st June it relieved the 2nd Royal Scots Fusiliers in the front line.

On the South African right lay the Australians, and on the night of 2nd June they carried out a minor operation in order to straighten their line ; while the South Africans co-operated by a *June 2.* pretended attack on Méteren. The Australians reached their goal without serious opposition. A German relief was in progress, and in consequence 5 officers and 250 other ranks, besides many machine guns and trench mortars, were captured. For the next few days the enemy front was stagnant, and on the night of the 5th the Brigade was relieved in the front line by the 26th, and moved back to the Hondeghem area for further training.

On 11th June the Composite Battalion marched to Thieushoek, and that night relieved the 7th Seaforth Highlanders in divisional reserve. Once again a German attack threatened. The South African Brigade front was now held by two battalions, and on the 17th the South African Battalion relieved the 9th Scottish Rifles, on the right of the front adjoining Méteren Becque.

The position at Méteren was far from comfortable, and Tanner, after conferring with the Australians on his right, submitted to General Tudor a proposal for a further adjustment of the line, which involved an advance of some 425 yards on a front of 750. The scheme was approved, but, since full artillery support was necessary, it had to be postponed till the night of 23rd June. The attack was to be delivered by the 1st Australian Brigade and by the South African Composite Battalion. Zero was fixed for half an hour after midnight on the 24th, in order that the troops should have sufficient time after nightfall to form up, and the remainder of the short midsummer dark for the consolidation of their gains.

At zero hour an accurate artillery and trench mortar barrage opened on the German front trenches, and
June 24. presently lifted a hundred yards. The attack, moving close to the barrage, succeeded at once, and the German machine guns were rushed and silenced as soon as they opened fire. Many small parties of Germans were found in the hedges and cornfields, who either fled or were quickly overpowered. The objective was soon reached, and consolidation began, and, with the assistance of a section of the 63rd Field Company R.E., by dawn the new line had been wired across its whole front. As a result of the operation 29 prisoners and 6 machine guns were taken, while 36 dead of the enemy were counted. The losses of the

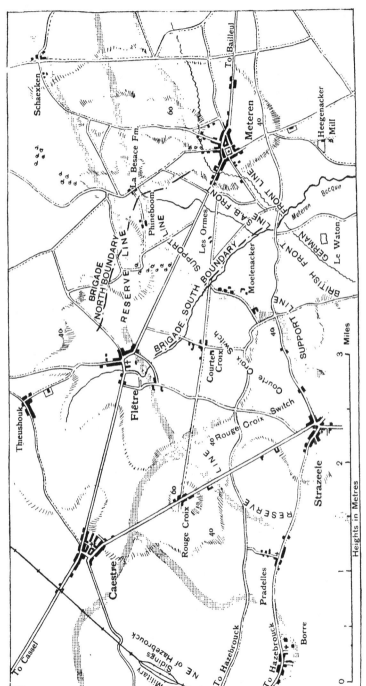

THE FIGHTING ABOUT METEREN.

Composite Battalion were 5 men killed, and 2 officers (Lieutenants Harvey and Uys) and 21 other ranks wounded. The following night the battalion was relieved by the 5th Camerons, and next day moved back to Hondeghem.

There the South Africans remained till the last day of June, when they came again into the front line to relieve one of the units of the 26th Brigade. *June 30.* At that moment the omens pointed to an elaborate German offensive on the whole front between the Forest of Nieppe and Ypres, with the Mont des Cats as one of the main objects of attack. But the assault tarried, and during the first days of July the front had never been quieter. This gave us leisure to improve our communication trenches and link up the outposts of the front line into one continuous trench—a most necessary work, for it had been resolved to attempt the capture of Méteren village in the near future, and the task had been entrusted to the 26th and South African Brigades.

The 10th of July was at first chosen as the day; but the weather grew bad, and the operation was postponed. On the night of the 12th the South African *July 12.* Brigade had been relieved by the 27th, and had returned to Hondeghem, with orders to be in readiness to move up at short notice. The two battalions of the Brigade selected for the assault—the South African Composite Battalion and the 2nd Royal Scots Fusiliers —rehearsed the business in complete detail. By the 17th the weather had improved, and on *July 18.* the night of the 18th the Brigade relieved the 27th in the right sector of the divisional front, and took up positions of assembly ready to move on the following day.

Zero was fixed for five minutes to eight on the morning of the 19th. At that hour the troops of assault left *July 19.* the trenches in artillery formation, and under cover of a smoke and high-explosive barrage rapidly over-ran the enemy front-line posts and prevented the use of his machine guns. One or two strong-points held out till they were enveloped on the flanks. The main attack, admirably led by the section commanders, bore down all resistance, and both battalions reached their objectives by the appointed time. One company of the Composite Battalion, which held the line on the extreme right, south of the point on which the operation hinged, had been ordered to watch for opportunities to harass the enemy while the main attack was proceeding, and, when the barrage ceased, to push up patrols along the front, and, if possible, capture the German trench between Méteren Becque and the road from Brahmin Bridge to Alwyn Farm. This they did with complete success, and took many prisoners and seven machine guns.

The main attack, having reached its goal, sent out patrols, who managed to establish themselves on a point some 200 yards north of the line between the Gaza crossroads and the Brahmin Bridge road. There was some stubborn fighting at Alwyn Farm and among the hedges north of it ; but in the afternoon the divisional artillery cleared the place. Under cover of this outpost line a position in Méteren village and on the ridge was rapidly established, and one of the most awkward corners of the British front made secure. During the latter part of the day our advance lines were heavily shelled, but no counter-attack developed. It appeared that the Germans had been taken by surprise. They expected only a gas discharge, and had in many cases put on gas masks, and were wholly unprepared to resist the rush of our infantry.

The night passed in comparative quiet. On the morning of the 20th the Composite Battalion was ordered to test the enemy front on the right of the division, which seemed to have retired. *July* 20. Fighting patrols were pushed out, and a line was established some 400 yards farther south. During this action Captain Scheepers was killed ; he had only rejoined the battalion two days before. The Brigade held their sector until the 24th, when they moved to the left of the divisional front, where for some days they were busy in restoring and draining the dilapidated trenches. On the night of the 30th the Composite Battalion was relieved by the 5th Camerons, and marched back to a rest area. *July* 30.

The capture of Méteren was a good example of a perfectly planned and perfectly executed minor action. The captured material consisted of 1 field gun, 13 trench mortars, and 30 machine guns, of which the Composite Battalion's share was 10 trench mortars and 23 machine guns. Between 200 and 300 prisoners fell to the Brigade. The casualties of the Composite Battalion were 130, of whom 27 were killed and 2 died of wounds. Besides Captain Scheepers, Second-Lieutenants Mackie, Anderson, Douglas, Male, and Keeley fell, and Lieutenant Mackay was wounded.

On 5th August the Composite Battalion was again in

the line on the right of the division, which by now extended beyond Méteren Becque, and included Le Waton. Little happened for the better part of a fortnight except patrol work along the Becque. On the

Aug. 18. 18th the 27th Brigade, with the 9th Scottish Rifles, attacked and captured the mill of Hoegenacker, taking 10 officers and 230 men prisoners. By way of retaliation the Germans heavily shelled the South African front, in spite of which Sergeant Thompson of the 4th Company of the Composite Battalion, with five men, raided and captured an enemy post during the morning. That night the battalion was relieved by the 8th Black Watch, and withdrew from the front.

On the day before the capture of Méteren, Foch on the Marne had delivered the great counter-stroke which decided the issue of the campaign. When on that morning the troops of Mangin breasted the Montagne de Paris they had, without knowing it, won the second Battle of the Marne, and with it the War. The final battle had been joined, and the greatest modern soldier had entered upon the first stages of that mighty contest, which in two months' time was to shatter all Germany's defences, and enable him to begin that deadly *arpeggio* on the whole front from the Moselle to the North Sea which brought her to her knees. It was fitting that South Africa should be represented by more than a battalion in the final march to victory. During August 1,000 reserves arrived at Lumbres from England, and

Aug. 28. it was now possible to consider the reorganization of the Brigade. On the 28th the Composite Battalion marched to Lumbres and prepared for disbandment. Since its formation on 24th April it had been almost continually in the line. Seventy-five officers had served with it at one time or another, and of these 7 had been killed and 11 wounded. Of the men, 84 had been killed, 27 had died of wounds, 329 had been wounded, and one was missing. For the operations in which it had taken part it had won two bars to the Military Cross, three Military Crosses, one Distinguished Conduct Medal, one bar to the Military Medal, and thirty Military Medals. The four months had been an interlude in the main story of the South Africans in France, but an interlude not without its own glory.

On 11th September the Brigade, now re-formed, was withdrawn from the 9th Division, with which the South Africans had served since their arrival in France. For the purpose of administration it was transferred to the VII. Corps, with which it trained till 22nd September. On that day it joined the 66th Division, which was then attached to the First Army. It was commanded, as before, by General Tanner, and in addition to the three infantry battalions contained the Signal Section, the South African Light Trench Mortar Battery, and the 1st South African Field Ambulance. The 1st Regiment was under the command of Major H. H. Jenkins, the 2nd under Lieutenant-Colonel H. W. M. Bamford, and the 4th under Lieutenant-Colonel D. M. MacLeod.

It was not easy for the South Africans to leave the 9th Division, or for the 9th Division to part with them. Together they had fought in the bitterest actions of the campaign, and their glory was eternally intertwined. I quote General Tudor's farewell letter to Tanner.

" I wish to express to you and to your officers, warrant officers, N.C.O.'s, and men of the Brigade under your command my great regret that the exigencies of the service prevented me seeing you all personally before you were transferred from the 9th Division, in order to say good-bye. For two and a half years your Brigade has shared the fortunes of the 9th Division. At Delville Wood, at Arras, at Ypres, in the Somme retreat, and finally at Méteren, it has fully contributed in establishing and maintaining the glorious record of this division. The South African Brigade bore the brunt of the attack on the divisional front on March 21, 1918, and its final stand at Bouchavesnes on 24th March, when it held out all day until all ammunition was exhausted, will live as one of the bravest feats of arms in the War. The cheery keenness and comradeship with which the South African Brigade has always worked and fought will be very much missed by me personally, and by all the 9th Division. We wish you and your Brigade the best of fortune, and know that you will always fully maintain the splendid name you have earned."

The division with which they were now brigaded had come later into the campaign than the 9th, but it had no mean record behind it. Under Major-General Neill Malcolm it had done gloriously in the retreat from St. Quentin, when it had been reduced to a handful. It was re-formed in the late summer under the command of Major-General H. K. Bethell, and, besides the South Africans, included the 198th and 199th Brigades, the units of which had been brought from Salonika. In the 198th Brigade were the 6th Lancashire Fusiliers, the 5th Royal Inniskilling Fusiliers, and the 6th Royal Dublin Fusiliers. In the 199th were the 18th King's Liverpool Regiment, the 9th Manchesters, and the 5th Connaught Rangers. The pioneer battalion was the 9th Gloucesters. The War brought the soldiers of South Africa into comradeship with all varieties of the New Armies of Britain. Hitherto they had fought side by side with the Scots ; the last stage was to be spent in a fighting fellowship, not less close and cordial, with the men of Ireland and the North of England.

CHAPTER XI.

THE ADVANCE TO VICTORY.
(September 28–November 11, 1918.)

Foch's Final Strategy—Progress of the Campaign in August and
September—The End of the Siegfried Zone—The 66th Division
in Action—The Fight of 8th October—The South Africans take
their Objectives—The Fight of 9th October—The Brigade
Captures Bertry, Maurois, and Reumont—The Line of the
Selle reached—The Enemy Position at Le Cateau—Preparation for the Attack—Lieutenant Hewat's Exploit—The
Battle of 17th October—South African Captures and Casualties—Splendour of the Achievement—The Last Stage in
the Campaign—Tanner's Mobile Column—The Last Shots
at Grandrieu—The Armistice.

AS the last stage in this record approaches, it is
necessary to gather up the threads of the campaign
and observe the position of the great Allied movement at the time when the South Africans appeared again
on the main front of battle. During the summer months
Foch had warded off Ludendorff's successive assaults,
and had accumulated a reserve, which at the end of
July, by the accession of the American troops, gave him
a final superiority both in men and material over anything
which the enemy could compass. He had also devised
a system of tactics which embraced all that was best in
the German plan, and avoided its defects. By his
counterstroke on 18th July against von Boehn's exposed

flank he had given the *coup de grâce* to Germany's offensive, wrested from her the initiative, and forced her back in some confusion on her defences. But the final blow could not yet be struck. It was the business of Foch to keep the battle " nourished," and at the same time to economize his forces till the moment came for the grand climax. He had to wear down the enemy methodically by attacks on limited fronts, ringing the changes over the whole battle-ground. The possession of abundant reserves and of such a weapon as his light tanks enabled him to " mount " a new action rapidly in any sector. After each blow he must stay his hand as soon as serious resistance developed, and attack instantly in another place. The enemy would thus be subjected to a constant series of surprises. Before his reserves could be brought up he would have lost heavily in ground and men ; his " mass of manœuvre " would be needed to fill up the gaps in his front, and by swift stages that " mass of manœuvre " would diminish. From 8th August to 26th September it was Foch's task to crumble the enemy front, destroy the last remnants of his reserves, force him behind all his prepared defences, and make ready for the final battle which would give victory.

The tale of that great achievement—one of the greatest in the history of war—can here only be sketched. The record of a brigade moves for the most part in the mist ; its story is of tactical successes, which may be only a minute part in the major purpose. Rarely, indeed, does it appear, like the South Africans at Marrières Wood, in the very centre of the stage, and the work of a small unit become the key to the strategical fortunes of an army. On 8th August Haig struck east of Amiens, followed by Humbert on the 9th, and Mangin on the 18th. On the 21st Byng's Third Army moved, and next day Rawlinson's Fourth Army, and on the 26th Horne's First Army astride the Scarpe. By the end of the month we had carried the Bapaume Ridge, the intermediate position which Ludendorff had hoped to hold till the coming of winter, when he could retire at leisure behind the Siegfried zone. On 2nd September the Canadians broke through the Drocourt-Quéant switch, and turned the Siegfried flank on the north. Steadily during the next week Haig forced the Germans behind the water line of the Canal du Nord, and inside the main Siegfried defences. On 12th September Pershing and the Americans far in the south put an end to the St. Mihiel salient. By the 24th Ludendorff was everywhere back in his last lines—the " granite wall " which the German army chiefs had told their countrymen could never be pierced. There he hoped to stand till such time as winter took the edge from the Allies' ardour, and disposed them to compromise.

He had not reckoned with Foch—nor with Haig, for on the 26th there began on the Meuse the *arpeggio* of attack which broke through the defences prepared during four years, and in six weeks brought Germany to surrender. On the 27th Haig struck at the main Siegfried zone from Cambrai to St. Quentin, and his blow was meant to shatter. It is no secret that the opinion of his Allies and of his own Government was not favourable to his boldness : even Foch, while he agreed that the plan was the right one, doubted its feasibility. The British Commander-in-Chief took upon himself the

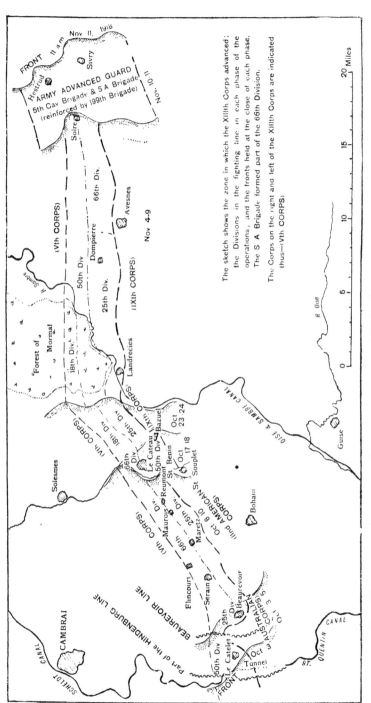

The sketch shows the zone in which the XIIIth Corps advanced; the Divisions in the fighting line in each phase of the operations, and the fronts held at the close of each phase. The S A Brigade formed part of the 66th Division.

The Corps on the right and left of the XIIIth Corps are indicated thus—(Vth CORPS)

THE VICTORIOUS ADVANCE. OPERATIONS OF THE XIII. CORPS UP TO 11TH NOVEMBER 1918.

responsibility of one of the most audacious operations of the War, and, daring greatly, greatly succeeded. That day Byng and Horne with the Third and First British Armies crossed the Canal du Nord, and next day reached the Scheldt Canal. On the 28th, too, the Belgians and Plumer's Second Army swept east from Ypres, and Mangin and Guillaumat opened a new battle between the Ailette and the Vesle. On the 29th came the main blow at the Siegfried citadel, when Rawlinson's Fourth Army, in conjunction with Byng and Débeney, crossed the Scheldt Canal, and stormed their way far into the fortified zone. In days of wind and cloud they enlarged this gap till St. Quentin fell, and Cambrai was utterly outflanked. On 30th October the Australians broke through the northern part of the Beaurevoir-Fonsommes line, the last of the Siegfried works, and looked into open country. Between the 27th September and the 7th October Haig had crossed the two great canals, and destroyed all but the final line of the Siegfried zone, while this final line in one part had been passed. The time had come for an advance on a broad front which should obliterate the remnants of the Siegfried works, and with them Germany's last hope of a safe winter position. Her nearest refuge would be the Meuse, and, shepherded by Foch's unrelenting hand, it was very certain that her armies would never reach the banks of that fateful river.

On 28th September the 66th Division had been transferred to Rawlinson's Fourth Army, and by the 5th October it had moved south to the old *Sept. 28.* Somme area, and was in the neighbourhood of Ronssoy. It was now part of Sir T. L. Morland's

XIII. Corps, which contained also the 18th, 25th, and 50th Divisions. Of these, the 25th was composed of troops brought from the Italian front, and the 50th, like the 66th, of battalions from Salonika and Palestine. Two of the divisions of the corps were, therefore, made up largely of men who had malaria in their bones, and there was some doubt as to how they would stand an autumn campaign in Picardy—a doubt which was soon to be put at rest. The 18th and 25th Divisions and the South African Brigade were well seasoned to northern warfare.

On 6th October the 66th Division was warned that it would be used presently in a major operation in which the Fourth and Third Armies would co-operate. The object was to destroy the remnants of the Beaurevoir line, and with it the Siegfried zone. The country was the last slopes of the Picardy uplands, where they break down to the flats of the Scheldt—wide undulations enclosing broad, shallow valleys. There was little cover save the orchards and plantations around the farms and hamlets, but there were many sunken roads, and these, combined with the perfect field afforded everywhere for machine-gun fire, made it a good land for rearguard fighting. The XIII. Corps was now the right flank of the Fourth Army, with the II. United States Corps on its right, and the British V. Corps on its left. The 66th Division was in the centre of the corps, and the task specially committed to it was the capture of Serain. General Bethell attacked with two brigades—the South African on the right and the 198th on the left, each on a two-battalion front. The starting-point was a line running north-west and south-east through the eastern outskirts of Beaurevoir village.

Oct. 6.

LIEUTENANT-COLONEL D. M. MACLEOD, D.S.O., M.C., D.C.M.,
Commanding 4th Regiment, South African Infantry.

In the South African Brigade the 2nd Regiment was on the right and the 4th on the left, with the 1st Regiment in support.

It was a wild, wet autumn morning when Byng and Rawlinson advanced on a seventeen-mile front, from south of Cambrai to Sequehart, while Débeney extended the battle four miles farther south. Zero hour for the Fourth Army was 5.10 ; for the Third Army, 4.30. The South African Brigade had moved on the 7th into the Siegfried lines at Bony, and by 3.30 a.m. on the 8th it had occupied its battle position. Unfortunately the assembly was not completed *Oct. 8.* without loss. A preliminary attack by the 38th and 50th Divisions on Villers and Villers-Outréaux brought down a retaliatory barrage from the enemy, and among the wounded was Lieutenant-Colonel Bamford, the commanding officer of the 2nd Regiment. His place was taken by Major Sprenger.

The attack at 5.10, covered by a creeping barrage, moved swiftly towards its goal, and by 7 o'clock the South Africans had their first objective. The enemy resisted stoutly, and made full use of the sunken roads, especially at the Usigny ravine, which was in the ground of the 2nd Regiment. There he disputed every yard with machine guns and snipers, and did not yield till all his posts had been killed or captured. The whippet tanks, moving in front of the infantry, were mostly put out of action by shell-fire at the start, but one arrived opportunely at the Usigny ravine, and helped to break down the last resistance there. The 2nd Regiment took at this stage nearly 500 prisoners, two anti-tank guns, seventeen machine guns, and four field-pieces. These last were captured by a few men under Lieutenant E. J. Brook and Sergeant Hinwood, who pushed forward and rushed the guns 400 yards south-east of Petite Folie farm, and then turned them on the retreating enemy. The 4th Regiment on the left had also to face heavy machine-gun fire, but it swept through the German position at La Sablonnière and Hamage Farm, taking no less than thirty-five machine guns.

As soon as the first objective was won the ground was consolidated. Covering posts were pushed out, and the two regiments were reorganized. The supporting battalion, the 1st Regiment, had been caught in the early morning barrage on the railway embankment north of Beaurevoir, and had suffered 23 casualties. Later it moved east of Beaurevoir, and provided a platoon to reinforce the 2nd before retiring to brigade reserve. The losses so far in the assaulting battalions had not been unduly heavy. The 2nd had suffered most in its commissioned ranks. Lieutenant R. G. A. M'Carter had been killed, and Lieutenant-Colonel Bamford, Captain Symons, Lieutenant Egan, and Second-Lieutenants Giddy, Birrell, Fernie, Roberts, Gunn, and Francis wounded, the last officer subsequently dying of his wounds. The 4th had 45 men killed, and 4 officers and 194 men wounded.

The first objective having been taken, the 199th Brigade, according to plan, took up the attack, leap-frogging the South African and 198th Brigades, and by 11 a.m. had taken Serain and reached the final line. For a little its left flank was exposed, for Villers-Outréaux was still in German hands. By three in the afternoon, however, the V. Corps had succeeded in carrying

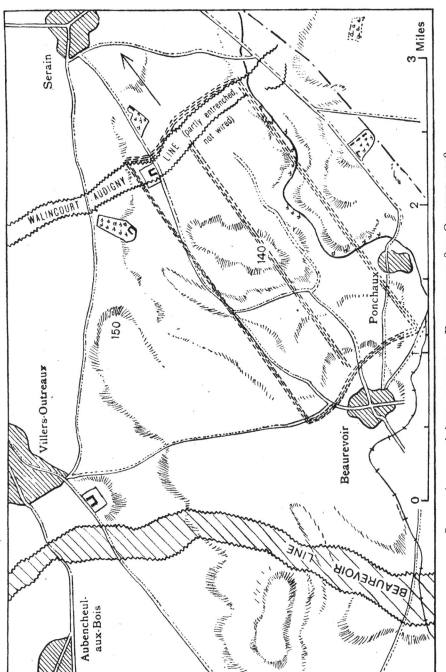

SOUTH AFRICANS' ATTACK BEYOND BEAUREVOIR, 8TH OCTOBER 1918.

that village, and the XIII. Corps was able to establish itself securely east of Prémont and Serain. It had been a day of unblemished success. Haig and Débeney had advanced between three and four miles, and the Siegfried zone had disappeared in a cataclysm. The enemy was falling back to the Oise and the Selle, and for the moment was in dire confusion. Every road converging upon Le Cateau was blocked with troops and transport, and our cavalry were galloping eastward to harass the retreat. Next day Cambrai fell, and the Germans retired behind the line of the Selle. The war of positions had ceased, and the combatants were now in open country.

On the 9th Byng and Rawlinson pressed their advantage against the stricken enemy, who had no position on which he could stand, short of the Selle river. The South Africans began the day in *Oct. 9.* reserve, the attack on Maretz being conducted by the 198th and 199th Brigades. By 10 o'clock Maretz, Avelu, and Elincourt had fallen, and half an hour later the South Africans passed through the two brigades and moved against the second objective, a line east of Maurois and Honnechy and Gattignies Wood. There was some hope that before nightfall the crossings of the Selle might be seized and the ridge to the east, which, it was clear, were the immediate objects of the German retreat. But though the enemy was disordered, he was not in rout, and his machine gunners fought stubborn rearguard actions. The 2nd Regiment on the right, now under Major Sprenger, came under heavy fire as soon as it emerged from the eastern skirts of Maretz. As its left approached Gattignies Wood, it was strongly opposed by machine guns and snipers, but by the assistance of two armoured cars the southern part of the wood was cleared. On the right the advance was held up for half an hour by enemy posts along the Le Cateau railway. To add to Sprenger's difficulties, the 4th Regiment, under MacLeod, on his left was compelled to veer north towards Bertry, since the troops on its left had fallen slightly behind and got out of touch. He was compelled to bring up one of his supporting companies, and presently established his line on the Cambrai railway, where many machine guns and prisoners were taken. Before him lay the villages of Maurois and Honnechy, which appeared to be lightly held, since some of the houses were flying white flags. Sprenger, with three companies in line and one in support, moved through the village with little opposition, and was received with wild enthusiasm by the French inhabitants. It was the first time the South Africans had liberated an area not cleared of its civil population. A little after 1 p.m. he reached his final objective, where he found his flanks exposed, since he had outrun the general advance.

Meantime MacLeod with the 4th Regiment had had severe fighting. His task was simple till he reached the northern edge of Gattignies Wood, which was held in strength by the enemy. By a flanking movement he overcame the resistance, and pushed on to the southwest skirts of Bertry. This village was not in the Brigade's area, but the delay in the advance of the division on its left made any further movement by the 4th Regiment impossible till Bertry had been taken. Accordingly Captain Tomlinson, commanding the left company, swung northwards and occupied the village. By 4.30 p.m. Mac-

Leod had reached his objective, and pushed outposts to link up with Sprenger. The Brigade was now established on a line east of Maurois and Honnechy.

The day had gone so well that it seemed as if more might be accomplished than had been forecast in the original plan. The cavalry was ordered to go through and ride for Le Cateau and beyond, in the hope of cutting the main enemy communications through Valenciennes. By 2 p.m. the Canadian Cavalry Brigade had gone forward, encircled Reumont, and formed a picket line beyond it. The South Africans were instructed to make good that village, and for the purpose Tanner brought up the 1st Regiment under Lieutenant-Colonel Jenkins. By dusk the work was accomplished, and Jenkins took over from the Canadian cavalry, occupying a line covering Reumont on the north and east. The more distant objective had proved impracticable. It was not possible to push through large bodies of cavalry, owing to the many strongly held machine-gun posts. That night the front of the 66th Division ran from the western skirts of Escaufourt, east of Reumont, to the east of Bertry station. For the South Africans it had been a day of distinguished achievement. The two battalions of assault had taken 150 prisoners, more than twenty machine guns, several anti-tank guns, and—at Bertry— a motor car containing a German officer. Their losses had been light. The 4th Regiment had one officer (Lieutenant R. Hill) and 23 other ranks killed, and 4 officers and 71 other ranks wounded. In the 2nd Regiment Second-Lieutenant H. Perry was the only officer casualty.

On the 10th the Brigade was in reserve at Reumont

and Maurois, where it was continuously shelled, the 1st
Regiment sustaining some twenty casualties.

Oct. 10.

That day the divisional advance was conducted by the 198th and 199th Brigades, who pressed
forward to the slopes above the Selle. By noon they held
the spurs overlooking Le Cateau from the west, and had
patrols in the environs of the town itself. But Le Cateau
was not to fall at the first summons. The 66th Division
found itself much harassed by artillery fire from the
high ground towards Forest in the north-east, which
overlooked its position. On its right the 25th Division
could do little so long as St. Benin was untaken, and
St. Benin was in the area of the II. United States
Corps, whose left division had been checked. The
G.O.C. 25th Division, Major-General Charles, attacked
St. Benin in the afternoon, and drove the enemy across
the Selle, but was unable to follow him owing to the
difficulty of the river crossings and the machine-gun
fire from the railway on the eastern bank. In the evening General Bethell, with the 199th Brigade, attempted to
carry the high ground east of Le Cateau and north-east
of Montay. The 5th Connaught Rangers reached the
railway east of the town ; the 18th King's Liverpool
Regiment reached Montay, but found the banks of the
Selle heavily wired and could not cross. General Bethell
accordingly withdrew the Connaught Rangers to the
west side of Le Cateau, where they held the line of the
Selle as it passed through the town.

That night the II. United States Corps took over
St. Benin, and the XIII. Corps lay north from it for the
most part along the western shore of the Selle. The
German 17th Reserve Division had arrived to rein-

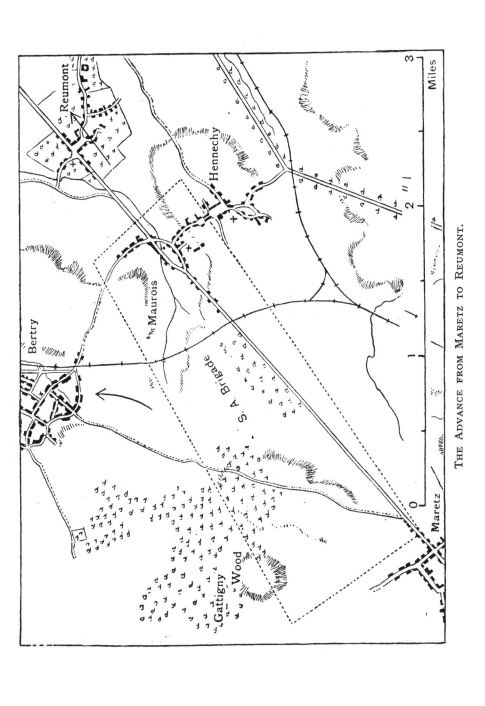

THE ADVANCE FROM MARETZ TO REUMONT.

force the enemy, and his front along the east bank of the river was very strong. The wreckage of the fallen bridges had dammed the stream and flooded the low-lying meadows. It was clear that the forcing of the Selle line was not a task which could be carried out by the pursuing army " in its stride," but required a careful and deliberate plan. For the enemy to stand awhile on the Selle was a matter of life or death, for otherwise he could not hope to extricate himself from Foch's pincers.

It was now the eve of the last great fight of the Brigade—the last, indeed, of the campaign in the West. To understand it we must note the configuration of the battleground. The valley of the Selle at Le Cateau has on each side slopes rising to plateau country some 200 feet above the bed of the river. On the west these slopes mount gently in bare undulations, but to the east they rise more abruptly, and the country in that direction is intersected with many orchards and hedges. A spur running north-east from Montay to Forest gives direct observation up the valley and over the eastern uplands. The Selle at Le Cateau is from fifteen to twenty feet wide, and usually about four feet deep, but with the recent heavy rains it was now rising fast. South of the town it flows through marshy meadows ; in the town itself the banks are bricked up, and it is spanned by two bridges ; farther north towards Montay it runs through firm pasture land. Le Cateau is a town normally of some 10,000 inhabitants, full of solidly built houses and factories, the greater part of which are on the slopes east of the river. On its eastern side runs the railway to Solesmes, which with its embankments and cuttings gave the enemy a position of exceptional strength. A formidable strong-point was the railway station and yard, which were bounded on the east by a bank thirty feet high, while a mound farther east, which could not be seen from the west bank of the Selle, gave good observation southwards.

The position from the point of view of the defence was all but perfect. The wiring was everywhere elaborate, the machine-gun posts had been prepared on a lavish scale, and the buildings and cellars were admirably adapted for a prolonged resistance. Four enemy divisions held the place, and two of them were fresh from reserve. The importance which the German High Command laid upon a stand on the Selle—which they knew as the " Hermann Line "—was shown by orders captured during our attack. One, issued by General von Larisch commanding the 54th Corps, announced that the Army would accept a decisive battle on that line, which must be held at all costs. An order of an artillery group declared that the possibility of an armistice being arranged depended on the battle coming to a standstill on the Selle. Still another artillery order warned the troops that if the Hermann Line were held, a favourable peace could be arranged ; otherwise there was no prospect of an end to the War. If the position was vital to the enemy, it was no less vital to the Allies. By 10th September the two main German salients—between the Lys and the Somme and between the Selle and the Argonne—had become precarious. Ludendorff had now but the one object, to protect the main lateral railway, from Lille by Valenciennes and Hirson to Mézières, long enough to permit of an orderly retreat. If it fell too soon, large parts of his front would be cut off. It was Haig's aim to cut that railway as soon as possible by forcing the Selle and pressing on to Maubeuge across the many rivulets which drain to the Scheldt from the Forest of Mormal.

On 11th October the position was that the XIII. Corps held ground in the skirts of Le Cateau west of the Selle and along the river line. A frontal attack was impossible, and the town must *Oct. 11.* be enveloped by its flanks. On the south the floods were extending, and a crossing place must be sought well upstream, so the Corps extended its right wing to St. Souplet. Simultaneously with any advance in the south there must be a movement on the north to capture the ridge north-east of the town. The immediate objective was the Solesmes-Le Cateau railway and the easterly ridge ; the ultimate goal the village of Bazuel.

Several days had to be spent in preliminary work. On the night of the 11th the South African Brigade moved up from Reumont and relieved the 198th and 199th Brigades. The 1st Regiment held the line opposite Le Cateau with the 2nd and 4th Regiments in support on right and left. Between the 12th and the *Oct. 12-15.* 15th the 1st pushed forward north of the town to the edge of the Selle. It was no easy task, for the western outskirts were not yet cleared of the enemy, and our positions were dominated by the high ground on the eastern bank and by the houses in the northern suburbs. In these days the 1st Regiment suffered some twenty casualties in officers and men, while a post of one N.C.O. and seven men was reported as missing. The next task was to establish bridgeheads in the area of the town itself, and in particular to hold the two ruined bridges. The capture of one of these was assigned to the 2nd Regiment, and Major Sprenger on the 15th ordered Second-Lieutenant R. D. Hewat, with one Lewis gun section and one rifle section, to establish posts east of the bridge on both sides of the road. Owing to the constant machine-gun fire the debris of the bridge could not be used, so Lieutenant Hewat and his men waded across the stream, heavily bombed all the while by the enemy, and carried out their instructions. During the 16th he was frequently attacked, but with seven survivors he held his ground, and when the general advance began next morning he was found engaged against three machine guns. Late that day he rejoined the Brigade after a most gallant feat of arms, having held out for over thirty-six hours.

The main attack of the XIII. Corps was fixed for the morning of the 17th. On the right the 50th Division, under Major-General Jackson, was to cross at St. Souplet and St. Benin, capture the railway embankment opposite them and the railway triangle, and then swing north and take the railway station. Their supporting troops were then to move on Bazuel. The South African Brigade was to cross the Selle north of the town, seize the railway, and link up with the 50th north of the railway triangle ; and, in the final stage, swing forward its right and establish itself on the spur east of Le Cateau. Since the V. Corps on the left was not attacking, arrangements were made to obscure the enemy observation from the high ground north-east of Montay by a smoke barrage.

Meantime, on the evening of the 16th, the 1st South African Regiment had attacked at 5.45 p.m. in order to win positions on the eastern bank, which would enable eight bridges to be thrown across the *Oct.* 16. river, since it was necessary that the assaulting position should be on that bank. This work was successfully accomplished by " A " and " B " companies under Lieutenants Gray and M'Millan. It was found that strong wire entanglements had been constructed on the east shore, through which openings had to be cut to permit of the assembly of the assaulting battalions.

At 8 p.m. that evening the 4th Regiment on the right and the 2nd on the left—together with " D " Company of the 1st under Captain Thomson, which had been detailed to follow the 2nd—began to move forwards. The crossing of the river was slow work, owing to the slender footbridges and the narrow gaps in the wire. The South Africans, when they reached the east bank, found themselves in places not fifty yards from the enemy, who held the railway embankment, and had pushed forward machine-gun outposts to the river-side road. By 4.30 on the morning of Tuesday the 17th the assembly was complete, and the South Africans laboured to make their position secure. They had little time for the work, for zero hour was approaching and their situation would have been perilous indeed but for the merciful interposition of the weather. Just before dawn a heavy mist rose from the valley, blinding the enemy's eyes, so that most of his artillery and machine-gun fire passed harmlessly over their heads. Casualties, however, could not be altogether avoided. Lieutenant M. E. Whelan, M.C., of the 2nd Regiment was severely wounded, and died on the following day; and Lieutenant

E. J. Brook of the same regiment was killed, his body, riddled with bullets, being found five yards from a German machine gun.

Zero hour for the 50th Division was 5.20 a.m., for it had much ground to cover before it could come into line with the 66th. The 151st Brigade crossed the river with ease, but met with a stubborn resistance at the station. The 149th Brigade followed for the attack on the second objective, and found like difficulties at the railway triangle. So soon as the news came that the 149th was over the Selle, it was time for the South Africans to advance. The Brigade had taken immense risks in its assembly, and escaped serious loss partly by the help of the fog, partly by the very boldness of the hazard, since it lay so close to the enemy that his fire was ineffective. But it was a welcome relief to officers and men when at 8.5 a.m. came the order to launch the attack.

Oct. 17.

The mist was still thick, and no man could see fifty yards before him. The first wave disappeared into the gloom, and those behind waited long before they got news of it. From the outset the attack had to face great belts of single and double apron wire, and heavy machine-gun fire from both flanks. After a hundred yards had been covered, the South Africans came upon a sunken road protected by a palisade, where the 4th Regiment was held up for some time, and suffered many losses. As they approached the railway they encountered another and more formidable obstacle—a belt of wire entanglements sixty yards deep. The railway at this point ran in a deep cutting, the sides of which were studded with machine-gun posts and rifle-pits. The South Africans rose to the emergency. They found a shallow trench used by the Germans as a route from the railway cutting to an outpost ; they found a tortuous path through the wire made for the use of German patrols, where Major Clerk of the 4th Regiment shot the two sentries on duty ; and by these roads slowly and patiently they filtered through to the railway. It was a magnificent feat of cool resolution, and it was performed under the most galling fire. Soon they were in the cutting, where stern fighting took place. It was Ludendorff's old device of " infiltration " in miniature, and at 9.15 Captain Jacobs of the 2nd Regiment reported to Major Sprenger that the first objective had been reached.

The situation, however, was still full of danger. The first objective was beyond the railway line ; but, since our troops could not dig themselves in in the open because of machine-gun fire, they were compelled to fall back to the railway itself, where they had some kind of cover, though the German field guns were accurately registered on it. Slowly they cleared the line, and by midday Tanner was able to inform General Bethell that he held the railway from a point 500 yards north of the railway triangle to the northern boundary of the XIII. Corps. Meanwhile " D " Company of the 1st Regiment, which had followed the 2nd, succeeded under great difficulties in its appointed task of establishing a defensive flank on the left between the railway and the Selle. Every officer of the company was wounded during the course of the day. The losses of the assaulting battalions had been high, and the 1st Regiment was now called upon to reinforce each with a company, while a little later the remaining company was sent forward to strengthen the left flank. One battalion of the 198th Brigade was busy clearing up in Le Cateau.

There could be no advance to the second objective yet awhile, for the 50th Division was in difficulties. It had not succeeded in carrying the railway triangle, and was involved in intricate fighting among the station buildings, much galled by machine-gun fire from the mound to the east. The 66th Division was called upon to help, and a battalion of the 198th Brigade was sent south of the town to attack towards the point where the Bazuel road crosses the railway. The Corps heavy artillery put down an intense bombardment from 3 p.m. to 3.30 p.m. on the station and the railway triangle, and it was proposed thereafter to send in the 150th Brigade. But at that moment came an enemy counterstroke against the junction of the 50th Division and the II. United States Corps, and the 150th Brigade had to be diverted south to restore the broken front. That evening, after fifteen hours of desperate fighting, the XIII. Corps held a line along the Arbre de Guise-Le Cateau road, through the east skirts of Le Cateau, and along the railway line to Baillon Farm, beyond which it bent back to the Selle. The town had been won, but not the vital ridge to the east.

The South African Brigade spent an uneasy night of "standing to." The enemy's bombing patrols were busy, his machine-gun and trench-mortar fire was accurate and intense, and his artillery fire, with light, heavy, and gas shells, was unceasing. At *Oct. 18.* 5.30 a.m. on the 18th the 50th Division again attacked, and carried all its objectives, establishing itself on the Le Cateau-Catillon road, with outposts

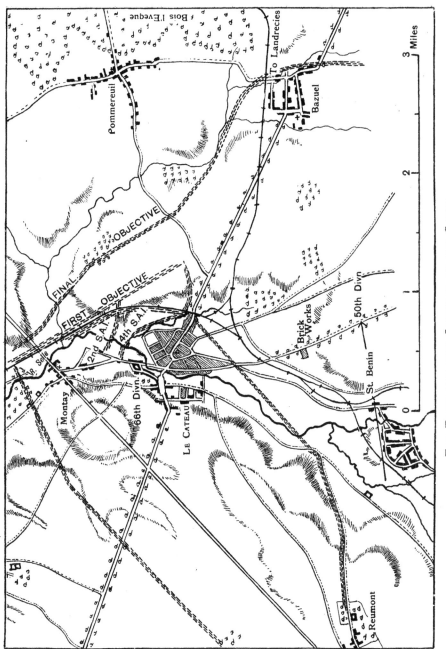

THE FIGHT FOR THE CROSSING OF THE SELLE.

east and north-east of Bazuel. During the afternoon
the 66th Division swung forward its right, and the task
originally allotted to the XIII. Corps was completed.
At 5 p.m. orders had been issued for a relief of the
South African Brigade by the 199th, but owing to the
lateness of the hour the relief was cancelled. Unfortunately this cancelling order did not reach " B " Company of the 1st Regiment till it had withdrawn, and in
returning to the line it lost thirteen killed, while Second-
Lieutenant R. MacGregor was mortally wounded. During
the night the 1st Regiment lost also Second-Lieutenant
C. H. Powell killed, while Second-Lieutenant C. H.
Perrem was severely wounded. The final objective of
the Brigade was established about 4.30 a.m. *Oct. 19.*
on the morning of the 19th, Captain King
of the 2nd being wounded during the operation.

Such was the part of the South Africans in the
forcing of the Selle, the last of their great battles. Between the 17th and 20th of October, in face of a most
gallant resistance, Byng, Rawlinson, and Débeney had
swept well beyond the river line and the Oise-Sambre
Canal, and the way was open for Haig's advance against
Valenciennes and the Forest of Mormal. In the XIII.
Corps area five brigades had in three days captured
7,000 yards of prepared positions defended by a difficult
water line, had advanced 6,000 yards, and utterly defeated four German divisions, taking 25 officers, 1,226
men, and 15 guns. In this work the South Africans
had played a pre-eminent part. Between the night of
7th October and the night of 19th October they had
taken prisoner 4 officers and 1,238 other ranks, and had
captured 367 machine guns, 19 trench mortars, 22 field

guns, 4 anti-tank guns, and a mass of other equipment. Their casualties were 47 officers and 1,229 men, of whom 6 officers and 184 other ranks were dead.

The achievement on the 17th is worthy to rank with their advance at Third Ypres as a brilliant feat of offensive warfare, and as such it was praised by their comrades in arms. Brigadier-General Ian Stewart of the XIII. Corps Headquarters Staff wrote to Tanner: " I shall always look on the capture of the railway embankment north of Le Cateau as one of the most astounding feats of the War. It will be good for South Africa to know what a brave part her contingent played in the closing chapter of the Great War, and it is no little honour to have been the foremost troops of the British Armies in France when the curtain fell on the greatest tragedy the world has seen." And when the war was over and the Brigade about to leave the 66th Division, Major-General Bethell wrote in his special order of the day : " In after life if any of you are up against what you imagine to be an impossible task of any description, call to mind the Boche position on the east bank of the Selle river north of Le Cateau, or ask some one who was there to depict it to you. Then remember that the South African Brigade crossed that stream and took that position, which the enemy thought impregnable to attack from that direction, and that, on looking back at it from the enemy's side, it was hard to understand how the apparently impossible had been done by you."

The fighting front of the XIII. Corps was now occupied by the 25th and 18th Divisions, and the 50th and

66th Divisions fell back into reserve. The South African Brigade was in rest billets at Serain till the 2nd November. Haig was now fairly embarked in open warfare, operating in a difficult country of large woods, many small villages, and an infinity of hedged enclosures. His first object was the line from Valenciennes to the Oise-Sambre Canal along the western edge of the Mormal Forest. The enemy had a strong water line in the canal and the Scheldt, and a good defensive position in the forest, but between the northern end of Mormal and the Scheldt was a gap of ten miles, and if Haig broke through the gap the position must crumble. On Wednesday, 23rd October, he struck on a front of fifteen miles, the Fourth Army using two corps, and the Third Army four. This was the beginning of the last great fight of the British Army, the Battle of the Rivers, fought in thick mists and drizzling rain. In two days Rawlinson, Byng, and Horne advanced six miles, and by the last day of October Haig was through the gap. Elsewhere, on the long front of the Allies, Débeney, Mangin, and Guillaumat were each some twenty-three miles from Hirson with an open country before them, and Gouraud and Pershing had broken the resistance in the tangled area west of the Meuse, and were ready for the final push on Mézières and Sedan. Meantime strange things were happening in Berlin. The new ministry which had come into power in Germany in the early days of October had opened feverish negotiations, and had made haste to recast the creed which had hitherto been Germany's faith. On 27th October Berlin accepted President Wilson's terms, which were that the only armistice to be considered must be one that made impossible the renewal of hostilities on the part of Germany, and was negotiated by a people's Government and not by the Great General Staff. The acceptance of such conditions was tantamount to an admission of defeat in the field. On Saturday the 26th Ludendorff resigned his command. The twilight of the gods had fallen upon his old proud world, and the direction of affairs had gone for good from the hands of him and his kind.

By now the condition of the German armies was in the last degree desperate. On 21st March they had had a reserve of eighty fresh divisions, and during the summer no division was returned to the line without at least a month of rest and training. By 30th October they had but one fresh division, and the intervals of rest had shrunk to nine days. There were divisions on their front which mustered less than 1,000 rifles, and the total shortage of rifles to establishment was not less than 500,000. Their casualties since March had been some 2,500,000, of which at least 1,000,000 represented permanent losses. Of the 18,000 pieces of artillery on their front on 15th July, a third had since been captured or destroyed. Worse still, they had been manœuvred into a position from which retreat was in the long run impossible. Pershing and Gouraud were about to cut their main trunk line in the south, and Haig's deadly pressure was shepherding them northward into the gap of Liége, where, unless an armistice intervened, on the scene of their worst infamies they would suffer a more terrible Sedan.

But it must not be thought that in those days the Allies, and especially the British, won easy victories. The enemy resisted with a gallantry and devotion worthy of a more honourable cause. Between the 27th September and the 11th November our First, Third, and Fourth Armies faced and defeated sixty-one divisions, of which twenty-one had been twice in the battle, eight thrice, and two four times. The rearguard actions by machine-gun posts were often brilliant and almost always resolute, and the defence of the Selle line, notably at Le Cateau, would have done credit to any troops. If we had broken through all the great prepared positions, we were none the less fighting in a country which allowed strong defences to be improvised, and the enemy did not fail to take advantage of it.

It should be remembered, too, that he massed his main strength against the British, for there, if anywhere, he must stand, since Haig was marching straight for Namur and the one narrow door still open to his frontiers. In especial he dared not weaken his artillery on that section, and Haig had to face the bulk of the dwindling complement of German guns. The shelling in those days seemed to many who had fought through the War to be the heaviest they had encountered. The South African Field Ambulance, which, under Lieutenant-Colonel Pringle and Major M. B. Power,* did magnificent work at that stage (it equalled its old record, for it was not in human power to surpass it), had a difficult task because of the steady German shell fire, which searched out all the back areas. As the advance grew faster, it became hard to keep up with the infantry, and to bring back the wounded expeditiously by ruined

* Major C. M. Murray, another distinguished officer, had been recalled in September to take up work in England. He was with the ambulance during the heavy fighting of the first half of 1918.

roads and broken bridges over distances unknown in the previous history of the campaign.

On 2nd November the South African Brigade moved forward from Serain. That day Valenciennes fell to the Canadians under Horne, and next day the German retreat increased its pace. By Monday the 4th, Pershing, who in three days had advanced twelve miles, had the southern railway at Montmédy and Longuyon under his fire. That bolt-hole had been closed. The time had come for Foch, as it came to Wellington on the evening of Waterloo, to give the signal for " everything to go in." On the 4th Haig attacked on the thirty-mile front between Valenciennes and the Sambre, and by the next day the Forest of Mormal was behind him. The enemy's resistance was finally broken, and his armies were not in retreat but in flight, with their two wings for ever separated. Through the fifty-mile pocket between Avesnes and Mézières the whole German forces in the south must squeeze if they would make good their escape, and the gap was hourly narrowing. Mangin and Guillaumat were close on Hirson, Gouraud and Pershing were approaching Mézières, and Haig had the Sambre valley as an avenue to Namur. Moreover, Foch had still his trump card to play, the encircling swing of a new American army north of Metz to cut off the enemy from his home bases. If a negotiated armistice did not come within the week, there would be a *de facto* armistice of collapse and surrender. On the 7th Byng was in Bavai, and on the 8th in front of Maubeuge. That day Rawlinson took Avesnes, and on the 9th the Guards entered Maubeuge, while farther north Condé and Tournai

Nov. 2–4.

Nov. 7–9.

were in our hands. On the 6th Gouraud was in Rethel, and on the 7th Pershing was in the western skirts of Sedan. On the 6th the German delegates, Erzberger and his colleagues, left Berlin on their embarrassed journey to Foch's headquarters. On the 9th came the revolution in Berlin, and the formation of a Council of National Plenipotentiaries under Ebert. Next day the Emperor fled from Main Headquarters to seek sanctuary in Holland.

On the morning of the 8th the South African Brigade was in reserve to the 66th Division at Dompierre, just west of Avesnes. Next day it marched by Beugnies to Solre-le-Château—an arduous journey, largely over field tracks, since most roads and bridges had been destroyed by the enemy. Tanner had been informed by his divisional commander that, owing to the new situation, it had been resolved to create a mobile column under his command. This column was to be part of an advanced guard to cover the Fourth Army front, which guard was to be under Bethell, and was to include the 5th Cavalry Brigade. Tanner's force was made up of his infantry brigade, " B " Battery 331st Brigade R.F.A. with six 18-pounders, " D " Battery of the same brigade with one section of 4.5 howitzers, the 430th Field Company R.E., " C " Company 100th Machine-gun Battery, two armoured cars, and two platoons of the XIII. Corps Cyclists. The general scheme was that the column should move on Beaumont, and cross the stream there, preceded by the 12th Lancers, while the remainder of the 5th Cavalry Brigade operated on its southern flank.

At 7 a.m. on the morning of Sunday, 10th November —about the time when the courier of the German delegates was reaching Spa with Foch's terms in his pocket —the column moved out from Solre-le-Château on the Beaumont road, Lieutenant-Colonel H. H. Jenkins, with the 1st Regiment, forming the advanced guard. A culvert a mile to the east had been blown up, and took some time to repair, so it was 9.30 before the head of the column reached Hestrud. The 12th Lancers, who were in possession, reported that the enemy was in considerable force on the high ground north and south of Grandrieu. Tanner accordingly halted the main body under cover at the Bois de Madame, and ordered the 1st Regiment after a brief reconnaissance to deploy for attack in order to clear the way for the column. The attack of the 1st on a three-company front began at 10.30 with the fording of the Thure river, the road-bridge having been destroyed. The enemy, part of the Guard Reserve Corps, opened the sluices of a reservoir upstream, with the result that the assaulting troops were cut off till the flood subsided. Presently it became clear that they were facing an organized rearguard position, strongly held by machine guns, and supported by artillery.

The flanks of the advance were exposed ; and since the bulk of the 5th Cavalry Brigade had not come up, General Bethell moved forward the 199th Brigade on the right of the South Africans in the direction of Sivry, where they were in touch with the 20th Hussars. The instructions of the advanced guard were to keep close to the enemy, but not to attack if he was found in a strong position. Accordingly Tanner did not force the advance, and in the afternoon the 1st Regiment was ordered to dig in. It was thought likely that the Germans

Nov. 10.

might retreat during the night, so vigilant patrolling was carried out ; but at dawn on the 11th the situation had not altered. In the meantime the bridge at Hestrud had been rebuilt by the Engineers.

The morning of Monday, 11th November, was cold and foggy, such weather as a year before had been seen at Cambrai. Very early, while the Canadians of Horne's First Army were entering Mons, *Nov. 11.* the 1st Regiment attacked, but could make little progress, though a patrol under Second-Lieutenant Cawood managed to gain some ground on the left flank. By 8 o'clock a considerable advance was made on the right, where the 20th Hussars were feeling their way through Sivry. At 10 a.m. Tanner received by telephone the news that an armistice had been signed. " Hostilities," so ran the divisional order, " will cease at 11 o'clock to-day, 11th November. Troops will stand fast on the line reached at that hour, which will be immediately reported by wire to Headquarters, Fourth Army Advance Guard. Defensive precautions will be maintained. There will be no intercourse of any description with the enemy until receipt of instructions." The news must have reached the enemy lines earlier, and he signalized its arrival by increasing his bombardment, as if he had resolved to have no surplus ammunition left when the hour of truce arrived.

Punctually at 11 o'clock the firing on both sides ceased. There came a moment of dramatic silence, and then a sound as of a light wind blowing down the lines —the echo of men cheering on the long battle front. The meaning of victory could not in that hour be realized by the weary troops ; they only knew that fighting had stopped, and that they could leave their trenches without disaster. The final " gesture " fell to the arm which from the beginning of the campaign had been the most efficient in the enemy service. At two minutes to eleven a machine gun opened about two hundred yards from our leading troops at Grandrieu, and fired off a whole belt without a pause. A German machine gunner was then seen to stand up beside his weapon, take off his helmet, bow, and, turning about, walk slowly to the rear.

At the hour of armistice the line reached by the advanced guard ran from Montbliart in the south, west of Sautain, through the Bois de Martinsart, round the eastern edge of Grandrieu to the western skirts of Cousolre. It represented the easternmost point gained by any troops of the British Armies in France. The South Africans had the honour of finishing the War as the spear-point of the advance to victory.

CHAPTER XII.

CONCLUSION.

The Price of Victory—The Special Strength of the Brigade—An Example of True Race Integration—The Nation and the Individual.

THERE is no need to pursue the chronicle of the Brigade through the slow months of demobilization, till in the following June the bulk of its members embarked for home in a German liner handed over to Britain under the terms of peace. When on that grey November morning the guns fell silent, it had accomplished the task to which it had dedicated itself in the summer of 1915. It had travelled a long road in the three years. Brought suddenly, after its short campaign in Egypt, into the thick of the fiercest struggle in the West, it had performed every duty allotted to it with whole-hearted devotion and supreme competence. Never more than a few thousand in numbers, and perpetually short of drafts, it had won for its country of origin a name in the field as proud as that of far larger and more populous territories. There is no soldier living who would deny that in quality the South Africans ranked with the best troops of any army. Twice by its own self-sacrifice the Brigade had been reduced to a handful, and had lost all semblance of a unit, and on each occasion its loss had been the salvation of the British cause. At Delville Wood, at Marrières Wood, and at Messines it had proved to what heights of resolution a defence may rise : in attack at Arras, at Third Ypres, and at Le Cateau it had shown the world, in Napier's famous words, " with what majesty the British soldier fights." The little contingent, one among some hundred British brigades, occupied small space on the battle-map. But scale must not be confused with kind ; the men of Leonidas were not the less Spartans because they were only three hundred.

In the long road to victory they had left many of their best by the wayside. The casualties in France were close on 15,000, nearly 300 per cent. of the original strength. Of these some 5,000 were dead. As evidence of the fury of the Western campaign, it may be noted that the South African contingent in East Africa was nearly twice the size of the forces in France from beginning to end, but its losses were not more than a quarter of theirs. How many, especially of the younger officers, whose names are recorded in the earlier actions, survived to advance on Le Cateau ? Yet the amazing thing is that in a Brigade which was so often severely engaged, and in which the uttermost risks were cheer-fully and habitually taken, any came through the three years' struggle. There are men who fought from Agagia to Le Cateau and have now returned to the mine and the farm to be living witnesses to their miraculous Odyssey.

Wherein lay the peculiar strength of the Brigade ? It has been a war of many marvels. We have seen pasty-faced youths from the slums of cities toughen into redoubtable soldiers, and boys new from office-stool and college classroom become on the instant leaders of men and Berserks in battle. The Brigade had the initial advantage of drawing upon men of a fine physique, and, in many cases, of practical experience in a rough and self-reliant life. Its recruits, too, as I have already said, showed a high average of education, and many who never left the ranks were well qualified for commissions. They developed rapidly a perfect *esprit de corps*, which, because they were so few and so far from home, was more than the solidarity of a fighting unit, and became something like the spirit of a race and a nation. I do not think a more perfect brotherhood-in-arms could have been found on any front. Lastly, they were commanded by officers who had their full confidence and affection. The successive brigadiers, the battalion and battery commanders, and every officer understood the meaning of " team-work," and loved and respected the troops they led.

There is one quality of the South Africans which deserves especial mention—I mean their curious modesty. A less boastful body of men never appeared in arms. They had a horror of any kind of advertisement. No war correspondent attended them to chronicle their doings ; no picturesque articles in the press enlightened the public at home. That may have been bad for the Allied cause ; but assuredly it was what they wished themselves. They had in a high degree the traditional British love of understatement, and no old regular was ever a greater adept at pitching things in a low key. To talk to them after a hard-fought action was to hear a tale of quite ordinary and prosaic deeds, in which little credit was sought for themselves but much given to others. They had that gentle and inflexible pride which is too proud to make claims, and leaves the bare fact to be its trumpeter. I believe that to be a quality of South Africa. She is so ancient a land that she does not need to brag and hustle like newer peoples, but comports herself with the quiet good-breeding of long descent. She has been through so many furnaces that she has won dignity and simplicity. These were most notably the traits of her forces on the Western front. They feared very little on earth except the reputation of heroes ; and if in this book I have done violence to that fine tradition, I can only make them my apology and plead the debt of the historian to truth.

The story which I have endeavoured to tell is to be regarded in the first place as the achievement of a people —that South African people in which the union of two race-stocks is in process of consummation. The war record of South Africa, from whatever angle it is regarded, is one to be proud of. To the different fronts she contributed over 136,000 white troops—nearly 10 per cent. of her total white population, and some 20 per cent. of her male white population. But, great as was her work in other battlegrounds, to my mind her chief glory is her achievement in France. The campaigns in German East and South-West Africa might be regarded as frontier wars, fought for the immediate defence of her borders and her local interests. But to come into line in the main struggle far away in Europe meant an understanding of the deeper issues of the Great War. Her sons in France did not fight in the narrow sense for Britain ; they fought for that liberal civilization of which the British

Commonwealth is the humble guardian; they fought for that South African nation which could not hope to live till Germany's challenge to liberty was answered. There were many in the Brigade who had still quick in their hearts an affection for the northern islands from which they had sprung ; but there were many to whom Britain was only a faint memory, and many in whom her name woke no enthusiasm. There were men of Dutch blood who had fought stoutly against us in the old South African War, and now fought like crusaders, not for our Empire, but for the greater faith by which alone that Empire can be justified. All honour to those who were not beguiled by the chatter of a shallow racialism, which, let it be remembered, is the eternal foe of nationality ; who, without the homely sentiment and intimate loyalties which inspired the British-born, battled for an austere faith and an honourable ideal of their country's future.

Ever since eighteen years ago I had first the privilege to know South Africa, I have cherished the belief that the Dutch stock there is one of the finest in the world, and the most akin in fundamentals to our own ; and that the future must bring to the two races some such union in spirit and in truth as links to-day the " auld enemies " of England and Scotland. The War has enlarged that hope. Never during its three years was there a spark of racial feeling in the ranks of the Brigade. No Dutchman ever cavilled at the appointment of an Englishman ; no Englishman or Scot but gave his full confidence to a Dutch superior. All were South Africans and citizens of no mean country. The Brigade was a microcosm of what South Africa may yet become if the fates are kind. It was a living example of true race integration.

The story may be regarded also as a record of plain human achievement, of what heights are possible in the " difficult but not desperate " life of man. To individuals, as to nations, comes at rare intervals the supreme test of manhood. It is often an open choice : there are excellent arguments why the smooth rather than the rough road should be taken. The men of the Brigade enlisted voluntarily, under no conscription of law—not even under the social coercion of universal recruiting ; their pay was the slender wage of the British regular ; they abandoned, most of them, good prospects in their different callings ; there was no reward before them save honour and a quiet conscience. They made, in another sense than Dante's Pope, the *gran rifiuto*, and preferred a rendezvous with death to comfort and ease. And having chosen, they were wholly resolved to endure to the end. Such a sacrifice is not made in vain, and against it the gates of death cannot prevail. The survivors face life with a new mastery over themselves and their fates, and the remembrance of the fallen will be a glory and inspiration to the generations to come.

Man cannot live always on the heights. It would not be well if he did, for the work of the world must be carried on among the flats beneath. But it is good to know that the hills are there, and it is better to have once sojourned among them. . . . In the bushveld under the scarp of the Berg one may move for days in a parched and thorny land, where the dust hangs in clouds over the road, and dank thickets fringe unwholesome rivers. But to the west above the foothills rise green lines of upland, which by day seem no more than the bare top of a mountain, but at sunset glow like jewels in the heavens. Such a sight is welcome to the traveller, for it tells him that somewhere, and not too distant, there is a land of cool meadows and shining streams; and from that secret country descend the waters which make fruitful the workaday plains.

APPENDICES

APPENDIX I.

THE HEAVY ARTILLERY.

AN apology is due for the relegation of so distinguished a service as the South African Heavy Artillery to an appendix, and for a sketch of a most honourable record which must necessarily be short and inadequate. To tell the story fully would involve the rewriting of the history of the campaign in the West from a special angle; and the point of view of a siege battery, which in action is stationary though not immobile, and is on all occasions ancillary to the infantry work, is not the best from which to follow the main movements of war. The story of a battery, too, should include many technical matters which cannot properly find their place in a general history. But it is greatly to be hoped that detailed records will be published of the different South African artillery units, such as has already been most admirably prepared for the 71st Battery. Some of them were engaged in battles in which the Infantry Brigade had no part, and when the artillery story is added, the South African records cover almost the whole career of the British Army in France and Flanders. In particular, the doings of the 73rd Battery at the southern gatepost during the Battle of the Lys is a fitting accompaniment to the exploits of the Infantry Brigade at Messines in the north.

We have already seen (Chapter I.) that the five batteries of the old South African Heavy Artillery Brigade were armed, on arriving in England, with 6-inch howitzers and affiliated to the Royal Garrison Artillery, becoming the 73rd, 74th, 71st, 72nd, and 75th Siege Batteries, R.G.A. In April 1916 a sixth battery, the 125th, was formed. Early in 1918 a seventh battery, the 542nd, and an eighth, the 496th, were created, but when they arrived in France they were broken up, and their guns and *personnel* dis-

268   APPENDIX I.

tributed, the first between the 75th and the 125th, and the second between the 72nd and 74th. A ninth battery, the 552nd, armed with 8-inch guns, was formed in the autumn of 1918, but the War ended before it could be brought into action. We have therefore to deal with six siege batteries, which were engaged in France from the summer of 1916 to the date of the armistice. At first the batteries were independent units, being allotted to widely separated corps and heavy artillery groups. It was not till the beginning of 1918 that they were brought together, and two South African Brigades formed, the 44th and the 50th—the 44th including the 73rd (S.A.), 71st (S.A.), 125th (S.A), and 20th Batteries; and the 50th, the 74th (S.A.), 72nd (S.A.), 75th (S.A.), and 275th. It will be convenient to take the doings of each battery separately up to January 1918, and thereafter to deal with the record of the two brigades.

THE 73RD SIEGE BATTERY, R.G.A.

This Battery, after its period of training in England, landed at Havre on May 1, 1916, under the command of Major Walter Brydon. On 9th May it reached Bienvillers-au-Bois, in the Somme area, where it took up a battle position under the command of the 19th Artillery Group. On 15th May it fired its first round for sighting purposes. On 1st July, when the First Battle of the Somme began, it covered the infantry advance on Gommecourt, attaining the record of thirty-two rounds in eight minutes with each gun. On 17th July it moved to the village of Berles-au-Bois, and was engaged in smashing enemy trenches and counter-battery work in the neighbourhood of Monchy-au-Bois and Ransart. On 25th August it moved back to Doullens, and thence to Albert, where it took up position in the ruins of La Boisselle. Here it supported the attack on Pozières, Courcelette, and Thiepval; and Major Brydon was wounded while observing for the Battery in the front trenches. In October it advanced its position to Pozières, where it suffered considerably from enemy fire, and had its fill of discomforts from the weather of that appalling winter. In February 1917 Major Brydon returned to duty; and on the 15th of that month two officers of the Battery, Lieutenant Campion and Second-Lieutenant J. Currie, advancing with the infantry to the capture of Boom ravine, rallied two companies whose officers had all been killed, and captured two strong machine-gun posts. Lieutenant Campion fell in this gallant exploit, and Second-Lieutenant Currie received the D.S.O.

In March, in a heavy snowfall, the Battery left the Somme and went north to the Arras area, where, in the Battle of Arras on 9th April, it supported the attack of the Canadians on Vimy Ridge. By noon the advance had progressed so far that the Battery was out of range, and moved forward first to Écurie and then to Thélus. Thélus proved a hot corner, and the Battery had many casualties, notably on 1st May, Major Brydon being wounded for the second time. Soon after it was relieved and retired to Houdain, its first spell out of the line since its arrival in France. It returned to Thélus on 28th May, Captain P. A. M. Hands being temporarily in command, and remained there till the last day of June, when it was transferred to Flanders. Its new position was in the Ypres salient, at the village of Zillebeke, close to Hill 60, where it was much exposed to the enemy's fire, and within 1,000 yards of his front lines. Owing to this, working parties had to be sent up overnight, going in single file for over three miles, past such places of proved unhealthiness as " Hell Fire Corner " and " Shrapnel Corner." The guns were in position by the 17th July, and on the 25th Major Brydon came back from hospital. The Battery was bombed night and day by enemy aircraft, and had no means of making shell-proof cover, for the water was only two feet below the surface of the ground. On 29th August it was relieved for a short space, but it was not till 1st November that it finally left Zillebeke and the Second Battle of Ypres. During the four months there it had nine guns put out of action by hostile fire. On 7th October Major Brydon was gassed, and went to hospital for the third time.

The Battery returned to its old ground at Thélus, which had now become a quiet area, and on 11th November moved to Liévin, west of Lens. Here it had comfortable quarters, and was busy preparing positions in anticipation of an attack. It pulled out for Christmas to Béthune, and on January 5, 1918, took up position at Loisne, where it received news of its inclusion in the new 44th (S.A.) Brigade, R.G.A.

THE 71ST SIEGE BATTERY, R.G.A.

The 71st Battery arrived at Havre on April 16, 1916, under the command of Major H. C. Harrison. It was destined for the impending operations on the Somme, and its first position was at Mailly-Maillet in the VIII. Corps area. On 2nd June, however, it was ordered north to Ypres, where the Canadians at the moment were heavily engaged. On the 18th it returned to Mailly-Maillet, where it participated in the opening days of the First Battle of the Somme. On 5th July it moved to Bécordel, and supported the attack on Mametz Wood, Ovillers, and Contalmaison, and the September attack on Martinpuich and Flers. On 20th September it moved forward to Bazentin, where till the close of the year it was engaged in battling with the problem of the Somme mud. After a short period of rest it was at Ovillers on January 2, 1917, and during February and March moved slowly eastward, following the German retreat. In April it was engaged against the Hindenburg line, and had a share in the fierce fighting around Bullecourt. In July and August it had a position at Croisilles, some 2,000 yards from the enemy front. One sector moved north on 31st August to a position just outside the Menin gate at Ypres, and the rest of the Battery followed on 15th September. There it took part in the Third Battle of Ypres, supporting the attack of the South African Brigade on 20th September, the first occasion when it was in action along with its own infantry. Its position was badly exposed, and it suffered many casualties from enemy shell fire and air-bombing, till it was relieved on 22nd October.

Much worn out, it now moved to Liévin, in the Lens area, where for a little it had a quieter life. On 8th November it handed over its guns to the 73rd (S.A.) Siege Battery, and with the guns of the latter went south to Bapaume. Its new position was in the outskirts of Gouzeaucourt, where, on 20th November, it shared in the Battle of Cambrai. The German counter-attack of the 30th came very near its position, and during those stormy days the Battery, under the command of Major P. N. G. Fitzpatrick, did brilliant work under great difficulties. Unhappily, on 14th December, at Beaumetz, Major Fitzpatrick was killed by a chance shell. On the 18th the guns were withdrawn to Beaumetz, and by the end of the month the Battery was on the front between Béthune and Lens, one section going to La Bourse, and the other to Beuvry. Here it became part of the 44th (S.A.) Brigade.

The 125th Siege Battery, R.G.A.

The 125th Battery was first organized on April 4, 1916, under the command of Major R. P. G. Begbie. It arrived at Havre on 21st July, and reached the Third Army area on 26th July, during the fourth week of the First Battle of the Somme. Its position was at Sailly-au-Bois, on the extreme left of the battle-ground, where its principal targets were the German batteries at Puisieux, Bucquoy, and Grandcourt. On 19th October it moved to the eastern edge of Englebelmer Wood, where it was attached to Sir Hubert Gough's Fifth Army. Here it "prepared" and participated in the attack on Beaumont-Hamel on 13th November. It was a difficult task, for its gun positions were remote from the road, and every 100 lb. shell had to be carried some 400 yards through a swamp, until eventually a line of rails was laid. On January 20, 1917, the Battery moved to a new position on the Auchonvillers road, half a mile north of Mailly-Maillet, where for the next few weeks it was engaged by enemy batteries and a German heavy calibre naval gun, and suffered many losses. On 22nd February it moved into Beaumont-Hamel, where it had better quarters.

On 22nd March, over impossible roads, the Battery moved north to Arras, where its first position was beside the Faubourg d'Amiens. On the second day of the battle of Arras it moved east to St. Sauveur, and on 16th April it went forward a mile east of Tilloy-lès-Mofflaines, on the Arras-Cambrai road. Here it was much exposed, and three days later it moved back to the wood of Tilloy. For the next month its guns were constantly in action by day and night. On 11th May it pulled out for a much needed rest, during which time it received reinforcements which brought it up to strength. On 18th June it moved to Roclincourt, in the Oppy section, where the first leave to England was granted. On 21st July it took up position at Vermelles-lès-Béthune, in the Lens area. Here it came under the First Army, and from the 15th to the 23rd August was heavily engaged in supporting the attack of the Canadians on Hill 70, east of Loos. On the evening of the latter day it moved forward into the ruins of Loos, and rendered brilliant service in the action of the 24th. Its cables were constantly cut by shell fire, and on 5th September it had 28 casualties from a deluge of

German gas shells. The *personnel* of the Battery was withdrawn to rest between the 9th and 21st of September, but from the latter date till 8th October it resumed its work in that section. When the four guns were brought back to Béthune, it was found that not one was fit for further action.

The Battery was now attached to the Belgian Army as one of the thirteen siege batteries constituting the XIV. Corps Heavy Artillery. Its position was in the swampy country in the neighbourhood of Steenvoorde and Oostkerke. On 3rd December it moved to the La Bassée area, and rejoined the First Army, taking up position at Annequin. On January 9, 1918, there came a short space of rest near Lillers. Major Begbie handed over the command to Major J. G. Stewart, and the Battery became part of the 44th (S.A.) Brigade.

THE 44TH (SOUTH AFRICAN) HEAVY ARTILLERY BRIGADE.

On January 29, 1918, Lieutenant-Colonel T. H. Blew, D.S.O., of the South African Defence Force, took command of the Brigade, with headquarters at Beuvry Château. The four batteries were in position east and south of Béthune. During February and March this was a quiet sector, but the batteries were busy preparing reserve positions in depth in view of a possible German attack. From the first day of April the guns were actively engaged in counter-battery work.

The German assault came on 9th April, and one of its main objectives was the right pillar of the British front at Givenchy, held by the 55th Division. All the battery positions of the Brigade, except that of the 125th, had been located by the enemy, who from the early morning drenched them with high explosives and gas shells. For a time all communications with Brigade Headquarters were cut. The falling back of the division on their left allowed the enemy to advance almost up to their gun positions. The 73rd Battery was in the most hazardous case, and owing to the shelling it was impossible to bring up motor transport to evacuate its guns. Major Brydon, who had returned the month before from hospital to the command of the Battery, was ordered to blow up his guns, but instead he served out rifles and a couple of machine guns to his men, and bade them stand to. At one time he had to send the breech-blocks to the rear for safety, but the attack was stayed before it reached the guns, and the breech-blocks were brought back. Though wounded and gassed, he refused to leave his Battery. Finally he was compelled to retire. The men dragged the guns for nearly a mile under cover of darkness, and by 2 a.m. on the morning of the 10th a new position had been found, and the Battery was again in action. The casualties of the Brigade that day were 13 men killed, and 6 officers and 29 men wounded.

The stand on the 9th checked the enemy for a time, and all batteries were able to take up less exposed positions. They suffered, however, from a continuous bombardment, and on the 12th the heroic commander of the 73rd was killed by a shell. He had left the doctor's hands when a severe burst of German fire began, and had hurried forward to see to his guns. No officer in the British Army had a finer record for gallantry and devotion to duty. His Battery was known everywhere on the front as " Brydon's Battery," and he was beloved by his men, for his only thought was for them. During the 9th, though wounded himself, he helped to dress the other wounded, and when the men at the guns began to show signs of exhaustion, he himself dealt out rum to them. Finally he went through a downpour of shells to find a doctor and more dressings. It was one of the many ironies of the war that he never received the Victoria Cross, for he won it a dozen times. Let his epitaph be the words of a gunner in his Battery, who had served with him only a few weeks, and who on the 9th had his arms and legs shot away. Major Brydon stopped and asked if he could do anything for him. The dying man raised himself on his stumps. " By God, Brydon," he cried, " you are a man. I'm only good for the parson now, but I'm proud to die under you."

The 18th of April saw another severe bombardment, when five officers of the 73rd Battery were gassed—Captain P. A. M. Hands, the second in command, and Second-Lieutenants Maasdorp and Brown dying of the effects. This meant a loss to the Brigade, since the 9th, of five officers dead. The expenditure of ammunition during that period had been enormous : the 71st Battery, for example, fired 11,000 rounds. The Brigade remained on the same front till the 27th June, when it was brought out to rest. On the 27th July Lieutenant-Colonel Blew relinquished his command, being succeeded temporarily by Major E. H. Tamplin, who, on

17th August, handed over to Lieutenant-Colonel G. M. Bennett, formerly commanding the 74th Battery.

On returning to the line on 2nd August, the Brigade took up positions farther south in the neighbourhood of Hulluch. On the 22nd its Headquarters were heavily shelled, and one member of the staff was killed. During August and September the batteries supported the steady pressure maintained along this sector in anticipation of the German retirement, all moving to forward positions. On the 2nd October the enemy fell back three miles to the line of the Haute-Deule Canal, and the advance of the Fifth Army began. As soon as roads were repaired, the guns moved up to Douvrin, Hulluch, and Wingles, and on the 12th October assisted in the capture of Vendin by the 15th Division. Owing to the difficulty of bridging the many canals, siege batteries could only follow very slowly, and the Germans were on the line of the Scheldt before they came again into action. The enemy kept up a heavy bombardment during the first week of November, and on the night of the 6th the Brigade suffered its last casualties in the war. The bridging of the Scheldt was in rapid progress, and the batteries were preparing to advance across the river, when on the 11th hostilities ceased.

The 74th Siege Battery, R.G.A.

The 74th Battery landed at Havre on April 30, 1916, under the command of Major Pickburn. It proceeded to Authuille, and on 4th May took up position at Bienvillers-au-Bois. On the first day of the First Battle of the Somme its four guns fired 1,733 rounds, supporting the unsuccessful attack of the infantry at Gommecourt. It then took over the position of the 73rd Battery, and later on, 27th August, moved to the Martinsart-Aveluy road for the operations against Thiepval. On 7th October it was in the orchard at Colincamp, a place without cover and a favourite target for the enemy. There it spent some desperate weeks. On 7th November the battery-commander, Major Pickburn, was killed. On the 20th November the enemy kept up a severe bombardment all day, and four gunners lost their lives. It was the same on the 29th, when an armour-piercing shell penetrated to a cellar protected by seven feet of earth and bricks, and killed the three occupants. The position was really untenable for a heavy battery, but it was held till early in December, when a move was made to Auchonvillers. It presently moved to Gouy-en-Artois, and then to Arras and the Faubourg d'Amiens. In the early weeks of the year it was at Rivière, opposite Ficheux, and then again in a suburb of Arras.

In the battle of Arras the Battery supported the advance of the South African Infantry Brigade, and on the 12th its right section was in the old German line at Point de Jour, supporting the fighting in the Oppy, Gavrelle, and Rœux area. At that time they were the farthest forward siege guns on the British front. There the Battery continued till the battle died away. Major Tamplin was gassed and returned to England, Major Murray-MacGregor taking over the command. By 5th July the whole Battery had moved to the Ypres neighbourhood, where it took up ground on the canal bank near "Shrapnel Corner." There, during the first stages of Third Ypres, it suffered the usual fate of combatants in the Salient. Major Murray-MacGregor was succeeded in the command by Major G. M. Bennett. Presently it moved to a position on the Verbranden-Molen road, and a little later to Hooge. This was its station during the remainder of the battle. It had many casualties from shell, fire, and gas, and the reliefs coming by the Menin road had to face an incessant enemy barrage. The total men available on each shift were only seventeen for all four guns, and had not three of the guns been knocked out the task would have been impossible. When at last the Battery was withdrawn, it was reduced to 1 gun and 70 men.

On 21st December the Battery, now brought up to strength, went back to the line as part of the 50th (S.A.) Brigade, R.G.A.

THE 72ND SIEGE BATTERY, R.G.A.

The 72nd Battery landed in France on April 21, 1916, under the command of Major C. W. Alston. Its first position was at Mailly-Maillet, where with a very short allowance of ammunition it entered upon its field experience. It was sent to Ypres on 3rd June along with the 71st to assist the Canadians, where it had some hard fighting, Major Alston being severely wounded, and Captain A. G. Mullins taking over the command. Returning to Mailly, it took part in the opening days of the First Somme, and then moved first to Englebelmer, and then to Authuille. This last was an excellent position, with a steep bank in front of the guns and the Ancre in the rear. The Battery remained there for eight months, until the retirement of the enemy enabled it to advance to Thiepval and Grandcourt.

On March 22, 1917, it moved to the Arras neighbourhood, taking up ground near Berthonval Wood, a few miles east of Mont St. Eloi. From this position the Battery shared in the battle for Vimy, after the fall of which it moved forward to Souchez, under the northern end of the ridge. On 30th April it retired to Houdain for its first spell of rest since it arrived in France. On 12th May it was at Thélus, and four days later it was transferred to the 1st Canadian Heavy Artillery Group, and took up position at Zouave valley, near Givenchy, in the Vimy area. There it remained for three months, supporting the Canadian attack at Lens.

On 25th October the Battery went north with the Canadian Corps to Ypres, where it relieved the 73rd (S.A.) Siege Battery in a peculiarly unhealthy spot between Zillebeke and Observatory Ridge. There, during the first twenty-four hours, it had twelve casualties. On 17th October the command was taken over by Captain C. P. Ward. On January 11, 1918, after a period of rest, the Battery took up position behind the Damm Strasse, near Wytschaete. It was now brigaded with the 50th (S.A.) Brigade.

THE 75TH SIEGE BATTERY, R.G.A.

The 75th Battery reached France on April 24, 1916, under the command of Major W. H. L. Tripp. It took up its position on the outskirts of the town of Albert, near the hospital, being attached to the III. Corps. It participated in the " preparation " for the First Battle of the Somme, and on 1st July fired 1,312 rounds before noon. On 14th July it moved to Bécourt Wood, and on the 29th to a position north of Fricourt Wood. Here it supported the attack of 15th September. On the 21st of that month it moved to the wood of Bazentin-le-Grand, where it was in touch with the South African Infantry Brigade during its fight at the Butte de Warlencourt. On January 29, 1917, it moved back to Albert,

Lieutenant-Colonel W. H. L. TRIPP, D.S.O., M.C.,
Commanding 75th Siege Battery, S.A.H.A., August 1915–January 1918,
then 50th (S.A.) Brigade, R.G.A.

and early in February went south of the Somme into the old French area. There it advanced as the Germans fell back, crossing the Somme at Péronne on 25th March, and occupying ground successively at Templeux-la-Fosse and Longavesnes. On 6th April, at St. Emilie, it fired its first shot against the Hindenburg Line, and remained in that area till the end of June, when it moved north to Flanders.

By 13th July all four guns were in position on the Vlamertinghe-Elverdinghe road, where, owing to the flat country, the Battery had great difficulty in finding suitable O.P.'s. On the night of 30th July it moved forward to the bank of the Ypres Canal, where it supported the opening of the Third Battle of Ypres. Later it advanced to the Pilckem ridge, where in a much exposed position it supported the attack on Houthulst Forest and Passchendaele. It was exceptionally fortunate, for in all the period from 31st July to 20th December it had only one officer casualty. In the middle of December it went south to the Zillebeke lake, and on January 11, 1918, it moved to the Damm Strasse, near Wytschaete. It was now part of the 50th Brigade.

THE 50TH (SOUTH AFRICAN) HEAVY ARTILLERY BRIGADE.

This Brigade was formed during January 1918, under the command of Lieutenant-Colonel W. H. L. Tripp, D.S.O., M.C., formerly of the 75th Battery. On 28th January it was attached to the Australian Corps, occupying positions between Zillebeke and Wytschaete. On 26th February it went into General Headquarters Reserve, being encamped near Bailleul. On 6th March the 496th (S.A.) Siege Battery arrived, and was split up between the 72nd and 74th Batteries, making these six-gun batteries. On 10th March the Brigade was ordered to prepare positions behind the Portuguese divisions, but the orders were cancelled. On 13th March it was attached to Sir H. Plumer's Second Army. On the 24th, after the great German attack had been launched at St. Quentin, it began to move southwards, and on the 28th was at Neuville St. Vaast during the German assault on Arras. On the 30th it was attached to the Canadian Corps.

During April the batteries were in position at Roclincourt, to the north-east of Arras, and settled down to the familiar type of trench warfare. Since the whole military situation was uncertain at the moment, much time had to be spent on the preparation of reserve battery positions. Five series were selected, varying from three to fifteen miles behind those in use. On 1st May the Brigade was ordered north, the 72nd and 74th Batteries joining the I. Corps near Mazingarbe, and the others going to the XIII. Corps, in the vicinity of Hinges. By the 3rd these orders were changed, and the whole Brigade was sent to Arras to the XVII. Corps. There it remained till the end of August, engaged in normal trench warfare. On 7th August Captain E. G. Ridley, M.C., was promoted major in command of the 74th Battery, to replace Major Bennett, who had gone to command the 44th Brigade.

On 26th August the Brigade supported the advance of the Canadian Corps and the 51st Division, which resulted in the capture of Monchy. The batteries now began to move forward along the Arras-Cambrai road, where they were engaged in cutting the wire of the Drocourt-Quéant switch. On 1st September the medical officer of the Brigade, Captain G. R. Cowie, was seriously wounded, and died two days later. On the 2nd the Canadians carried the Drocourt-Quéant switch, all the guns in the Brigade assisting in the preliminary bombardment and the subsequent barrage. Next day the Brigade passed under the XXII. Corps, which held the line of the Sensée, in order to protect the flank of the Canadian thrust towards Cambrai. No serious operations took place for more than three weeks; but on the 27th came the great advance of the Canadian and XVII. Corps towards and beyond Cambrai, and it became clear that a general enemy retirement was a matter of days. On 3rd October Major Ridley left for England to form a new 8-inch S.A. battery, and his place in command of the 74th was taken by Major C. J. Forder. On the 11th the Brigade came under the Canadian Corps.

On the 12th the batteries advanced, first to Tortequesne, and then to Estrées and Noyelle. On the 19th they were at Lewarde. On the 20th a section of the 74th Battery moved to Wallers to support the Canadian attack. This was the last engagement of the Brigade in the War, for on the 24th it was placed in army reserve, and remained there till the armistice on 11th November.

APPENDIX II.

THE SOUTH AFRICAN SIGNAL COMPANY (R.E.)

INCEPTION AND ORGANIZATION—AUGUST–OCTOBER 1915.

AT the beginning of the war the service of communications in the Imperial Army was organized as the Signals Branch of the Corps of Royal Engineers. This provided and maintained all communications, comprising Telegraphs, Telephones, Visual Signalling, and Despatch Riders (Horse, Motor-Cycle, and Cycle). A Signal Service Company, suitably equipped and organized for its multifarious duties, was provided in war establishments as a part of the headquarters of each of the higher formations—Division, Corps, and Army. The development of scientific trench warfare on the Western Front vastly increased both the importance and the complexity of the communications of the contending armies ; and when, towards the close of the campaign in German South-West Africa, the composition of the Union Oversea Contingent was decided, the offer of a Divisional Signal Company was willingly accepted by the Imperial authorities.

The raising of this Company was entrusted to Major N. Harrison, Engineer-in-Chief of the Union Post Office, who had acted as Director of Signals to the Union Forces during the Rebellion and the German South-West African Campaign. For the acceptance of his recruits Major Harrison set such a high standard of specialized knowledge, character, intelligence, and military experience, that the assembling of the two hundred and thirty men of the original Company occupied the whole of August and September 1915. Eventually a magnificent body of picked men were assembled in Potchefstroom Camp fully representative of all South Africa, from the Zambesi to Cape Town. In view of the technical nature of the new unit's duties, it was natural that a high proportion of the recruits should come from the Transvaal, and particularly the Witwatersrand. The relative figures were—

Recruited in Transvaal . . . 53.7 per cent.
   (Of these, 64 per cent. from Johannesburg.)
Cape . . . . 25 ,,
Natal . . . . 12.7 ,,
Orange Free State . . . . 6.6 ,,
Rhodesia, etc. . . . . . 2 ,,

The standard of physique was very high, and fully correspondent to the maturity shown by an average age of 28.4 years. The backbone of the Company consisted of skilled telegraphists and linemen from the Union Post Office, the majority of whom had served in German South-West Africa, and in previous wars. The drivers, whose excellent horsemanship impressed every one at the training centre in England, were recruited mainly from the farming population, and included many young Dutchmen.

By the beginning of October all the officers, who had been selected from officials of the engineering branch of the post office and electrical engineers of the Witwatersrand, had joined, and on the 17th October the unit, in company with the S.A.M.C. and details of the South African Brigade and S.A.H.A., sailed for England on the *Kenilworth Castle*, with a strength of six officers —Major N. Harrison commanding—Lieutenants J. A. Dingwall, R. H. Covernton, J. Jack, F. H. Michell, F. M. Ross—and 229 other ranks. The Company arrived at Bordon Camp, Hants, on 4th November.

REORGANIZATION AND TRAINING OF THE COMPANY IN ENGLAND— NOVEMBER 1915–APRIL 1916.

Owing to the demands of the German East African Campaign, in which the Union Government was now engaged, there was no prospect of infantry units for the Western Front beyond the one brigade already in England. As the South African Brigade would, therefore, constitute only one-third of the infantry of some Imperial division, the Company could not serve with the Infantry Brigade

:n the capacity of a divisional signal company, as originally contemplated. On the other hand, new army corps were in course of formation, and corps signal companies had to be raised and trained for them. A corps signal company requires a high proportion of skilled technicians in the ranks, and as, owing to the commanding officer's care in selecting his recruits, the company possessed such a proportion, the War Office decided that it should be reorganized in order to form a Corps Signal Company, and proceed to the Signal Service Training Centre in Bedford for the necessary specialized training. The Company accordingly entrained for Hitchin on the 23rd November, and during the next few days was reorganized.

A Corps Signal Company exists primarily . provide communication between the headquarters of an army corps and the infantry divisions with their associated divisional field artilleries which constitute a corps. For this purpose it staffs and equips a Corps Headquarters Signal Office, including telephone exchange, telegraph and despatch rider offices ; constructs such telegraph and telephone lines to divisions as may be necessary or possible ; provides operators at the divisional ends of the lines, and runs and maintains local telephone lines to the different sections of the corps staff, and to the different units of the corps troops. The corps troops—which are those units directly commanded by corps headquarters—though negligible at the beginning of the war, increased enormously with the development of the Heavy Artillery, the Flying Corps, and the rest of the complicated technique of modern position warfare, until finally their communications dwarfed all others. In addition, the Corps Signal Company acts as a repair workshop, and issue store for the signal material and apparatus required by all units and formations within the corps ; assists with and correlates their signal arrangements, and provides electric lighting for corps headquarters.

To provide for the night and day working and the manning of an advanced headquarters, the Headquarter Section was organized in three reliefs, each under a sergeant superintendent. To increase the number of lines which can be simultaneously run out during a general move, both Air Line and Cable Sections were divided into two detachments, each under a sergeant or corporal. Each air line detachment carried material for five miles of poled line on its lorries, and, after training, became capable of erecting this line at the rate of a mile an hour. Each cable detachment carried nine miles of cable, and learned to lay this out at the gallop when necessary, or at a normal rate of three miles an hour along roads where precautions for the preservation of the line had to be taken.

On January 17, 1916, all sections were concentrated in order to continue their training as a company, and billeted in the small villages of Clifton, Shefford, and Broome, a few miles from Haynes Park. The following months were spent in continuous unit training, interspersed with periods of combined training, known as " Signal Schemes." In these " schemes " numbers of signal units awaiting their turn for oversea were organized as armies—imaginary in all except their communications—and flung a moving network of lines across the Eastern Counties. It was an extremely valuable and realistic training for mobile warfare. The drawing of the Company's mobilization equipment and the completion of the motor transport, with the A.S.C. *personnel* to operate it, followed the news of Verdun, and the day of embarkation for France was eagerly awaited. The men grew restive at the idea that the Infantry Brigade had already been in action in Egypt while they were still training in England.

Towards the end of March Major Harrison went to France in order to acquire the atmosphere of the trenches. During his absence the great blizzard of 1916 destroyed much of the post office and railway telegraph systems in the Midlands. All experienced men in the Company were turned out to assist in repairs, and the order to move to Southampton for France arrived when 51 Air Line and portions of all cable sections were scattered on this work up to a radius of forty miles from headquarters. Nevertheless the Company was assembled in a few hours, and was ready to move off at noon next day, with its mass of stores packed complete in all respects. The headquarters and 51 Air Line moving by road in their lorries, and the cable sections by train from Hitchin, reassembled at Southampton on the 10th April, and, sailing in the S.S. *Investigator* with one of the S.A.H.A. batteries, landed at Havre on the 21st.

IN FRANCE : THE FRICOURT SECTOR—APRIL 1916.

After a day at Havre the move was continued—motor transport sections by road and cable sections by train—to Vignacourt.

At this village in the Somme Valley, between Abbeville and Amiens, the headquarters of the newly constituted XV. Corps was concentrating under Lieutenant-General Horne, and Major Harrison, on the 23rd April, was appointed Assistant Director of Army Signals—*i.e.* Staff Officer for Signals to the Corps Commander. The Company now became the XV. Corps Signal Company, and served continuously with that Corps throughout the remainder of the war. A few days later the Corps moved into line between the III. and XIII. Corps, becoming a part of the Fourth Army under General Sir H. Rawlinson, and took over the sector fronting Fricourt and Mametz, between Bécourt and Carnoy. On the 30th April the Company took over from the XIII. Corps Signal Company at Heilly, a village on the Ancre, near Corbie. B.F. and B.G. sections were sent to join the headquarters of the two divisions in line—the 7th and 21st respectively—and B.F. section proceeded to Ville-sur-Ancre, where Brigadier-General Napier, commanding the Corps Heavy Artillery, had his headquarters, and took charge of the Heavy Artillery's communications on the 27th April.

The experience of previous battles had shown that, next to an adequate artillery, the primary technical condition for a successful offensive was good and reliable communication between the assaulting infantry, the directing staffs, and the supporting artillery. Overground wires, no matter how multiplied, failed immediately under the counter-barrage. Visual signalling, slow at the best, was generally ineffective because of the smoke and dust of the barrage, the exposure of the *personnel*, and the unsuitability of the terrain, so faith was now pinned on cables laid in deep trenches for thousands of yards in rear of the front line, carrier pigeons, and runners. As soon as the area could be thoroughly surveyed, a programme of work was drawn up covering :—

(*a*) Reconstruction of and additions to the inadequate open wire routes in the back area, from Corps headquarters up to behind Méaulte, Morlancourt, and the Bois des Tailles, sufficient to cope with the number of units and formations to be thrown in for the battle, and suitably designed and located for rapid extension along the probable roads of the anticipated advance.

(*b*) A complete network of cable trenches extending from the heads of the open wire routes to the front line, providing telephone communication down to company and battery command posts and artillery observation posts.

In the early part of 1916 the deficiencies of technical equipment, in the supply of materials and of labour, were still great. The Signal Sections were then equipped for mobile warfare only, and found themselves carrying out heavy semi-permanent work with scarcely any of the usual tools and appliances. The work of the Ministry of Munitions had not yet produced its full fruits in supply, and though the Deputy-Director of Army Signals—Colonel R. G. Earle—did everything possible to meet the Company's requirements, signal material—particularly cable—was scanty, and deliveries of a hand-to-mouth order. The Labour Corps was then a thing of the future, and, therefore, the whole of the massive works required for the offensive—roads, railways, dumps, dug-outs, etc.—had to be performed by the infantry in their turns out of the line. In such circumstances there was never enough labour to go round, and it required all the commanding officer's tact and persuasiveness to secure the minimum of digging labour required for the cable trenches ; all other unskilled work had to be thrown on the skilled sappers of the Company, and to free the outdoor men for construction, the telegraphists, after a long day at their instruments, had often to spend half the night loading and off-loading in the forward area masses of cable, poles, and line material.

Labour for the Heavy Artillery cable trenches was not secured till June, when two battalions from each division were placed under the direction of Lieutenant Ross for this work. Digging the trenches and laying cable were then pressed forward continuously night and day. Much of the work was only possible at night, as the ground was under direct observation, and the few skilled sappers available, after working most of the night with infantry digging parties, had to be turned out again at dawn, day after day, to take charge of scratch cable-laying parties made up from the signallers of batteries. The Heavy Artillery allotment for the XV. Corps in the coming battle was twenty-three batteries, organized in five groups, and an independent railway battery. The tactical conditions made the communication problem one of peculiar difficulty, because they enforced the siting of the batteries in two main clusters—one in the valley of the Ancre and the other in

Happy Valley—both on the extreme flanks of the Corps' frontage. Further, owing to the enemy's tenure of the Fricourt salient, many batteries, to carry out their work, had to establish communication with observation posts sited on the opposite flank of the Corps area to the position of the batteries, and the most favourable O.P. positions lay far outside the Corps boundaries. The fact that many of the batteries only took position and settled on their O.P.'s in the last few days was an additional complication.

When these difficulties had been more or less successfully disposed of and laying commenced, a minor but vital detail in the material threatened disaster. The cable coming forward proved to be mainly single D 5—*i.e.* the standard army cable as supplied for overground use in mobile warfare, when few lines are laid and there is no objection to the earth constituting the return circuit. The results already known to have been obtained by the enemy in picking up our messages through earth by means of sensitive listening telephone apparatus, had already caused the issue of stringent orders that all lines within 1,600 yards—later increased to 3,000 yards—of the front line must be metallic circuits—*i.e.* each line had to consist of a pair of insulated wires. Also, owing to inductive effects when a number of pairs of wires are laid closely parallel to each other, as in a trench, a conversation over one pair will be heard in the other circuits unless each pair is twisted. The use of the single cable, therefore, not only doubled the work of laying (as each line necessitated two separate wires), but the untwisted pairs so formed would render the lines noisy and possibly entirely unworkable. Utilizing the frame of a cable wagon trail, and one of its wheels as a foundation, a machine was rapidly improvised by the section on which the drums of single cable were mounted as received, spun into twisted cable, and simultaneously reeled off on other drums for the laying parties. This apparatus was kept going and running at high pressure by the section wheeler, Sapper Page, with a few Artillery Headquarters' grooms and batmen as his only available assistants.

By such strenuous efforts the programme was completed, and when the preparatory bombardment opened, 500 miles of cable had been laid and joined up in over twenty miles of cable trench, and every battery had excellent and reliable communication forward to its observation posts and back to its group commander. Two dug-outs had been constructed on each flank, into which all O.P.

lines were led and terminated on special switchboards, designed and made up at the Company Headquarters.

Through these O.P. exchanges any battery could be connected to any O.P. for control of fire, which proved most valuable in the changing circumstances of the fighting. At that date the establishment of neither groups nor batteries included switchboards for metallic circuit lines. The necessary number—over thirty—were improvised in a few days at the Company workshops out of electric light fittings purchased in Amiens.

Meanwhile the other sections working at similar high pressure had completed the main communications from Corps Headquarters to the Battle Headquarters of the divisions, the 7th in dug-outs near Groveton, and the 21st in dug-outs on the edge of the plateau above Méaulte, and B.F. section had established and staffed a Corps Advanced Exchange at Morlancourt. The Carrier Pigeon Service had been organized and arrangements made for the systematic distribution of pigeons to the assaulting brigades from the main lofts in Heilly, Albert, and Méaulte, and the most rapid circulation from the pigeon lofts to all staffs concerned of information contained in messages brought by the birds returning from the front line.

A wireless detachment was supplied from Fourth Army Signals, and the *personnel* completed by skilled operators selected from the Company. The Headquarters Station was fixed on the high ground near the Bray-Albert road on the cable trench between the two O.P. exchanges, and provided with direct communication to Corps through the underground system, and mobile stations were attached to the Signals of the attacking divisions. The Corps Staff Observation Posts in Péronne Avenue trench and the Grand Stand above Bonte Redoubt were connected by direct lines to the General Staff at Headquarters in Heilly, about ten miles off, and the special linemen provided to look after these lines kept them through without interruption during the attack.

THE SOMME BATTLE—JULY–NOVEMBER 1916.

In the early morning of the 1st July, after a continuous bombardment from the 25th June, the XV. Corps attacked with the 7th Division on the right, the 21st on the left, and the 17th in sup-

LIEUTENANT-COLONEL N. HARRISON, C.M.G., D.S.O.,
Commanding South African Signal Company (R.E.).

port. Hopes of a decisive victory ran high, and all signal arrangements for a rapid advance were in readiness, including the lines necessary to divert communications to Vivier Mill, outside Méaulte, which was to be the first bound of the Corps Headquarters, while the cable sections stood by with wagons packed during the morning. In spite of the gallantry of the infantry assault—which several of the Company were privileged to witness from the advanced trenches—by the evening it was clear that no great depth would be attained.

The village of Fricourt was still holding out, and had repulsed a frontal attack with heavy loss, while the converging attacks of the 7th and 21st Divisions on the flanks of the salient, which were to have pinched it out, had carried Mametz, but just failed to link up behind Fricourt. The III. Corps on our left had taken La Boiselle and entered Ovillers, but had been driven out again ; Montauban had fallen to the XIII. Corps on the right, but heavy fighting continued. Fricourt was bombarded all night by heavy howitzers, and deluged with a new gas shell by a brigade of French 75's, which, together with an additional brigade of heavies, had been attached to the Corps Heavy Artillery shortly before the battle. When the infantry advanced next morning the village was found evacuated, and a party from B.E. section were able to make a preliminary reconnaissance for pushing forward the artillery routes. Our tenure of the high ground between Mametz and Montauban was now sufficiently secured, and the roads Méaulte-Fricourt and Carnoy-Mametz repaired to such an extent as to permit the advance of the heavy batteries to positions about our old front line. The artillery moves having thus begun, B.E. section thenceforward found itself taxed to the limit to keep pace with them. There were now seven groups to keep in touch, including the two attached French groups.

It was evident from the map that while the fighting for Mametz Wood continued, the new centre of observation would be about Pommiers Redoubt—the highest point of the Mametz-Montauban ridge—and after a hasty reconnaissance which located our advanced line down the forward slope about Caterpillar Wood, it was decided to lay a few pairs of armoured cable up the old German trenches from the new battery positions about Carnoy and Fricourt. The only armoured cable to be obtained was a portion of that already laid in the trench between the two O.P. exchanges.

A few signallers having been collected from the batteries, this heavy armoured cable was recovered from the trench, conveyed forward by wagon, and again laid out up to Pommiers Redoubt. In doing this work the effect of the appalling road and traffic conditions which clogged all effort throughout the Somme was first clearly appreciated. The XV. Corps was unfortunately placed, in that no main road ran forward through its front. From beginning to end of the battle, the only traffic artery was the narrow country by-road from Méaulte to Fricourt, and thence by Mametz to Montauban.

Such transport conditions bore more hardly on signals than any other service. With activities spread over the whole area, a very limited *personnel* and transport, and ever-changing conditions, which often stultified by nightfall all the laborious effort of the day, the difficulty of getting parties to a given spot at a given time, co-ordinating the supply of materials and labour, controlling the working parties and switching them to meet emergencies as they arose, was a splendid schooling in patience, temper, and too often in resignation to fate. This remained the paramount factor in the Company's experience throughout the Somme. As an example, a cable wagon of B.E. section took its place in a melancholy queue at 7 a.m., and arrived at its working point near Montauban at 2 p.m., to lay a short line required urgently at noon, and involving about half an hour's work. The party returned *via* Carnoy in accordance with the traffic circuit, and encountering similar conditions, reached headquarters near Méaulte at 10 p.m., with horses and men exhausted. Under the same difficulties, 51 Air Line Section was engaged in following up the advance with a light open wire route up to Fricourt, and B.G. and B.F. Sections were worked with the 21st Division Signals and the Corps Observers respectively.

The commencement of active operations brought the work of the operators and the despatch riders at headquarters and with the heavy artillery to a point of extreme pressure, which was maintained with little variation throughout the following months. Up to two thousand telegrams, and a larger number still of D.R.L.S. packets, were received or despatched daily. The telephone exchanges at Corps and Heavy Artillery Headquarters, with over sixty and thirty connections respectively, worked hard day and night, handling urgent priority calls ; but so keen and expert were the operators that a service was maintained equal, if not superior, to the highest civilian standard. The destruction of lines by hostile shelling and traffic was met by the skilful use of alternative routes and by the quickness and energy of the maintenance linemen. However, the incessant strain to which the operators were subjected soon began to affect their nerves, and before the Company was withdrawn men resting off duty could be heard answering imaginary calls in their sleep.

On the 10th July B.G. Section, under the command of Lieutenant Covernton, did a notably fine performance in laying and maintaining lines through the intense barrages surrounding Mametz Wood. One of the first Valve Amplifying Listening Sets supplied to the British forces for use in intercepting enemy messages, by picking up weak leakage or induced currents through earth or along parallel conductors, had been issued to the Company for trial. As a large number of enemy cables ran through Mametz Wood, and some extended to enemy territory behind it, favourable results seemed probable. Lieutenant Collins took up the set, and tracing the cables into No Man's Land, tapped in there. Though, owing to the excellent discipline of the enemy in obeying the limitations prescribed for use of wire communication in the front line, no tactical messages were obtained, this officer afterwards obtained recognition of his courageous and enterprising efforts.

On the 14th July another general assault secured the line along the ridge between Bazentin-le-Petit and Longueval. Accordingly, heavy batteries were moved up as far as Caterpillar Wood in the valley in front of Montauban, and on the 15th a party of B.E. section reconnoitred for lines to Bazentin-le-Petit, in which village it was proposed to establish H.A. Headquarters. The German reaction had, however, already begun, and the party found the conditions in the village highly unsuited for a headquarters, so much so that a warm infantry combat was proceeding in the outskirts. High Wood had to be evacuated as too advanced to hold, and the memorable struggle of the South African Infantry Brigade for Delville Wood had begun. Nevertheless, over a mile of ground had been gained, and the corresponding extension of communications necessarily taxed all sections to their limit. The advanced headquarters of divisions moved up to the famous dug-outs in the chalk under the ruins of Fricourt Château, in which, thirty feet underground, with the amenities of electric light, panelled walls, and artificial ventilation, the German Staff had dwelt during the bombardment of the village. A twenty-four wire heavy route was rapidly constructed by the 4th Army Signals from Méaulte to this point, and thence to Mametz, in readiness for the advance, and the wire light route built by the Company was extended by the Air Line Section past Fricourt, up Death Valley, to Mametz Wood. The next deep advance was not, however, to occur till two months later, as the corps front was now becoming a salient, and it was necessary to clear the flanks and broaden the base of the attack. Therefore, while the Anzac Corps and III. Corps on the left, and the XIII. Corps succeeded by the XIV. Corps on the right, hammered away round Pozières and Ginchy respectively, the XV. Corps was engaged in continuous auxiliary attacks, and its heavy artillery co-operated largely with the operations of the flanking corps.

This situation did not bring any relaxation to the Signal Company. The German artillery, whose work behind the front line had been feeble immediately after the 1st July, had now been heavily reinforced, and the salient position of the Corps inevitably drew much enfilade fire. One of the effects was the continuous destruction of lines back to points thousands of yards from the front. In moving up after the 14th July, all units had finally passed beyond the buried cables laid down for the battle. Forward lines were now entirely overground, and if not blown up by direct hits, were cut by the smallest splinters.

As the month of July wore on the demand for additional forward communication and the strength of the hostile fire increased. It was obvious that no satisfactory communication could be secured beyond Fricourt except by burying, and Major Harrison finally succeeded in securing a small labour party from the Corps Cyclist Battalion for this purpose. It was decided to commence by burying sixteen pairs of armoured cable from the head of the open route at Mametz to Pommiers Redoubt dug-outs, where there were now Brigade Headquarters and Divisional Report Centres. The work was entrusted to B.G. Section and proved difficult, not only because of the maze of old trenches, barbed wire, and shell-holes through which the cable trench had to go, but also because of the frequent shelling of Mametz and along the ridge. On the 28th Lieutenant Covernton, while superintending this work, was badly wounded. Lieutenant Baker took over B.G. Section, completed the trench, and subsequently extended the cables to Caterpillar Trench. At the same time, 51 Air Line Section diverted the open wire route between Fricourt and Mametz, by constructing a substantial pole route skirting both villages, which carried eight pairs of twisted D 5 cables hung in slotted boards. This cable route was not only much less frequently shelled down—a daily occurrence with the open route—but could be quickly repaired, as the cable when cut could be rejointed and worked, even if lying on the ground.

This method of substantial poled cable routes could and would have been used to a greater extent but for the deficiency of material. The consumption of cable by units in line was appalling. Artillery Observation Post Lines, laid overground, were badly cut about by shell fire, and had to be renewed every few days, and sometimes daily. In the case of the heavy batteries, these lines were often of great length, and ran to more than one O.P. For instance, the 34th Siege Battery, sited to the left of Fricourt, had about this period lines out to O.P.'s at Longueval and at the windmill in front of Bazentin-le-Grand, a total line length of over eleven miles.

During the comparative lull towards the end of July the shelling of the Fricourt area became so pronounced that, pending the next general attack, the headquarters of the divisions in line were moved back to Bellevue Farm—between Méaulte and Albert—and the opportunity was at once taken to transfer the Corps Exchange in Fricourt into the dug-outs so vacated. The Armstrong hut had luckily escaped so far, but several shells had pitched within a few yards of it, and the operators deserved great credit for the way they stuck to their duties without the slightest protection through the periodical shellings. A new route was built by 51 Air Line from Bellevue Farm to link up this new position with the main forward route at Vivier Mill, and was calculated on a scale sufficient to meet requirements in the event of the headquarters of the Corps moving to Bellevue Farm when the advance resumed.

Throughout the war, but particularly in this earlier period, the difficulties of Signals did not arise exclusively from the terrain and from enemy action, but to a great extent from careless and thoughtless conduct on the part of the other arms. Much damage to lines was done by cross-country traffic at night, largely unavoidable but much also avoidable, if a better understanding of the importance of communication had existed in the non-technical units. When an infantryman found himself in reserve a few thousand yards behind the front line, and lacking a piece of cord to fix up his bivouac, cut a few yards out of a cable which had been strung across the ground in his vicinity, he did not realize that the line so put out of action might well be the observation line of a heavy battery, that the damage he had done in a few seconds might take an over-worked lineman hours to locate and repair, and that meanwhile the battery would be blinded and his comrades in the front line deprived of its instant and effective support. A typical instance occurred on the night of the 3rd July. The group of French 75's attached to Corps Heavy Artillery had moved suddenly late in the evening to support operations at Mametz Wood next morning. Communication was established through one of the buried trenches by 10 p.m., but an hour later this and other lines in the trench went full earth. At 3 a.m., after tracing the cable inch by inch through a dark night, and tapping in at intervals as he progressed, the exhausted lineman found that a company in support had decided that the cable trench would make a good temporary cook-house, and, of course, had burnt all the twelve pairs of wires in the trench. To the infinite relief of the H.A. Signal Officer, this proved to be the only damage done, and the wires were set going again before dawn and in time for the operations.

Long before the Somme Battle, the exigencies of trench warfare had altered the original organization of army corps. The corps had ceased to be a unit composed of specific divisions, and divisions were no longer affiliated permanently to one corps, but moved at frequent intervals from quiet sectors to active ones to take part in an offensive, and after a short period of heavy losses and extreme exertion would be again withdrawn to another quiet sector or a training area for rest, recruitment, and refit. Therefore, on a front like the Somme, a continuous stream of divisions passed through the corps, each taking its share of the fighting and being in turn relieved. As the Corps Signal Company, like the brook, " went on for ever," it had to fit each fresh division into the frame of the existing communications as they chanced to stand at the moment, and assist the divisional signals to pick up and utilize the available lines. The organization had, also, to be elastic enough to meet the requirements of administering anything from two to seven divisions simultaneously. During the Somme, nineteen different divisions passed through the XV. Corps, and as many of them went through the furnace more than once, there were altogether fifty-three divisional changes.   What work this involved to the Corps Signal Company in the transferring of lines, the directing of traffic, the continuous alteration of records, and the supply of material can be readily imagined.

The excellence of the work of the B.E. Section with the Heavy Artillery was recognized in a communication addressed to Major Harrison, in which the Corps commander stated that he much appreciated the work done by Lieutenant Ross and his party, and considered that the work of this section was typical of the whole South African Signal Company.   When General Horne himself left the Corps at a later date, to take command of the First Army, he had evidently seen no reason to alter his opinion of the Company, for in taking leave of the A.D.A.S. he congratulated him on commanding a unit second to none in France.

The operations continued to be hampered by rain at each of the critical phases, but by the beginning of September the flanking corps had made the necessary progress and everything was in readiness for the great attack of 15th September.   The vital importance of secure communication being fully appreciated by the Staff, the necessary labour was made available for a considerable buried scheme.   A buried water-pipe laid by the enemy between Longueval and Montauban had been located, and considerable effort was expended by B.F. section in investigating the possibility of using this pipe for running cable through.   It was finally decided that its exploitation would not be justified in view of the small depth of the bury, and the extensive damage already done by shell fire.   The first section of the new bury consisted of a six-foot-deep cable trench, extending from Pommiers Redoubt via the famous Cosy Corner, where the Carnoy and Mametz roads join outside Montauban, and thence to York Trench on the left of Longueval. This trench had nine framed test points let into the walls every four hundred and forty yards, and contained forty-five pairs of cable.   The accumulation of the necessary quantities of cable suitable for the work presented great difficulty, and the trench probably set up a record for the number of different varieties it contained—from nineteen pair V.I.R., as thick and heavy as a hawser and supplied on drums weighing over half a ton each, to one pair G.P. Twin about as stout as a double boot-lace. The actual digging was done by a battalion of the 7th Division, the work being under the charge of Lieutenant Collins, assisted by Lieutenant Baker, with B.G. section and most of the sappers of B.E. and W.W. sections. The mud of the Somme will go down to history : and as the line of the trenches included some excellent samples of it, the distribution along the trench of the heavy cable drums and the pipes for crossing under tracks presented great difficulties. The jointing, terminating, and testing of the wires had to be completed against time, and with a limited number of expert men, as the maintenance of the widespread network for which the Company was responsible had absorbed many of the best men out of all sections. The lines were, however, ready in time for the divisions who had moved Headquarters up again to Fricourt and Pommiers Redoubt, with Advanced Headquarters at York Trench, and also for the Heavy Artillery, most of whose batteries took positions along the Mametz-Montauban ridge and in folds of the forward slope towards Caterpillar Wood and Longueval. To cope with the steady forward drift of the Corps units, and to provide another advance maintenance point, a new Corps Forward Exchange was established in a dug-out at Pommiers, and after the attack B.E. section staffed this exchange and maintained the area.

The attack on 15th September proved highly successful and not too costly in life, a depth of over a mile being made good, including the villages of Courcelette, Martinpuich, and Flers. Communications held well throughout the day, and the good liaison between infantry and artillery so secured played an important part in the result. The recently introduced Power Buzzers for transmitting high-power buzzer signals through earth to be picked up by Valve Amplifying Receivers at distances up to three thousand yards, were used with fair success in the advance. These sets were controlled by the Wireless Section, but the forward stations were manned by signallers of the attacking battalions. The comparative inexperience and lack of special training of these signallers prevented the best being got out of the instruments, but the limited establishment of the Signal Service prevented any other procedure.

The advance rendered a further extension of the cable trench urgent, but for the moment suitable cable for a permanent bury was not available. Another section of trench, however, was dug immediately in order that units might have the benefit of its protection in running temporary field cables forward. This section extended from York Trench through the corner of Delville Wood to Switch Trench, and the digging proved a gruesome task, as Delville Wood and neighbourhood was a huge graveyard. In the sides of the trench were visible more than one pitiful reminder that our heroic comrades of the Infantry Brigade had fought and died there. To prevent confusion and facilitate maintenance, the left-hand side of the new trench was assigned to divisions and the right to the Heavy Artillery, the Headquarters Signals of which prepared and erected along the trench fixtures for cables in the shape of angle iron high-wire entanglement pickets, each having a piece of two-inch by two-inch wood screwed to it with a dozen diagonal slots cut in it for the cable. The cutting and slotting of so many pieces—upwards of one thousand five hundred—was a task beyond hand methods, but was accomplished in three days by obtaining a power-band saw from a factory in Albert, and connecting it up with the water wheel at Vivier Mill by a belt extemporized from the driving bands of the cable wagon winding gears.

During this period occurred a noteworthy performance in rapid repair of cable routes. The main cable trench about midnight received a direct hit from a large shell, severing all communication ; but fortunately a party of B.E. section was returning down the trench from forward work, and came on the shell crater soon after-wards. Though already worn out with a long day's work and struggling through the mud, they at once started to dig up the cable ends, sending a man to summon assistance by tapping in at the next test point in the trench, and succeeded in getting all the forty-five pairs of wires rejointed and working again in *three hours*.

Liaison lines had grown formidably in numbers. Direct lines were now demanded not only between Heavy Artillery Head-quarters and the Artillery Headquarters of all divisions in line, but between the divisional artilleries and the majority of the Heavy Artillery Groups. There had been a great development of the service of Observation in the shape of artillery aeroplanes, kite balloons, of which there were now three sections attached to the Corps and Observation Groups of the R.E. Survey battalion. Whenever possible lines were now required from these units, not only to the artillery groups, but to the batteries specially assigned for counter-battery work. To co-ordinate and render fully effective this work of the systematic location and destruction or neutralization of hostile batteries, a special staff, commanded by a colonel, had been added to the H.A. Headquarters, and this staff, in its turn, required additional direct lines and communication facilities to enable it to function promptly and effectively.

The evil luck that, except in the initial push, caused every successful attack to be followed by broken weather, still held good and hampered all preparations for the assault on the next entrenched line ; but by herculean efforts the necessary organization for another general attack on the 25th September was completed. Road conditions up to a certain point forward were now beginning to improve under the triple influences of the introduction of Décauville tramways for the conveying of the heavy ammunition in the forward area, the extension of broad-gauge ammunition railheads to Fricourt and Caterpillar Wood, and the removal of water lorries from the roads by the completion of a vast system of pipe lines extending back to the Ancre and the Somme through which the river water was pumped after treatment in chlorinating plants.

On the 25th the intermediate German line, including Morval, Lesbœufs, and Gueudecourt, succumbed, and the Corps front again advanced over a mile. On the 26th the victory was completed by the Fifth Army's capture of Thiepval, and once again the roseate prospect of a great victory and of reaching Bapaume before winter cheered the tired troops, and kept the Signal Company's hands full with preparations for forward moves of all headquarters. The weather, however, intervened on the side of the Germans, and breaking decisively on the 26th, remained miserably cold and wet thenceforward, and largely stultified the heroic efforts repeatedly made throughout October.

During this period, the heavy batteries of some of the H.A. Group Headquarters moved up to and in front of Longueval, necessitating the running of many new cable lines. Permanent cable was laid in the second section of the main cable trench up to Longueval, and a third section of trench was dug forwards to the sugar works at Factory Corner in front of Flers. An experimental trench was started near Longueval, with a trench excavator loaned by the French, which was, in effect, a small land dredge mounted on a motor lorry chassis and driven by its engine. This machine could excavate a cable trench eighteen inches wide and up to seven feet deep in ordinary soil with ease, but it was immobile on the terrain of the Somme, and could not be manœuvred except with the assistance of an artillery caterpillar tractor. Consequent on this trial improved machines were ordered from America for next year's campaign, but the Corps Signal Company did not have the opportunity of using them.

At the end of October the Anzac Corps, under General Birdwood, relieved the XV. Corps commanded by Sir John Ducane since the departure of General Horne. As there was then no other Corps Signal Company in France formed from Colonial troops, it appeared possible that the Company would be retained in line with the Anzacs. It is no disparagement of the spirit of the men to state that every one heaved a sigh of relief when it became known that " K " Corps Signal Company was to take over. In truth, nearly all were bone-weary and temporarily played out, and every section badly needed a spell out of the line to reorganize and refit. There had been no leave granted in the line, and those with ties in England eagerly anticipated its reopening.

In view of the extensive system to be taken over, the relief by " K " Corps Signal Company was conducted gradually, and B.E., the last section to leave the line, did not reach the new headquarters at Long until the middle of November. Long proved to be a tiny old-world village on the left bank of the Somme a few miles upstream from Abbeville. A liberal allotment of leave permits was soon issued, and a batch of men were sent off daily, while the less fortunate ones overhauled, cleaned, and repaired equipment, improved billets and horse standings, and carried out the signal work still required. For Signal Companies in the field there is no such thing as " complete rest," even in the rest area.

On Major Harrison's promotion, Captain Dingwall now assumed the executive control of the Company, but scarcely had the sections completed their refit, when orders were suddenly received for the Corps to take over a portion of the French front in the Péronne sector, with the 4th, 8th, 33rd, and 40th Divisions then in rest.

THE WINTER CAMPAIGN ON THE SOMME—

16TH DECEMBER–17TH MARCH.

The move into line commenced on the 3rd December, and was completed on the 6th. The cable sections, so depleted by the large numbers on leave that they were unable to fill the saddles of the mounted men, moved with the Divisional Signal Companies, and were directed—B.E. and B.G. on Bray, and B.F. on Maricourt.

Headquarters and the air line section joined the Corps Headquarters at Etinehem, a village on the right bank of the Somme, a mile or so west of Bray. In their weakened condition all sections had a most strenuous time taking over communications as released by the French, testing the routes out, reorganizing the lines and connecting up units as they arrived. The Corps front extended from the XIV. Corps boundary on the north at Combles, previously the extreme right of the British line, to near Bouchavesnes, and ran in front of St. Pierre Vaast Wood, where the most desperate French attacks in the autumn had, like our own in the north, been stifled in the mud. The terrain as a whole was of similar nature and condition to that in the Longueval sector, but the roads were better, Décauville tramways existed, and best of all, from a signal point of view, a very fair network of deep cable trenches had been dug in the forward area. Though the cable used in these " buries " —mainly one pair lead covered with impregnated paper insulation— proved unreliable in insulation, and much trouble was caused and many circuits lost thereby, yet the "buries" proved very useful, and, supplemented by the construction system of several new open routes in rear, enabled a communication system to be rapidly completed, sufficient for the needs of the defensive winter campaign. Corps forward exchanges were established with the Heavy Artillery Headquarters in excellent French dug-outs at Bois Louage in front of Maurepas, as at Maricourt, in charge of B.F. section, and with B.G. section at Bray, where the horse lines of all cable sections were shortly concentrated. The sappers of B.E. section remained with H.A. Headquarters under Lieutenant Collins, who replaced Captain Ross as H.A. Signal Officer, while the latter did duty at Headquarters during the successive sick leaves of Lieutenant-Colonel Harrison and Captain Dingwall.

Etinehem proved a most miserable headquarters. The village was much overcrowded, and the billets so wretched that some of them did not even afford an adequate shelter from the weather of the most severe winter known in France for over twenty years. The only redeeming feature of the place was that its situation on the river enabled the many tons of heavy signal stores now in the Company's possession to be brought up the Somme from Long by barge, so releasing the lorri·s for urgent construction work. The pressure of duty on the limited numbers of men available, as well as the shortage of material, fuel, and of daylight, made it difficult for some time to improve conditions. Authority for additional blankets and for the issue of waterproof clothing to the linemen was obtained, but the poor conditions, the severity of the weather, and the lowered vitality, due to the lack of a sufficient recuperative period after the summer campaign, resulted in a heavy and increasing sick list, reaching forty daily, and the evacuation of considerable numbers to hospital with pulmonary complaints. This state of affairs, coupled with difficulties experienced in obtaining reinforcements, kept the Company much below normal strength for several months.

During December it was understoo·' that the French contemplated launching an attack against Mont St. Quentin and Péronne, and to this end they retained a frontage on both banks of the Somme. However, early in January 1917 the project was abandoned, and orders were received for the XV. Corps to extend its front to the right, taking over to the river by Cléry, and simultaneously handing over a divisional frontage on the left to the XIV. Corps. The divisional sectors were taken over successively, and the move completed by the 22nd January without interference by the enemy, the Headquarters of divisions in line being established at P.C. Chapeau and P.C. Jean, ex-French divisional command posts judiciously and inconspicuously sited under the high bank running parallel to the Somme bank. H.A. Headquarters with B.E. section moved also to P.C. Chapeau, and the Corps Forward Exchange at Maricourt was transferred with B.F. section to Suzanne. This change of frontage was a nasty jar to the Company, as nearly all the new routes, on which the sections had toiled early and late to complete the communication scheme for the winter, were now outside the Corps area, and the same work had to be started afresh in the bitter frosts of January. The weather, that had been vilely cold and wet from the beginning of December, now turned to snow and hard frost. The latter penetrated the ground to such an extent that by the end of the month all digging became impossible, and work on a buried cable trench between Ouvrages and Oursel, to provide forward communications for the 33rd Division, had to be suspended. The ex-French bury forward of P.C. Jean proved very faulty, and a section of twelve pair open-wire heavy route was put in hand early in February, running forward to Monac, partly to supplement the bury and partly to carry forward the head of the main route in anticipation of the advance next spring. The ground was found to be frozen as hard as concrete to a foot from the surface, and after ineffectual struggles with picks and crowbars, excavations for the pole holes were finally blasted with gun-cotton. As the forward end of this route came under direct observation, the last few hundred yards were run in cables hung on short stakes, each cable from a small bobbin insulator nailed to the side of the stake. This method was copied from the French, who had used it extensively in the area, and proved very satisfactory in this instance.

In the meantime, aeroplane night-bombing and the shelling of back areas by long range guns, initiated in the latter stages of the Somme Battle, had developed to an unpleasant extent. Rarely did a day pass without some main route suffering from one or other of these agencies, and the consequent necessity for diverting the limited working parties from urgent construction to still more urgent repairs. The railheads of Maricourt and Bray were favourite targets, and again and again the unfortunate sappers were turned out of their blankets to stumble along a route in the pitch black night, and then struggle for hours with numbed fingers to evolve order out of a chaos of tangled wire and broken poles.

This hostile aeroplane activity caused a rapid increase of anti-aircraft units. Batteries and searchlights were now dotted over the area, and the installation and maintenance of a separate and complete system of communication for the Anti-Aircraft Defence of the Corps area was now added to the Company's duties, and the H.A. Signal Officer found himself occupied with communications for the Survey Groups and the installation of lines to their O.P.'s, and to the Microphone positions of the Sound Ranging Section now added to the H.A. Counter Battery organization.

Though the duties of the H.A. Signal Officer were somewhat reduced by the appointment, in January, of a R.E. Signal Officer to each H.A. Group, the commencement by the enemy of systematic counter battery work, in imitation of the British methods initiated in the previous year, made it more than ever difficult to keep the forward lines in continuous operation. A scheme for the forward extension of the buried system, till recently used by the French, was prepared under the greatest transport difficulties, the drums having to be man-handled about half a mile across country by night, and a portion of the material was got up to Marrières Wood, next year the scene of the South African Brigade's fine stand in the March retreat. But the deep crust of frozen ground prevented digging, and the important local attack of the 8th Division on the 4th March on Fritz Trench above Bouchavesnes had to be carried through without the assistance of the new buried communication, and as most of the above-ground cables were cut, the first news of the assaulting troops was brought by pigeon to the Corps Loft at Etinehem. The attack was fully successful, and the effective use made by the artillery of the excellent observation secured by it, no doubt expedited the general retirement of the enemy in this sector.

A few days later symptoms of this retreat became obvious in the shape of villages burning and large transport movements in the enemy back area. The general withdrawal began on the 15th March, the enemy falling back on the Corps front across the Canal du Nord. As the Fourth Army was not destined to play a part in the spring offensive, it had been heavily depleted both to swell the concentration northwards in preparation for the coming Arras battle, and to take over additional ground from the French, the sector on the XV. Corps right south of the Somme having been occupied by the III. Corps during February. Apart, therefore, from the tremendous transport difficulties due to continuous wet weather succeeding the frost, and the methodical destruction of bridges, roads, and railways, there was not sufficient strength to press the enemy closely, but the advance was conducted methodically, touch with the enemy rearguards on the Corps front being maintained by the Wiltshire Yeomanry and the Corps Cyclist Battalion until a Cavalry Division could come up.

The Signal Company's share in the work was first to maintain direct touch between the Corps Staff and the advanced troops, for which purpose D.R.'s were attached to the cavalry, but by a special effort of B.E. section direct telephone communication was soon secured and maintained. Secondly, the main communication network had to be extended forward at the same rate as the advance, and, as a counter-attack was very possible, the full organization for position warfare accompanied the Corps. The Signal difficulties were doubled on the 25th March, by the sudden withdrawal from line of the XIV. Corps on the right and the consequent extension of the already wide Corps frontage which then stretched from Péronne to Le Transloy.

The Imperial Signal Sections attached for assistance at intervals during the winter had been withdrawn, and, worst of all, the needs of the fighting fronts northwards entirely shut off for a time the supply of line construction material. Consequently, before a single pole or wire could be erected, it had to be released from service in rear, salvaged, and transported forward by the company's lorries over extremely bad and congested roads. Much heavy material had again to be relayed forward over tracks impassable to lorries by teams from the cable sections, and finally carried on the sappers' shoulders over shell-shattered ground impassable even for wagons. Under such handicaps, and in the teeth of continuous blizzards of snow, sleet, and rain, which continued till the end of April, over forty miles of poled route, including much of a heavy permanent nature carrying twenty-four wires, was erected, and two successive moves of the Headquarters of Corps and all subordinate formations accomplished without any loss of communication. The skill, endurance, and ready zeal of the A.S.C. Motor Transport drivers attached to the Company played a great part in the results achieved. They had never failed to meet the severe calls made upon them from time to time during the Somme fighting, but now both the distances and the masses of material to be moved were greater, and the road conditions but little, if any, better.

Early in April the advance reached its limit, and was definitely held up in front of La Vacquerie and Havrincourt—outlying strong points of the Hindenburg Line. On the 17th, Corps Headquarters was established in hutments and tents near Haute-Allaines, after a short interval at P.C. Chapeau. Then the weather at last broke, and with a genial spring sun overhead, a rapidly drying country underfoot, and good news coming through from the Arras front, life under canvas, even in this devastated zone, became pleasant.

Little relaxation of effort was possible however. The Germans on their retreat had accomplished as thorough work in the demolition of signal communications as in their wanton spoliation of civilian property. As every house and every fruit tree was destroyed, so was every pole sawn through when not bodily removed. Scarcely a yard of usable line—cables or open wire—existed in the new area, and the whole of the immense network of communications for stationary warfare had to be reconstituted under continuing supply and transport difficulties, while the hasty work done in the advance had to be overhauled and made permanent.

Scarcely was this task well under way when orders were received to prepare signal plans for an offensive and commence the necessary works as early as possible. The position in regard to materials was alleviated in May by the organization of a temporary Corps Signal Salvage Unit, composed of B.F. section, a platoon of a Labour Company, and the necessary horse and motor Transport under Lieutenant Jack. This made it possible to push forward work on two heavy open-wire routes, running from Corps Headquarters, through Nurlu and Fins, and through Sève Wood, Liéramont, and Heudicourt respectively, with the necessary spur and lateral routes. To economize cable, which remained very short in supply, the subsidiary routes were run as far as possible in light iron wire (60 lb. to the mile), on air line or light hop poles, and considerable use was made of a light type of French cable with all copper conductors salvaged in the back area. This use of low resistance conductors, and the maintaining of good line conditions, made clear speech possible between O.P.'s and H.A. Headquarters, and on special occasions Corps Headquarters, a point of great value in securing rapid and effective counter-battery work. Up to this time all the British field cables, except D 5—too heavy and too scarce for ordinary forward use—had steel conductors, and were, therefore, of high resistance, and good speech could only be obtained on short lines. Plans were also elaborated for a buried cable scheme covering the area between the front line and heads of open wire behind Gouzeaucourt and Gonnelieu respectively. The permanent routes had progressed beyond Fins and Heudicourt, when, towards the end of May, orders arrived for the XV. Corps to hand over to the III. Corps and proceed to Villers-Bretonneux. The cable sections of the Company joined various divisions, and, at the end of May, accompanied them out of the area to unknown destinations.

The remainder of the Company reached Villers-Bretonneux on the 3rd June, and settled down very comfortably in this pleasant little town, destined to be the storm centre of the fighting for Amiens next spring. A small allotment of leave was obtained, making it possible to send away some of the men who had now been fifteen months continuously in the field. The usual refitting proceeded, and opportunity was taken to complete the reorganization necessitated by certain changes in signal establishments that had recently taken effect, and by the increasing numbers of valuable and experienced N.C.O.'s and men who left to take up Imperial commissions in the various branches of the service. The numbers so lost to the Company constituted a striking testimony to the high quality of its *personnel*, and aggregated over eighty before hostilities ceased.

The great and continuing growth in the demands on the Signal Service, particularly in connection with the Heavy Artillery, had for long unduly taxed the available *personnel*, and increase in establishments was overdue. To the Corps Signal Company was, therefore, now added a Heavy Artillery Headquarters Signal Section, with a strength of one officer and thirty-seven other ranks. The *personnel* for this section was obtained from drafts built up on a nucleus of experienced men, mainly from R.E. section. At the same time, a signal sub-section of one officer and twenty-seven other ranks was formed for each H.A. Group, but as H.A. Groups were frequently moved from Corps to Corps, these sub-sections were organized from Imperial R.E. *personnel*. The Company Headquarters Section was also strengthened by the withdrawal of four telegraphists from each cable section, the vacancies being filled with additional pioneers. The Signal Section forming part of the Headquarters of S.A. Infantry Brigade was now affiliated to the Company, and thenceforward drew its reinforcements therefrom. This Section was originally formed by Lieutenant F. W. S. Burton of the Union Post Office and the 3rd Regiment from signallers selected from the infantry battalions. As, however, the Brigade only chanced to serve for two short periods in the same formation as the Signal Company, the story of this Signal Section is that of the Brigade and need not be separately recounted.

The signal instruction for infantry and artillery units, commenced at Long, and so abruptly suspended by the move into line, had during the spring become a permanent feature of the Company's activities. Classes in Carrier Pigeon work had been immediately resumed at Etinehem, and were thenceforward carried on till the end of the war under Lieutenant Egleton and Corporal Jorgenson, with the most valuable results. In the middle of March the

Corps Signal School was reconstituted at Chipilly, with a separate establishment, and Lieutenant Johnson was seconded as Commandant with a staff of four Sergeant-Instructors from the Company. The School then constituted continued to function till after the Armistice, moving with the Corps from point to point, and many hundreds of officers and men passed through the six weeks' courses held at it with a most marked and beneficial effect to the efficiency of Signal work among the fighting troops. Lieutenant Johnson's vacancy was filled by the promotion of C.Q.M.S. C. H. Ison, whose untiring energy had done much to help the Company through its difficulties in the past year.

The interlude at Villers was abruptly cut short by orders to move on the 10th June for a secret destination. As there were no cable sections to accompany, all *personnel* travelled in lorries, and the move was accomplished in two days. The secret was extremely well kept, however, and not until the convoy actually entered Dunkirk on the 11th was it realized that the Corps was to take over the Nieuport Sector—the important bit of line running from the sea along the Yser, which had been held by the French since the momentous days of the first battle of Ypres. Corps Headquarters were established on the 11th in the Casino of Malo-les-Bains, a suburb of Dunkirk, and arrangements for the relief of the 36th French Corps at once put in hand.

THE BELGIAN COAST AND THE BATTLE OF THE DUNES—NOVEMBER 1917.

Though this sector had been for a long period a quiet one, the German artillery concentration opposite it was already great, especially in heavy long range guns, partly because the arc of many of their coast defence batteries covered more or less of the land front, and for the most part were already behind concrete emplacements. Normal trenches in this terrain were impossible, and both sides stood behind breastworks that in the dunes were merely gabions filled with sand ; but here, as on the Ypres front, the liberal use of concrete by the enemy had given his front-line troops, as well as his batteries and command posts, the protection of many " pill-boxes " and concrete shelters of various forms. For a long period the French had held the sector comparatively lightly ;

consequently the whole of the titanic task of mounting a trench warfare offensive fell on the incoming corps. On such terrain the preparations presented extreme and unique difficulties, and those of Signals were enhanced by the fact that not only did the nature of the ground forbid deep cable buries, but very few shallow ones existed ; while the existing communications—naturally inadequate—were almost entirely open wire to within four thousand yards of the front line, and sited along roads certain to be heavily shelled.

British divisions began to arrive in the area on the 15th, bringing the absent cable sections of the Company with them, and between the 20th and 23rd the French divisions in line were relieved by the 1st and 32nd Divisions. Thereafter the Corps Heavy Artillery commenced to move in, the H.A. Signal Section and B.E. Section proceeding to the late French Heavy Artillery Headquarters, D.C.A.L. to a small copse about two miles south of Nieuport, and B.G. Section to Coxyde to prepare for the establishment of a forward exchange.

After a rapid survey of the area, a communication scheme to meet the needs of Corps, Divisions, and the Heavy Artillery on a hitherto unprecedented scale was prepared. Meanwhile the various sections toiled at the familiar task of connecting up the units that were streaming into the area daily, and preparing the new Corps Headquarters at Bray-Dunes Plage—a small wateringplace south of La Panne. The H.A. Section had, even with the assistance of B.E. Section, a particularly strenuous task in coping with the concentration of eleven groups of " heavies," and found it necessary to endeavour to bring into use at once the incomplete French buries. By an evil stroke of luck, the material ordered for this purpose was delayed over a fortnight by the truck containing it being railed to Péronne instead of Dunkirk, owing to the extreme secrecy that enshrouded the movements of the Corps.

The movement of Corps Headquarters to Bray-Dunes was effected on the 29th June, having been somewhat expedited by one of the periodical shellings of Dunkirk by a German long range gun. On the morning of the 27th a twelve-inch shell dropped on the Corps Offices in the Casino at Malo, and inflicted a number of casualties—luckily for the Company, it just missed the Signal Office. A few days later the Heavy Artillery Quarters moved back to the village of Oost Dunkirk, about six thousand yards from the line, and occupied the Villa Rosarie. During the first week in July a considerable increase in hostile shelling was noted, but not to an alarming extent, though a direct hit on the H.A. sections' store rooms put a few telephones *hors de combat;* and no immediate operations were anticipated.

The enemy, however, had decided to nip our attack in the bud by taking the initiative himself, and had only delayed to complete a crushing artillery concentration. Thus about 9.30 a.m. on the 10th July, when many batteries were not yet in position and many others not yet ready for action, an intense bombardment dropped over the whole Corps area up to nine thousand yards behind the front line. With the most admirable accuracy and thoroughness, every village and battery position was searched, and every road of approach swept by heavy shell fire. Forward communications failed almost at once, the bridges across the Yser below Nieuport were destroyed, the breastwork trenches melted away before the storm of high explosive, and when the infantry assault was delivered about 7 p.m. few survivors of the Brigade of the 1st Division that held the trenches across the Yser in front of Nieuport Bain, remained to resist, and the German front line was established on the Yser bank in this sector. On the other flank, at Lombartzyde, the 32nd Division managed by desperate fighting to retain most of the ground in front of Nieuport, but the main German object was achieved ; the approaches to the bridgehead were now limited to the single entry of Nieuport, and the bridgehead itself was so reduced in area as to make a serious attack in force a very desperate venture.

This day was naturally a most trying one for the Signal *personnel.* Nearly all wire communication was lost in the first two hours, and all formations from Corps downwards had to fall back on despatch riders and runners. Very fine work was done by the Company's despatch runners on the shell-swept roads, while the sections strove to patch up and keep going the vital command lines. Thanks to cool and quick repair work by the sappers, and to the use of a short piece of cable trench completed on the previous day, touch was kept with most of the Heavy Artillery Groups continually throughout the day. The observation lines could not, however, be kept going, and thus the batteries not put out of action were blinded, and could not effectively support the infantry across the river. Oost Dunkirk village suffered heavily, and after nightfall the H.A. Staff were forced to move into the sand dunes half a mile to the flank, when temporary cables were run back to the signal office at the Villa Rosarie, which enjoyed protection in a sand-bagged shelter behind the house. As this shelter was the only place in the village enjoying any degree of protection, it became during that day and night a temporary aid post for wounded and a refuge for the few remaining villagers. Amid these conditions, and deafened by the crashing explosions of the shells among the houses, the telephonists managed to carry on with wonderful efficiency for twenty-four consecutive hours. Conditions at Coxyde Signal Office with B.G. section were very similar.

Much to the general surprise, the attack was not resumed on the following day, and while every nerve was strained to get the existing lines restored, work on the new communications began and was pressed forward night and day. The buried scheme originally planned provided for four forward trenches, one along the sea coast, one through the dunes, one partly French and already dug through the polder area, and one consisting of cable laid in the bed of the Nieuport Canal—all to be connected by a lateral trench running through H.A. Headquarters, which was to become the chief maintenance and test point. Lieutenant Collins with B.E. section and a rapidly increasing number of Imperial sections, loaned from Army Signals, was entrusted with this work, assisted by Lieutenant Dobson. In view of the experiences of the 10th, two additional trenches were added to the plan, one from a main open route junction point behind Coxyde, forward along the fringe of the dunes to H.A. Headquarters, and the other along the sea-beach above highwater mark from Corps Headquarters at Bray-Dunes to the same point.

This latter trench, which contained twenty-five pair dry core cable, was completed by Lieutenant Hill with skilled cable jointers from 51 Air Line. Labour was made freely available by the Corps Staff, and as material now came forward rapidly, up to two thousand men a day were employed on these works. The forward portion of the scheme presented great difficulty, as the area was now so sown with batteries that it was almost impossible to trace the trenches so as to avoid battery positions and the shelling which they attracted. The greater part of the work could only be done by night because of enemy observation ; and, further, time did not admit of the usual detailed preparation for the working parties.

Nevertheless, all works were completed for the attack ; and taking into account the continuous heavy shelling, with light casualties.

The experiment made on the Somme of using a kite balloon to maintain communication with the front line, was now repeated ; and as a separate balloon was now placed at the disposal of Second-Lieutenant Wilson and a visual signalling party, the result was satisfactory.

Though all other preparations were well advanced, including the seclusion of the 1st Division in a " hush " camp on the coast, where they were specially rehearsed in landing operations from the sea, the attack was postponed from date to date, until it finally became evident by the transfer of a large proportion of the heavy batteries to the Ypres front, that the slow progress made there owing to weather and " pill-boxes " was likely to postpone the Nieuport offensive indefinitely.

During the interval, the rival artilleries waged a furious and continuous duel. The forward buried system, unavoidably shallow from the nature of the ground, was continuously broken by shell fire. During September the cable trenches were blown up by direct hits on the average nearly twice a day. The repairs were most difficult and laborious owing both to the persistent shelling and the rise of the water level everywhere after the wet weather of August. Even with the sappers of three cable sections—B.F., B.E., and A.U. Imperial Cable Section, and two area Signal Detachments from the Fourth Army, it became impossible to keep going satisfactorily the network of forty miles of trenches containing 1,200 miles of cable ; and finally the assistance of the Corps Cyclist Battalion was obtained to dig diversion trenches in the worst shell areas, and a new trench in the Belgian area in substitution of the cable laid in the Nieuport Canal, the insulation of which began to fail soon after laying.

During this period the sappers stationed at the forward test points had a most trying experience. Owing to the frequent breakdowns, they were perpetually working on the cable trenches by day and by night, employed in testing and substituting lines. The frequent use of gas shell made it necessary that at their isolated points they should secure the gas blankets of their dug-out entrances at night, and this inevitably produced an atmosphere little inferior to the gas itself. Two concreted test points in the " polder " area, taken over from the French, were conspicuous after shelling had destroyed all arboreal cover. The Germans apparently decided that these were gun positions, and favoured them with special attention, managing finally to secure three direct hits—two innocuous, however unnerving to the inmates ; but the third on P.C. 6 burst square on the roof, and though only slightly bending the steel rails embedded in the concrete, killed a sapper of B.F. section inside. One small dug-out on the canal bank, P.C. 18, disappeared altogether after an eleven-inch howitzer bombardment of a neighbouring battery, but fortunately there was no occupant at the time.

Corps Headquarters moved to La Panne at the beginning of September ; but the location had evidently been given away by a spy, as it was heavily shelled by a long range gun a fortnight later, and consequently retransferred to Bray-Dunes. Though as the autumn drew on activity in the sector died down, all ranks had reason to welcome the relief of the Corps by the XXXVI. French Corps that commenced on the 19th November. On the 20th the Headquarters of the Company, under Captain Dingwall, who had been acting as A.W. Signals since September during Lieutenant-Colonel Harrison's absence on sick leave, moved to Hinges near Béthune, and commenced to take over from the XI. Corps—then under orders for Italy—a sector between Béthune and Armentières.

THE LYS AREA.

After some readjustments of frontage in December, the XV. Corps settled down to hold the sector in front of the Lys, from Houplines to Laventie, with the Portuguese Corps on the right and the Anzac Corps on the left. In January 1918 Corps Headquarters were shifted from Hinges to La Motte-aux-Bois in front of the Forest of Nieppe, and Heavy Artillery, with the H.A. and B.E. sections, to Estaires, where 51 Air Line was already established. A further reorganization of the Company now took place. As cable sections rarely, if ever, performed the mobile work for which their horse transport was provided, the decision was reached to disband one cable section in each Corps, to reduce the strength of the Corps air line section to forty-two all ranks with one heavy and two light lorries, and with the surplus *personnel* so accruing form an additional air line for each Corps. B.G. section was, accordingly, converted into the nucleus of the new 91 Air Line Section, to which Lieutenant

Dobson was appointed. At the same time, " Q " Wireless Section became an integral portion of the Signal Company, and was taken over by Lieutenant McArthur, with 2nd Lieutenant Fitzgeorge as second officer, the Imperial *personnel* being rapidly replaced by South Africans. A second officer was also authorized for the Heavy Artillery Section, and Lieutenant M. Cohen, who had been attached to a brigade of the 8th Division since his arrival from England in November 1917, was appointed.

The communications here were such as would serve on a thinly held and lightly shelled front. Buries were few and becoming inefficient with age ; the light open-wire routes which formed the bulk of the communication were run close up to the front line. The defection of Russia made it certain that the Allies would be thrown on the defensive in the spring ; and as the Lys covered Hazebrouck and the direct route to Calais, it was probable that the sector would become a main front of attack. Ample and secure communications were, therefore, a first necessity, and a complete scheme was prepared on a scale of magnitude and thoroughness which surpassed any previous performance. All trenches were to be seven feet deep and carry no less than thirty pairs of wires.

Work could not be commenced before the 25th January, owing to the whole Lys Valley, which is very low lying, becoming waterlogged by heavy rain. At first the labour available was very limited, owing to the urgent demands for defence works in the battle zone, and for the construction and wiring of a new emergency line of five trenches on the north bank of the river. Early in February the labour position improved, and frequently over one thousand five hundred men were employed simultaneously. The sappers had a strenuous time, and, but for the assistance of a party from the Corps Cyclists, who by long association with Signals had become relatively skilled, could not have kept up the pace. By unremitting effort the Corps Section of the trenches was completed by the beginning of March, and a portion of the work originally assigned to divisions taken over.

While the other sections were so engaged, B.F. was employed on another section of the scheme in and around Armentières itself. In this town a considerable underground sewer system existed, and though not comparable with the underways of Arras, yet these sewers proved extremely valuable as affording ready-made covered ways for cable. B.F. accordingly spent two months in laying

312 APPENDIX II.

securely many miles of cable. The new 91 Air Line Section meanwhile pushed on the necessary additions to the open-wire routes forward from Corps Headquarters. Hostile artillery activity began to increase considerably in March, and about the middle of the month became so marked that from this and other symptoms an immediate attack was expected. This cut off the supply of labour, but the sappers were busier than ever in bringing the cables already laid into use by temporary joints, without waiting for the construction of the test dug-outs.

This alarm proved for the time false, the offensive commencing instead on the Third and Fifth Army fronts on the 21st March. The immediate effect was the withdrawal of all the divisions in the Corps, and their replacement with exhausted divisions from the south—the 34th and 40th—who naturally could provide no labour. The greatest anxiety was now felt lest the communication should not be finished in time, and work was rushed day and night. With the assistance of the Corps Cyclists temporary sandbagged test points were erected where the concrete work was still lacking, and when the storm finally broke on the 9th April practically all cable laid had been joined up and was working, and three-quarters of the original scheme had been completed.

The attack began at 4.30 a.m. with an intense bombardment extending back to and beyond the river, followed by an infantry assault about 7 a.m., which immediately broke through the Portuguese on the Corps right. There were no reserves available to man effectively the new line dug on the northern bank, and during the afternoon the enemy crossed at Bac St. Maur, and by 7 p.m. had forced our firing line back behind the signal test point at Croix de Bac. Communications had held well so far; the 34th Division was still maintaining its ground on the left round Armentières, and there was hope of an immediate restoration of the situation by counter-attack. The lineman at this point—Corporal Shepherd of the H.A. section—was, therefore, instructed not to destroy the lines, but to leave them all through, and fall back on the next test point. He did so, but omitted to put through one of the lines. On ascertaining this when he reached H.A. headquarters, he voluntarily returned and managed to re-enter the dug-out, which was now in No Man's Land, and put the line through. Though this dug-out passed into the enemy's hands during the night, and after a temporary reversal of fortune again next morning, direct communication from Corps headquarters to troops in Armentières was maintained over the cables passing through it till afternoon on the following day, when the evacuation of the town began.

By next morning the Germans had forced the river to Estaires. This town had been intensely shelled all day, and B.E. Section billet was blown up early in the morning. Nevertheless, the Corps Exchange was kept going till a late hour that night by Lieutenant Hill with 51 Air Line and a party of operators from the Headquarters section.

During the following days, the 10th, 11th, and 12th, the Corps was steadily driven back by the heavy thrust made by the enemy for Hazebrouck. The 29th and 31st Divisions and the 4th Guards Brigade were successively thrown in, but their desperate fighting only succeeded in slowing the German advance, until the entry into line of the 1st Australian Division on the night of the 12th, when the enemy was finally brought to a stop on the edge of the Nieppe Forest. Thereafter the storm centre shifted gradually to the northward round Kemmel and Messines, while on the Corps front the battle died down to local combats.

The effort to keep up communications during these days tested every one to the limit. Units were changing location like figures in a kaleidoscope, and nearly the whole of the existing system of lines had passed into the enemy's hands. However, by the most strenuous efforts, touch was maintained throughout the retreat, and the good work done was recognized by the Corps commander ; for in a letter addressed to Colonel Harrison, he conveyed his appreciation of the work carried out by all ranks of the Company during the recent operations. He added that he realized that, owing to the untiring energy and devotion to duty shown by all ranks, a very high standard of communication was maintained, and thanked all for the efforts made and the results achieved. The general commanding the Heavy Artillery also made reference in a special order of the day to the particularly good work done by the H.A. Signal Section, under Lieutenant Collins, in the following words :—

" That the Heavy Artillery was able to cover the whole Corps front with its fire during each day, and to withdraw to fresh positions each night, testifies also to the excellence of the staff work—especially in connection with telephonic communication."

On the 11th Corps Headquarters fell back to Wardrecques, between St. Omer and Hazebrouck, leaving an advanced Signal Office at La Motte until the evening of the 12th. During the next few days it became evident that the front was established again—at any rate temporarily—and the work of restoring the normal network of communication at once commenced, at first with great shortage of material, as all forward signal dumps had been captured.

Captain Dingwall, whose health had suffered under the continuous strain in France, now left the Company to join L Signal Battalion, and was replaced by Captain Ross, who was relieved of the Heavy Artillery Section by Lieutenant Collins. Lieutenant Hill took up duty at headquarters, and Lieutenant McArthur left the Wireless Section for 51 Air Line.

At this time also Lieutenant-General Sir J. P. Ducane was summoned to replace Sir Henry Rawlinson on the Versailles Council, and the XV. Corps was henceforward commanded by Lieutenant-General Sir B. de Lisle. The departure of General Ducane was much regretted by the Company, as he had always taken a close interest in communications, and showed keen appreciation of the work done, as is shown by the following extract from a letter written by him to Colonel Harrison after the termination of hostilities :—

" In the many bright spots of the XV. Corps, I have always maintained, and always will maintain, that the Signal Service was far away the best Signal Service of any other organization in France. Not only was there a very thorough grasp of the work, but always—what was so pleasant to find—there was a desire to go out of your way to help. It is with the greatest pleasure that I write to say how much I always appreciate having the South African Signal Company in the XV. Corps. They were not only highly efficient in all departments of this work, but I can honestly say they were the most energetic, hard-working, well-disciplined, and courteous body of men that I have come across in my experience of the Army.

" I always felt in dealing with you that nothing was ever too much trouble for you or your men, and that no matter how exacting the demands made upon you—and they were often very heavy indeed—no effort would be spared to carry them through successfully. Never were we let down during the most trying times—on the Somme, on the coast, or on the Lys. During the enemy's attack on the Lys in April 1918, the truly remarkable way in which all our communications held out for three days, till we were compelled to abandon La Motte, greatly facilitated the exercise of the command of the Corps during those difficult days, and was an eloquent testimony of the thoroughness and skill with which the work of preparation had been carried out."

The final holding up of the Germans at Kemmel on the 28th April made it possible to commence effective work on the defences at Hazebrouck, and during the next few months successive lines of trenches and belts of wire came into existence, and seamed the country as far back as St. Omer. The Company's share in these preparations was work on a buried cable scheme which started early in May, and gradually developed as labour and material were obtainable, until, when the advance began, a network of trenches extended across the whole Corps area for 13,000 yards in depth and 7,000 in breadth, embodying thirty miles of seven-foot deep trench and nearly 1,200 miles of pair cable. This work, though never tested by another offensive, was of great value during the prolonged artillery duel which followed the Battle of the Lys. The open-wire routes were continuously shelled or bombed down, for in this sector, as on the coast, aeroplane bombing was a nightly event.

The series of successful minor operations carried out by the Corps in July and August, including the capture of Méteren, and the devastating effect of our superior and incessantly active artillery, no doubt quickened the German decision to evacuate the Lys salient. This evacuation commenced at the end of August, and thenceforward all ranks were occupied in the rapid restoration of communications through the devastated area, now as broad as the old Somme battlefield. An attempt was made to utilize the old buries laid down by the XV. and other Corps before the retreat ;

but these were too effectively destroyed by the enemy to admit of rapid restoration.

After the successful attack of the Belgian and Second British Armies at the end of September, in which the XV. Corps co-operated on the right flank, headquarters were moved to St. Jans-Cappel on the 4th October, and on the 21st, to Mouvaux, near Tourcoing, following the rapid retreat of the enemy to the Scheldt. On this occasion a fast piece of work was done by 91 Air Line and B.E. Cable Section, two lines being completed across the Lys to the new headquarters—a distance of nearly twenty miles—in one day.

The Signal portion of the preparations for forcing the passage of the Scheldt filled the period up to the 10th November; but as the enemy retired during the night, and the Armistice was proclaimed the following day, they proved unnecessary.

The Corps was not selected to accompany the advance to the Rhine, and so it fell to the lot of B.E. Section on the 12th to lay the last and farthest forward cable in France, from the Scheldt, crossing at Pecq to an observation point on the eastern side.

APPENDIX III.

THE MEDICAL SERVICES.

WHEN the South African Expeditionary Force was organized on the termination of the campaign in German South-West Africa, Colonel P. G. Stock was appointed S.M.O., and in addition to the South African Medical Corps *personnel* who volunteered for regimental duties, arranged for the mobilization of one Field Ambulance and one General Hospital. The former, under the command of Lieutenant-Colonel G. H. Usmar, S.A.M.C., assembled at Potchefstroom with the 1st South African Infantry Brigade; while the General Hospital was formed at Wynberg, the *personnel* being largely composed of volunteers from the staffs of No. 1 General Hospital, Wynberg, and No. 2 General Hospital, Maitland, and included representatives from each of the four provinces of the Union. It subsequently provided the *personnel* for the Depot in England, and the South African Military Hospital at Richmond, which was afterwards built and organized.

No hospital equipment was available in South Africa, but the official Advisory Committee on Voluntary Aid, of which Sir Thomas Smartt was chairman, met the difficulty by voting £15,000 to purchase it on arrival in England, and a further £1,500 to augment the equipment taken by the Field Ambulance.

Both units accompanied the Infantry Brigade to England, the General Hospital embarking on H.M.T. *Balmoral Castle* at Cape Town on 25th September, and the Field Ambulance on H.M.T. *Kenilworth Castle* on October 10, 1915. On arrival there, they proceeded to the R.A.M.C. Depot at Twezeldown, near Aldershot. At the depot the training of the Field Ambulance proceeded under its own officers, and, with the rest of the Brigade, it was present at Bordon when her Majesty the Queen reviewed the troops on December 2, 1915. On 29th December the unit proceeded by route march to Farnham, there entraining for Devonport, where it embarked on H.M.T. *Corsican* for Egypt, Alexandria being reached on January 13, 1916.

In the meantime, the *personnel* of No. 1 General Hospital—which had been particularly fortunate in securing the services of some of the leading surgeons and physicians and most experienced nurses in South Africa—was temporarily detailed to strengthen the staffs of various Imperial hospitals in England. On 20th December, however, the unit was reassembled at Bournemouth, where it took over and staffed the Mont Dore Military Hospital, which, under an Imperial officer as commandant, had just been equipped for 520 patients.

In February 1916 the control of the " Grata Quies " Auxiliary Hospital was transferred to the Mont Dore, which became a " Central Hospital," and on April 1, 1916, seventeen additional auxiliary hospitals, situated in the districts of Poole, Wimbourne, Swanage, Sherbourne, and Yeovil, were affiliated, increasing the number of beds controlled to over 1,200.

The first patients from overseas were admitted on 8th January, the majority being medical cases, and although a number of severe cases of " trench feet " from Gallipoli were taken in, few wounded were received up to the time the unit left on July 3, 1916, when it proceeded to Aldershot preparatory to joining the British Expeditionary Force in France.

When the decision to send South African troops to England became known, a number of prominent South Africans in London formed a committee under the chairmanship of Lord Gladstone—until recently the Governor-General—to start a fund for the establishment of a hospital and for the general comfort of the troops. On the arrival of the contingent in England this movement received renewed attention, a proposal then being under consideration to erect huts to accommodate some three hundred patients, as a South African wing to the Royal Victoria Hospital at Netley. On further investigation, however, it was found that the site, although in many respects an ideal one in the summer, would not have been suitable for South African troops during the winter, and further search had to be made. Many places and buildings were inspected, and finally a site in Richmond Park, for which his Majesty the King was graciously pleased to grant the necessary permission, was selected, and no more beautiful, convenient, and healthy spot could possibly have been obtained.

Colonel P. G. STOCK, C.B., C.B.E.,
D.D.M.S., South African Forces.

Much of the success of this hospital was due to the time and care spent over the plans, and Mr. Allison, the chief architect of the Office of Works, was always ready to adopt any recommendations made by Lieutenant-Colonel Stock and the expert sub-committee of officers of No. 1 General Hospital who were dealing with the project. The desire was to provide 500 beds, but for financial reasons it was decided to start with 300, on the basis of plans which provided for future necessary extensions.

The construction was begun early in March, and on June 16, 1916, the hospital was formally opened by its patroness, H.R.H. Princess Christian, being then taken over fully equipped as a gift from South Africans by the D.D.M.S., London District, on behalf of the Army Council.

On the opening of the hospital, the S.A.M.C. Depot in England was transferred to Richmond, and a redistribution of the *personnel* of No. 1 General Hospital carried out, which enabled a South African Staff to be placed in charge of Richmond without interfering with the efficiency of the former unit. Major Thornton, the adjutant and registrar of No. 1 South African General Hospital, succeeded Lieutenant-Colonel Stock in command at Richmond, and Captain Basil Brooke was appointed adjutant and registrar of No. 1 General Hospital. Before, however, proceeding further with the history of the South African Hospital at Richmond, it will be convenient to follow the fortunes of the units which left England.

On January 13, 1916, No. 1 South African Field Ambulance arrived at Alexandria on H.M.T. *Corsican*, and marched the following day to Mex Camp, where the rest of the Brigade was encamped. Its history is included in that of the South African Infantry Brigade, with which it was associated from this date until the cessation of hostilities.

On the arrival of No. 1 South African General Hospital at Aldershot, the final touches were given to the unit, and about 400 shipping tons of stores and equipment drawn, which, by a special arrangement with the Army Council, had been paid for out of the £15,000 voted by Sir Thomas Smartt's Committee in Cape Town.

On 12th July the unit entrained for Southampton, there to embark on H.M.T. *Huntcraft*. The ship berthed at Havre about 10.30 a.m. on the 13th, and as she was urgently required elsewhere, the unloading at once commenced; and on the following day the unit—together with its stores and equipment—left for Abbeville, which was reached on 15th July.

Here it was found that the hospital would be established next to No. 2 Stationary Hospital, an Imperial unit which had been there for some time. The necessity for not interfering with the ripening harvest considerably curtailed the choice of a site, the ground allotted being a ploughed field on the slope of the hills overlooking the valley of the Somme. Abbeville itself lay about a mile away in the valley, but the railway station and "triage" were on the far side of the town and must have been nearly three miles from the hospital.

Some hospital marquees had already been erected, but the lay-out of the hospital was greatly handicapped by the cramped area of ground then available. As the corn was reaped more ground became vacant, and, later on, by frequent striking and repitching of tents, the hospital gradually took a more symmetrical and workable shape.

When the unit arrived in France the First Battle of the Somme had begun, and hospital accommodation was urgently required for the large number of casualties. So, in the absence of any kind of building, a store tent was converted into an operating tent; an improvised sterilizing shelter erected; and within forty-eight hours of arrival patients were admitted and every available surgeon hard at work.

In those early days the wide surgical experience and considered judgment of Lieutenant-Colonel Ritchie Thomson proved invaluable. He had accepted the post of chief surgeon when the hospital was mobilized in South Africa, and many a sorely wounded man owes his life and limb to his skill and judgment.

The initial difficulties were many: buildings and engineering services were almost impossible to obtain, and it was not until the end of November that the operating block—the first building to be erected—was completed. All, however, were willing workers, and it was not long before additional tentage was pitched and Major Merritt had organized the kitchens, stores, and a hundred and one odd things appertaining to the Quartermaster's Department, all of which mean so much to the efficiency and comfort of any hospital.

Until early in August the hospital was without its own nursing Sisters—these services being performed by members of the

Q.A.I.M.N.S., the Canadian Military Nursing Service, and English V.A.D.'s, who did all that hard work and devotion to duty could do to make up for the shortage in number. On 5th August, however, Matron Creagh and twenty-one members of the S.A.M.N.S. arrived from England, and the greatest difficulties in this respect were over. The nurses' camp had to be pitched in the wooded ground of a château some little distance off; but when the storm clouds rolled up the valley, and the winter rains set in, they had perforce to be billeted in the town until the huts which were contemplated for them were completed.

Situated as it was at the advanced base in a convenient position for their reception, the hospital, during the autumn of 1916, received a large number of wounded direct from the Somme battlefield. Amongst the earliest admissions in July 1916 were South Africans wounded at Delville Wood, and towards the end of July General Lukin was one of the first officer patients.

The most severely wounded journeyed by specially-fitted hospital barges, which, from the casualty clearing stations around Corbie, floated down the Somme to Abbeville, where the patients were disembarked and taken by motor ambulances to the hospital. The use of barges was restricted to those cases who were unable to stand the strain of a journey by train. Usually they travelled in pairs, but on more than one occasion during the autumn of 1916 patients from six barges were admitted during the twenty-four hours. Towards the end of 1916 the barges ceased running, as the winter rains had rendered the passage down the Somme too dangerous, and they were not again employed, as the advance in the spring of 1917 carried the fighting away from the river.

Fortunately, during the first few weeks after the arrival of the unit in France, the weather was fine, but even then difficulties were experienced in regard to the main road leading to the hospital. For part of the way this was formed by " sleepers," but as the supply of them gave out beech planking had to be substituted. This quickly " warped," and becoming displaced with the constant traffic, was always a source of trouble, as the underlying chalk during the dry weather quickly powdered to a fine dust, and later, when the rains set in, turned into a particularly greasy form of mud.

As soon as materials and labour became available, the " sleeper track " was continued, and a large " triage " constructed on which the ambulance wagons could turn; but it was not until many months later that it became possible to build a macadamized road connecting the hospital with the Route d'Amiens. The old entrance was then utilized as an exit for empty wagons, and the original signboard of the hospital, on which Major Merritt had painted the Springbok badge, was removed to the new entrance.

Progress was gradually made in the erection of temporary buildings, and by the end of 1916 there was accommodation in huts for 120 patients. It was obvious, however, that for that winter at least the majority of beds would be under canvas, and a particularly successful form of sliding door with windows at the top was designed; and with the funds available a local contractor was engaged, who quickly fitted them at each end of the tented wards. At the same time the Royal Engineers undertook the installation of stoves and wood flooring, and with doors closed and the sides of the tents fastened down the tented wards were really most comfortable. "Duck" boarding also gradually became more plentiful.

During the period July 23, 1916, to December 31, 1916, the total admissions were 6,436, of whom 3,032 were "battle casualties" and 3,404 "sick." During the same period 5,719 were "discharged hospital." Of these 673 were returned to duty; 548 transferred to convalescent depots; 3,306 evacuated to the United Kingdom; and 1,192 transferred to hospitals at other bases in France. Five hundred and eighty-eight major operations were performed; and there were in all, for the same period, 236 deaths, or—calculated on the number of admissions—a percentage of 3.68. This comparatively high mortality is explained by the fact that practically every case admitted to this hospital was seriously wounded—the barges, from which the large majority of cases were received, only carrying those cases which were unfit to travel by other means of transport. The mortality was further increased owing to the fact that this hospital was the nearest General Hospital to the Somme front, and many moribund patients were taken off ambulance trains on account of their being too ill to travel to more distant bases. By the end of the year, in addition to the operation block, hutted accommodation for 120 patients was erected, and in the early part of 1917 hutted quarters for the nursing staff and rooms for officers', sergeants', and men's messes were added, as well as buildings for part of the quartermaster's stores.

Early in the year instructions were received from General

Headquarters that the hospital was to be enlarged from 520 beds to a normal capacity of 1,120 beds, with a " crisis expansion " to 1,500 beds. The hospital remained on this basis, and during the latter part of 1917, and not infrequently during 1916, as many as 1,600 to 1,700 patients were accommodated at one time.

The total admissions for the year 1917 were 19,109, of which 7,613 were battle casualties and 11,496 were sick. During the same period there were 18,277 discharges. Of this number 2,638 were returned to duty, 4,253 were transferred to convalescent depots, 8,749 were evacuated to the United Kingdom, and 2,637 were transferred to hospitals at other bases in France. One thousand two hundred and ten major operations were performed during the year 1917. For the same period, including eleven cases brought in for burial, there were 181 deaths in the hospital. Of these 128 were due to wounds—a percentage of 1.68 ; and 53 were due to sickness— a percentage of .46. The death rate from all causes for this year worked out at .94 per cent.

Promises of hutted accommodation, both for patients and personnel, were current for at least twelve months. Nothing, however, happened in this direction, except that an administration block and a new kitchen for the hospital were built ; and in October 1917, with keen remembrances of the previous winter, it was decided to erect such huts as was possible with labour supplied by the staff of the hospital. A start was made, with the idea of housing the men of the company who were over forty years of age, and a hut was built, using discarded telegraph poles as the principals, covered with corrugated iron and lined with wood—the lining being bought from funds provided by the South African Hospital and Comforts Fund at a cost of, approximately, £120.

Stimulated by the success of the first, the building of the second hut was then taken in hand; and eventually, with the assistance of the engineer services, comfortable quarters for all the personnel were erected. In January 1918 six hospital " Adrian " huts were erected, but were not completed until the end of March, chiefly owing to the lack of labour and uncertainty as to whether the hospital would have to be evacuated. Three double " Nissen " hospital huts were subsequently added—the last not being quite finished when the armistice was signed. The erection of a further eight, which would have completed the building programme of the hospital, was cancelled.

For the first few months all traffic to the hospital had to pass through a neighbouring hospital—No. 2 Stationary, R.A.M.C.—this being not only inconvenient, but leading to congestion. Later, a metalled road was made through the South African Hospital leading to the Amiens road and looping within the hospital. This meant that traffic was easily managed, and made the handling of convoys infinitely easier.   In the summer of 1918 a tarred surface was put on to this road, which proved a great help in keeping down the dust.

The necessity for a special railway siding for the three large hospitals in this area to avoid the long, rough, and frequently interrupted journeys by ambulance from and to the main station was also met.

A church was erected within the precincts of the hospital, the cost of which was defrayed partly by subscriptions received from the patients and personnel, and partly by a donation of £75 from the South African Hospital and Comforts Fund, London. It was dedicated in the name of St. Winifred to the memory of the late staff nurse—Miss Winifred Munro, South African Military Nursing Service—and as a tribute to her devotion to duty.

In December 1917 the hospital was specially selected for the reception and treatment of cases of fracture of the femur. Beds for the accommodation of 200 such cases were provided—50 being reserved for officers, and 150 for other ranks. The special bed and technique devised at the hospital were afterwards adopted as the standard for the British Army.

During the German offensive of 1918 the hospital passed through what was its period of most intense activity. The medical staff was depleted to replace casualties in the South African Field Ambulance and other units in the forward areas, while reinforcements from the male personnel were sent to the Field Ambulance. Practically all the female nursing staffs from this district were withdrawn, on account of the enemy advance and the frequent bombing at night by hostile aeroplanes of the back areas. Thus the number of medical officers in charge of wards was reduced to 8 instead of the normal 22 ; the male personnel fell to 188—the normal establishment being 212 ; while the female nursing staff, with a normal establishment of 88, was reduced to 8.

With this depleted staff it would have appeared almost impossible to look after a normal number of patients, but many more than normal had to be dealt with during the last week of March, 1,820 being admitted and 2,365 discharged.

Many of these received at the hospital their first medical attention since leaving the battlefield, and a very large number had to be operated upon immediately.

This involved teams working in the operating theatre day and night, but all members of the unit rose to the occasion and worked with a splendid will and cheerfulness under these trying conditions.

The huts recently erected for accommodating the *personnel* had to be evacuated by them to make room for patients, of whom as many as ninety slightly wounded were packed into one hut on stretchers. The men were crowded into the remaining three huts, and the overflow slept on the football field.

Nor did the work end here, for, owing to the threat of hostile air attacks, it became urgently necessary to dig protective trenches for patients, sisters, officers, and other ranks, and also to erect sandbagged revetments around the wards which contained the helpless patients. Outside assistance at this time was unprocurable, as all labour was fully employed in the digging of a defensive system at Flixecourt to protect the town of Abbeville, and the task therefore fell on all ranks of the *personnel*. Soon after this air alarms became an almost nightly occurrence, and even when raids did not actually take place, sleep was broken. But the nursing staff and all inmates of the hospital passed through this prolonged period of physical and mental strain without failing to respond adequately to the demands made on them. Though no definite attack was made by hostile aircraft on the hospital, bombs on several occasions fell uncomfortably near, one actually falling inside the grounds. This fortunately buried itself before exploding, and, beyond tearing the roof of a tent used as a carpenter's shop, did no damage.

The approach of the enemy and the frequency of bombing raids made the retention of cases of fracture of the femur in this hospital inadvisable, and on that account as many as possible were evacuated to the United Kingdom, together with the greater portion of the special equipment used for these cases.

Not long after the last consignment was despatched the Allied offensive began, and the heavy influx of fractured femur cases— amounting to more than 150 in the hospital at one time— made it necessary to use improvised apparatus for dealing with a number increased to this extent, in spite of the fact that as many of these cases as possible were at once evacuated to the United Kingdom.

During the months of June and July 1918 the admissions of sick to the hospital were large, owing to an epidemic of influenza. Since then admissions steadily increased, both of sick and wounded, due to the offensive which began in the latter part of July and which continued up to the signing of the armistice.

During September the admissions reached the figure of 3,276, while in October they numbered 3,214, and the discharges 3,318. For the period of January 1 to November 30, 1918, the total admissions were 20,089. Of these 8,716 were battle casualties, and 11,373 were sick; discharges for the same period amounted to 19,921. Of these, 4,196 were returned to duty; 4,229 were transferred to convalescent depots; 9,028 were evacuated to the United Kingdom; and 2,468 were transferred to other hospitals in France.

All the tented wards were equipped with sliding doors, the first of which were provided out of South African funds. These were made by a French contractor to our design, and the type was afterwards adopted for all hospitals in this area. The engineer services eventually supplied the remainder of the wards with similar doors.

A considerable amount of extra equipment was also provided out of South African funds, notably, an extra operating table, portable ray apparatus for use in the fractured femur wards, additional surgical instruments, and the apparatus necessary for Ionic medication.

The appearance of the hospital grounds improved from year to year, grass lawns and flower-beds being laid out, and vegetable gardening being carried on each year on a progressively larger scale.

From the early days of the unit in France a field adjoining the hospital was available for purposes of recreation, the rent being paid from hospital funds. During all seasons of the year it was made full use of by the unit for football, hockey, cricket, and other games. Badminton and tennis courts were constructed in the officers' and sisters' quarters, and a tennis court was made on ground adjoining the recreation field for the use of other ranks of the unit.

In June 1917 a surgical team for duty at a casualty clearing station was provided by the unit, and performed continuous duty in the forward areas until December of that year. Since then a surgical team performed duty in the front areas on eight occasions. In addition, nursing sisters from time to time were detailed for duty on ambulance trains and for nursing duties and as anæsthetists at casualty clearing stations.

On July 10, 1917, the hospital was honoured by a visit from her Majesty the Queen and his Royal Highness the Prince of Wales. Her Majesty inspected three of the wards in the Hospital and the operating theatre block, and before leaving was graciously pleased to express her entire satisfaction with the work of the Hospital.

To return to the South African Military Hospital at Richmond. In September 1916 the Army Council, on its own account, proposed to add to the accommodation; the Committee, however, considered that, in view of the fact that the provision of 500 beds had been originally contemplated, the additional accommodation proposed should be undertaken by the Committee. This necessitated a further appeal for funds; but, to avoid delay, Mr. Otto Beit generously gave a very substantial contribution. Eventually the total donations received from the issue of the second appeal assured the extension being carried through. The work was pressed forward, and the extension was opened for patients in February 1917. It was, however, hardly in use when a demand was made for further beds. This was met by the Committee converting into wards the quarters originally built for orderlies, and by renting a neighbouring house as an annex, so that in April 1917 the total accommodation for patients had increased to 620 beds.

Early in 1918 the War Office, seeing that the Richmond Military Hospital was almost entirely filled with South African patients, proposed to the Committee that the South African and the Richmond hospitals should be amalgamated, the combined hospitals to be known as the South African Military Hospital. The Committee readily agreed, and the two hospitals were completely amalgamated on July 1, 1918.

The enlarged hospital provided 1,098 beds; but even this was not sufficient, and 250 emergency beds were added by billeting patients in the neighbourhood. In addition, four auxiliary hospitals were attached, bringing the total number of beds to 1,321, or, including billets, 1,571.

The Park section of the combined hospitals stood on an enclosed site of about twelve acres, the actual area of the building being about two and one-third acres. The construction throughout was of timber with felt and weather-board linings on the outside, and asbestos board-sheeting on the inside of the walls and ceilings of all wards and principal rooms. A special feature of this section was the bath ward, with six fire-clay continuous baths for the treatment of patients suffering from severe wounds.

The Grove Road extension was a brick building, and consisted for the most part of modern infirmary wards supplemented by additional wards in old buildings.

The equipment of the Park section was entirely provided by the Committee, while that of the Grove Road section was found by the Board of Guardians and the War Office, and was only where necessary supplemented by the Committee.

Towards the end of 1916 the Committee offered the privilege of naming a bed in the hospital to any persons or institutions making a gift of £25, and of naming a ward for a donation of £600. The appeal resulted in 99 beds and 8 wards being thus named, approximately 265 of the beds being the gifts of schools in South Africa, the organization for these being initiated and carried out by Mr. Maskew Miller of Cape Town.

The principal corridors and rooms in the hospital were named after well-known streets or places in South Africa, all the principal towns in the Union being represented. The result of this, and of placing the tablets over the beds, was that familiar names greeted the South African visitor—a happy idea on the part of the Committee, and one which was much appreciated by the sick and wounded of the contingent.

The Committee expended approximately £45,000 on building the hospital and its extensions, and £19,000 on equipment. The former figure, however, includes a sum of approximately £2,000 expended in erecting a concert hall and certain workshops, while the latter figure includes considerable sums spent on replacements. That the money was well spent is shown by the fact that the hospital was always regarded as one of the model war hospitals in the United Kingdom.

The medical staff consisted of thirteen officers of the South African Medical Corps, and eleven civilian practitioners, who for various causes were not eligible for commissions in the S.A.M.C.

Various changes naturally occurred in the staff owing to inter-changes being effected from time to time with the units in France. When Lieutenant-Colonel Thornton took over the command he was succeeded as registrar by Captain Coghlan, S.A.M.C., who in turn was succeeded by Major J. C. A. Rigby, S.A.M.C. The first quartermaster was Major G. Merritt, S.A.M.C., who left, however, with No. 1 South African General Hospital when that unit proceeded to France, his duties being taken over by Captain Lunney, S.A.M.C. In the autumn of 1917 Captain Lunney relieved Major Merritt in France, and Major Merritt then returned to Richmond, where shortly after he was promoted to the rank of Lieutenant-Colonel.

The nursing staff under the matron—Miss Jackson, R.R.C., Q.A.I.M.N.S.—consisted of 2 assistant matrons, 23 nursing sisters, 55 staff nurses, and 88 probationers, the larger proportion of whom were South Africans. The trained members of the staff mostly belonged to the Q.A.I.M.N.S. (Res.), or to the S.A.M.N.S. The subordinate *personnel* consisted, with a few exceptions, of N.C.O.'s and men who, having been invalided owing to wounds or sickness in the field, did duty at the hospital while regaining health and strength.

The hospital also served as the depot for the S.A.M.C. subordinate *personnel;* and 18 drafts, comprising 423 men, were sent to France as reinforcements for the First South African General Hospital and the First South African Field Ambulance.

The number of patients admitted up to October 31, 1918, was 274 officers and 9,412 other ranks—a total of 9,686. This does not include any patients admitted to the Richmond Military Hospital prior to the date of amalgamation. Of the 9,686 patients, 2,628 belonged to Imperial units, but included a good many South Africans, and 7,058 were members of the South African Contingent; 8,260 patients were discharged, including 6,230 members of the Contingent.

The total number of operations performed under a general anæsthetic was 2,125, and the number of medical boards held was 1,559.

Most of the swabs and bandages used in the hospital were manufactured in the South African workrooms, organized by a group of ladies attached to the South African Comforts Committee. The ladies responsible for these workrooms made most of the curtains and other similar articles required to equip the hospital, and undertook most of the mending. Under Mrs. Friedlander they rendered most valuable assistance to the hospital since its foundation, and their help was much appreciated by all concerned.

From the very first the Committee spared neither trouble nor money to provide for the comfort and welfare of the patients. At first the work of visitation and entertainment was organized under Lady (Lionel) Phillips, but later it was taken over by the Red Cross sub-committee of the Fund. For those sufficiently convalescent to enjoy them, every possible variety of amusement was provided. On four or five nights a week some form of entertainment was given in the large concert hall, while every week theatres or places of interest were visited, a special feature being the river trips arranged by the " African World " War Comforts Service, who also very generously provided gifts of fruit and other comforts. Further, in order that nothing should be left undone, Lady Phillips founded a riverside club in close proximity to the hospital, for the benefit of those patients sufficiently convalescent to enjoy the delights of its garden and picturesque river views.

Arrangements for bedside occupational work were, in the early days of the hospital, made by lady visitors. Material for fancy work and needlework was generously provided, and the making of regimental crests and other work of a like nature helped patients to pass in bed many a weary hour when they were still too weak to be doing the more serious vocational work.

Shortly after the hospital was opened the problem of dealing with the permanently disabled men of the Contingent had to be faced. After negotiations with the War Office, it was arranged that a Vocational Training School should be established in connection with the hospital. A commencement was made in November 1916, and the school was finally opened in February 1917. The scheme involved awakening the men while still in bed to interest in their future, so that when well enough they might go to the classrooms and undertake extensive courses of training. The South African Military Hospital was the first primary hospital in the United Kingdom in which permanently disabled men, while being restored to the best possible physical condition, were trained, with due regard to their disabilities, for a civil career to enable them on discharge from the army to become self-supporting members of the community. There was what was perhaps a natural reluctance on the part of the Home Government in giving sanction to this new venture, which was for many months looked upon as being at the best an interesting experiment. The New Zealand authorities, however, quickly saw the advantages of the methods, and in August 1917 a similar scheme for their hospitals was adopted.

The desirability of training permanently disabled soldiers while still undergoing hospital treatment was finally endorsed at the Inter-Allied Conference on Disablement Problems, held in London in May 1918, and committees were subsequently formed in each Command to organize similar work throughout the hospitals of the United Kingdom.

The South African Vocational Training Scheme was carried on side by side with the work of the hospital, and was successful both in improving the mental attitude—especially of limbless men—and in training many disabled men of the Contingent who would otherwise have been unproductive to the community.

The cost of the erection of the workshops—amounting to £2,335—was borne by the South African Hospital and Comforts Fund and the Governor-General's Fund.

Much of the equipment was either given or lent, but about £1,200 had to be expended to obtain such tools and appliances as could not otherwise be obtained. The latter expenditure was defrayed by the Governor-General's Fund. The scheme also necessitated the hiring of four houses in the vicinity of the hospital for housing students who had been discharged from hospital ; the cost of the equipment of these, amounting approximately to £1,400, was also met by the two funds.

These hostels were managed by a small committee appointed by the General Committee. The expenditure on rents, rates, and taxes for the hostels was shared by the local fund and the Governor-General's Fund, but all other expenditure was met by the sub-committee which received through the High Commissioner the sum of £1 per week for each inmate. This sum represented a ration allowance of 1s. 9d. per head per diem received from Defence Votes, the balance being made up by the Governor-General's Fund. The Union Government also made itself responsible for the pay and allowances of the inmates, and entirely relieved the Imperial Government of all financial responsibility for the period during which the men were undergoing training after discharge from hospital. The number of crippled men who attended classes since their commencement was 393. Of these 167 remained on October 31, 1918, and 226 had left. Of those remaining, 112 were out-students—that is, men discharged from hospital—and 55 were patients still in hospital. The number of out-students dealt with was 215, of whom 103 have left.

The school was at first under the direction of Mr. Charles Bray, but on his resignation owing to ill-health, Staff-Sergeant Newell, B.Sc., of the S.A.M.C., and in civil life on the staff of the Natal Education Department, was appointed as educational organizer. He was subsequently granted honorary commissioned rank in the Union Defence Force. The propaganda work in the wards and the ward teaching were in the hands of Miss Edith Hill, also of the Natal Education Department.

The hostels for housing out-students were managed by a matron —Mrs. Lennox, of Lovedale—and a staff of ladies, whose efforts were attended with every success.

But the success of the school, in spite of many initial difficulties, was due to the keenness of the men themselves and to the excellent co-operative work of the whole staff of the hospital, with the result that in a number of cases of limbless men the earning capacity was undoubtedly increased as a result of the training they received at Richmond.

APPENDIX IV.

THE RAILWAYS COMPANIES AND MISCELLANEOUS TRADES COMPANY.

In 1916 the railways, roads, canals, and docks in the British zone in France were brought under the control of " Transportation," which was under the command of Sir Eric Geddes. The War Office appealed to the Dominions for Railway Operating Sections, or Companies, each consisting of three officers and 266 men. In South Africa the position was such that the railways could, at the time, only spare sufficient men to form one company, but it was arranged to form a second from those not actually in the railway service but who had railway experience, or were in other ways fitted for the particular work required of them.

The first company assembled at Potchefstroom in November 1916, under Captain H. L. Pybus, and the second at Robert's Heights, Pretoria, under Captain W. McI. Robinson. Fifty locomotive drivers and a similar number of firemen and guards formed the backbone of each company, the balance being composed of traffic controllers, blockmen, signalmen, with the necessary mechanics and clerical staff to enable each company to operate as a separate and a complete unit.

Lieutenant-Colonel F. R. Collins—a mechanical superintendent in the South African Railways—was appointed in command, and left for England in December 1916, the companies following later under the command of Captain (Acting Major) Robinson, and arriving at Bordon, Hampshire, in March 1917, at which place the depot was formed.

Both companies arrived in France at the end of March 1917, and were detailed for light railway work, which was then in its initial stage. The first section was renumbered " No. 7, South African Light Railway Operating Company," and the second,

" No. 8, South African Light Railway Operating Company," the former being sent to Romarin on the Belgian border, while the latter proceeded to Savy, in the Arras district. Twenty-five drivers and a like number of firemen from each company were transferred to the Broad Gauge, and remained on that work throughout the war. No. 7 Company stayed at Romarin until the operations in connection with the taking of Messines Village and Ridge were completed in June 1917, during which time the Ploegsteert Light Railway system was built, over which the company was responsible for all traffic, the bulk being ammunition with delivery points at the different batteries. The 8th Company took over the Light Railway work from Marœuil to the north and north-east of Arras, whence lines were extended after the Vimy Ridge operations. In June 1917 both companies proceeded to Audruicq preparatory to taking up Broad Gauge work, and were designated No. 92 and No. 93 Companies respectively.

During most of this period Lieutenant-Colonel Collins was attached to Transportation Headquarters, and in May 1917 was appointed Assistant-Director of Light Railways, Fifth Army, which was then operating in the Bapaume sector. On the transfer of this Army to Belgium to take part in the series of operations known as the Third Battle of Ypres, light railways, in addition to serving batteries and Royal Engineers, were now required to prepare to follow up any advance. For this purpose the services of the 92nd and 93rd South African Companies were loaned to Light Railways, and took their place with five Imperial Operating Companies in the Fifth Army area. They shared in the operations up to November 1917, when the offensive ceased.

During this time the 92nd Company was employed on the system north-east of Ypres, eleven of the members being awarded Military Medals for individual acts of gallantry and devotion to duty. The 93rd Company worked from Elverdinghe through Boesinghe to Langemarck, and among other duties was responsible for the placing of field gun ammunition in position in front of the field guns on the eastern slopes of the Pilckem Ridge and in the Steenbecque Valley prior to the attacks during September and October 1917, which led to the front being advanced to the edge of the Houthulst Forest. Seven members received the Military Medal during this time.

In January 1918 the Fifth Army took over the sector of forty-

LIEUTENANT-COLONEL F. R. COLLINS, D.S.O.,
Commanding South African Railway Companies.

five miles on the extreme south of the British front, and, in anticipation of an enemy offensive, light railway construction on a considerable scale was undertaken under Lieutenant-Colonel F. Newell. Later, on the division of this system, Lieutenant-Colonel Collins took over the northern area—the 92nd and 93rd Companies being ordered south from Belgium. The 93rd arrived early in March and was sent to Noyon, where it remained until the 23rd, when, retirement being forced by the enemy advance, the company proceeded by route march to Flexicourt, west of Amiens, and was employed on the construction of defence works in company with many other transportation units whose usual employment had been suspended for a like reason. Later, they were employed on railway construction necessitated by the altered conditions. In July 1918 the Company Headquarters were established at Ligny, east of St. Pol, and the operation of the main trunk lines to Arras was undertaken. The German retreat caused a forward move, and the company, since November, operated over the section Douai to Mons inclusive, with headquarters at Somain.

The 92nd Company, after concentrating in Belgium in March for its projected move south, subsequently cancelled owing to the enemy's advance, went to Crombeke and from there assisted in railway construction and other duties, until in September, when, with Berguette as headquarters, the operation of the newly-constructed line towards Merville and later towards Armentières was undertaken. In November the Company moved forward to Lille, and with headquarters at Tourcoing worked the section from Tourcoing to Tournai.

In 1917 the South African Union Government consented to the formation of a Miscellaneous Trades Company for service in France. This company began to assemble at Potchefstroom in June, and, as recruiting was brisk, it was able to embark fully organized at Cape Town as early as 25th July, under the command of Captain C. E. Mason, S.A.E.

Arriving at Bordon on 28th August, the company was given a short course of training at the Royal Engineers' Depot there, and sent to France on 14th October. Here the company was re-numbered the 84th Miscellaneous Trades Company, R.E. (South African), and sent to the Director-General of Transportation, Chief Mechanical Engineer Department, Locomotive Workshops, situated at St. Etienne-du-Rouvray, near Rouen, where five companies of the Royal Engineers, under the command of Lieutenant-Colonel Cole, R.E., were already stationed.

These were the largest locomotive workshops attached to the British Armies in France, and, by reason of its large percentage of skilled *personnel*, the 84th Company was enabled to take a very considerable share in the activities of the shops, Captain Mason being appointed Erecting Works' Manager, and the N.C.O.'s of the Company in many instances being entrusted with positions of responsibility. On the recall of Captain Mason to South Africa, Captain N. S. Weatherley, S.A.E., succeeded to the command of the Company. When the armistice was signed in November 1918, Lieutenant-Colonel Cole ordered a special parade of the Company, in order to express to all ranks his high appreciation of their services, which he characterized in the most complimentary terms.

A depot for the companies in France was originally established at Bordon, and was temporarily under the charge of Lieutenant Arthur, of the 1st section. Advantage was taken of the Instructional Establishment at Longmoor to train as many men as possible in the operation of petrol tractors, which were largely used in place of steam locomotives in the forward areas on light railways. In June 1917 the depot was taken over by Captain M. J. Byrne, who, on his transfer to France in July 1918 to command the 93rd Company, was succeeded by Captain H. E. Greaves, M.C., R.E., the depot about the same time being transferred from Bordon to Longmoor.

APPENDIX V.

THE CAPE AUXILIARY HORSE TRANSPORT COMPANIES.

IN February 1917 the Government of the Union of South Africa was asked by the War Office to raise eight companies of Cape coloured drivers for service with the Army Service Corps in France. The *personnel* originally required was :—

Officers	50
Warrant officers	6
Non-commissioned officers	60
Artificers	131
Drivers . . . . . . , . .	2,316

but this was eventually increased to—

Officers	67
Warrant officers	23
Non-commissioned officers	92
Artificers and drivers	3,482

Towards the end of February Lieutenant-Colonel J. D. Anderson (an officer who had considerable experience in transport work) was asked to take command, and to arrange for the recruiting and organization of the eight companies. Kimberley was selected as the most convenient centre for mobilization, and De Beers Corporation gave the use of its Nos. 1 and 3 Compounds. These had hutting accommodation for approximately two thousand men. They were provided with a hospital, kitchens, washing-rooms—in fact everything required—and there is no doubt that the loan of these compounds not only facilitated mobilization and saved a great deal of expense, but probably accelerated the departure of the contingent by at least two months. Lieutenant-Colonel Wynne was appointed camp commandant, with Captain MacKeurton as paymaster, and Captain Cooper as officer in charge of the Records, and by the 12th March everything was in readiness for recruiting to begin.

The results were at first disappointing, as recruiting for the Cape coloured battalions for service in German East Africa was at this time being undertaken, and recruiting committees for this purpose were at work at all the principal centres in South Africa. In addition there were many questions, such as the appointment of coloured N.C.O.'s, increased rates of pay, the rejection of all coloured drivers other than Cape coloured drivers, recognition by the Governor-General's Fund, and other details, all of which had to be settled before the Coloured Recruiting Committees would lend their assistance. There was also a lack of Cape Auxiliary Horse Transport officers to conduct a special recruiting campaign. However, these difficulties were soon overcome, and recruiting proceeded with great rapidity. Johannesburg, where Captain Barlow, Captain and Chaplain Rogers, and Lieutenant Graham Moore inaugurated a vigorous recruiting campaign ; Cape Town, where Lieutenants Gillam and Sawyer, Second-Lieutenant Tracey, S.S.M. Simmons, and C.S.M. Creagh met with considerable success ; and Knysna, with Second-Lieutenant Anderson and C.Q.M.S. Steytler as recruiting officers, each produced five hundred recruits in a short time.

At the beginning the amount of clerical work entailed was very heavy, the work being increased owing to the necessity of having to reject a large number of drivers who were attested but subsequently found unsuitable. Every officer, warrant officer, and N.C.O., however, assisted the Records' officer to such an extent that by the middle of April 1,500 men were ready to leave for overseas. Unfortunately, shipping could only be found for 867, and these sailed in the *Euripides* on the 20th April. These were shortly followed by drafts under the command of Majors Jenner and Barnard, and a reinforcement draft under Lieutenant Smith.

On the arrival of the first detachment in France on 23rd May, the Director of Transport decided that the contingent should release for other service, and take the place of, the Army Service Corps *personnel*, forming the following companies :—

No. 22 Auxiliary Horse Transport Company, A.S.C., stationed at Dunkirk and Calais.

No. 5 Auxiliary Horse Transport Company, A.S.C., stationed at Boulogne.

No. 2 Auxiliary Horse Transport Company, A.S.C., stationed at Havre.

No. 8 Auxiliary Horse Transport Company, A.S.C., stationed at Rouen.

No. 10 Auxiliary Horse Transport Company, A.S.C., stationed at Rouen.

No. 11 Auxiliary Horse Transport Company, A.S.C., stationed at Rouen.

Arrangements were also made for a base depot to be established at Havre.

The reorganization was commenced at once, one company of the first draft going to Calais and the two others to Rouen. As other drafts arrived they were sent to the base depot for three weeks, where they were equipped, and went through a course of training before being distributed to the various A.S.C. companies. Thus by the 31st August the Cape Auxiliary Horse Transport detachments had released the whole of the white *personnel* of six companies of the Army Service Corps, with the exception of five officers and a certain number of warrant officers and N.C.O.'s, whose services it was proposed permanently to retain, while after a few months in France the reorganized companies were all commanded by officers of the detachment.

Though the men did very excellent work at the base posts, Colonel Anderson felt that there were strong arguments in favour of them being moved to divisional trains or Army Auxiliary Horse Transport companies actually working in the army areas. The arguments in favour of the move from a South African point of view were unanswerable. The environments at the base posts were not good, and the work of the men chiefly lay in the lower quarters of the towns where liquor-sellers and their customary associates resided. It is greatly to the credit of the men that their general conduct was exemplary in spite of the adverse conditions under which many of them worked.

The views of the military authorities in France did not, however, coincide with those of Colonel Anderson. All the commandants of the bases at which the companies were employed recommended that they should remain where they were, and wrote highly of the men's behaviour, bearing, and discipline. It was a great disappointment to all that the companies were not at once employed in the army areas ; but a promise was given that, if reinforcements proved sufficient, an experiment would be made in employing them nearer to the actual scene of fighting. This was eventually done, and the 1st, 3rd, and 5th Army Auxiliary Horse Companies were taken over, the experiment proving an unmitigated success. The work of these companies consisted in conveying ammunition and supplies to the firing lines, and transporting metal for the new roads which had to be constructed as the armies advanced.

Of the other companies which were employed on the lines of communication, Numbers 2, 5, 8, and 22 Companies were employed at the docks, the bulk of the work consisting in conveying munitions and supplies from the docks to the different distributing centres. The work was hard, the hours long, and the drivers much exposed to weather conditions.

Numbers 10 and 11 Companies were designated as " Forest Companies," and were employed almost entirely in hauling logs from the place where they were felled to dumping centres. In a report on the work in the forests in France, Lord Lovat, the Director of Forests, wrote that, without prejudice to other units, he wished to remark on the work done by the Horse Transport Companies manned by South African (Cape coloured) *personnel*, who had shown throughout both practical knowledge of the work and patriotic devotion to duty.

During their stay in France the health of the officers, N.C.O.'s, and men was much better than could reasonably have been expected. Casualties were estimated at 1 per cent. per month, but this figure was reduced by half.

APPENDIX VI.

VICTORIA CROSSES WON BY SOUTH AFRICANS DURING THE WAR.

LIEUTENANT (ACTING CAPTAIN) ANDREW WEATHERBY BEAUCHAMP-PROCTOR, D.S.O., M.C., D.F.C., No. 84 Squadron, Royal Air Force.

Between August 8, 1918, and October 8, 1918, this officer proved himself victor in twenty-six decisive combats, destroying twelve enemy kite balloons, ten enemy aircraft, and driving down four other enemy aircraft completely out of control.

Between October 1, 1918, and October 5, 1918, he destroyed two enemy scouts, burned three enemy kite balloons, and drove down one enemy scout completely out of control.

On October 1, 1918, in a general engagement with about twenty-eight machines, he crashed one Fokker biplane near FONTAINE and a second near RAMICOURT ; on 2nd October he burnt a hostile balloon near SELVIGNY ; on 3rd October he drove down completely out of control an enemy scout near MONT D'ORIGNY, and burned a hostile balloon ; on 5th October, the third hostile balloon near BOHAIN.

On October 8, 1918, while flying home at a low altitude after destroying an enemy two-seater near MARETZ, he was painfully wounded in the arm by machine-gun fire ; but, continuing, he landed safely at his aerodrome, and after making his report was admitted to hospital.

In all, he has proved himself conqueror over fifty-four foes, destroying twenty-two enemy machines, sixteen enemy kite balloons, and driving down sixteen enemy aircraft completely out of control.

Captain Beauchamp-Proctor's work in attacking enemy troops on the ground and in reconnaissance during the withdrawal following on the battle of St. Quentin, from March 21, 1918, and during the victorious advance of our armies commencing on 8th August, has been almost unsurpassed in its brilliancy, and as such has made an impression on those serving in his squadron and those around him that will not be easily forgotten.

Captain Beauchamp-Proctor was awarded the Military Cross on June 22, 1918 ; the Distinguished Flying Cross on July 2, 1918 ; a bar to the Military Cross on September 16, 1918 ; and the Distinguished Service Order on November 2, 1918.

Captain William Anderson Bloomfield, Scouts Corps, South African Mounted Brigade.

At Mlali, East Africa, on August 24, 1916. For most conspicuous bravery. Finding that, after being heavily attacked in an advanced and isolated position, the enemy were working round his flanks, Captain Bloomfield evacuated his wounded and subsequently withdrew his command to a new position, he himself being among the last to retire. On arrival at the new position he found that one of the wounded—No. 2475, Corporal D. M. P. Bowker —had been left behind. Owing to very heavy fire he experienced difficulties in having the wounded corporal brought in. Rescue meant passing over some four hundred yards of open ground, swept by heavy fire, in full view of the enemy. This task Captain Bloomfield determined to face himself, and unmindful of personal danger, he succeeded in reaching Corporal Bowker and carrying him back, subjected throughout the double journey to heavy machine-gun and rifle fire. This act showed the highest degree of valour and endurance.

No. 1630, Sergeant Frederick Charles Booth, South African Forces, attached Rhodesia Native Regiment.

At Johannesbruck, near Songea, East Africa, on February 12, 1917. For most conspicuous bravery during an attack, in thick bush, on the enemy position. Under very heavy rifle fire, Sergeant Booth went forward alone and brought in a man who was dangerously wounded. Later, he rallied native troops who were badly disorganized, and brought them to the firing line. This N.C.O. has, on many previous occasions, displayed the greatest bravery, coolness, and resource in action, and has set a splendid example of pluck, endurance, and determination.

No. 4073, Private William Frederick Faulds, 1st Regiment, South African Infantry.

At Delville Wood, France, on July 18, 1916. For most conspicuous bravery and devotion to duty. A bombing party under Lieutenant Craig attempted to rush across forty yards of ground which lay between the British and enemy trenches. Coming under very heavy rifle and machine-gun fire, the officer and the majority of the party were killed or wounded. Unable to move, Lieutenant Craig lay midway between the two lines of trenches, the ground being quite open. In full daylight Private Faulds, accompanied by two other men, climbed the parapet, ran out, picked up the officer and carried him back, one man being severely wounded in so doing.

Two days later Private Faulds again showed most conspicuous bravery in going out alone to bring in a wounded man and carrying him nearly half a mile to a dressing-station, subsequently rejoining his platoon. The artillery fire was at the time so intense that stretcher bearers and others considered that any attempt to bring in the wounded man meant certain death. This risk Private Faulds faced unflinchingly, and his bravery was crowned with success.

Lieutenant Robert Vaughan Gorle, " A " Battery, 50th Brigade, Royal Field Artillery.

For most conspicuous bravery, initiative, and devotion to duty during the attack at Ledeghem on October 1, 1918, when in command of an eighteen-pounder gun working in close conjunction with infantry. He brought his gun into action in the most exposed positions on four separate occasions, and disposed of enemy machine guns by firing over open sights under direct machine-gun fire at five hundred to six hundred yards range.

Later, seeing that the infantry were being driven back by intense hostile fire, he without hesitation galloped his gun in front of the leading infantry, and on two occasions knocked out enemy machine guns which were causing the trouble. His disregard of personal safety and dash were a magnificent example to the wavering line, which rallied and retook the northern end of the village.

Major (Acting Lieutenant-Colonel) Harry Greenwood, D.S.O., M.C., 9th Battalion, King's Own Yorkshire Light Infantry.

For most conspicuous bravery, devotion to duty, and fine leadership on October 23–24, 1918. When the advance of his battalion on the 23rd October was checked, and many casualties caused by an enemy machine-gun post, Lieutenant-Colonel Greenwood, single-handed, rushed the post and killed the crew. At the entrance to the village of OVILLERS, accompanied by two battalion runners, he again rushed a machine-gun post and killed the occupants.

On reaching the objective west of DUKE'S WOOD, his command was almost surrounded by hostile machine-gun posts, and the enemy at once attacked his isolated force. The attack was repulsed, and, led by Lieutenant-Colonel Greenwood, his troops swept forward and captured the last objective with one hundred and fifty prisoners, eight machine guns, and one field gun.

During the attack on the " Green Line," south of POIX DU NORD, on 24th October, he again displayed the greatest gallantry in rushing a machine-gun post, and he showed conspicuously good leadership in the handling of his command in the face of heavy fire. He inspired his men in the highest degree, with the result that the objective was captured, and in spite of heavy casualties the line was held.

During the advance on Grand Gay Farm Road, on the afternoon of 24th October, the skilful and bold handling of his battalion was productive of most important results, not only in securing the flank of his brigade but also in safeguarding the flank of the Division.

His valour and leading during two days of fighting were beyond all praise.

CAPTAIN PERCY HOWARD HANSEN, ADJUTANT, 6th (Service) Battalion, the Lincolnshire Regiment.

For most conspicuous bravery on August 9, 1915, at YILGHIN BURNU, Gallipoli Peninsula. After the second capture of the " Green Knoll " his battalion was forced to retire, leaving some wounded behind, owing to the intense heat from the scrub which had been set on fire. When the retirement was effected, Captain Hansen, with three or four volunteers, on his own initiative, dashed forward several times some three hundred to four hundred yards over open ground into the scrub, under a terrific fire, and succeeded in rescuing from inevitable death by burning no less than six wounded men.

LIEUTENANT (ACTING CAPTAIN) REGINALD FREDERICK JOHNSON
HAYWARD, M.C., Wiltshire Regiment.

Near FREMICOURT, France, on March 21–22, 1918. For most
conspicuous bravery in action. This officer, while in command of
a company, displayed almost superhuman powers of endurance
and consistent courage of the rarest nature. In spite of the fact
that he was buried, wounded in the head, and rendered deaf on
the first day of operations, and had his arm shattered two days
later, he refused to leave his men (even though he received a third
serious injury to his head), until he collapsed from sheer physical
exhaustion.

Throughout the whole of this period the enemy were attacking
his company front without cessation, but Captain Hayward continued to move across the open from one trench to another with
absolute disregard of his own personal safety, concentrating entirely
on reorganizing his defences and encouraging his men. It was
almost entirely due to the magnificent example of ceaseless energy
of this officer that many most determined attacks upon his portion
of the trench system failed entirely.

No. 8162, LANCE-CORPORAL WILLIAM HENRY HEWITT, 2nd Regiment, South African Infantry.

At east of YPRES on September 20, 1917. For most conspicuous
bravery during operations. Lance-Corporal Hewitt attacked a
" pill-box " with his section and tried to rush the doorway. The
garrison, however, proved very stubborn, and in the attempt this
non-commissioned officer received a severe wound. Nevertheless,
he proceeded to the loophole of the " pill-box " where, in his attempts
to put a bomb into it, he was again wounded in the arm. Unde-
terred, however, he eventually managed to get a bomb inside,
which caused the occupants to dislodge, and they were successfully
and speedily dealt with by the remainder of the section.

SECOND-LIEUTENANT (ACTING CAPTAIN) ARTHUR MOORE LASCELLES,
3rd (attached 14th) Battalion, Durham Light Infantry.

At MASNIÈRES, France, on December 3, 1917. For most conspicuous bravery, initiative, and devotion to duty when in command
of his company in a very exposed position. After a very heavy
bombardment, during which Captain Lascelles was wounded, the
enemy attacked in strong force but was driven off, success being

due in a great degree to the fine example set by this officer, who, refusing to allow his wound to be dressed, continued to encourage his men and organize the defence.

Shortly afterwards the enemy again attacked and captured the trench, taking several of his men prisoners. Captain Lascelles at once jumped on the parapet, and followed by the remainder of his company, twelve men only, rushed across under very heavy machine-gun fire and drove over sixty of the enemy back, thereby saving a most critical situation.

He was untiring in reorganizing the position, but shortly afterwards the enemy again attacked and captured the trench and Captain Lascelles, who escaped later. The remarkable determination and gallantry of this officer in the course of operations, during which he received two further wounds, afforded an inspiring example to all.

CAPTAIN OSWALD AUSTIN REID, 2nd Battalion, Liverpool Regiment, attached 6th Battalion, Loyal North Lancashire Regiment.

At DIALAH RIVER, Mesopotamia, on March 8–10, 1917. For most conspicuous bravery in the face of desperate circumstances. By his dauntless courage and gallant leadership he was able to consolidate a small post with the advanced troops, on the opposite side of a river to the main body, after his lines of communication had been cut by the sinking of the pontoons.

He maintained this position for thirty hours against constant attacks by bombs, machine-gun and shell fire, with the full knowledge that repeated attempts at relief had failed, and that his ammunition was all but exhausted. It was greatly due to his tenacity that the passage of the river was effected on the following night. During the operations he was wounded.

MAJOR (ACTING LIEUTENANT-COLONEL) JOHN SHERWOOD-KELLY, C.M.G., D.S.O., Norfolk Regiment, Commanding 1st Battalion, Royal Inniskilling Fusiliers.

At MARCOING, France, on November 20, 1917. For most conspicuous bravery and fearless leading, when a party of men of another unit detailed to cover the passage of the canal by his battalion were held up on the near side of the canal by heavy rifle fire directed on the bridge. Lieutenant-Colonel Sherwood-Kelly at once ordered covering fire, personally led the leading company of his battalion across the canal, and, after crossing, reconnoitred under heavy rifle and machine-gun fire the high ground held by the enemy.

The left flank of his battalion, advancing to the assault of this objective, was held up by a thick belt of wire, whereupon he crossed to that flank and with a Lewis-gun team forced his way under heavy fire through obstacles, got the gun into position on the far side, and covered the advance of his battalion through the wire, thereby enabling them to capture the position.

Later, he personally led a charge against some pits from which a heavy fire was being directed on his men, captured the pits, together with five machine guns and forty-six prisoners, and killed a large number of the enemy.

The great gallantry displayed by this officer throughout the day inspired the greatest confidence in his men, and it was mainly due to his example and devotion to duty that his battalion was enabled to capture and hold their objective.

CAPTAIN (ACTING LIEUTENANT-COLONEL) RICHARD ANNESLEY WEST, D.S.O., M.C., late North Irish Horse (Cavalry Special Reserve) and Tank Corps.

At COURCELLES and VAULX-VRAUCOURT, France, on August 21, 1918, and September 2, 1918. For most conspicuous bravery, leadership, and self-sacrifice. During an attack, the infantry having lost their bearings in the dense fog, this officer at once collected and reorganized any men he could find and led them to their objective in face of heavy machine-gun fire. Throughout the whole action he displayed the most utter disregard of danger, and the capture of the objective was in a great part due to his initiative and gallantry.

On a subsequent occasion it was intended that a battalion of light Tanks, under the command of this officer, should exploit the initial infantry and heavy Tank attack. He therefore went forward in order to keep in touch with the progress of the battle, and arrived at the front line when the enemy were in process of delivering a local counter-attack. The infantry battalion had suffered heavy officer casualties and its flanks were exposed. Realizing that there was a danger of the battalion giving way, he at once rode out in front of them under extremely heavy machine-gun and rifle fire and rallied the men.

In spite of the fact that the enemy were close upon him, he took charge of the situation and detailed non-commissioned officers to replace officer casualties. He then rode up and down in front of them in face of certain death, encouraging the men and calling to them, " Stick it, men ! Show them fight ! and for God's sake put up a good fight ! " He fell riddled by machine-gun bullets.

The magnificent bravery of this very gallant officer at the critical moment inspired the infantry to redoubled efforts, and the hostile attack was defeated.

LIEUTENANT-COLONEL G. HELBERT, C.B.E.,
Military Staff Officer, South African Expeditionary Force.

APPENDIX VII.

LIST OF HONOURS WON BY THE SOUTH AFRICAN FORCES IN FRANCE.

The ranks shown were those held at the date of the bestowal of the different awards.
Each asterisk denotes an additional mention.

V.C.

Faulds, No. 4073, Private W. F. . . . . Infantry.
Hewitt, No. 8162, Lance-Corporal W. H. . . Infantry.

K.C.B.

Lukin, Major-General Sir H. T. . . . . Staff.

C.B.

Lukin, Brigadier-General H. T. . . . . Staff.
Tanner, Brigadier-General W. E. C. . . . Staff.

C.M.G.

Dawson, Lieutenant-Colonel F. S. . . . . Infantry.
Jones, Lieutenant-Colonel F. A. . . . . Infantry.
Pritchard, Colonel S. A. M. . . . . . S.A.N.L.C.
Tanner, Lieutenant-Colonel W. E. C. . . . Infantry.
Thackeray, Lieutenant-Colonel E. F. . . . Infantry.
Thomson, Lieutenant-Colonel G. R. . . . S.A.M.C.

BAR TO D.S.O.

Dawson, Brigadier-General F. S. . . . . Staff.

D.S.O.

Baker, Major J. M.	Staff.
Bennett, Major G. M.	Heavy Artillery.
Blew, Lieutenant-Colonel T. H.	Heavy Artillery.
Brydon, Major W.	Heavy Artillery.
Bunce, Captain H.	Infantry.
Christian, Lieutenant-Colonel E.	Infantry.
Cochran, Major F. E.	Infantry.
Collins, Lieutenant-Colonel F. R.	S. A. Engineers.
Currie, Lieutenant J.	Heavy Artillery.
Dawson, Brigadier-General F. S.	Staff.
Edwards, Major S. B.	Heavy Artillery.
Forbes, Lieutenant E. C.	Infantry.
Greene, Captain L.	Infantry.
Hands, Major P. A. M.	Heavy Artillery.
Harrison, Major H. C.	Heavy Artillery.
Harrison, Major N.	Signal Coy.
Heal, Lieutenant-Colonel F. H.	Infantry.
Heenan, Major C. R..	Infantry.
Hemming, Major H. S. J. L.	Infantry.
Jacobs, Captain L. M.	Infantry.
Jenkins, Lieutenant-Colonel H. H.. . . .	Infantry.
Maasdorp, Major L. H.	Heavy Artillery.
MacLeod, Lieutenant-Colonel D. M. . . .	Infantry.
Mullins, Major A. G.	Heavy Artillery.
Murray, Major C. M..	S.A.M.C.
Ormiston, Major T.	Infantry.
Power, Major M. S.	S.A.M.C.
Pringle, Lieutenant-Colonel R. N.	S.A.M.C.
Sprenger, Captain L. F..	Infantry.
Tanner, Lieutenant-Colonel W. E. C. . . .	Infantry.
Thackeray, Lieutenant-Colonel E. F. . . .	Infantry.
Tomlinson, Captain L. W.	Infantry.
Tripp, Major W. H. L.	Heavy Artillery.
Ward, Lieutenant-Colonel A. B.	S.A.M.C.
Ward, Major C. P.	Heavy Artillery.

C.B.E. (MILITARY DIVISION).

Anderson, Lieutenant-Colonel J. D. . . .	Cape Aux. Horse Transport.
Baker, Lieutenant-Colonel J. M.	Staff.
Duff, Colonel C. de V.	General List.
Helbert, Lieutenant-Colonel G. G.	Staff.
Stock, Colonel P. G.	S.A.M.C.
Thornton, Lieutenant-Colonel E. N. . . .	S.A.M.C.

O.B.E. (MILITARY DIVISION).

Baker, Major H. C.	S.A.M.C.
Balfour, Lieutenant-Colonel H. H.. . . .	S.A.M.C.
Bamford, Lieutenant-Colonel H. W. M. . .	Infantry.
Bowles, Captain E.	General List.
Cameron, Captain and Quartermaster C. S. .	S.A.N.L.C.
Collins, Captain F.	S. A. Engineers.
Deane, Major R.	Infantry.
Emmett, Lieutenant-Colonel J. J. C. . . .	S.A.N.L.C.
Fawcus, Lieutenant-Colonel A.	S.A.N.L.C.
Geddes, Captain W. L.	S.A.N.L.C.
Green, Major J. A.	Staff.
Harris, Major J. J. F.	Infantry.
Jacobsby, Lieutenant-Colonel J.	S.A.N.L.C.
Jenner, Major L. W.	Cape Aux. Horse Transport.
Knight, Acting Major R. C..	General List.
Lennox, Captain and Chaplain J.	S.A.N.L.C.
Long, Captain W.	Cape Aux. Horse Transport.
Marshall, Captain H. E.	C.C.L.C.
Mills, Major H. P.	Infantry.
Pearson, Major M. G.	S.A.M.C.
Pepper, Major A. L.	Staff.
Rann, Major A. E.	Heavy Artillery.
Rigby, Major J. C. A.	S.A.M.C.
Ross, Captain F. M.	Signal Coy.
Sandes, Major T. L.	S.A.M.C.

Sproule, Major H. . . . . C.C.L.R.
Thornton, Lieutenant-Colonel E. N. . . . S.A.M.C.
Usmar, Lieutenant-Colonel G. H. . . . . S.A.M.C.
Wakefield, Major H. S. . . . . General List.

M.B.E. (MILITARY DIVISION).

Balfour, Lieutenant-Colonel H. H.. . . . S.A.M.C.
Bowles, Captain E. . . . . S. A. Pay Corps.
Coghlan, Captain G. S. . . . . S.A.M.C.
Deane, Major R. . . . . Infantry.
Ellis, Lieutenant N. N. . . . . S. A. Pay Corps.
Jamieson, Captain E. C. K.. . . . . . S. A. Pay Corps.
Kimberley, No. 17409, Reg. Sergt.-Major H. . S.A.M.C.
Knibbs, Lieutenant A. R. . . . . . . Staff.
Legge, Captain E. A. . . . . Infantry.
Rann, Major A. E. . . . . Heavy Artillery.
Sandes, Major T. L. . . . . S.A.M.C.
Tucker, Captain W. E. . . . . Infantry.
Walker, Captain E. B. . . . . Infantry.
Walker, No. X235, Staff Sergeant-Major J. H.. Staff.
Whyte, Captain J. E. . . . . S.A.N.L.C.

BAR TO M.C.

Green, Lieutenant G. G.. . . . . . . Infantry.
King, Captain W. L.. . . . . Infantry.
Lawrie, Captain M. B. . . . . S.A.M.C.
Morrison, Lieutenant R. E. . . . . . Infantry.
Neille, Lieutenant P. C.. . . . . . . Infantry.
Phillips, Second-Lieutenant S. G. . . . . Infantry.
Ridley, Captain E. G. . . . . Heavy Artillery.
Roffe, Captain T.. . . . . Infantry.
Smith, Captain W. . . . . S.A.M.C.
Ward, Captain A. E.. . . . . Infantry.

M.C.

Allen, Second-Lieutenant V. W.	Infantry.
Backeberg, Second-Lieutenant H. W. . . .	Infantry.
Bailey, Lieutenant H.	Heavy Artillery.
Bamford, Captain H. W. M.	Infantry.
Begbie, Major R. P. G.	Heavy Artillery.
Begley, Lieutenant E. R.	Infantry.
Beverley, Lieutenant R..	Infantry.
Beyers, Captain G. A.	S.A.M.C.
Boustead, Second-Lieutenant H.	Infantry.
Bower, Second-Lieutenant E. W.	Heavy Artillery.
Browne, Captain C. M.	Infantry.
Burgess, Captain E. J.	Infantry.
Burton, Second-Lieutenant F. W. S. . . .	Infantry.
Carding, Lieutenant W. H.	Infantry.
Cawood, Second-Lieutenant R. C.	Infantry.
Charlton, Captain W. D.	Infantry.
Cohen, Lieutenant M.	Signal Coy.
Collins, Second-Lieutenant F.	Signal Coy.
Connock, Second-Lieutenant C. O.. . . .	Infantry.
Covernton, Lieutenant R. H.	Signal Coy.
Cragg, Second-Lieutenant J. C.	Infantry.
Crooks, Lieutenant A. S.	Infantry.
Culverwell, Second-Lieutenant D.	Heavy Artillery.
Davies, Captain E. A.	Infantry.
Dickson, Second-Lieutenant E. G. H.. . .	Infantry.
Dingwall, Captain J. A..	Signal Coy.
Dobson, Lieutenant F. L.	Signal Coy.
Duminy, Second-Lieutenant F. J. van H.. .	Heavy Artillery.
Elias, Lieutenant D. H..	Infantry.
Ellis, Captain P. H.	Infantry.
English, Second-Lieutenant F. H.. . . .	Infantry.
FitzGeorge, Lieutenant F. S. L.	Signal Coy.
Forbes, Captain A. G.	S.A.M.C.
Forbes, Lieutenant L. H.	Infantry.
Goodwin, Lieutenant B. W..	Infantry.
Gray, Lieutenant S. E. G.	Infantry.
Green, Lieutenant A. P..	Heavy Artillery.

Green, Second-Lieutenant G. G.	Infantry.
Greene, Captain L.	Infantry.
Hallack, Lieutenant M. H.	Infantry.
Hands, Captain P. A. M.	Heavy Artillery.
Harris, Captain and Chaplain H.	S. A. Chap. Dept.
Harris, Second-Lieutenant W. E.	Infantry.
Hatchard, Second-Lieutenant F. H. F. . .	Infantry.
Heeley, Lieutenant H. N.	Infantry.
Hennessy, Second-Lieutenant B. P. . . .	Infantry.
Hewat, Second-Lieutenant R. D.	Infantry.
Hill, Captain and Chaplain E. St. C. . . .	S. A. Chap. Dept.
Hill, Lieutenant J. L.	Signal Coy.
Humphrey, Captain J. T.	Infantry.
Ingarfield, Lieutenant G. P.	Infantry.
Jack, Lieutenant J.	Signal Coy.
Keith, No. 2300, Reg. Sergt.-Major P. . .	Infantry.
Kilpin, Second-Lieutenant T.	Heavy Artillery.
King, Second-Lieutenant W. L.	Infantry.
Kirby, Second-Lieutenant W. H.	Infantry.
Kirkham, Captain G. H.	Infantry.
Lawrence, Captain H. R.	S.A.M.C.
Lawrie, Captain M. B.	S.A.M.C.
Leighton, Second-Lieutenant G. A. . . .	Infantry.
Lewell, Second-Lieutenant E.	Infantry.
Liebson, Captain S.	S.A.M.C.
Lunn, Captain W. S..	Heavy Artillery.
Maasdorp, Lieutenant A.	Heavy Artillery.
Macfarlane, Lieutenant B. N.	Infantry.
MacFie, Second-Lieutenant T. G.	Infantry.
Mackie, Second-Lieutenant D. C.	Infantry.
Maddison, Lieutenant E. A. J..	Heavy Artillery.
Marshall, Captain R. B.	Infantry.
Martin, Second-Lieutenant H. A.	Infantry.
M'Donald, Captain A. W. H.	Infantry.
M'Gregor, Major A. M.	Heavy Artillery.
M'Intosh, Second-Lieutenant R.	Infantry.
M'Lean, Lieutenant W.	Infantry.
Mellish, Lieutenant F. W.	Heavy Artillery.
Meredith, No. 5755, Reg. Sergt.-Major G.. .	Infantry.
Methven, Second-Lieutenant N. W. . . .	Infantry.

Middleton, Lieutenant E.	Infantry.
Miller, Second-Lieutenant R. S.	Heavy Artillery.
Mitchell, Captain F. McE.	Infantry.
Money, Lieutenant A. G.	Infantry.
Morrison, Second-Lieutenant R. E. . . .	Infantry.
Murray, Second-Lieutenant A. S.	Heavy Artillery.
Neille, Second-Lieutenant P. C.	Infantry.
Nicholson, Lieutenant C. F. S.	Infantry.
Page, Second-Lieutenant P. T. A.	Heavy Artillery.
Pentz, Second-Lieutenant H. F.	Infantry.
Pepper, Captain A. L.	Staff.
Perrem, Second-Lieutenant C. H.	Infantry.
Peters, Second-Lieutenant J.	Infantry.
Phillips, Second-Lieutenant E. J.	Infantry.
Phillips, Second-Lieutenant S. G.	Infantry.
Poole, Lieutenant R. P.	Signal Coy.
Pougnet, Second-Lieutenant V. N.	Infantry.
Rann, Captain A. E.	Heavy Artillery.
Reid, Captain E. L.	S.A.M.C.
Ridley, Captain E. G.	Heavy Artillery.
Roberts, Second-Lieutenant C. W.	Infantry.
Roddy, Captain G.	Infantry.
Roffe, Captain T.	Infantry.
Roper, Captain A. W. F.	Heavy Artillery.
Rose-Innes, Second-Lieutenant F. G. . . .	Heavy Artillery.
Ross, Captain F. H.	Infantry.
Ross, Captain F. M.	Signal Coy.
Rushforth, Lieutenant A. H.	Heavy Artillery.
Sampson, Captain B.	S.A.M.C.
Saphir, Second-Lieutenant M.	Infantry.
Scheepers, Second-Lieutenant J. C. . . .	Infantry.
Shenton, Lieutenant J. L.	Infantry.
Smith, Captain W.	S.A.M.C.
Sprenger, Captain L. F.	Infantry.
Solomon, Lieutenant A. C.	Heavy Artillery.
Stapleton, Lieutenant P. R.	Infantry.
Stewart, Lieutenant J. G.	Heavy Artillery.
Style, Captain S. W. E.	Infantry.
Sumner, Lieutenant H. L.	Infantry.
Symons, Captain T. H.	Infantry.

Thomas, Second-Lieutenant W. F. G. . . Infantry.
Thorburn, Lieutenant W. . . . . . . Infantry.
Unwin, Captain H. W. . . . . Heavy Artillery.
Van Ryneveld, Second-Lieutenant T. V. . . Infantry.
Vincent, Lieutenant S. C. . . . . . . Infantry.
Vivian, Captain E. V. . . . . Infantry.
Walker, Captain E. B. . . . . Infantry.
Walsh, Second-Lieutenant F. G. . . . . Infantry.
Walshe, Captain and Chaplain P. J. . . . S. A. Chap. Dept.
Ward, Lieutenant A. E. . . . . . . Infantry.
Wardill, No. 907, Batt. Sergt.-Major A. J. . Heavy Artillery.
Wells, No. 6163, Reg. Sergt.-Major R.. . . Infantry.
Welsh, Captain T. . . . . S.A.M.C.
Whales, Second-Lieutenant G. . . . . . Heavy Artillery.
Whelan, Second-Lieutenant M. E.. . . . Infantry.
Wilson, No. 5266, Reg. Sergt.-Major J. . . Infantry.
Wood, No. 6386, Company Sergeant-Major J.. Infantry.

THE ROYAL RED CROSS.

MEMBERS.

Bester, Nursing-Sister H. L. . . . . . S.A.M.N.S.
Creagh, Matron E. R. . . . . S.A.M.N.S.
Fynn, Nursing-Sister M. A. . . . . . S.A.M.N.S.
Purcell, Matron A. M. . . . . Q.A.I.M.N.S. (Res.)
Wessels, Nursing-Sister E. S. . . . . . S.A.M.N.S.

ASSOCIATES.

Barber, Nursing-Sister M. E. . . . . . S.A.M.N.S.
Blake, Nursing-Sister E. C.. . . . . . S.A.M.N.S.
Campbell, Nursing-Sister M. H. . . . . S.A.M.N.S.
Conyngham, Nursing-Sister A. B. . . . . S.A.M.N.S.
Francis, Staff-Nurse G. E. . . . . . . S.A.M.N.S.
Goulden, Nursing-Sister K.. . . . . . S.A.M.N.S.
Loosemore, Nursing-Sister A. H. M. . . . S.A.M.N.S.
Redpath, Staff-Nurse V. M.. . . . . . S.A.M.N.S.

Ross, Nursing-Sister K. . . . . S.A.M.N.S.
Tilney, Nursing-Sister M. E. . . . . . S.A.M.N.S.
Wagstaff, Staff-Nurse B. . . . . . . S.A.M.N.S.

BREVET RANK.

BREVET-LIEUTENANT-COLONEL.

Green, Major J. A. . . . . Staff.
Pearson, Major M. G. . . . . S.A.M.C.
Purcell, Major (Temp. Col.) J. F., D.S.O. . Infantry.
Sandes, Major T. L. . . . . S.A.M.C.

BREVET-MAJOR.

Jamieson, Major E. C. K. . . . . . . S. A. Pay Corps.

D.C.M.

Alexander, No. 2471, Sergeant C. G. . . . Infantry.
Beckman, No. 4768, Sergeant G. H. W. . . Infantry.
Bell, No. 4699, Company Sergeant-Major F. . Infantry.
Borland, No. 6016, Reg. Sergt.-Major J. C. . Signal Company.
Brown, No. 5258, Company Sergeant-Major D. Infantry.
Cawthorn, No. 5573, Lance-Corporal W. . . Infantry.
Chapman, No. 689, Corporal R. L.. . . . Heavy Artillery.
Craig, No. 902, Corporal J. . . . . . . Infantry.
Dacombe, No. 5099, Batt. Sergt.-Major S. G. . Heavy Artillery.
Davis, No. 9996, Battery Sergeant-Major W. . Heavy Artillery.
Dewar, No. 3110, Corporal W. R. . . . . Infantry.
Dollery, No. 700, Gunner R. N. . . . . Heavy Artillery.
England, No. 3558, Sergeant W. J. . . . Infantry.
Fernie, No. 2658, Sergeant G. S. . . . . Infantry.
Fisher, No. 5664, Sergeant M. H. . . . . Infantry.
Govan, No. 972, Private F. G. . . . . . Infantry.
Guest, No. 5913, Sergeant W. . . . . . Heavy Artillery.
Healey, No. 1106, Private W. . . . . . Infantry.
Hean, No. 11511, Corporal D. McK. . . . Infantry.
Hilson, No. 2179, Sergeant J. C. . . . . Infantry.

Hodges, No. 469, Sergeant E. C. . . . . Heavy Artillery.
Hogarth, No. 13004, Sergeant F. . . . . Infantry.
Hope, No. 5293, Private C. J. . . . . . Infantry.
Horne, No. S6, Lance-Corporal F. C. . . . Infantry.
Howells, No. 1010, Sergeant W. K. . . . Heavy Artillery.
Hughes, No. 572, Bombardier F. . . . . Heavy Artillery.
Hurr, No. 571, Sergeant B. F. . . . . . Heavy Artillery.
Hutchins, No. 6165, Sergeant F. G. . . . Infantry.
Ison, No. 3161, Coy. Q.M.-Sergeant C. H. . Signal Company.
Jordan, No. 8431, Coy. Sergeant-Major A. J. . Infantry.
Keit, No. 4916, Coy. Sergeant-Major M. W. . Infantry.
Keith, No. 2300, Company Sergeant-Major P. Infantry.
King, No. 5540, Reg. Q.M.-Sergeant M. . . Infantry.
King, No. 3782, Coy. Sergeant-Major W. L. . Infantry.
Lilford, No. 920, Lance-Corporal A. F. . . Infantry.
Loubser, No. 4152, Private A. J. . . . . Infantry.
Mack, No. 15543, Sergeant J. G. . . . . Infantry.
Mallett, No. 5575, Sergeant H. F. P. . . . Infantry.
Marshall, No. 2834, Sergeant G. E. . . . Infantry.
Meyer, No. 2299, Sergeant J. W. . . . . Infantry.
Mundy, No. 9175, Sergeant P. . . . . . Infantry.
Naisby, No. 1813, Sergeant J. . . . . . Infantry.
Prebble, No. 348, Coy. Sergeant-Major E. E. . Infantry.
Rodgers, No. 6612, Coy. Sergeant-Major A. F.. Infantry.
Rynhoud, No. 12781, Lance-Corporal F. A. . Infantry.
Schroeder, No. 10907, Sergeant A. E. . . . Infantry.
Shapcott, No. 4914, Lance-Corporal H. . . Infantry.
Sinclair, No. 509, Sergeant W. N. . . . . Heavy Artillery.
Smith, No. 4087, Sergeant A. . . . . . Infantry.
Spence, No. S4, Sergeant F. H. . . . . Infantry.
Stafford, No. 9089, Private T. . . . . . Infantry.
Starke, No. 834, Corporal S. J. . . . . Infantry.
Stewart, No. 713, Lance-Sergeant T. T. . . Infantry.
Stuart, No. 7389, Corporal W. . . . . . Infantry.
Tanner, No. 1607, Private G. G. . . . . Infantry.
Thomson, No. 3058, Coy. Sergeant-Major J. M. Infantry.
Townes, No. 5241, Private L. A. . . . . Infantry.
Tye, No. 362, Sergeant R. C. . . . . . Heavy Artillery.
Vlok, No. 429, Private N. J. . . . . . Infantry.
Walsh, No. 216, Staff-Sergeant L. H. . . . S.A.M.C.

Warman, No. 50, Batt. Sergeant-Major H. G..   Heavy Artillery.
Watson, No. 1546, Sergeant J. . . . . .   Heavy Artillery.
Wellensky, No. X633, Private B. . . . .   Infantry.
Wilkie, No. 3657, Company Sergeant-Major F.   Infantry.

BAR TO MILITARY MEDAL.

Black, No. 3309, Sergeant A. J. . . . .   Infantry.
Cawthorn, No. 5573, Lance-Corporal W. . .   Infantry.
Cole, No. 8334, Private H. J. . . . . .   Infantry.
Cox, No. 588, Corporal H. F. . . . . .   Infantry.
Edgar, No. 68, Sergeant C. W. E.. . . . .   S.A.M.C.
Evans, No. S2, Corporal S. D. . . . . .   Infantry.
Flack, No. 2024, Corporal C. . . . . .   Infantry.
Hoaston, No. 6286, Corporal A. . . . .   Infantry.
Lang, No. 13287, Corporal B. G. . . . .   Infantry.
Langlands, No. 5032, Private W. G. . . .   Infantry.
MacLachlan, No. 2302, Corporal G. H. . .   Infantry.
M'Gregor, No. 498, Lance-Sergeant D. . .   Infantry.
Pullen, No. 823, Gunner C. E. . . . . .   Heavy Artillery.
St. George, No. 10599, Private R. T. . . .   Infantry.
Stober, No. S20, Lance-Corporal F. . . .   Infantry.
Willcocks, No. 4979, Corporal W. . . . .   Infantry.

MILITARY MEDAL.

Adlam, No. 4618, Private C. E. . . . .   Infantry.
Allen, No. 7018, Sergeant T. H. . . . .   Infantry.
Allen, No. 5471, Private V. W.. . . . .   Infantry.
Anderson, No. 441, Bombardier H. K. . .   Heavy Artillery.
Arnold, No. 5925, Private C. M. . . . .   Infantry.
Aupias, No. 2422, Private F. G. . . . .   Infantry.
Badcoe, No. 550, Sergeant T. J. . . . .   Infantry.
Bain, No. X282, Sergeant C. S.. . . . .   Signal Company.
Baker, No. 893, Private G. F. . . . . .   Infantry.
Baker, No. 4798, Private G. T.. . . . .   Infantry.
Ballantyne, No. 5329, Lance-Corporal A. . .   Signal Company.
Ballot, No. 1181, Gunner D. W. F. E.. . .   Heavy Artillery.
Baragwanath, No. 7958, Private A. J. . .   Infantry.

Barrable, No. 2436, Lance-Sergeant E. M. V.   **Infantry.**
Bayman, No. 3853, Private W.. . . . .   Infantry.
Becker, No. 16871, Private L. D. . . .   Infantry.
Bell, No. 4250, Sergeant T.. . . . .   Infantry.
Benson, No. 3871, Sergeant R. H.. . .   S.A.M.C.
Bertram, No. 9016, Corporal F. S. . .   Infantry.
Bester, No. 16897, Private C. . . .   Infantry.
Bettison, No. 1251, Gunner C. M. . . .   Heavy Artillery.
Biccard, No. 1326, Private R. C. . . .   Infantry.
Biebuyck, No. 2915, Lance-Corporal M. F. .   Signal Company.
Black, No. 3309, Lance-Corporal A. J. . .   Infantry.
Black, No. 26, Sergeant S. C. . . . .   S.A.M.C.
Boden, No. 12, Private T. H. . . . .   S.A.M.C.
Borchers, No. 14586, Private O. . . .   Infantry.
Botha, No. 8548, Private C. . . . .   Infantry.
Botterill, No. 4865, Corporal H. . . .   Infantry.
Bowen, No. 76, Corporal E. J.. . . .   Infantry.
Bowley, No. 2025, Corporal D. D. H. . .   Infantry.
Brampton, No. 8505, Sergeant T. C. . .   Infantry.
Brand, No. 533, Bombardier T. J.   . .   Heavy Artillery.
Brickhill, No. 5570, Coy. Sergt.-Major F. H. .   Infantry.
Broussow, No. 6896, Private E. J.   . .   Infantry.
Brown, No. 10557, Sergeant N. F.   . .   Heavy Artillery.
Burgess, No. 265, Gunner S. . . . .   Heavy Artillery.
Butler, No. 1831, Sergeant J. D. A. . .   Infantry.
Cabrita, No. 133, Lance-Corporal W. M. . .   Engineers.
Calder, No. 3252, Corporal K. . . .   Infantry.
Carlson, No. 5170, Private W. . . .   Infantry.
Carter, No. 536, Lance-Corporal E. . .   Infantry.
Casey, No. 3464, Corporal T. P. . . .   Infantry.
Cawthorn, No. 5573, Lance-Corporal W. . .   Infantry.
Celliers, No. 7379, Private J. D. . . .   Infantry.
Christie, No. 697, Gunner J. . . . .   Heavy Artillery.
Church, No. 2498, Sergeant J. . . .   Infantry.
Clarke, No. 629, Gunner A. D. . . .   Heavy Artillery.
Clarke, No. 9572, Private W. W. . . .   Infantry.
Cleverley, No. 3821, Private F.. . . .   Infantry.
Cloete, No. 1826, Lance-Corporal S. B. . .   Infantry.
Coaton, No. 1303, Gunner W. H. . . .   Heavy Artillery.
Codd, No. 11434, Corporal E. W. . . .   Infantry.

Coetzee, No. 12073, Private A. J. P. . . .	Infantry.
Coetzee, No. 14633, Lance-Corporal J. D.. .	Infantry.
Cole, No. 8334, Private H. J.	Infantry.
Collins, No. 769, Sapper H. P.	Engineers.
Collins, No. 9040, Private R. M.	Infantry.
Collocott, No. 4269, Sergeant C. D. . . .	Infantry.
Conacher, No. 16232, Private A. J. . . .	Infantry.
Conradie, No. 32, Private J. A.	S.A.M.C.
Cook, No. 427, Private T.	Infantry.
Coomber, No. 5303, Sergeant E. L. . . .	Infantry.
Cooper, No. 9226, Private C.	Infantry.
Cosser, No. X568, Gunner S. C. A. . . .	Heavy Artillery.
Cox, No. 588, Corporal H. F.	Infantry.
Cragg, No. 698, Lance-Corporal J. B. . . .	Infantry.
Croft, No. 8625, Private J. B.	Infantry.
Cronje, No. 2290, Private J. J.	Infantry.
Cummings, No. 4503, Sergeant A.	Infantry.
Cunningham, No. 923, Lance-Sergeant J. J. .	Infantry.
Cuthill, No. X290, Sapper J. D.	Signal Company.
Davenport, No. 54, Lance-Corporal J.. . .	Engineers.
Davies, No. 192, Gunner W. A.	Heavy Artillery.
Davies, No. 12354, Private W. J.	Infantry.
Davis, No. 2022, Corporal C. S.	Infantry.
Davis, No. 423, Corporal W. J.	Heavy Artillery.
Dawson, No. 228, Lance-Corporal A. E. . .	Engineers.
Dawson, No. 16888, Sergeant J. E. . . .	Infantry.
De Beer, No. 13451, Private W. A. . . .	Infantry.
Dent, No. 13263, Corporal H. C.	Infantry.
Dey, No. 12783, Private H..	Infantry.
Dickson, No. 611, Corporal J.	Heavy Artillery.
Dignon, No. 10336, Private H. A.	Infantry.
Dinnes, No. 3240, Lance-Corporal J. . . .	Infantry.
Dixon, No. 3488, Lance-Corporal C. . . .	Infantry.
Doig, No. 197, Sapper E. H.	Engineers.
Dowaithe, No. 3100, Private R.	Infantry.
Doyle, No. 669, Sapper J. R.	Engineers.
Duffy, No. 709, Gunner J.	Heavy Artillery.
Duncan, No. 1579, Private R.	Infantry.
Dunstone, No. 1186, Private S. T. . . .	Infantry.
Du Preez, No. 5636, Private F. J.. . . .	Infantry.

Du Toit, No. 3882, Private J. J.	Infantry.
Edgar, No. 68, Sergeant C. W..	S.A.M.C.
Edgar, No. 15959, Private H. M. S. . . .	Infantry.
Egan, No. 6514, Sapper C. D.	Signal Company.
Ellis, No. 1356, Gunner A. W. J.	Heavy Artillery.
Ellis, No. 11522, Private G. W. J.. . . .	Infantry.
Ellwood, No. 7062, Private W. B. M. . . .	Infantry.
Erlank, No. X613, Private G.	Infantry.
Estment, No. 4787, Lance-Corporal A. . .	Infantry.
Evans, No. 3185, Sergeant J. A.	Infantry.
Evans, No. S2, Lance-Corporal S. D. . . .	Infantry.
Fairburn, No. 112, Lance-Corporal G. . .	Infantry.
Farmer, No. 17744, Private E. F. C. . . .	Infantry.
Fennessy, No. 90, Private C. E.	Infantry.
Ferreira, No. X297, Sapper B. P.	Signal Company.
Flack, No. 2024, Private C.	Infantry.
Flanagan, No. 546, Lance-Corporal W. N. .	Infantry.
Flannagan, No. 17182, Lance-Corporal W. M.	Infantry.
Foden, No. 8451, Corporal G. W.	Infantry.
Forbes, No. 2175, Private J.	Infantry.
Forman, No. 2177, Lance-Sergeant J. L. . .	Infantry.
Fourie, No. 624, Sapper J. J.	Engineers.
Fritz, No. 6407, Private E. H.	Infantry.
Gardiner, No. 7628, Sergeant T. H. . . .	Infantry.
Gardner, No. X727, Private E. H.. . . .	Infantry.
Garland, No. 3241, Lance-Corporal F. L. . .	Infantry.
Gaskon, No. 8130, Corporal A. H.	Infantry.
Gaston, No. 11342, Lance-Corporal J. A. . .	Infantry.
Gerber, No. 6155, Sergeant H. J.	Infantry.
Gibson, No. 8523, Private P. A.	Infantry.
Giles, No. 1064, Gunner E. H.	Heavy Artillery.
Glennie, No. 15130, Private S. A.	Infantry.
Goldsworthy, No. 8455, Private F.. . . .	Infantry.
Goodwill, No. 3865, Corporal H. P. . . .	S.A.M.C.
Gourlay, No. 6210, Lance-Corporal J. H. . .	Signal Company.
Graham, No. 14829, Private C. F.	Infantry.
Granger, No. 4418, Private J. L.	Infantry.
Gray, No. 425, Private A.	Infantry.
Gray, No. 591, Corporal W. A..	Infantry.
Green, No. 9672, Lance-Corporal G. P. . .	Signal Company.

Greenhough, No. 6346, Corporal P. R.   . .   Infantry.
Greenish, No. 8752, Lance-Corporal M. T.   . Infantry.
Grenfell, No. 8970, Private G. A. . . . .   Infantry.
Guerini, No. 6874, Corporal V. . . . . .   Infantry.
Hall, No. 3351, Private J. . . . . . .   Infantry.
Hamilton, No. R1783, Private B. B. . . .   Infantry.
Hammond, No. 6310, Corporal L. H. . . .   Signal Company.
Hands, No. 9626, Sergeant C. . . . . .   Infantry.
Hansen, No. 6213, Sergeant W.   . . . .   Signal Company.
Hansen, No. X149, Gunner W. C. . . . .   Heavy Artillery.
Hardwick, No. 7065, Sergeant R. E. S.   . .   Infantry.
Hare, No. 888, Private H. L. . . . . .   Infantry.
Harris, No. 5027, Private W. F. . . . .   Infantry.
Harris, No. 5687, Lance-Corporal W. S. . .   Infantry.
Harrison, No. 3458, Private R. W.   . . .   Infantry.
Hart, No. 4278, Lance-Corporal G. A.. . .   Infantry.
Hawke, No. 2955, Sergeant W. C. . . . .   Infantry.
Hawkins, No. 1004, Private C. W.   . . .   Infantry.
Hawthorne, No. 7368, Lance-Corporal J. . .   Infantry.
Healy, No. 7785, Private P. W.   . . . .   Infantry.
Heathcote, No. 880, Lance-Corporal L. S.   .   Infantry.
Hein, No. 466, Gunner B. . . . . . .   Heavy Artillery.
Hemmings, No. 749, Gunner W. . . . .   Heavy Artillery.
Hendry, No. 54, Sergeant A. . . . . .   Heavy Artillery.
Henning, No. 9468, Corporal J. A.. . . .   Infantry.
Heunis, No. R1769, Sergeant C. M.   . . .   Infantry.
Hincks, No. X154, Sergeant H. T.. . . .   Heavy Artillery.
Hinwood, No. 128, Sergeant S. J. . . . .   Infantry.
Hoaston, No. 6286, Corporal A.   . . . .   Infantry.
Hodgson, No. 793, Private J. . . . . .   Infantry.
Holborn, No. X15, Sergeant J. S. . . . .   Infantry.
Holdsworth, No. 4476, Private W.. . . .   Infantry.
Holiday, No. 906, Private T. H. . . . .   Infantry.
Hollenbury, No. 5726, Private W. . . . .   Infantry.
Holliday, No. 12768, Private M. A.   . . .   Infantry.
Hollington, No. 5381, Private E. E.   . . .   Infantry.
Holmes, No. 4399, Private R. J. . . . .   Infantry.
Hook, No. 746, Private T. C. . . . . .   Infantry.
Hopkins, No. 1785, Gunner D. A. J.   . . .   Heavy Artillery.
Hosking, No. 14070, Private J. F.. . . .   Infantry.

Howard, No. 16253, Private C. L.	Infantry.
Howard, No. X121, Bombardier H. W. . .	Heavy Artillery.
Hugo-Brunt, No. 196, Gunner H.	Heavy Artillery.
Hume, No. 4855, Private D. M.	Infantry.
Humphries, No. 8573, Private W.	Infantry.
Hunter, No. 259, Sergeant W. F.	Engineers.
Huntley, No. 12798, Private W. B. . . .	Infantry.
Hurd, No. 15058, Private H. K.	Infantry.
Huskisson, No. 100, Sergeant D. S. . . .	S.A.M.C.
Ind, No. 8484, Private H. G.	Infantry.
Inglis, No. 15436, Lance-Corporal W. B. . .	Infantry.
Jackson, No. 4825, Sapper V. D.	Signal Company.
Jacobs, No. 123, Private C. J.	S.A.M.C.
James, No. 5956, Sergeant W. N.	Infantry.
Johnson, No. 1358, Private J.	Infantry.
Jones, No. 10162, Corporal A.	Infantry.
Jones, No. 583, Lance-Corporal A.	Engineers.
Jones, No. 8861, Private P. D.	Infantry.
Jordan, No. 5088, Private M.	Infantry.
Jorgensen, No. 527, Sergeant W. H. . . .	Signal Company.
Juul, No. 10624, Sergeant A. W.	Infantry.
Keates, No. 150, Lance-Corporal F. J. . .	Engineers.
Kerwin, No. 15150, Private A. T. K. . . .	Infantry.
Kikillas, No. 1592, Private T. N.	Heavy Artillery.
Kirkland, No. 125, Private F. G.	S.A.M.C.
Kirkland, No. X286, Corporal J.	Signal Company.
Kretschmer, No. 12216, Lance-Corporal H. F.	Infantry.
Kriel, No. 2965, Sergeant J.	Infantry.
Kruger, No. 8449, Private P. S.	Infantry.
Lagerstroom, No. 5211, Lance-Sergeant J. .	Infantry.
Laidler, No. 7606, Lance-Sergeant J. . . .	Infantry.
Lang, No. 13287, Private B. G.	Infantry.
Langlands, No. 5032, Private W. G. . . .	Infantry.
Laverack, No. 4706, Sergeant A.	Infantry.
Lawrence, No. 11941, Private R. J. . . .	Infantry.
Lazarus, No. 7843, Private C. M.	Infantry.
Lee, No. 16767, Lance-Corporal F. E. . .	Infantry.
Lee, No. 10130, Corporal J.	Infantry.
Lees, No. X233, Gunner J. S.	Heavy Artillery.
Leith, No. 295, Gunner G. B. A.	Heavy Artillery.

Lerche, No. 16796, Private H. F. . . . . Infantry.
Levey, No. 16114, Private H. G. . . . . Infantry.
Levinson, No. 2656, Private L.. . . . . Infantry.
Liebenberg, No. 1707, Private B. J. . . . Infantry.
Lotz, No. 14169, Private J. C. . . . . . Infantry.
Loubser, No. 1138, Lance-Corporal J. J. . . Infantry.
Lowe, No. 12481, Private C. V. . . . . Infantry.
Lowings, No. 22, Private B. A.. . . . . Infantry.
Lubbe, No. 4920, Private G. J. J. . . . . Infantry.
Lubbie, No. 1266, Corporal T. A. . . . . Infantry.
Lumb, No. 651, Sapper F. . . . . . . Engineers.
MacDonald, No. 8591, Sergeant D. . . . Infantry.
MacGuire, No. 3304, Private J. N.. . . . Infantry.
MacIntosh, No. 4691, Private A. G. M. . . Infantry.
Mackay, No. 10415, Private W. . . . . Infantry.
Mackay, No. 12432, Private D.. . . . . Infantry.
MacLachlan, No. 2302, Private G. H. . . . Infantry.
Magnussen, No. 453, Private M. A. . . . S.A.M.C.
Makepeace, No. 4106, Private R. B. N. . . Infantry.
Maloney, No. 3760, Private W.. . . . . Infantry.
Manzie, No. 13533, Private A. J. . . . . Infantry.
Marshall, No. X305, Lance-Corporal C. E. . Signal Company.
Martin, No. 8473, Private A. . . . . . Infantry.
May, No. 3614, Private G. H. . . . . . Signal Company.
M'Clelland, No. 6852, Lance-Corporal J. . . Infantry.
M'Donald, No. 6845, Sergeant W. S. . . . Infantry.
M'Donald, No. 13351, Private C. A. . . . Infantry.
M'Dougall, No. XIII, Gunner J. S. . . . Heavy Artillery.
M'Gregor, No. 498, Lance-Sergeant D. . . Infantry.
M'Innes, No. 6462, Sergeant N. . . . . Infantry.
M'Kendrick, No. 159, Lance-Corporal M. . . Infantry.
M'Kenna, No. 157, Lance-Corporal J. P. . . Engineers.
M'Kenzie, No. 14203, Private A. C. . . . Infantry.
M'Lean, No. 7069, Lance-Sergeant D. . . Infantry.
M'Lellan, No. 6987, Sergeant A. W. . . . Infantry.
M'Millan, No. 4074, Private J. . . . . . Infantry.
Meggy, No. 761, Lance-Corporal R. S. . . Infantry.
Messum, No. 1600, Gunner G. G. . . . . Heavy Artillery.
Meyers, No. 6571, Private L. C. C.. . . . Infantry.
Milella, No. 8346, Sergeant O. A. . . . . Infantry.

Miller, No. 3479, Sergeant D. H. C. . . . Infantry.
Mills, No. 1281, Corporal S. G. . . . . . Infantry.
Mitchell, No. 6291, Lance-Corporal G. F. . . Infantry.
Mitchell, No. 8453, Private T. . . . . . Infantry.
Monoran, No. 1356, Private F. G. . . . . Infantry.
Moore, No. 7814, Sergeant C. V. . . . . Infantry.
Moreton, No. 2898, Corporal H. B. . . . Signal Company.
Munro, No. 300, Gunner G. W.. . . . . Heavy Artillery.
Munro, No. 8928, Private H. W. . . . . Infantry.
Murray, No. 6067, Corporal J. W.. . . . Infantry.
Nelson, No. 161, Private R. W. . . . . S.A.M.C.
Nicholl, No. X124, Gunner G. . . . . . Heavy Artillery.
Nicholls, No. 5444, Sergeant H. . . . . Infantry.
Nicholls, No. 1941, Sergeant T. H.. . . . Infantry.
Nicholson, No. 2418, Private L. . . . . Infantry.
Nicolle, No. 4817, Corporal J. . . . . . Signal Company.
Noble, No. 3198, Corporal C. A. . . . . Infantry.
Noble, No. 1458, Lance-Corporal J. E. T. . Infantry.
Norvall, No. 6415, Sergeant W. A.. . . . Infantry.
O'Boyle, No. 16, Gunner L. N. . . . . Heavy Artillery.
O'Connor, No. 3886, Lance-Corporal C. J. . Signal Company.
Oliver, No. 5291, Corporal S. . . . . . Infantry.
Oosthuizen, No. 10386, Private W. J. J. . . Infantry.
Orsmond, No. 16703, Lance-Corporal S. . . Infantry.
Owen, No. 7102, Corporal A. E. . . . . Infantry.
Paddock, No. 9082, Private J. R. . . . . Infantry.
Page, No. 7032, Corporal R. . . . . . Infantry.
Page, No. 1591, Corporal S. A. . . . . Signal Company.
Pains, No. 590, Gunner J. F. . . . . . Heavy Artillery.
Parfitt, No. 165, Private F. W.. . . . . S.A.M.C.
Parfitt, No. 145, Lance-Corporal W. H. . . Engineers.
Parker, No. 118, Sergeant E. H. . . . . Heavy Artillery.
Parkinson, No. 1512, Lance-Corporal J. G. . Infantry.
Patience, No. 12998, Private J. . . . . Infantry.
Paton, No. 211, Gunner R. . . . . . . Heavy Artillery.
Patterson, No. 3140, Sergeant W. . . . . Infantry.
Pownall, No. 3863, Driver C. . . . . . S.A.M.C.
Peacock, No. 827, Bombardier E. M. . . . Heavy Artillery.
Pearce, No. 172, Private H. S. . . . . . S.A.M.C.
Pearce, No. 8182, Private W. C. . . . . Infantry.

Pentz, No. 10516, Lance-Corporal H. F. . . . Infantry.
Perrett, No. 614, Sergeant W. J. . . . . Heavy Artillery.
Perrie, No. 705, Lance-Corporal J.. . . . Infantry.
Prentice, No. 5097, Private W.. . . . . Infantry.
Preston, No. 17806, Lance-Corporal S. . . Infantry.
Price, No. 84, Corporal S. . . . . . . Heavy Artillery.
Pringle, No. 6617, Private G. G. . . . . Infantry.
Pritchard, No. 17620, Private E. E. . . . Infantry.
Pullen, No. 823, Gunner C. E. . . . . . Heavy Artillery.
Raats, No. 11230, Private P. J. . . . . Infantry.
Reece, No. 704, Corporal A. O.. . . . . Engineers.
Reingold, No. 8446, Lance-Corporal J. . . Infantry.
Rennie, No. 5827, Private A. . . . . . Infantry.
Reynolds, No. 12281, Sergeant G. J. . . . Infantry.
Rhodin, No. 12739, Private W. H.. . . . Infantry.
Richardson, No. 7961, Lance-Corporal J.. . Infantry.
Richardson, No. 7955, Private T. L. . . . Infantry.
Ritchie, No. 5762, Private F. . . . . . Infantry.
Robertson, No. 5250, Sergeant F. . . . . Infantry.
Robinson, No. 409, Corporal H. E. B.. . . Heavy Artillery.
Rodgers, No. X295, Sapper H. C. . . . . Signal Company.
Ross, No. 1534, Lance-Corporal F. W. . . Infantry.
Ross, No. 841, Gunner W. T. W. . . . . Heavy Artillery.
Rowley, No. 9013, Sergeant E. . . . . Infantry.
Rundle, No. 15860, Private S. P. . . . . Infantry.
Ryder, No. 3114, Corporal A. . . . . . Infantry.
St. George, No. 5599, Private J. C. . . . Infantry.
St. George, No. 10599, Private R. T. . . . Infantry.
Salsbury, No. 869, Corporal E. . . . . Heavy Artillery.
Scholes, No. 213, Bombardier C. E. . . . Heavy Artillery.
Schultz, No. 11904, Private H. . . . . Infantry.
Schuur, No. 544, Gunner H. M. . . . . Heavy Artillery.
Scott, No. 10114, Lance-Corporal R. C. . . Infantry.
Seddon, No. 4725, Lance-Corporal L. J. . . Infantry.
Shapcott, No. 1971, Lance-Corporal F. R. . Infantry.
Sharman, No. 522, Coy. Sergt.-Major W. . . Engineers.
Shearer, No. 10437, Sergeant J. . . . . Infantry.
Shepherd, No. 6479, Sapper J. . . . . . Signal Company.
Sheppherd, No. 7491, Private G. S. . . . Infantry.
Sherman, No. 423, Private H. J. . . . . Infantry.

Simpson, No. 7703, Sergeant J. N.	Infantry.
Sinclair, No. 509, Sergeant W. N.	Heavy Artillery.
Sjoberg, No. 373, Private A. B.	Infantry.
Slade, No. X302, Bombardier A. J. . . .	Heavy Artillery.
Smith, No. 979, Sergeant A.	Infantry.
Smith, No. 4087, Sergeant A.	Infantry.
Smith, No. 7217, Private A. W. C.	Infantry.
Smith, No. 6796, Sergeant H. C.	Infantry.
Smuts, No. 582, Private M. R.	Infantry.
Snibbe, No. 9742, Sergeant M. J.	Infantry.
Sobey, No. 8116, Private W. N.	Infantry.
Somerville, No. 2291, Corporal W. . . .	Infantry.
Spangenberg, No. 10074, Private J. M. . .	Infantry.
Speed, No. 4683, Lance-Corporal T. H. . .	Infantry.
Spencer, No. 8032, Private J. G. A. . . .	Infantry.
Sprague, No. 15663, Private H. G. R. . .	Infantry.
Stafford, No. 9089, Sergeant T.	Infantry.
Steele, No. 877, Bombardier G.	Heavy Artillery.
Steele, No. 1905, Private H.	Infantry.
Stephen, No. 1052, Lance-Sergeant R. G. . .	Infantry.
Stephen, No. 616, Bombardier W.	Heavy Artillery.
Stewart, No. 713, Lance-Sergeant T. T. . .	Infantry.
Stewart, No. 2037, Private W. A.	Infantry.
Still, No. 13, Sergeant J. F.	Infantry.
Stober, No. 20, Lance-Corporal F.	Infantry.
Strickland, No. 4959, Lance-Corporal G. C. .	Infantry.
Sumner, No. 3677, Corporal H. L.	Infantry.
Super, No. 451, Private E. S.	S.A.M.C.
Surman, No. 9537, Corporal M. W. . . .	Infantry.
Sutherland, No. 2542, Corporal N. . . .	Infantry.
Suttie, No. 3811, Private L. H.	Infantry.
Swan, No. 9351, Private V. E.	Infantry.
Swanepoel, No. 16823, Private J. J. F. . .	Infantry.
Swaraston, No. 50, Sergeant H. D. . . .	Engineers.
Swart, No. 14796, Private J. J. L. . . .	Infantry.
Symonds, No. 10661, Sergeant J.	Infantry.
Tanner, No. 101, Lance-Corporal A. D. . .	Engineers.
Tasker, No. 631, Gunner G. T. B.	Heavy Artillery.
Taylor, No. 6285, Private H. M.	Infantry.
Taylor, No. X24, Corporal J. H.	Infantry.

Taylor, No. 886, Sergeant O. . . . . . Heavy Artillery.
Taylor, No. 2581, Corporal W. . . . . . Infantry.
Tennant, No. 8064, Sergeant J. R.. . . . Infantry.
Thomas, No. 9335, Private C. D. . . . . Infantry.
Thompson, No. 160, Private B. . . . . Infantry.
Thompson, No. 7747, Sergeant D. . . . . Infantry.
Thompson, No. 11114, Private J. . . . . Infantry.
Thompson, No. 290, Sergeant W. G. . . . Infantry.
Thomson, No. 6586, Private A. . . . . Infantry.
Thomson, No. 5871, Lance-Corporal A. R. . Infantry.
Thorpe, No. 5835, Corporal H. S. . . . . Infantry.
Thow, No. 212, Private J. M. . . . . . S.A.M.C.
Thurgood, No. 9092, Sergeant A. H. . . . Infantry.
Thurman, No. 416, Bombardier E. G. . . Heavy Artillery.
Tomsett, No. 213, Private R. . . . . . S.A.M.C.
Topp, No. 885, Gunner R. M. . . . . . Heavy Artillery.
Tregonning, No. 890, Gunner W. J. . . . Heavy Artillery.
Trehoeven, No. 8711, Private W. H. . . . Infantry.
Tucker, No. 205, Private S. . . . . . S.A.M.C.
Tuer, No. 4969, Sergeant J.. . . . . . Infantry.
Turnbull, No. 3875, Driver D. . . . . . S.A.M.C.
Turnbull, No. 11, Bombardier J. M. M. . . Heavy Artillery.
Twynham, No. 11928, Lance-Corporal W. C.. Infantry.
Usborne, No. 7981, Batt. Sergt.-Major H. H. Heavy Artillery.
Van Buuren, No. 10383, Sapper N. A. A. . Signal Company.
Van Heerden, No. R1678, Lance-Cpl. J. L. . Infantry.
Van Rensburg, No. 16820, Private P.. . . Infantry.
Van Rensburg, No. 258, Sapper J. A. J. . . Engineers.
Van der Walt, No. 11990, Private N. . . . Infantry.
Vice, No. 51, Sergeant J. H. B. . . . . Heavy Artillery.
Vimpany, No. X193, Private A. . . . . Infantry.
Walker, No. 7455, Private J. . . . . . Infantry.
Wall, No. 7701, Sergeant A. W. . . . . Infantry.
Wanliss, No. 4197, Private J. . . . . . Infantry.
Ward, No. 9511, Sergeant E. . . . . . Infantry.
Waterhouse, No. 11935, Private J. . . . Infantry.
Wattrus, No. 585, Bombardier C. E. . . . Heavy Artillery.
Waugh, No. 11078, Private P. . . . . . Infantry.
Wells, No. 11860, Sapper A. . . . . . Signal Company.
Wentzel, No. 9704, Sapper E. J. . . . . Signal Company.

Whillier, No. 16599, Private C. E. . . . . Infantry.
White, No. 10216, Private J. R. . . . . Infantry.
White, No. 4122, Sergeant W. M. . . . . Infantry.
Wilkins, No. R1473, Sergeant W. T. . . . Infantry.
Willard, No. 7944, Private W. F. . . . . Infantry.
Willcocks, No. 4979, Corporal W. . . . . Infantry.
Williams, No. 15300, Private A. R. . . . Infantry.
Williams, No. 315, Bombardier C. . . . . Heavy Artillery.
Williams, No. 5752, Corporal G. W. . . . Infantry.
Williams, No. 913, Staff-Sergeant W. . . . Heavy Artillery.
Wood, No. 13123, Corporal T. C. P. . . . Infantry.
Woolgar, No. 217, Private C. S. . . . . S.A.M.C.
Wright, No. 4116, Corporal A. J. . . . . Infantry.
Wright, No. 13860, Corporal C. H.. . . . Infantry.
Wright, No. 17091, Private G. F. . . . . Infantry.
Young, No. 5095, Sergeant J. J. . . . . Infantry.
Yuill, No. 652, Corporal A. . . . . . . Engineers.
Zahn, No. 7440, Sergeant F. S. T. . . . . Infantry.

MERITORIOUS SERVICE MEDAL.

Barends, No. 959, Lance-Corporal H. A. . . Labour Corps.
Bayne, No. 3346, Coy. Q.M.-Sergeant W. . . Infantry.
Berry, No. 4554, Staff-Sergeant A.. . . . Infantry.
Blackwell, No. 266, Bombardier M. C. . . Heavy Artillery.
Bonacina, No. 6148, Sergeant L. . . . . Infantry.
Bothwell, No. 5051, Sergeant-Major H. . . Pay Corps.
Boyce, No. 3189, Sergeant D. R. . . . . Infantry.
Brown, No. 3504, Sergeant J. . . . . . Infantry.
Burton, No. 5639, Lance-Corporal J. . . . Signal Company.
Burton, No. 6211, Sapper R. J. . . . . Signal Company.
Butlin, No. 83, Reg. Q.M.-Sergeant H. . . Labour Corps.
Clatworthy, No. HT4185, Coy. Sgt.-Maj. W. M.   Cape Aux. Horse
                                               Transport.
Clews, No. 4, Company Sergeant-Major J. C. . Labour Corps.
Coombes, No. 3121, Sergeant A. S. . . . Infantry.
Craig, No. 1347, Reg. Sergt.-Major W. . . Infantry.
Cruickshank, No. 4812, Coy. Q.M.-Sergeant P.   Signal Company.
Dalton, No. 6334, Sergeant W. J. . . . . Signal Company.

Evans, No. 4180, Sergeant W. D. . . . . Infantry.
Ferguson, No. 2004, Coy. Q.M.-Sergeant A. . Infantry.
Field, No. 129, Sergeant W. C. . . . . Labour Corps.
Forsyth, No. X12, Sergeant J. R. . . . . Infantry.
Gadd, No. 167, Sergeant W. P.. . . . . Labour Corps.
Glencross, No. 3120, Sergeant C. M. G. . . Infantry.
Gonsalves, No. 5026, Coy. Q.M.-Sergt. M. A. . Infantry.
Gordge, No. 80, Quartermaster-Sergeant J. H. S.A.M.C.
Greenwood, No. 21654, Private J. H. . . . Infantry.
Guy, No. 1361, Sergeant E. A.. . . . . Heavy Artillery.
Hall, No. 5332, Sergeant P. C. W.. . . . Signal Company.
Hickman, No. 6294, Reg. Q.M.-Sergt. C. S. . Infantry.
Holborn, No. X15, Corporal J. S. . . . . Infantry.
Horridge, No. 19322, Sergeant-Major J. D. . Staff.
Hudson, No. 2817, Sergeant-Major T. . . Infantry.
Jamieson, No. X503, Staff-Sergeant T. C. . Labour Corps.
Kenny, No. 2330, Staff-Sergeant P. . . . Infantry.
Knox, No. 306, Quartermaster-Sergeant A. J. S.A.M.C.
Lightfoot, No. 344, Staff-Sergeant R. . . . S.A.M.C.
Lowe, No. 4700, Sergeant T. E. . . . . Infantry.
M'Callum, No. 3650, Sergeant J. A. . . . Signal Company.
M'Dowell, No. 41, Reg. Sergt.-Major A. H. . Labour Corps.
M'Farlane, No. 4317, Sergeant J. . . . . Infantry.
M'Feggans, No. 125, Colour-Sergeant A. . . Labour Corps.
M'Pherson, No. 4011, Sergeant C.. . . . Infantry.
Melrose, No. 20, Superintendent-Clerk G. M. . Labour Corps.
Orchard, No. 165, Coy. Q.M.-Sergeant A. O. . Labour Corps.
Phillips, No. 11764, Corporal L. D. . . . Infantry.
Powell, No. X523, Staff-Sergeant H. E. . . Pay Corps.
Reeves, No. 10585, Sergeant J. H.. . . . Infantry.
Rhind, No. 53, Company Sergeant-Major F. . Staff.
Ritchie, No. 6658, Sergeant H. . . . . Signal Company.
Roxburgh, No. 1, Reg. Sergt.-Major A. . . Labour Corps.
Russell, No. 9110, Coy. Q.M. Sergt. E. E. R.. Infantry.
Sayer, No. 3112, Colour-Sergeant A. . . . Infantry.
Sheard, No. 3616, Sergeant O. F. . . . . Signal Company.
Shepherd, No. 4340, Coy. Sgt.-Major D. D. . Infantry.
Sowden, No. 4716, Sergeant C. H. V. . . . Signal Company.
Stanley, No. 75, Colour-Sergeant A. E. . . Labour Corps.
Stearns, No. 2164, Private E.. . . . . Infantry.

372 APPENDIX VII.

Stirton, No. V50, Sergeant-Major S. A. . . Engineers.
Stokell, No. 1929, Coy. Sergt.-Major E. R. . Infantry:
Summers, No. 1046, Gunner H. . . . . Heavy Artillery.
Thompson, No. 160, Private B. . . . . Infantry.
Trimmer, No. 1375, Reg. Q.M.-Sergt. H. W. . Infantry.
Truss, No. 955, Sergeant W. G. . . . . Heavy Artillery.
Walker, No. X235, Sergeant-Major J. H. . . Staff.
Watson, No. 7546, Lance-Corporal W. . . Infantry.
Weddell, No. 425, Staff-Sergeant A. C. . . S.A.M.C.
White, No. 408, Quartermaster-Sergeant J. H. S.A.M.C.
White, No. 896, Bombardier T. W. . . . Heavy Artillery.
Wilkinson, No. 910, Sergeant F. . . . . Labour Corps.
Williams, No. 5906, Sergeant A. E. . . . Infantry.
Willson, No. 6393, Sergeant H. B. . . . Signal Company.
Wilson, No. HT2499, Coy. Sergt.-Major. H. J. Cape Aux. Horse
                                          Transport.
Witney, No. 3536, Coy. Sergt.-Major. A. W. . Infantry.
Woodhead, No. 3208, Sergeant H. C. . . . Infantry.
Zeederberg, No. 85, Superintendent-Clerk H.. Labour Corps.

MENTIONED IN DESPATCHES.

OFFICERS.

Allin, Captain H. G. W. . . . . . Labour Corps.
Alston, Lieutenant-Colonel C. W.. . . Heavy Artillery.
Anderson, Lieutenant-Colonel J. D. . . Cape Aux. Horse
                                       Transport.
Bailey, Lieutenant H. . . . . . . Heavy Artillery.
*Baker, Lieutenant-Colonel J. M. . . . Staff.
Barnard, Major A. J. C. . . . . . Labour Corps.
Bendlestein, Lieutenant A. . . . . Heavy Artillery.
*Bennett, Lieutenant-Colonel G. M. . . Heavy Artillery.
Blaine, Captain C. H. . . . . . . Heavy Artillery.
Blew, Lieutenant-Colonel T. H. . . . Heavy Artillery.
Bond, Lieutenant C. H. . . . . . Heavy Artillery.
Brydon, Major W. . . . . Heavy Artillery.
Cameron, Q.M. and Hon. Captain C. S. . Labour Corps.
Campion, Lieutenant R. R. . . . . Heavy Artillery.
Chester, Second-Lieutenant R. S.. . . Heavy Artillery.

Christian, Lieutenant-Colonel E. . . . Infantry.
*Cochran, Major F. E. . . . . . . Infantry.
Collins, Lieutenant F. . . . . . . Signal Company.
*Collins, Lieutenant-Colonel F. R. . . Engineers.
Cooke, Lieutenant F. A. . . . . . Signal Company.
Crooks, Q.M. and Hon. Lieutenant A. S. Infantry.
Currie, Second-Lieutenant J. . . . . Heavy Artillery.
Davis, Captain F. M. . . . . . . Infantry.
****Dawson, Brigadier-General F. S. . . . Staff.
Dickerson, Captain F. J. . . . . . Labour Corps.
Drummond, Captain J. . . . . . S.A.M.C.
Duff, Colonel C. de V. . . . . . . Labour Corps.
*Edwards, Major S. B. . . . . . . Heavy Artillery.
Ellis, Captain P. H. . . . . . . Infantry.
Emmett, Lieutenant-Colonel J. J. C.. . Labour Corps.
Farmer, Lieutenant P. D. . . . . . Infantry.
Farrell, Captain T. . . . . Infantry.
*Fawcus, Lieutenant-Colonel A. . . . Labour Corps.
*Forbes, Lieutenant E. C. . . . . . Infantry.
Geddes, Captain W. L. . . . . . Labour Corps.
Goodwin, Second-Lieutenant B. W. . . Infantry.
Gordon, Captain W. L.. . . . . . S.A.M.C.
Grady, Captain E. E. D. . . . . . Infantry.
Green, Second-Lieutenant A. P. . . . Heavy Artillery.
Greene, Captain L. . . . . Infantry.
*Hands, Major P. A. M.. . . . . . Heavy Artillery.
Harris, Major J. J. F. . . . . . . Infantry.
Harrison, Lieutenant-Colonel N. . . . Signal Company.
Heal, Lieutenant-Colonel F. H. . . . Infantry.
Heenan, Major C. R. . . . . . . Infantry.
Hemming, Major H. S. J. L. . . . . Infantry.
Hill, Lieutenant W. J. . . . . . . Infantry.
*Hunt, Major D. R. . . . . Infantry.
Hunt, Second-Lieutenant V. A. . . . Infantry.
Ison, Lieutenant C. H. . . . . . Signal Company.
Jackson, Captain J. W. . . . . . Infantry.
Jacobs, Captain L. M. . . . . . . Infantry.
Jacobsby, Lieutenant-Colonel J. . . . Labour Corps.
*Jenkins, Lieutenant-Colonel H. H. . . Infantry.
Johnson, Captain W. J. . . . . . Signal Company.

Jones, Lieutenant-Colonel F. A. . . . . Infantry.
Joseph, Second-Lieutenant H. A.. . . Infantry.
Kernick, Second-Lieutenant R. G. . . Infantry.
King, Second-Lieutenant F. . . . . Infantry.
Lawrence, Second-Lieutenant G. G. J. . Infantry.
Lawrence, Captain H. R. . . . . . S.A.M.C.
Lawrie, Captain M. B. . . . . . . S.A.M.C.
*Lennox, Captain J. . . . . . . Chaplains Dept.
**Lukin, Major-General Sir H. T. . . . Staff.
Maasdorp, Major L. H.. . . . . . Heavy Artillery.
MacLeod, Lieutenant-Colonel D. M. . . Infantry.
Mallett, Lieutenant S. . . . . . . Infantry.
Marshall, Captain H. E. . . . . . Labour Corps.
M'Lean, Lieutenant W. . . . . . Infantry.
Medlicott, Second-Lieutenant G. H. . . Infantry.
Mellish, Second-Lieutenant F. W. . . Heavy Artillery.
Miller, Captain R. S. . . . . . . Heavy Artillery.
Mills, Second-Lieutenant F. E. . . . Infantry.
*Mullins, Captain A. G.. . . . . . Heavy Artillery.
Mullins, Major H. R. . . . . . . S.A.M.C.
*Murray, Major C. M. . . . . . . S.A.M.C.
Murray-M'Gregor, Lieutenant A. . . . Heavy Artillery.
Ormiston, Major T. . . . . . . Infantry.
Owen, Captain J. W. W. . . . . . Chaplains Dept.
*Page, Lieutenant P. T. A.. . . . . Heavy Artillery.
Palmer, Major J. E. . . . . . . Labour Corps.
Pickburn, Major W. H. . . . . . Heavy Artillery.
*Power, Major M. S. . . . . . . S.A.M.C.
Preston, Lieutenant W. G. . . . . Labour Corps.
*Pringle, Major R. N. . . . . . . S.A.M.C.
*Pritchard, Colonel S. A. M. . . . . Labour Corps.
Purcocks, Captain G. F. . . . . . Heavy Artillery.
Pybus, Captain W. H. L. . . . . . Engineers.
Rann, Major A. E. . . . . Heavy Artillery.
Richardson, Q.M. and Hon. Lieut. W. . S.A.M.C.
Ridley, Captain E. G. . . . . . . Heavy Artillery.
Roberts, Second-Lieutenant C. W. . . Infantry.
Roper, Captain A. W. F. . . . . . Heavy Artillery.
Roseby, Lieutenant P. R. . . . . . Infantry.
*Ross, Captain F. M. . . . . . . Signal Company.

Ross-Garner, Lieutenant-Colonel C. R. J.   Labour Corps.
Scheepers, Captain J. C. . . . . . Infantry.
Solomon, Lieutenant A. C.. . . . . Heavy Artillery.
Sprenger, Major L. F. . . . . . . Infantry.
Sproule, Major H. . . . . Labour Corps.
Symmes, Major H. C. . . . . . . Infantry.
****Tanner, Brigadier-General W. E. C. . . Staff.
Tarboton, Second-Lieutenant C. C. . . Infantry.
Tatham, Second-Lieutenant E. V. . . Infantry.
**Thackeray, Lieutenant-Colonel E. F.. . Infantry.
Theron, Captain F. H. . . . . . . Infantry.
Thomas, Second-Lieutenant W. F. G. . Infantry.
*Thomson, Lieutenant-Colonel G. R. . . S.A.M.C.
Tomlinson, Captain L. W. . . . . Infantry.
Tripp, Major W. H. L. . . . . . Heavy Artillery.
Unwin, Second-Lieutenant H. W. . . Heavy Artillery.
Usmar, Lieutenant-Colonel G. H. . . S.A.M.C.
Van der Byl, Lieut.-Colonel V. A. W.. . Labour Corps.
*Van Ryneveld, Captain T. V.. . . . Infantry.
Wakefield, Major H. S.. . . . . . Infantry.
Walsh, Captain F. G. . . . . . . Infantry.
Ward, Lieutenant-Colonel A. B. . . . S.A.M.C.
*Ward, Major C. P. . . . . Heavy Artillery.
*Williamson, Captain E. . . . . . Labour Corps.
*Wolff, Lieutenant-Colonel H. P. . . . Labour Corps.

NURSING STAFF.

Bester, Nursing-Sister H. L.. . . . . S.A.M.N.S.
Brookshaw, Staff-Nurse F. . . . . S.A.M.N.S.
Burgess, Nursing-Sister E.. . . . . S.A.M.N.S.
Child, Assistant-Matron J. C. . . . . S.A.M.N.S.
Conyngham, Nursing-Sister A. B. . . S.A.M.N.S.
Creagh, Matron E. R. . . . . . . S.A.M.N.S.
Dawson, Nursing-Sister L.. . . . . Q.A.I.M.N.S.R.
Freshney, Nursing-Sister F. H. . . . S.A.M.N.S.
Gilson, Nursing-Sister M. A. . . . . S.A.M.N.S.
Johnson, Nursing-Sister M. E. . . . Q.A.I.M.N.S.R.
Kingon, Nursing-Sister H. A.. . . . S.A.M.N.S.
*Northard, Staff-Nurse C. A. . . . . S.A.M.N.S.

Northard, Nursing-Sister M. . . . . S.A.M.N.S.
Thomson, Probationer Nurse D. M. . . S.A.M.N.S.
Van Niekerk, Nursing-Sister D. N. K. . S.A.M.N.S.
Waters, Nursing-Sister I. G. . . . . S.A.M.N.S.

WARRANT OFFICERS, N.C.O'S, AND MEN.

Anderson, No. 271, Staff-Sergeant R. D.. S.A.M.C.
Atwood, No. 12731, Sergeant E. E. . . Infantry.
Bantjes, No. 4371, Private M. J. . . . Infantry.
Barker, No. 3877, Private J. G. . . . Infantry.
Beasley, No. 3855, Coy. Q.M.-Sergt. N. . Infantry.
Bentley, No. 5846, Sergeant P. . . . . Infantry.
Blackie, No. 2878, Lance-Corporal F. T.. Signal Company.
Borland, No. 6016, Coy. Sgt.-Major J. C. Signal Company.
Brown, No. 49, Coy. Sergeant-Major J. . Labour Corps.
Butler, No. 16, Colour Sergeant F. . . Labour Corps.
Cullen, No. 2913, Lance-Cpl. R. V. V. . Signal Company.
Cursley, No. 5811, Private F.. . . . Infantry.
Dalton, No. 6334, Sergeant W. J. . . Engineers.
Davis, No. 1895, Sergeant J. . . . . Infantry.
Elliott, No. 382, Sergeant R. P. . . . Heavy Artillery.
Emery, No. 17, Lance-Corporal E. H. . Infantry.
Ewin, No. 2142, Sergeant E. F. . . . Infantry.
Ferguson, No. 1580, Corporal J. . . . Heavy Artillery.
Gattens, No. V35, Sergeant J. . . . Engineers.
Gillholm, No. 59, Coy. Sergt.-Major H. P. Labour Corps.
Gordge, No. 80, Q.M.-Sergeant J. H.. . S.A.M.C.
Grant, No. 78, Sergeant J. A. F. . . . S.A.M.C.
Hall, No. 3613, Coy. Sergeant-Major A. . Infantry.
Hall, No. 5332, Sergeant P. C. W. . . Signal Company.
Harrison, No. 289, Sergeant J. G. . . Heavy Artillery.
Helfrick, No. 3977, Private W. . . . Infantry.
Henderson, No. 5351, Sergeant W. . . Infantry.
Hewitt, No. 141, Reg. Sgt.-Major W. H.. Labour Corps.
Hopkins, No. 540, Staff-Sergeant C. . . Heavy Artillery.
Hughes, No. 572, Gunner F. . . . . Heavy Artillery.
Hukins, No. 242, Colour Sergeant L. C. . Labour Corps.
Hulett, No. 179, Coy. Sergt.-Major A. C. Labour Corps.
Jessop, No. 107, Colour Sergeant W. H. . Labour Corps.

Jones, No. 10951, Private W. E. . . .	Infantry.
Jorgensen, No. 527, Corporal W. H. . .	Signal Company.
Kenyon, No. 4807, Corporal A. J. . .	Signal Company.
Krige, No. 1067, Gunner P. H. . . .	Heavy Artillery.
Lee, No. 1491, Gunner F. L. F. . . .	Heavy Artillery.
Lenz, No. 388, Sergeant F.	Labour Corps.
Lodge, No. 1838, Sergeant H. . . .	Infantry.
Long, No. 1665, Lance-Corporal C. E. .	Infantry.
Lowe, No. 4700, Sergeant T. E. . . .	Infantry.
Loxton, No. 5620, Lance-Corporal C.. .	Infantry.
Mackay, No. 622, Batt. Q.M.-Sergeant A.	Heavy Artillery.
Magor, No. 282, Sergeant H. C. . . .	Labour Corps.
M'Conachie, No. 1933, Sergeant J. . .	Infantry.
Meredith, No. 5755, Reg. Sgt.-Major G. .	Infantry.
Morgan, No. 245, Private R. H. . . .	Infantry.
Munro, No. 3890, Corporal W. . . .	Signal Company.
Nicholls, No. 45, Reg. Q.M.-Sergt. G. R. F.	Infantry.
Nicolle, No. 4817, Corporal J. . . .	Signal Company.
Northend, No. 5330, Corporal G. F. . .	Signal Company.
Parsley, No. 7728, Staff-Sergeant A. J. .	Infantry.
Perrett, No. 614, Sergeant W. J. . . .	Heavy Artillery.
Petters, No. 497, Sergeant A. T. . . .	Heavy Artillery.
Prebble, No. 348, Coy. Sergt.-Major E. E.	Infantry.
Price, No. 745, Sergeant F. W. . . .	Labour Corps.
Prior, No. 1998, Private E. C.. . . .	Infantry.
Purcell, No. 6031, Lance-Corporal I.. .	Signal Company.
Ritchie, No. 6658, Sergeant H. J. . .	Signal Company.
Robey, No. 5275, Coy. Sergt.-Major J. E.	Infantry.
Rowe, No. 3655, Corporal H. J. . . .	Engineers.
Salsbury, No. 869, Gunner E. . . .	Heavy Artillery.
Schoeman, No. 18, Private A. J. . . .	Infantry.
Schuring, No. 3550, Sergeant D. . . .	Infantry.
Sewell, No. 545, Sergeant-Major W. E. .	Heavy Artillery.
Shaw, No. 2, Colour Sergeant R. G. . .	Labour Corps.
Skinner, No. 4146, Sergeant W. T. . .	Infantry.
Stidworthy, No. 8781, Sergeant G. A. .	Infantry.
Truss, No. 955, Sergeant W. G. . . .	Heavy Artillery.
*Van Hoof, No. 2893, Sergeant A. C. . .	Signal Company.
Vlok, No. 429, Private N. J.	Infantry.
Walter, No. 9004, Corporal B. C.. . .	Infantry.

Wedderburn, No. 3188, Sergeant A. . . Infantry.
Westley, No. 14561, Private L. F. C.. . Infantry.
Whitnall, No. 4280, Q.M.-Sergt. E. C. . Infantry.
Wilson, No. 5266, Reg. Sergeant-Major J. Infantry.
Beckman, No. 4768, Sergeant G. H. W. . Infantry.
Dewar, No. 3110, Lance-Sergeant W. R. Infantry.
Hilson, No. 2179, Sergeant J. C. . . . Infantry.
Husband, No. 2146, Lance-Sgt. W. J. M. Infantry.
King, No. 3782, Coy. Sergt.-Major W. L. Infantry.

MENTIONED IN WAR OFFICE COMMUNIQUÉS.

OFFICERS.

Ashmead, Lieutenant J. E. W. . . . Infantry.
Balfour, Lieutenant-Colonel H. H. . . S.A.M.C.
Bamford, Lieutenant-Colonel H. W. M. . Infantry.
Byrne, Captain M. J. . . . . . . Engineers.
Chave, Lieutenant A. F. . . . . . Infantry.
Covernton, Captain R. H. . . . . . Signal Company.
Davison, Major G. L. . . . . . . Labour Corps.
Deane, Major R. . . . . Infantry.
Ellis, Lieutenant N. N.. . . . . . Pay Corps.
Jamieson, Captain E. C. K. . . . . Pay Corps.
Knibbs, Lieutenant A. R. . . . . . Infantry.
Legge, Captain E. A. . . . . . . Infantry.
Macdougal, Major I. . . . . . . Infantry.
Marillier, Second-Lieutenant F. L. . . Infantry.
M'Cubbin, Captain J. S. . . . . . Infantry.
Metelerkamp, Second-Lieutenant L. . . Infantry.
Millar, Captain E. S. . . . . . . Infantry.
Mills, Major H. P. . . . . Infantry.
Money, Captain A. G. . . . . . . Infantry.
Montgomery, Captain H. . . . . . Infantry.
Paxton, Captain A. L. . . . . . . Infantry.
Rae, Lieutenant N. E.. . . . . . Infantry.
Rigby, Major J. C. A. . . . . . . S.A.M.C.
Riley, Captain J. W. . . . . . . Infantry.
Thomson, Captain A. M. . . . . . Infantry.
Tucker, Captain W. E. . . . . . Infantry.

Young, Lieutenant-Colonel B.. . . .	Infantry.
Walker, Major E. B.	Infantry.
Whiting, Captain E.	Infantry.
Whyte, Captain J. C.	Labour Corps.

NURSING STAFF.

Adendorff, Staff-Nurse M. A.	S.A.M.N.S.
Allen, Staff-Nurse P. W.	S.A.M.N.S.
Aves, Staff-Nurse D.	S.A.M.N.S.
Cloete, Probationer-Nurse R. F. . . .	S.A.M.N.S.
Donaldson, Nursing-Sister A. E. . . .	S.A.M.N.S.
Fraser-Wood, Nursing-Sister K. . . .	Q.A.I.M.N.S.R.
Pearson, Staff-Nurse E. M.	S.A.M.N.S.
Thom, Probationer-Nurse H.	S.A.M.N.S.

WARRANT OFFICERS, N.C.O.'S, AND MEN.

Ardouin, No. 10758, Corporal W. . .	Infantry.
Augustus, No. 200, Q.M.-Sergeant I. S. .	Pay Corps.
Bailey, No. X558, Staff-Sergeant J. S. .	Pay Corps.
Bell, No. 4699, Coy. Sergeant-Major F. .	Infantry.
Blackmore, No. 8667, Corporal W. . .	Infantry.
Boam, No. 1918, Staff-Sergeant H. N. .	Pay Corps.
Bothwell, No. 5051, Staff-Sergeant H. .	Pay Corps.
Brampton, No. 8505, Sergeant T. C. . .	Infantry.
*Bromehead, No. 2098, Sergeant E. C. .	Infantry.
Bruno, No. 2779, Corporal H. A. . . .	Infantry.
Buchanan, No. 5562, Sergeant D. K.. .	Infantry.
Burns, No. X661, Staff-Sergeant J. F. .	Pay Corps.
Burns, No. 8673, Sergeant W. R. . .	Infantry.
Burrage, No. 3144, Staff Q.M.-Sergt. F. L.	Pay Corps.
Church, No. 6298, Q.M.-Sergeant R. L. .	Infantry.
Cooper, No. 6811, Sergeant W. P. . .	Infantry.
Coyne, No. X44, Sergeant W. B. M. . .	Infantry.
Craig, No. 1347, Reg. Sergt.-Major W. .	Infantry.
Crocker, No. 4558, Sergeant W. T. H. .	Infantry.
Crowson, No. 6299, Q.M.-Sergeant E. .	Infantry.
Dagnin, No. 1623, Lance-Sergt. A. A. F.	Infantry.
Davenport, No. 6074, Reg. Sgt.-Major B.	Infantry.
*Davidson, No. X19, Sergeant C. . . .	Infantry.

Driver, No. 8522, Sergeant E. M. . .	Infantry.
Easterbrook, No. 6262, Lance-Cpl. E. H.	Infantry.
Fearnhead, No. 400, Staff-Sergeant E. A.	Pay Corps.
Fletcher, No. 13834, Lance-Corporal C. A.	Infantry.
Foster, No. 11594, Sergeant W. M. . .	Infantry.
Fromant, No. 4893, C. Q.M.-Sgt. J. W. G.	Infantry.
*Furley, No. 1518, Sergeant E. H.. . .	Infantry.
Glencross, No. 3120, Sergeant C. M. G. .	Infantry.
Hall, No. 1474, Sergeant O. H. . . .	Infantry.
Harris, No. 1065, Sergeant E. W.. . .	Heavy Artillery.
*Hickman, No. 6294, Reg. Q.M.-Sgt. C. S.	Infantry.
Hudson, No. 2817, Coy. Q.M.-Sergeant T.	Infantry.
Impellezzenie, No. 13957, Private G. A. .	Infantry.
Janion, No. 1058, Lance-Corporal J. R. .	Infantry.
Johnstone, No. 4456, C. Sgt.-Major C. E.	Infantry.
Kelly, No. X256, Staff-Sergeant G. . .	Pay Corps.
Levell, No. 787, Q.M.-Sergeant W. J. .	Heavy Artillery
*Lightfoot, No. 344, Staff-Sergeant R. .	S.A.M.C.
Murgatroyd, No. 3207, Lance-Cpl. T. C. .	Infantry.
Newall, No. 478, Sergeant W. . . .	S.A.M.C.
Pauley, No. X255, Staff-Sergeant H. E. R.	Pay Corps.
Phillips, No. 2946, Staff-Sergeant D. T. .	Infantry.
Pool, No. 10093, Lance-Corporal W. . .	Infantry.
Popkiss, No. 3146, Staff Sergt.-Major R. J.	Pay Corps.
Pretorius, No. 6238, Corporal J. L. . .	Infantry.
*Priest, No. 388, Sergeant-Major F. D. .	S.A.M.C.
Reid, No. 3315, Sergeant H.	Infantry.
Rhind, No. 53, Sergeant F.	Staff.
*Rose, No. 414, Private R.	S.A.M.C.
Rowley, No. 5883, Reg. Q.M.-Sergt. A. B.	Infantry.
Russell, No. 9110, Coy. Q.M.-Sergt. E. E.	Infantry.
Sayer, No. 3112, Sergeant A.	Infantry.
Scherger, No. 5711, Corporal B. . . .	Infantry.
Shearer, No. 10077, Sergeant J. . . .	Infantry.
Sherman, No. 423, Corporal H. J. . .	Infantry.
Shires, No. 2212, Corporal A.	Infantry.
Sim, No. 11041, Lance-Corporal A. E. .	Infantry.
**Smith, No. 315, Staff-Sergeant C. G. W..	S.A.M.C.
Stead, No. 15343, Corporal F. H. . .	Infantry.
Swanby, No. X23, Staff-Sergeant C. F. .	S.A.M.C.

Thomas, No. 639, Bombardier B. J. A. . Heavy Artillery.
Tuck, No. 9122, Lance-Corporal F. G. . Infantry.
*Walker, No. X235, Staff Sgt.-Major J. H. Staff.
Walton, No. X522, Staff-Sergeant A. E. Pay Corps.
Wasser, No. 2673, Private J. . . . . Infantry.
White, No. 403, Corporal H. W. S. . . S.A.M.C.

FOREIGN DECORATIONS.

FRENCH HONOURS.

CROIX DE GUERRE.

Clunnie, No. 4080, Sergeant R. J. . . . . Infantry.
Edwards, Major S. B. . . . . Heavy Artillery.
Fraser, No. 6212, Corporal C. M. . . . . Signal Company.
Glascock, No. 6317, Sergeant E. W. . . . Infantry.
Goodwin, Second-Lieutenant B. W. . . . Infantry.
Harrison, Major N. . . . . Signal Company.
Hunter, No. 1197, Private H. P. . . . . Infantry.
Maasdorp, Major L. H. . . . . Heavy Artillery.
Meredith, No. 5755, Reg. Sergeant-Major G. . Infantry.
Nelson, No. 943, Sergeant T. D. . . . . Heavy Artillery.
Ross, Lieutenant F. M. . . . . Signal Company.
Smith, No. 4087, Sergeant A. . . . . . Infantry.
Sowdon, No. 4716, Sergeant C. H. V. . . . Signal Company.
Steele, No. 1905, Private H. . . . . . Infantry.
Thackeray, Lieutenant-Colonel E. F. . . . Infantry.
Wilkie, No. 3657, Coy. Sergeant-Major F.. . Infantry.
Wilson, Lieutenant C. K. . . . . . . Signal Company.

LÉGION D'HONNEUR, CROIX D'OFFICIER.

Collins, Lieutenant-Colonel F. R. . . . . Engineers.

MÉDAILLE MILITAIRE.

Davenport, No. 6074, Reg. Sergeant-Major B. Infantry.
Hodges, No. 468, Bombardier T. E. . . . Heavy Artillery.
Mann, No. 13298, Sergeant A. . . . . . Heavy Artillery
Stevens, No. 7071, Private J. B. . . . . Infantry.

BELGIAN HONOURS.

ORDRE DE LA COURONNE.

Little, Second-Lieutenant H. G. . . . . Heavy Artillery.

CROIX DE GUERRE.

Clegg, No. X93, Corporal W. D. . . . . Heavy Artillery.
L'Estrange, No. X123, Bombardier G. E. F. . Heavy Artillery.
Little, Second-Lieutenant H. G. . . . . Heavy Artillery.
Stiger, No. 968, Corporal W. T. M. . . . Heavy Artillery.
Tanner, Brigadier-General W. E. C. . . . Staff.
Truss, No. 955, Sergeant W. G. . . . . Heavy Artillery.

Rowe. B. Sergt 3655
Dalton. 6334. ORDRE- DE LÉOPOLD. *Engineers*

Tanner, Lieutenant-Colonel W. E. C. . . . Infantry.
Truss, No. 955, Sergeant W. G. . . . . Heavy Artillery.

DÉCORATION MILITAIRE.

Gourlay, No. 6210, Sergeant J. H. . . . Signal Company.
Page, No. 1591, Private S. A. . . . . . Signal Company.

ITALIAN HONOURS.

SILVER MEDAL FOR MILITARY VALOUR.

Charlton, Captain W. D. . . . . . . Infantry.
Shenton, Captain J. L. . . . . Infantry.
Unwin, Lieutenant H. W. . . . . . . Heavy Artillery.

BRONZE MEDAL FOR MILITARY VALOUR.

Allison, No. 3554, Lance-Corporal C. J. . . Infantry.
Knowles, No. 777, Gunner J. D. . . . . Heavy Artillery.

SERBIAN HONOURS.

ORDER OF THE WHITE EAGLE.

FOURTH CLASS WITH SWORDS.

Christian, Lieutenant-Colonel E. . . . . Infantry.

FIFTH CLASS WITH SWORDS.

Pepper, Captain A. L. . . . . Staff.

CROSS OF KARAGEORGE.

FIRST CLASS WITH SWORDS.

Wells, No. 563, Coy. Sergeant-Major F. W. . Infantry.

SECOND CLASS WITH SWORDS.

Jenner, No. 3447, Lance-Corporal D. . . . Infantry.

GOLD MEDAL.

Hoy, No. 1469, Lance-Corporal J. D. . . . Infantry.
Pringle, No. 4137, Private N. . . . . . Infantry.
Tuer, No. 4969, Sergeant J.. . . . . . Infantry.

SILVER MEDAL.

Bower, No. 4225, Private T. . . . . . Infantry.
Hunter, No. 142, Private H. J.. . . . . Infantry.

MONTENEGRIN HONOURS.

ORDER OF DANILO.

FIFTH CLASS.

Medlicott, Captain R. F. C. . . . . . Infantry.

SILVER MEDAL FOR MERIT.

Morgan, No. 245, Private R. H. . . . . Infantry.
Naisby, No. 1813, Sergeant J. . . . . . Infantry.

EGYPTIAN HONOURS.

ORDER OF THE NILE.

THIRD CLASS.

Lukin, Brigadier-General H. T.. . . . . Staff.

ROUMANIAN HONOURS.

MÉDAILLE BARBATIE SI CREDINTA.

SECOND CLASS.

Digby, Second-Lieutenant C. R. . . . . Cape Aux. Horse
Transport.

CHEVALIER OF THE ORDER OF THE CROWN OF ROUMANIA.

Havery, Lieutenant J. N. . . . . Infantry.

SUMMARY.

1. V.C.	2
2. K.C.B.	1
3. C.B.	2
4. C.M.G.	6
5. Bar to D.S.O.	1
6. D.S.O.	35
7. C.B.E. (Military Division).	6
8. O.B.E. (Military Division)	29
9. M.B.E. (Military Division)	15
10. Bar to M.C.	10
11. M.C.	134
12. D.C.M.	64
13. Bar to M.M..	16
14. M.M.	431
15. M.S.M.	75
16. Royal Red Cross	16
17. French Decorations	22
18. Belgian Decorations	11
19. Italian Decorations	5
20. Serbian Decorations	9
21. Montenegrin Decorations	3
22. Roumanian Decorations	2
23. Egyptian Decorations	1
24. Brevet Rank	5
25. Mentioned in Despatches	218
26. Mentioned in War Office Communiqués .	107

INDEX.

INDEX.

PRINTED IN GREAT BRITAIN AT
THE PRESS OF THE PUBLISHERS.

Lightning Source UK Ltd.
Milton Keynes UK
UKOW06f2232260317

297499UK00011B/55/P